michel
Christian

P9-BYV-041

The Blue Guides

Please write in with your comments, suggestions and corrections for the next edition of the Blue Guide. Writers of the most helpful letters will be awarded a free Blue Guide of their choice.

Provence &
the Côte d'Azur

Paul Stirton

A&C Black • London
WW Norton • New York

BLUE GUIDE

1st edition © Paul Stirton, September 1999
Published by A & C Black (Publishers) Limited
35 Bedford Row, London WC1R 4JH

Maps and plans drawn by Carto Graphics, © A&C Black

Illustrations © Colin Ross

A CIP catalogue record of this book is available from the British Library.

ISBN 0–7136–3981–4

Published in the United States of America by
WW Norton and Company Inc.
500 Fifth Avenue, New York, NY 10110

Published simultaneously in Canada by
Penguin Books Canada Limited
10 Alcorn Avenue, Toronto
Ontario M4V 3B2

ISBN 0–393–31931–8 USA

The authors and the publishers have done their best to ensure the accuracy of all the information in Blue Guide Provence and the Côte d'Azur; however, they can accept no responsibility for any loss, injury or inconvenience sustained by any traveller as a result of information or advice contained in the guide.

Cover photograph: Lavender field at Simiane-la-Rotonde, by Edmund Nägele, FRPS. **Title page illustration**, Man with truffling pig.

Paul Stirton was educated at the University of Edinburgh and the Courtauld Institute of Art in London. He is currently Senior Lecturer in the History of Art at Glasgow University and Visiting Professor at the Bard Graduate Center in New York City. Among his many publications on aspects of European art and design are *Renaissance Painting* (1979), *William Blake and his Circle* (1994) and, with Michael Jacobs, critical guides to the art galleries of Great Britain and France (1985).

Printed and bound in England by Butler & Tanner Ltd., Frome and London.

Preface

In the past, travellers from the north have tended to see the journey to Provence in metaphorical terms. It was a journey of the soul or the mind as much as the crossing of a country and it generally resulted in a change of outlook, a new feeling about their surroundings. For Stendhal and Corot in the 1830s, descending from the Massif Centrale to the landscape of the Mediterranean meant leaving the cares of a cold climate behind and entering a world permeated by ancient Rome. Some fifty years later, Van Gogh sought the future of modern art in Arles and he was followed by the great procession of masters including Matisse, Picasso, Bonnard, Renoir and Chagall, all of whom found the light, the colour, the very atmosphere of the region liberating after their days in Paris. In the 1920s, it was the coastal strip, particularly the Cote d'Azur, that represented a carefree, hedonistic life to the American expatriates Gerald and Sara Murphy and their circle of friends such as Scott Fitzgerald, Ernest Hemingway, Cole Porter and the luminaries of the Jazz Age. Finally, in 1947 the British writer Charles Graves could not feel that the war was really over until he had arrived on the Riviera to sense the warmth of the south and the return to such forbidden pleasures as fresh seafood and delicious white wines.

My own first journey to the south was as a teenager in the mid sixties, but travelling in the back of a windowless van I was unable to appreciate the sense of release, the gradual change in the colouring, the flora and the temperature that signals one's approach to the latin culture of the Mediterranean. Over the years I returned many times to the south of France but it was not until I spent a magical holiday there with my daughter, visiting a friend on the Luberon, that I began to recognise the particular character of this area.

It is a region of fantasies in so far as outsiders have tended to project their desires onto it. It has offered a setting for various types of escapism but they are mostly artificial. Peter Mayle's popular account of life in a rural community, *A Year in Provence*, was only the most recent of these fantasies. This is not to say that he invented it, but like Brigitte Bardot in the 1950s, Scott Fitzgerald in the 1920s or Van Gogh in the 1880s, Provence and the Côte d'Azur served to fulfill the expectations of outsiders. This is odd when you consider that Provence has its own very distinctive culture; a culture which, moreover, seems to encompass contrary tendencies. In that sense 'Old Provence' in the west is often seen as an essentially peasant and traditional region, while the Riviera is regarded as modern, flashy and superficial. As with all clichés, there is a grain of truth on both sides. It does not take long in the area, however, to recognise that the popular image of these areas is both fake and real at the same time. Le Style Provençal with its distinctive cuisine and printed cottons is as much an invention of modern advertising as is the Riviera, while beneath its surface the Cote d'Azur has a great deal that is both traditional and historic. To many people seeking an 'authentic' Provence, this can be disappointing but to the open-minded visitor, this is part of the appeal of the region. The interplay between fantasy, history and a vibrant, dynamic culture is what make the South of France more than simply a holiday resort or museum.

My aim in writing this guide was to introduce something of the complexity and contradiction of the region—the historic and the modern, the traditional and the superficial—while trying to remain as open as possible to the new experiences that contemporary Provence has to offer. Even if I wanted to, I could not have been entirely unbiased in my choices but I would like to think that there are travellers who would welcome information on the flamboyant villas of the Second Empire as well as the Romanesque chapels or Modernist houses. I have also tried to introduce a slightly more international view of the South of France. The British and North Americans have exerted a huge influence on the history and culture of Provence but we were not the only travellers to colonise it. As a result, the reader will encounter the Spanish writer Blasco Ibàñez, Chekhov and Alma Mahler as well as Edward, Prince of Wales and Scott Fitzgerald.

The South of France has been the playground for cultural and political figures for well over a century but there is one art form in which it has excelled above all others. Almost every major French painter of the twentieth century has passed some time there and Provence can claim, with some justification, to be the heartland of modern French art. Artists, therefore, do figure prominently throughout the chapters, as well as in the museums and monuments that are such a highlight of the region as a whole.

Acknowledgements

Over the years I have had the good fortune to be introduced to many aspects of Provence and the Riviera by people who know it much better than myself. Michael Jacobs has been a companion and guide on several occasions and I am very grateful to him for suggesting that I write this book. John and Christiane O'Keeffe have been generous hosts and equally stimulating guides. In Hyères, I was introduced to several unusual features of the area by Janine and Jean-Claude Gaudin and in Toulon I was able to use the fascinating library of Les Amis du Vieux Toulon. While staying in Provence I had the benefit of numerous visitors, including Zoe and Michael Stirton, Anna Raab, Clair McFadden and the late Sheenah Smith. Back in Britain, I have benefitted from the knowledge of my colleagues in Glasgow University, the book collections of Jolyon Hudson and Barry Bergdoll, and from the technical expertise of Corinna Kinchin. I am also very grateful for the patience and support of the editorial team of Gemma Davies, Judy Tither and Alison Effeny. Finally, my greatest debt is to Juliet Kinchin, my constant companion who has contributed more to this book than I could ever acknowledge adequately.

Paul Stirton
August 1999

Contents

The Languedoc border 90

Northern Vaucluse and Alpes de Haute-Provence 132

The central region 174

Along the southern coast 132

The Riviera and its hinterland 248

Into the mountains 299

Index 311

Maps

Practical information

Planning your trip

When to go

The south of France has more reason than most to be regarded as an all-year-round destination. The region first became popular among foreigners and particularly northern Europeans as a winter resort, where they could escape from the cold and wet of the northern climate. The famous resorts of the Victorian period—Nice, Cannes, Menton and Hyères—attracted the wealthy and the sick who could enjoy the mild Mediterranean winter. In the 20C, with the rise of the sun tan and the bikini, it has been turned into perhaps the most famous summer holiday centre in the world. In each of the intermediate seasons there have also been regular visitors, particularly those who wish to walk in the very diverse landscape, visit the plentiful antique and medieval remains, or undertake any number of hobbies and pursuits from botany to gambling. The south of France has plenty to offer at all times of the year and can accommodate visitors as and when most suitable for their preferred activities.

If you intend to travel in old Provence, to visit the great centres such as Arles or Avignon, you may find the early autumn to be preferable. The crowds have generally thinned out from their height in July and August, the temperature has eased to a pleasant, less than stifling heat and it is still warm and dry enough for you to enjoy the outdoor sights. Similarly, in September and October the coastal resorts are still warm enough for those not overused to the intensity of midsummer and the beaches are less crammed with sunbathers. One word of warning, however. Winter in Provence can be severe, particularly in the inland areas of the Rhône Valley which are prone to the Mistral wind.

Average temperatures in the region

Central Provence

Jan	Feb	Mar	Apr	May	June	July	Aug	Sept	Oct	Nov	Dec
12.2	11.9	14.2	18.5	20.8	26.6	28.1	28.4	25.2	22.1	16.8	14.1

Rhône Valley

Jan	Feb	Mar	Apr	May	June	July	Aug	Sept	Oct	Nov	Dec
7.4	6.7	10.8	15.8	17.3	25.6	27.6	27.6	23.5	16.5	10.4	7.8

Côte d'Azur

Jan	Feb	Mar	Apr	May	June	July	Aug	Sept	Oct	Nov	Dec
12.2	11.9	14.2	18.5	20.8	26.6	28.1	28.4	25.2	22.1	16.1	14.1

Information

The French Government Tourist Office in the UK produces an annual *Reference Guide for the Traveller* with good factual information on most general aspects of travelling or holidaying in France. This is available by contacting their office in London. They also have a range of more specific brochures on different regions, services and activities.

- **UK**. 178 Piccadilly, London W1V OAL ☎ (0891) 244 123, fax (0171) 493 6594.
- **USA**. 444 Madison Avenue, 16th Floor, New York, NY 10022, ☎ 900 990 0040, fax 212 838 7855.
- **Canada**. 1981 Avenue McGill College, Suite 490, Montreal, Québec H3A 2W9 ☎ (514) 288 4264, fax (514) 845 48 68; 30 St Patrick's St, Suite 700, Toronto, Ontario M5T 3A3 ☎ (416) 593 4723.

While Government Tourist Offices hold information on various types of holidays and accommodation this is probably better pursued in local travel agencies and in the advertising columns of national newspapers.

For cultural tours led by specialist lecturers, particularly those with an emphasis on art and architecture, try the following agencies:
- **Martin Randall Travel**. 10 Barley Mow Passage, London W4 4PH. ☎ (0181) 742 3355.
- **Prospect Music and Art Tours Ltd**. 36 Manchester Street, London W1M 5PE. ☎ (0181) 995 2151.
- **Swan Hellenic**. 77 New Oxford Street, London WC1A 1PP. ☎ (0171) 831 1515 cover similar ground in a less specialist manner.

Passports and visa requirements
No visa is required for citizens of EU countries but a passport is needed for identification. North Americans and New Zealanders require only a passport if staying less than three months in France. Members of Commonwealth countries should check visa requirements with their nearest French consulate before departing.

Visas are of three types, valid for two months (transit visa), for 90 days after the date of issue (*court séjour*) or for multiple stays of 90 days over three years (*long séjour*). Non-visa visitors staying longer than 90 days should apply for a *Carte de Séjour*, for which you'll need to show proof of income.

Disabled travellers
Like most countries in Europe, France has become increasingly aware of its reponsibilities to disabled travellers and, although hardly ideal, the situation regarding access and support services is improving. Blind people may be able to take a companion free of charge, and some tour operators have special facilities on offer. Check with your carrier or tour company. Most of the major tourist sights are now accessible although in the more remote and rugged areas wheelchair travellers may be confined to the car. The main cities, although very busy, have turned substantial areas over to pedestrians which at least ensures the freedom of the surface. Most of the larger museums are also accessible with lifts and other services to assist disabled people. The same cannot be said of the older hotels, the public transport and even the toilets which can be inaccessible.
- **RADAR (Royal Association for Disability and Rehabilitation)**. 12 City Forum, 250 City Road, London EC1V 8AF ☎ (0171) 250 3222.
- **APF (Association des Paralysés de France)**. 11 allée Alphée-Carter, Marseille ☎ 04 91 08 08 28; 90 avenue du Général-Nogués, Toulon ☎ 04 94 62 97 75; 3 rue du Marquis-de-Calvières, Avignon ☎ 04 90 89 41 92; HLM Les Serrets, Manosque ☎ 04 92 72 34 37.

Maps

There is a good standard map covering the whole of Provence and the Côte d'Azur in the Michelin 1/200,000 Yellow series (No. 245). This indicates the major and minor roads, plus most of the monuments and places of interest. The same area is divided between four smaller Michelin maps to the same scale (Nos 80, 81, 83 and 84), which may be more convenient. More attractive and useful still is the series of maps produced by the Institut Géographique National (IGN) which, at a scale of 1/100,000, provide more detail and a better indication of the terrain (Nos 60, 61, 66, 67 and 68). For even more detailed coverage, IGN also produce maps at 1/50,000 and 1/25,000 scale, and even a 1/10,000 map.

Tourist offices in towns usually have a small street map that is given out free of charge. Likewise in villages, the local *syndicat d'initiative* or *office du tourisme* will generally have a small map of the area with a few notable sights and routes marked.

 # Money

After a period of great strength in the early 1990s, the French *franc* has weakened against the pound and dollar giving slightly more favourable **exchange rates** to visitors. Nevertheless, Provence, and particularly the Côte d'Azur, is a fairly expensive area when compared to the rest of rural France. The high life on the coast has retained its high prices while losing much of its prestige. Bearing this in mind, however, Provence can still offer very good value in accommodation, eating out and general travelling expenses. As ever, the lower-rated hotels, private accommodation and fixed-price menus are less expensive than their equivalents in Britain or North America.

All of the principal **credit cards** are widely accepted in shops, hotels, restaurants and petrol stations. They are also accepted for payment of tolls on motorways. When paying by credit card, check the amount which appears on the receipt: in France, no decimal point is shown between *francs* and *centimes*. Cash can be withdrawn from relevant cash-dispensing machines in France using UK pin numbers. Most banks in France no longer accept Eurocheques and there are complicated arrangements and charges for bank cheques from foreign countries. French *franc* **travellers' cheques** are still a convenient and reliable method of changing money; there should be no further commission charges in France and they are often accepted as cash.

The banks tend to offer fairly similar exchange rates but the Banque Nationale de Paris has a reputation for being the most favourable. When assessing the relative rates between banks and the currency booths, check the commission; many have a flat surcharge or commisssion of c 30FF for every transaction. Automatic currency exchange machines are convenient but offer a very poor rate. When changing money it is likely that you will be given high denomination notes which are often awkward to use for everyday expenses. Try to ensure that you have some smaller notes and change to pay for such things as buses or taxis.

Customs and currency regulations

Unlimited currency may be taken into France but must be declared if bank notes to the value of 50,000FF or more are likely to be re-exported.

Getting to Provence

By air

There are regular daily services **from the UK** by British Airways ☎ (0345) 222 111, Air France ☎ (0181) 742 6600, Easyjet ☎ 0990 29 29 29 and British Midland ☎ (0345) 554 554 between the main London airports and the two international airports in the south of France, Nice and Marseille. The same airlines operate some direct flights from other British airports such as Manchester, Birmingham, Edinburgh or Glasgow, or else have routes with a change in either London or Paris.

There is one airline, Delta ☎ (800) 241 4141, which flies into Nice direct **from New York**. Otherwise, flights from North America or Australia require a change in London or Paris, depending on the carrier.

The French tend to discourage the burgeoning package tour and charter trade but there are a few **charter companies**, such as Avro Manchester, offering flight-only deals to Nice related to package tours in the summer. These are best traced through the independent travel agencies such as STA Travel, Campus Travel or Trailfinders, with branches throughout Britain (see below). Late bookings can occasionally produce bargains in the so-called 'bucket shops', but high summer tends to be booked well in advance. On occasion you can find inexpensive flight-only charters offered in the columns of national newspapers. These are relatively rare to Provence but are good value if available. A recent additional option is that of flying into Paris (Charles de Gaulle) and continuing to Provence by high-speed train (TGV), directly from the airport.

• **STA Travel**. 86 Old Brompton Road, London SW7 3LH ☎ (0171) 361 6161; 75 Deansgate, Manchester M3 2BW ☎ (0161) 834 0668; 25 Queens Road, Bristol BS8 1QE ☎ (0117) 929 4399; 38 Sidney Street, Cambridge CB2 3HX ☎ (01223) 366 966; 184 Byres Road, Glasgow G12 ☎ (0141) 338 6000; 36 George Street, Oxford OX1 2OJ ☎ (01865) 792800.
• **Campus Travel**. 52 Grosvenor Gardens, London SW1W OAG ☎ (0171) 730 3402; 541 Bristol Road, Bournbrook, Selly Oak, Birmingham B29 6AU ☎ (0121) 414 1848; 53 Forest Road, Edinburgh EH1 2QP ☎ (0131) 225 6111.
• **Trailfinders**. 215 Kensington High Street, London W8 6BD ☎ (0171) 937 5400; 58 Deansgate, Manchester M3 2FF ☎ (0161) 839 6969; 254–84 Sauchiehall Street, Glasgow G2 3EH ☎ (0141) 353 2224; 48 Corn Street, Bristol BS1 1HQ ☎ (0117) 929 9000.

By rail

The Eurostar passenger service **from London Waterloo** to Paris Gare du Nord takes just three hours but you must cross Paris to link up with the rest of the rail network. For bookings and information ☎ (0990) 300 003. The best rail link to the south is the TGV (*Train à Grande Vitesse*) from the Gare de Lyon: this has a very good service and network of routes, taking between three and a half and six hours depending on your destination. A specific time and seat reservation is compulsory on this service.

France has one of the finest rail systems in the world and there are other regular, if slower, services to Provence and the Côte d'Azur. For information and booking on all routes contact The Rail Shop ☎ (0990) 300 003. This office can also give information on concessionary fares or **travel passes** such as the Eurodomino Rover Ticket which allows unlimited travel by train for certain fixed periods. There are concessions for students, travellers under 26 and senior citizens.

If you are planning to travel further than Provence, it may be worth considering the Eurail Pass which allows **unlimited travel** throughout Europe. A number of other rail passes exist for North American visitors but must be purchased in the USA or Canada.

For group travel by train with special reductions, contact the Group Travel section of Rail Europe, ☎ (0171) 633 9000. To take your **car by rail** from Folkestone to Calais through the Channel Tunnel, book with Le Shuttle ☎ (0990) 353 535 or buy your ticket at the terminal outside Folkestone. This service can connect with Motorail to transport your car from Calais or Paris to a holiday destination in the south of France, ☎ (0181) 880 8161 or (0171) 203 7000.

By bus

There are very few long-distance bus companies in France, partly due to the scale and efficiency of the train service, but Eurolines operates between Paris and the main cities of Provence. For information in the UK ☎ 01582 404511 ☎ 0990 808080. Tickets from most parts of Britain can be purchased through National Express. The main coach tours to the region are operated by firms from outside France and should therefore be booked as a complete package holiday from Britain.

By car

Provence is a great area to explore by car but there are many disadvantages and obstacles which can mar a driving holiday. The first of these is the journey out. Fortunately, crossing the Channel is now easier and less expensive than at any time in the past. Three **ferry companies** serve the Dover–Calais route alone: P&O (☎ 0990 980980), Sea France (☎ 01304 212696) and Stena Sealink (☎ 01233 647022), and there are other crossings which may be more convenient, depending on the starting-point of your journey. Hoverspeed operate **hovercrafts** Dover–Calais and Folkestone–Boulogne. Le Shuttle carries cars via the **Channel Tunnel** between Folkestone and Calais (see above). The cost of the crossing by each of these methods varies depending on the time of year and the time of day or night that you travel.

On arrival in France you have to cover the considerable distance of some 1000km to reach Provence. The first destination is Paris, the outer ring road (*periphérique*) being the hub of the main motorway network. Provence is linked to Paris and the north by the formidable but rather unpopular **Autoroute du Soleil**. Unpopular because at certain times of the year, particularly midsummer and at the key French holidays, it is very busy. Even with half a dozen lanes in some stretches it can be congested. Tearing down this immense motorway hemmed in by cars, motorcycles and container lorries, all apparently travelling at over 80mph, is not a relaxing way to start any holiday. If this encourages the driver to consider transporting the car by train to the south, French Railways operate a Motorail service from Calais or Paris to most major centres, although this is expensive (see above).

Apart from the price of petrol, which is slightly more than that in Britain and considerably more than that in North America, the motorway has **tolls** (*péages*) from Calais to the south coast, the overall charges on the route being approximately 350–400 francs.

Hiring a car in Provence is an alternative to the long drive from the north and it may be worth it as a relief from the *autoroute* or if you do not have much time. Car hire is, however, more expensive than in Britain or North America although there are slight reductions if booked through a travel agent before you leave. All the leading car hire firms have offices in the main towns and at airports and railway stations in Provence. There is also a fair range of local firms which are slightly cheaper and generally reliable. 'Fly-drive' deals, giving a special rate for car hire, can be arranged from most countries when booking flights. Most of the conditions regarding mileage and insurance that operate in Britain or North America are found in France. The minimum age for drivers wishing to hire a car is generally 21.

Before your departure it may be useful to consult either the AA or RAC, or the French Tourist Board, regarding specific **rules or restrictions** about driving in France. There are a few simple points which should be borne in mind. Drivers from EU countries require only their national licence but non-EU drivers require an International Driving Licence. Car ownership and insurance documents should be carried and a national identity sticker should be fixed to the rear of your vehicle. The speed limits are 130kph (80mph) on toll motorways, 110kph (68mph) on dual carriageways, 90kph (55mph) on other roads and 50kph (30mph) in towns. There is a minimum speed of 80kph (50mph) on the outside lane of motorways. A sliding scale of fines is imposed for speeding with a reduction if paid immediately.

Seat belts must always be worn. A reflective 'triangle' must be carried at all times and used to warn other motorists if you have to pull over to the side of the road for minor repairs. The headlight beam must be adjusted for driving on the right to avoid glare; masking patches can be purchased before leaving and a yellow stain, while not compulsory, is often recommended over the headlight glass. To avoid misunderstandings it is best not to rely on informal signs or practice. If a driver flashes his headlights in France, for example, he is generally signalling that he has priority and you should give way, contrary to standard practice in Britain.

Accommodation

As perhaps the oldest true holiday destinations in the world, Provence and the Côte d'Azur are well provided with accommodation at all levels and categories. There is a considerable range to choose from and the recommendations in this guide give only a selection of the more interesting or reliable. Many of the hotels in remote or country areas have not been listed here, but this does not mean that they should be ignored, as they are often the most attractive and personable. The French operate a fairly simple system of **star rating** for hotels, from no stars to four-star luxury, but it is often inconsistent. For example, a one-star room with minimal facilities in a town like Avignon is likely to be more expensive than a well-appointed two-star room in a more remote hotel. Prices are posted on the back of the room door but they can vary somewhat even within a single street. If you are arriving without a reservation it is advisable to take advantage of viewing the room before accepting. You should also check the view and the proximity to the street even in expensive hotels; town traffic can be very noisy in France. Car **parking** in towns is another problem and, if available at the hotel, it is generally reflected in the price.

Most of the hotel chains are consistent in what they offer and the prices they charge. If there is a restaurant attached the better or higher-rated hotels may expect you to take full board but, again, the simpler hotels are generally happy with demi-pension or bed-and-breakfast alone. The popularity of Provence in the summer means that it is becoming increasingly difficult to move around the region finding accommodation as you go. July and August are the busiest months but in other periods a special festival or attraction in the area can fill the available rooms. For travel in the summer it is often best to book accommodation of any sort, even camping, in advance.

Lists of hotels for each region are available from the French Government Tourist Offices, as is the brochure of **Logis de France** listing over 4000 family-run hotels, mostly one- or two-star, throughout the country.

Gîtes or self-catering accommodation is becoming increasingly popular for family holidays in all parts of France. This is operated by a range of agencies and can often be booked through local travel agents. To book direct, try Vacances en Campagne ☎ (01798) 869433 or Lagrange ☎ (0171) 371 6111. Another source is the advertising columns of national newspapers or the various published listings such as *French Farm and Village Holiday Guide: The Gîtes Guide* by FHG Publications, available from bookshops.

There are numerous **camping and caravanning** sites in the south of France, also graded according to the facilities they offer. Agencies and guides which have reasonably detailed lists are the *Guide Officiel Camping & Caravanning*, the *Good Camps Guide* or the *Michelin Green Guide: Camping/ Caravanning France*, available from bookshops. The British firm Canvas Holidays, ☎ (01383) 644000 specialises in French campsites, and others such as Eurocamp ☎ (01565) 625544 or Keycamps ☎ (0181) 395 4000/7525 have a good selection.

Details on all the various types of holiday mentioned above can be obtained from French National Tourist Offices, which in some cases can arrange bookings although they generally refer enquiries to the relevant organisation.

Getting around Provence

By car

Arriving in Provence by the motorway gives little impression of the range of roads and landscapes you can encounter when driving within the region. Nevertheless, for the committed driver the **motorways** are, themselves, quite an experience. Just before Marseille, there is a turn-off from the *Autoroute du Soleil* to the east. This is the *Autoroute La Provençale* which runs to Ventimiglia at the Italian border and gives access to all the resorts along the coast. Like the *Autoroute du Soleil* it is a toll road but the scenery through the mountains and the view over the sea can be worth it, especially if you do not have much time. The coast road is almost always congested in summer. For a truly spectacular driving experience, the three Corniche roads between Nice and Menton are unparalleled and have come to represent the Riviera for motorists from the early 20C to the present day. Motorists from Isadora Duncan to James Bond have had experiences along this stretch. One famous narrow escape was an evening journey along the Corniche made by Scott and Zelda Fitzgerald in 1929. At the height of her depression after a party, Zelda seized the steering-wheel to force their car off the cliff into the sea. Scott was able to recover control but in his diary he records how this prompted one of Zelda's spells in a clinic. Isadora Duncan was less fortunate. Her scarf caught in the wheelnut of an open-topped sports car and she was strangled to death.

Elsewhere driving in Provence is rather like driving in other parts of France except that it is generally busier. The region is nevertheless very large and it is not difficult to find remote and quiet districts to explore in the *arrière pays* back from the coast. In certain parts, such as the mountainous reaches of Haute-Provence, and the road network around the *Route Napoléon*, a car is virtually the only way to get around. These areas offer unique and breathtaking natural sights from the edge of the road but other popular sights, such as the Gorges de Verdon or the single road through Moustiers, can be one constant traffic jam.

On a practical note, petrol is generally cheaper off the main roads or motor-ways and the best prices are probably found at supermarkets. There are still many small **garages** in France and they tend to offer a very good repair service. If you have a breakdown check the local garage in any town or village. Otherwise look under *Dépannages* in the telephone directory.

Taxis are well marked and freely available in the towns: there is a rule that they should only pick up passengers from ranks but they will overlook this restriction. The rates vary from town to town but make sure there is a meter and that it is running properly when you get into the taxi. In villages, the taxi service can be rather quaint. Sometimes you will have to book your taxi well in advance, only to find that the driver is the mechanic or petrol-pump attendant whom you originally asked.

By rail and bus

The rail network in Provence is good, making it easy and convenient to travel between towns. There is, for example, a line along much of the eastern coastal area linking the resorts. The main lines back into the heart of the region tend to follow the river valleys and this has, to some extent, defined the rail network much as it shaped the older road system. The train is less convenient if one wishes to gain access to some of the more spectacular scenery and the railway system does not reach many of the parts which are readily accessible by car. In this case bus services can be more useful but they are less frequent than many tourists and travellers would like and tend to operate within self-contained districts. This means that there is a lack of the central timetabling information which would allow for more elaborate route-planning across a wide area. For detailed information on local bus services you must check at the bus station (*gare routière*) or at the tourist information office in each town.

By bicycle

You can always see bikes in every part of Provence but on the higher roads cycling can appear more like an endurance test than a mode of transport or a relaxing pursuit. The coastal roads are too congested with cars in summer to offer the freedom and flexibility that a bicycle seems to invite. For these reasons, therefore, the most suitable area for the cyclist is old Provence and the Rhône valley in the west. Not only is this part relatively flat, particularly round the area of La Crau, but there are numerous interesting sites to visit, from Classical remains or ruined abbeys to the landscapes once painted by Van Gogh. Bicycles are widely available for hire at the main bus and train stations or through local tourist information offices. Mopeds, motorcycles and scooters are also readily available for hire.

Walking

Despite its popularity, Provence offers many walks which take the rambler out of sight and earshot of the general tourist traffic. Not only are many of these just a short distance from the coast but they are often well marked and mapped out. Most of the local tourist offices have a map of their immediate area with good walks of various lengths of time or difficulty. I have always found the area of Haute-Provence around Digne or the Lubéron to be best for walking. Others find the spectacular heights of the Gorges du Verdon more exciting.

The **Sentiers de Grande Randonnée** (GR), an organisation dedicated to planning and preserving some of the longer historic routes, have a list of walks that should engage the serious cross-country walker. Six of these major routes (GR4, 6, 9, 92, 98 and 99) come into the region of Provence and the Côte d'Azur: these are detailed in *Walks in Provence* (Robertson McCarta, London, 1989), or contact:

Comité National des Sentiers de Grandes Randonnées. 64 rue de Gergovie, 75014 Paris ☎ 01 45 45 31 02

It is often claimed that the French are less conscious of private property and of the laws of trespass than the English. This may be true but the presence of fierce **dogs**, which are generally kept for security purposes, not as pets, is a major deterrant to the adventurous rambler. A large stick is useful to fend off unwanted attentions. For walking in the wilder parts of Provence you will need proper boots, a hat and some water to counteract the heat in summer.

 # Health

There are no specific health concerns when travelling in France beyond the normal advice to travellers in general. The French are probably more conscious of care in preparing food than others but everyone is prone to stomach problems when in a different country. Unless marked *eau non potable* most water is drinkable. In general, however, you should drink bottled water, a habit pioneered by the French.

There are reciprocal health and medical arrangements between EU countries. UK citizens can obtain emergency cover under form E111, available from post offices. In any case, travel insurance is recommended. Travellers from North America should check that their insurance covers all medical expenses. Make sure you obtain the relevant forms or receipts (feuille des soins) for an insurance claim.

You may be charged for the use of an ambulance but this should be covered in any insurance policy. For a doctor, consult the police station (*gendarmerie*) or local telephone directory under the category *Urgences* or *SOS Médecins*. First aid advice is generally available from pharmacies which are marked by a Green Cross.

In case of accident, emergency telephone numbers are as follows:

Ambulance (SAMU) ☎ 15   **Police** ☎ 17
Fire ☎ 18   **Operator** ☎ 13
Directory Enquiries ☎ 12.

Telephone and postal services

You can make local, national and international calls from the **telephone boxes** or *cabines* in the street or at post offices. Many of these will only operate with phone cards, available from *tabacs* and newsagents (50 units for 40FF), but some accept coins. France has a new telephone system involving 10-digit numbers which is explained in three languages in the telephone box. (If phoning from Britain you do not dial the first 0, that for the area code.) To make an international call from Provence, dial the international access code 00, then the national code of the country (UK 44, USA 1, Canada 1, Australia 61), then the number minus the first 0. The off-peak period with cheaper rates is 22.30–08.00, and weekends starting at 14.00 on Saturdays. Mobile phones can be used from France if they are digital but the scale of charges will be altered.

A very useful adjunct to the French telephone system is **Minitel**, a computerised information service which gives access to many directories, timetables, programmes and databases. It is found in many French homes and can be used in post offices.

Postal services are very straightforward. There are **post offices** in every town and village, with all the facilities you would expect: letter and parcel post, fax, *poste restante*, etc. Stamps can be purchased at *tabacs* as well as at post offices and their staff are familiar with the rate for letters and postcards. The small, yellow post boxes are easily visible in the streets.

Additional information

Crime and personal security

Petty crime is very common in the south of France and particularly along the coastal strip. Much of this is opportunistic theft of purses and bags but there is a virtual epidemic of **car break-ins**. As in most countries, do not leave valuables in cars if at all possible, and certainly do not leave bags and other belongings in full view. Thefts from hotel rooms and campsites are also quite common, so you should leave valuables in a safe. As a general rule, try not to carry large amounts of money. Traveller's cheques are safer and can be replaced.

If you have to report a crime, go to the *gendarmerie* or *commisariat de police* where a form can be filled out for insurance purposes.

Embassies and consulates

• **British Consulate**. 24 avenue Prado, 13006 Marseilles ☎ 91 15 72 10, fax 91 37 47 06.

• **US Consulates.** 12 boulevard Paul-Peytral, 13006 Marseilles ☎ 91 54 92 00 and 31 rue Maréchal-Joffre, 06000 Nice ☎ 93 88 89 55.

Other nationalities should consult the relevant embassy or consulate in Paris.

Newspapers

Most British newspapers and the *International Herald Tribune* are available from newsagents in the larger towns, usually on the day after publication. Of the French newspapers, *Le Monde* and *Le Figaro* are the main national broadsheets, but there is great loyalty to local or regional newspapers in the south. In the great age of Anglo-American tourism there were several English-language newspapers on the Côte d'Azur. Nowadays, a few local versions like the *Riviera Reporter* still operate but they are rather parochial.

Opening hours

Banks are open 09.00–12.00 and 14.00–16.00 on weekdays and closed either Monday or Saturday. They also close early on the day before a public holiday.

Post offices are open 08.00–19.00 on weekdays and 08.00–12.00 on Saturdays.

Shops. Most food shops are open 07.00–18.30 or 19.30 with some variations. Clothes shops and department stores are open from c 09.00–19.00. The large supermarkets are often open till 21.00 or 22.00 in the evening. Many shops close on Mondays or else take a half day.

National art galleries and museums in France tend to close on Tuesday. To complement this, or to confuse the visitor, most of the **local or municipal museums** close on Monday. Virtually all museums are closed on national holidays. To further complicate matters, a number of châteaux are still in private hands and may have their own calendars of opening. State buildings tend to be closed from mid-December to the end of February and have longer opening hours in high summer. The best advice is to check locally.

Churches and cathedrals are open most days but they often close at lunchtime. Treasuries or any sections with an entrance fee may have restricted opening hours.

Public holidays

The following dates are the main public holidays (*jours fériés*) in France. Museums and other monuments may be closed on these days and you should expect reduced services.

The French tend to take their summer holidays in August. This is a particularly busy time on the roads and on all forms of public transport, as are the various annual festivals (see p 25).

1 January New Year's Day	**14 July** Bastille Day
Easter Sunday and Monday	**15 August** Assumption
1 May May Day	**1 November** All Saints' Day
8 May VE Day	**11 November** Armistice Day
21 May Ascension Day	**25 December** Christmas Day
Whit Sunday and Monday	

Public toilets

The notorious French *pissoirs* of British humour have largely disappeared to be replaced by corrugated concrete cubicles in the street. They cost a *franc* and claim to be hygienic but beware those that malfunction. There are some proper public toilets in towns with an attendant who may expect a small tip on the plate. An alternative is to make use of the WCs in the basements of cafés.

Tipping

Most restaurants now incorporate in the bill a percentage for service, usually 12% or 15%. As with most things, however, a sort of inflation applies and it is becoming increasingly expected that customers will want to give a further gratuity for an individual waiter. You should also tip taxi drivers, porters and the attendants at public toilets.

Tourist information

Offices du Tourisme or *Syndicats d'Initiative* (SIs) exist in all towns and in many of the villages of Provence. For locations, see the individual entries in the guide. They can provide information on accommodation, restaurants, local transport and the most important sights or entertainment in the area. In many cases they can also book hotel rooms or local bed-and-breakfast accommodation. The central offices in each Provençale *département* are:
• **Bouches-du-Rhône**. 13 rue Roux-de-Brignolles, 13006 Marseille ☎ 04 91 13 84 13.
• **Gard**. 3 place des Arènes, BP 122, 30011 Nîmes ☎ 04 66 21 02 51.
• **Côte d'Azur**. 55 promenade des Anglais, BP 602, 06011 Nice ☎ 04 93 44 50 59.
• **Monaco**. 2A boulevard des Moulins, 98000 Monaco ☎ 04 93 50 60 88.
• **Var**. 1 boulevard Maréchal Foch, BP 99, 83003 Draguignan ☎ 04 94 68 58 33.
• **Vaucluse**. BP 147, 84008 Avignon ☎ 04 90 86 43 42.

Food and drink

Provençal cuisine is distinguished from the rest of France by its **Mediterranean character**. Not only is there an abundance of the type of fruit, vegetables and above all herbs that can only be grown on the fringes of the northern Mediterranean basin, the culture which has developed there has also placed great emphasis on certain combinations and methods of cooking food. Provençal cuisine is often closer to Italian and Spanish cooking than it is to the food of other parts of France. Perhaps for this reason it has had to wait longer for recognition and is still occasionally referred to as a provincial, peasant or primitive style of cooking as opposed to the *haute cuisine* upon which the French pride themeselves. But this attitude has changed and the rise of an international market for French country cooking, promoted above all by the famous book of the same name by Elizabeth David, has given Provençal food a justly famous position.

There are perhaps three ingredients which, more than anything else, help to define Provençal cuisine. **Olives** were planted in Provence by the Greeks and, ever since, the trees have occupied a symbolic position in the life of the area as well as being a conspicuous feature of the landscape. Olive oil underlies virtually all the major dishes, whether meat, fish or vegetable. Alongside this **garlic** appears just as prominently and in the past helped to characterise the peasant fare as coarse, smelly and somehow crude. Fortunately the Anglo-Saxon aversion to garlic has receded and its rich tang, which runs through most dishes, is now prized rather than lamented by visiting palates. Garlic is the principal ingredient of *aïoli*, often described as 'Provençal butter', which is an accompaniment to many dishes and is celebrated in village festivals. The third element is the fresh **herbs** that are widely available in the south of France, and which are now collectively marketed in sachets as *Herbes de Provence*. Any walk in the country-side of the *arrière pays* will reveal plenty of rosemary, sage, thyme, bay and fennel growing by the path and it is understandable that this natural harvest should be used widely in cooking.

It would be wrong, however, to see Provençale cuisine as something fixed or universal. In fact the reverse is true. One of its main features is the sheer diversity of styles and ingredients as one moves across the region. This is perhaps to be expected, given the local differences in climate, landscape and even political allegiance. Perhaps for this reason the area around Nice, which only returned to France from Italy in 1860, is felt to have the most distinctive and celebrated cuisine of the whole area. By the same token the inland areas have little in common with the coast and it is not unusual for towns to have developed dishes in direct contradiction to the tastes of their neighbours. Another aspect is the introduction of exotic elements which seem to have settled into the diet as if they were natural products of the area. Many **Spanish dishes** were introduced to the coastal towns and the hinterland of the Luberon by an influx of Spanish settlers in the 19C. Similarly, the presence of a large Arab population from North Africa has introduced new features that have found their place.

Provençal cooking has grown out of a peasant culture and as a result its dishes have often developed out of necessity and the availability of certain unusual ingredients. For example, one of the most famous dishes is *bouillabaisse*, a rich fish and seafood stew made in Marseille and Toulon. Far from being the expensive delicacy it is now, it was probably inspired by the need to make something of those parts of the fisherman's catch that could not be sold.

Nevertheless, to recreate a traditional Provençal peasant meal is probably to indulge in myth-making. Despite the attempts of the poet Mistral to fashion a folk tradition out of fragments of evidence, there was no such thing. There are however, distinctive dishes that have come to represent a peculiarly Provençal pattern to dining, whether in the family home or in a restaurant. A typical opening to the meal would be **tapenade**, a paste of olives and anchovies which can be eaten with celery or bread. The starters might include **salade Niçoise**, one local dish which has become international, although many claim it has been corrupted. (According to Jacques Médecin, erstwhile mayor of the city, the true version of this salad consists of boiled eggs, olives, tomatoes and anchovies, but definitely not potatoes.) Another famous local starter is the thick vegetable soup known as **soupe de pistou**. Close to Italian minestrone, this is filled out with beans but it is the basil and olive-oil sauce (*pistou* is the Provençal for the Italian *pesto*) that gives it its distinctiveness. *Soupe de pistou* can be so filling that the rest of a meal might consist solely of local vegetables such as the delicious asparagus or ubiquitous chard.

A more elaborate but actually quite simple use of vegetables is **ratatouille**, also from Nice, which consists of tomatoes cooked with onions, aubergines, courgettes and peppers in garlic, oil and herbs. These vegetable dishes apart, several rich meat and fish dishes are still widely eaten in the south. Beef stews, known as **daubes**, are quite common, although they were more often made with pork or mutton in the villages. Another version uses the wild boar that is hunted in the autumn; when available this can produce a particularly rich and tangy stew but it is often so laden with gravy that it loses its taste. A more famous and, in summer, appetising dish is the fish and seafood stew known as

bouillabaisse. There are versions of this along the whole length of the Côte d'Azur but, strictly speaking, it is made best in the stretch between Marseille and Toulon. The main ingredients are garlic, water seasoned with saffron, and various shellfish which are added whole to the pot. The key to true bouillabaisse, however, is the rascasse, a grotesque, spiky fish unique to that part of the Mediterranean. Bouillabaisse takes a long time to cook and you will have to order it in advance, often the day before, if it is to be done properly. It is also very expensive for everyday meals, so the more modest **bourride** (a stew of white fish) or the noted **soupe de poissons** of St-Tropez may be more appropriate.

Provence is one of the great market gardens of France and its **fruit** is noted all over the country. This extends to specific towns and villages which are famous for their produce. Cherries from Lourmarin, melons from Cavaillon, figs from Marseille and oranges from Nice are an excellent way to finish a meal. There is a range of goat's **cheeses** (*chèvres*), flavoured with herbs, and some unusual **sweets** like the *calissons* of Aix or the crystallised chestnuts (*marrons glacés*) of Collobrières.

Wine

Even more than the cuisine, the **wines** of Provence have suffered from the snobbery and elitism of many wine buffs. While they will never rival the great centres of Burgundy and Bordeaux, Provençal wines have been improving steadily over the last couple of decades to create a distinctive character for the region. Reds are most common, tracing their origins back to the Greeks who introduced the Syrah grape to the region in the 5C BC. The true founders of viticulture in Provence, however, were the clergy who cultivated both the grape and the refining processes during the Middle Ages. The greatest testament to this are the famous vineyards of Chateauneuf-du-Pape near Avignon, which grew up on land owned by the popes. The castle was ruined by fire in the 16C but the vineyards continue to thrive long after the popes moved back to Rome. In fact it was the wine-growers of this district who in the 1920s campaigned successfully for protection of their identity, introducing the system of *appellation contrôlée* that now governs the assessment of all French wines. Of the four categories most Provençal wine is in the 2nd class (*Vin de Qualité Supérieure*), or 3rd class (*Vin de Pays*). Recommendations of specific labels do not necessarily help in choosing wines with a meal but the Côtes-du-Rhônes are notable, and the Lubérons and Côtes-du-Ventoux are heavy reds with an improving reputation. For everyday drinking the *vin du maison*, served in an unlabelled carafe, is likely to be quite palatable and probably good value. The whites of Provence are less successful but the region is known for its *rosés* which can be very light and refreshing. Of a different category altogether is the famous **sweet wine** known as Muscat de Beaumes-de-Venise, mainly drunk as an aperitif. The traditional aperitif of the region, however, is the local version of aniseed spirit that in Greece is known as ouzo and in Turkey as raki. In Provence it is called *anis* but such is the success of one local producer that it has become collectively known as **pastis**. Drunk on an evening while you overlook one of the outstanding views of this area, nothing seems more natural or perfectly suited to the place and time. Only when you get *pastis* back to northern climes do you wonder why it seemed so perfectly refreshing and delicious.

Restaurants

France's justified reputation for the quality of its cuisine is reflected in the range and standard of its **restaurants**. It is true that many of the better restaurants, particularly those with the coveted Michelin stars, can be pricey but in France you generally get what you pay for when eating out. Having said this, there is no doubt that the overall standard is better than that in Britain or North America and that at the bottom end of the market it is cheaper and easier to have a good meal with wine in France than in almost any country in Northern Europe.

The *Michelin Red Guide* gives information on the better restaurants, grading them according to a series of stars. Those listed can be expensive but they are worth it for a culinary experience. You should note that the French themselves take the **Michelin listing** very seriously and it is important to book in advance. Lower down the scale there is every type of eating-place imaginable. There are still many small restaurants owned and run by families who offer a reasonable menu and a range of set meals, while others specialise in regional or local cuisine which, in Provence, is one of the most distinctive in all France. Obviously, the best seafood restaurants are near the coast but other types of local cooking are found in the inland areas.

There are generally two ways of ordering a meal in France which, nowadays, are adopted in many other countries. To eat **à la carte** is to choose from the full menu in which each dish is priced individually. Most of the smaller and many larger restaurants will also have a **menu du jour** or set menu with a limited range of dishes and an overall fixed price. It is generally advisable to check the *menu du jour* because the chef will have composed this from what is in season or readily available from the market and it is, therefore, often the best value and the freshest. Look out also for dishes that may be unique to that chef or restaurant. In towns it is often advisable to eat in bars or cafés at lunchtime. This is where the local working people generally eat and you will find many establishments which offer only lunch to a set menu in the back room. Cafés also offer snacks and sandwiches through most of the day.

Tourist restaurants have acquired something of a poor reputation in many of the coastal areas and, increasingly, at the more popular sights of inland Provence. It is difficult to say whether this is the natural result of over-popularity or a lack of discrimination which has driven prices up and standards down. Certainly, there has been a huge rise in fast food chains during the last 20 years which have undermined the more traditional restaurants, cafés and bistros. The best advice is to look at the menu, generally posted outside, and weigh up the establishment from its overall appearance and prices. For some guidance, see the restaurants recommended in the guide.

Sports and leisure

Given its climate and landscape, the south of France is particularly well suited to outdoor sports and there are facilities for virtually every pursuit imaginable. All of these, from water sports to rock-climbing, can be followed up at local *syndicats d'initiative* or *offices du tourisme*, which should have the addresses of local facilities and an indication of prices.

All types of **sailing** are available with tuition along the Côte d'Azur and the rocky coastline round Marseille is very popular for **scuba-diving**. By contrast, **fishing** is less easy in Provence. The rivers suffer from variable water levels and do not offer the range of locales that you would find in other parts of France. Anglers must obtain a permit and observe any local regulations. Sea-fishing is probably better done by boat than from the shore. Activities that are pursued on the rivers of Provence are **canoeing and rafting**, restricted to the stretches that are deemed safe. Again, consult the local tourist offices for details of local firms with canoes for hire or expeditions led by specialists.

For **rock-climbing**, the Dentelles de Montmirail offer a range of ascents and there are other specific heights throughout the region that appeal to different tastes. The Club Alpin Français has an office at 12 rue Fort-Notre-Dame, 13007 Marseille ☎ 04 91 54 36 94 which has information on climbing and potholing. **Riding** is popular in most parts of upper Provence but it is probably most associated with the Camargue. There are stables hiring out horses for varying lengths of time in Stes-Maries-de-la-Mer, the main agency being the Association des Loueurs de Chevaux de Camargue at Mas de Lys, Route d'Arles, Stes-Maries-de-la-Mer, ☎ 04 90 97 86 27. Despite the aridity of much of the Provençal landscape, there are a number of **golf** courses in the south. The best known are in the area inland of Cannes, notably at Mandelieu-la-Napoule. These course are now organised rather in the style of American country clubs and a round of golf can be very expensive.

Petanque or **boules** is the principal local sport that you see played in the hard gravel squares of every town and village in Provence. It is taken seriously, however, and the grizzled locals do not take favourably to outsiders who wish to join in. If you wish to play, the space is free and you can purchase *boules* of varying quality from local shops.

With regard to competitive or spectator sports, there are numerous **tennis** tournaments in the south, particularly at Nice and Monaco in April. Two of the leading French **football** teams, Olympique de Marseilles and Monaco, are based here and many other towns and villages have a local team. A different sort of sport altogether, **bullfighting**, is played out in the old Roman amphitheatres of Arles and Nîmes throughout the summer. Traditionally, the Provençal bullfight does not lead to the killing of the bull, but many fights are now conducted in the more bloodthirsty Spanish style.

High and popular culture are well catered for throughout the south of France. As well as the range of **arts festivals** listed in the calendar (see above), there are numerous theatres, cinemas and concert halls in all the main towns. Check with the tourist offices for a programme of forthcoming events. A particular development of the last two decades is **open-air concerts** in ancient sites such as the amphitheatres in Arles, Nîmes or Fréjus. These encompass chamber music to heavy metal rock concerts as well as a range of theatre productions and dance performances. The great theatre at Orange is an experience in itself, often overpowering the performance. At the other end of the scale, the *fêtes* held in every village in Provence at some point during the year will have local musicians, dance troupes and performers appearing on a makeshift stage in the main square and culminating in a dance to one of the local bands in the evening. These are well worth attending for a glimpse of village life only partially packaged for the tourist market.

Events and festivals

Fêtes are a recurring feature of life in Provence as in other parts of France. They originally related to certain saints' feast days, to local customs or to the season in which particular produce such as grapes, fruit or rice was harvested. This is still the case and in many instances the *fêtes* are remarkably well supported by local people. The **bravade** is perhaps the most typical of the Provençal festivals, involving processions to and from church and a series of competitions from bull-chasing to fights over water. Alongside this there is usually a special market offering a colourful and at times delicious alternative to the public entertainment. In recent years, however, arts festivals of one sort or another have been identified as a great aid to tourism with the result that there is scarcely a town in Provence which does not have an arts, folklore, music or jazz festival at some point in the year. The models for these are the great international festivals at Avignon, Aix and Antibes

The following list includes only the major festivals and those which are either traditional or unique. Dates are approximate and may vary by a few days each year. More detailed information on each event and on those not mentioned in the list are available from local *syndicats d'initiative* or *offices du tourisme*.

January
17 January	**Barjols** Festival of St Marcel, lasting a week
27 January	**Monaco** Festival of St Devota in the Condamine
Last weekend	**Valbonne** Festival of the Grape and the Olive

February
2 February	**Marseilles** Candlemas Procession (*Fête de la Chandeleur*)
2 February	**Grimaud** Candlemas Festival
Mid-February	**Nice** Carnival and Battles of Flowers. There are flower festivals in other towns at this time, including Bormes-les-Mimosas and Mandelieu
Mid-Feb to March	**Menton** Lemon Festival

March
Good Friday	**Roquebrune** Procession of the Entombment of Christ
Easter	**Arles** Easter Festival with bullfights in the Spanish style
Easter	**Vence** Festival of Folklore
End March or early April	**Hyères** Floral procession

April
3rd Sunday after Easter	**Fréjus** *Bravade St-François*, with procession
End of April	**Villeneuve-Lès-Avignon** Feast of St Mark, with processions

May
1 May	**Arles** *Gardians'* festival
Ascension Day	**Grimaud** Wool Fair
2nd week	**Cannes** Film Festival
Mid-May	**Monaco** Grand Prix

Mid-May	**Nîmes** *Féria*
16–18 May	**St-Tropez** *Bravades*
Third weekend	**Grasse** Rose Festival
24–26 May	**Stes-Maries-de-la-Mer** Gypsy pilgrimage and festival
Whitsun(late May early June)	**Apt** Music Festival and equestrian cavalcade
Whitsun	**Nîmes** Festival or *Féria*
Whit Monday	**St-Rémy** Festival of Transhumance

June

June	**Toulon** Music Festival
15 June	**St-Tropez** Spanish Procession
Last weekend	**Tarascon** Tarasque festival: folklore, processions and bull fights
Late June	**St-Tropez** Fishermen's Festival

July

	L'Isle-sur-la-Sorgue and surrounding villages Music and Drama Festival
	Arles Festival
	Villeneuve-Lès-Avignon Events and performances at the Chartreuse
	St-Rémy Organ Festival
	Vence Classical Music Festival
1st Saturday	**Martigues** Venetian Festival, with aquatic displays
1st weekend	**Villefranche** Feast of St Peter
2nd Sunday	**Tende** Feast of St Eligius, patron saint of muleteers
1st fortnight	**Marseille** Festival of Folklore at Chateau-Gombert
1st or 2nd Sunday	**Cap d'Antibes** Seamen's Festival at La Garoupe
Mid-July	**Carpentras** Festival of Our Lady of Good Health, with processions
Mid-July	**Le Cannet** Flower Festival
Mid-July to early August	**Avignon** Festival
Mid-July to early August	**Orange** Choir Festival
Mid to end July	**Aix-en-Provence** Festival
2nd fortnight	**Antibes** International Jazz Festival
2nd fortnight	**Arles** Festival of Photography
2nd fortnight	**Uzès** Music Festival
Mid-July to mid-August	**Cotignac** La Falaise Theatre Festival
21–22 July	**La Ste-Baume** Feast of St Mary Magdalene
End July to early August	**Marseille** Boules Competition at Borély Park
July and August	**Cannes** American Festival
July and August	**Brignoles** Summer Festival

August

	Sylvacane Abbey Piano Festival
	Menton Chamber Music Festival
1st fortnight	**Abbaye du Thoronet** Poetry Festival
1st fortnight	**Ramatuelle** Theatre Festival
1st Sunday	**Grasse** Jasmine Festival
1st Sunday	**Fréjus** Grape Festival
5 August	**Roquebrune-Cap-Martin** Passion procession
Mid August	**St-Rémy** *Féria*
2nd fortnight	**Barjols** Leather Fair
End August	**Aigues-Mortes** Feast of St Louis
Tues in late August	**Monteux** St John Fireworks Display

September

	Cannes Festival of Sailing
1st Sunday	**Peille** Folk Festival
2nd week	**Arles** Rice Festival and procession
8–9 September	**Cogolin** Provençal Fair
3rd week	**Le Castellet** Motorcycle races
3rd Sunday	**Taradeau** Festival of New Wine
19 September	**Lorgues** Festival of St Ferréol
Last week	**Nîmes** Grape Harvest Festival
29 September	Many villages hold fairs on or around Michaelmas

October

6 October	**Fréjus** Garlic Fair
Late October	**Grasse** Perfume Fair
Sunday nearest 22 October	**Stes-Maries-de-la-Mer** Procession and blessing of sea

November

Monday after 11 November	**Collobrières** St Martin's Fair
End November and December	**Marseille** Santons Fair
30 November	**Ramatuelle** St Andrew's Fair

December

1st Sunday	**Bandol** Wine Festival
24 December	Midnight Mass celebrated in most towns in Provence but special events at Les Baux, Lucéram, St-Rémy, La Ste-Baume and Tarascon.

Background information

History of Provence

Chronology

c 1800–600 BC	Area of Provence settled by Ligurian tribes during Bronze Age
c 800–600 BC	Infiltration of Celts from Northern Europe
c 600 BC	Foundation of Massalia (Marseille) by Phocaeans
218 BC	Hannibal crosses the Rhône *en route* to Italy from North Africa
125–23 BC	Sextius overruns Salyan citadel at Entremont and founds Aquae Sextiae (Aix), the first Roman settlement in Provence
102 BC Aix	Roman General Marius defeats huge Teuton army near to consolidate Roman imperial power in Gaul
58–51 BC	Invasion of Gaul by Julius Caesar
49 BC	Marseille besieged and taken by Julius Caesar in war with Pompey
19 BC the	Erection of the Pont du Gard carrying fresh water from Eure to the Roman colony at Nîmes
313	Emperor Constantine grants freedom of worship to Christians in Edict of Milan
314	First Council of Christian Bishops in Arles
321	Capital of Empire moved from Rome to Byzantium
400	Roman Emperor Honorius declares Arles capital of the 'Three Gauls' (France, Britain and Spain)
410	Foundation of monastery on Iles de Lérins by Honoratus
416	St John Cassian founds Abbaye St-Victor at Marseille
471	Arles overrun by Visigoths
476	Collapse of the Western Roman Empire; overall control of Provence falls to Visigoths
536	Provence ceded to the Franks
725	Abbot and monks of St-Honorat massacred by Moors
732–39	Region passified and Moors driven out by Charles Martel
843	Treaty of Verdun presents Provence and Burgundy to Lothair, grandson of Charlemagne
855	Provence declared a kingdom for Lothair's son Charles the Bald
879	Boson crowned King of Provence; declares Arles capital
949	Provence united with Burgundy under Duke Conrad
972–79	Guillaume liberates Provence from the Saracens and declares himself Marquis
1032	Provence annexed to the Holy Roman Empire under Conrad II

1112	Marriage of Douce and Raymond Bérenger III brings Provence under counts of Barcelona
1125	Provence divided between Counts of Toulouse and Barcelona
1176	Pierre Valdo of Lyon founds Waldensian (Vaudois) religious sect
1178	Emperor Frederick Barbarossa crowned King of Arles in Cathédrale St-Trophîme
1213	Nîmes surrenders to Simon de Montfort in the 'crusade' against the Albigensians in southwest France
1246	Charles of Anjou becomes Count of Provence through marriage to Beatrice of Provence; the start of the Angevin dynasty
1248	Seventh Crusade leaves Aigues-Mortes for Holy Land under St Louis
1274	Comtat-Venaissin ceded to the papacy following the Albigensian 'crusade'
1286	First meeting of the Estates-General of Provence at Sisteron
1303	Foundation of University of Avignon by Pope Boniface VIII
1308	Grimaldi family from Genoa purchase Monaco
1309	Pope Clement V leaves Rome for lands in Provence
1316–76	Period of papal residence in Avignon, the 'Babylonian Captivity'
1327	Petrarch sees Laura at church of Ste-Claire in Avignon
1348	Avignon purchased by Pope Clement VI from Queen Jeanne
1378–1417	Great Schism with rival popes in Rome and Avignon
1388	Nice secedes from Provence to become part of the County of Savoy
1409	Foundation of the University at Aix-en-Provence
1434	René d'Anjou, the exiled king of Naples, becomes Count of Provence ('Good King René')
1480	Death of René d'Anjou
1481	County of Provence bequeathed to King Louis XI of France
1486	Union of Provence with Kingdom of France ratified by Estates-General at Aix
1501	Inauguration of Parlement and Supreme Court establishes Aix as effective administrative capital of Provence until 1790
1536	Invasion of Provence by Emperor Charles V
1539	Villers-Cotterêts Statute imposes French as the official language of Provence

1545	Suppression and massacres of the Vaudois in the Luberon
1567	Massacre of Catholics in Nîmes
1598	Edict of Nantes grants religious tolerance to Huguenots
1680	Louis XIV visits Provence
1685	Louis XIV revokes Edict of Nantes and renews persecution of Huguenots
1720	Plague of Provence ravages Marseille and other towns
1731	Principality of Orange incorporated into France
1789	Comte de Mirabeau elected to the Estates-General for Aix-en-Provence
1790	Marseille declared new regional capital of Provence
1791	Papal lands of Comtat-Venaissin and Avignon annexed to France
1792	In Paris revolutionary supporters from Marseille sing new battle hymn, *La Marseillaise*
1793	Napoleon achieves fame during siege of Toulon
1799	Napoleon lands at St-Raphael after abortive Egyptian campaign
1815	Napoleon lands at Golfe-Juan from Elba to begin march north to Paris, the *Route Napoléon*
1822	British colony in Nice finance the building of the Promenade des Anglais
1830	Revolution brings Louis-Philippe to power
1834	Lord Brougham 'discovers' Cannes and builds villa, confirming the Anglo-Saxon adoption of the Riviera as a holiday resort
1848	Revolution in France
1851	Coup of Napoleon III ends the Second Republic
1854	Foundation of Provençal literary movement, the Félibrige
1855	Louis Napoleon declared emperor; the 'Second Empire'
1860	Plebiscite restores Nice to France after almost 600 years as part of House of Savoy
1862	Casino set up in Monte Carlo
1868	Railway extended to Menton, reaching all the resorts along the Riviera
1869	Opening of Suez Canal boosts Marseille as principal port for trade with the Orient
1887	Poet Stephen Liegeard describes Riviera as the 'Côte d'Azur'
1888	Vincent Van Gogh settles in Arles
1904	Frédéric Mistral awarded Nobel Prize for Literature
1906	Death of Paul Cézanne at his home in Aix-en-Provence
1911	First Monte Carlo Rally

1922	*Train Bleu* begins luxury sleeper service from Paris to Côte d'Azur
1925	Gerald and Sara Murphy build Villa America on Cap d'Antibes
1934	F. Scott Fitzgerald's novel *Tender is the Night* published, describing the life of expatriate Americans on the Côte d'Azur
1936	Introduction of paid holidays for French workers changes character of tourism in Provence
1940	German victory and occupation; creation of Vichy regime
1942	Vichy territory occupied by German troops; French fleet sunk at Toulon
1944	Allied landings near St-Tropez; Provence liberated within two weeks
1946	First Cannes Film Festival
1947	Upper valley of the Roya, behind Menton, ceded to France from Italy
1954	Death of Henri Matisse at Nice
1956	The film *And God Created Woman* with Brigitte Bardot revitalises St-Tropez and the Côte d'Azur as a hedonistic playground
1962	Independence of Algeria leads to return of c 800,000 colonists (*pieds-noirs*), many of whom settle in Provence
1966	Architect Le Corbusier drowns while swimming off Roquebrune
1970	Creation of new local government region, Provence-Alpes-Côte d'Azur
1973	Death of Pablo Picasso at Mougins, burial at Vauvenargues
1980	Completion of *Autoroute La Provençale*
1981	The TGV high speed train network links Paris and Mediterranean
1982	Death of Princess Grace of Monaco in a car accident
1990	Jacques Médecin, mayor of Nice for 25 years, flees to South America under charges of corruption
1997	Election of Front National member of parliament for Vitrolles, near Marseille
1998	France win World Cup; riots of English football fans in Marseille

Rulers of Provence

771–814	Charlemagne, Holy Roman Emperor, King of the Franks
843–55	Lothair I
855–63	Charles, son of Lothair
863–75	Louis II, King of Italy
875–81	Charles the Bald, Holy Roman Emperor
879–87	Boson of Vienne, King of Provence
890–926	Louis ('the Blind'), Holy Roman Emperor
926–47	Hugh of Arles
948–1032	Rights of County of Provence to Burgundy; Conrad of Burgundy (947–93) and Rudolph III, the Idler (993–1032) divide rule of Provence between three counts; rise of local dynasties
(979–	Guillaume 'le Libérateur', declares himself Marquis of Provence)
1032–1113	Incorporated into Holy Roman Empire (but again divided between local dynasties of Toulouse and Barcelona)

The Catalan Counts
1113–31 Raymond Bérenger I
1131–44 Raymond Bérenger II
1144–66 Raymond Bérenger III

The House of Barcelona
1166–96 Alphonse I
1196–1209 Alphonse II
1209–45 Raymond Bérenger V

The House of Anjou
1246–85 Charles I
1285–1309 Charles II
1309–43 Robert the Wise
1343–82 Queen Jeanne

The second House of Anjou
1382–84 Louis I
1385–99 Regency of Marie de Blois
1400–1417 Louis II
1417–34 Louis III
1434–36 Isabelle de Lorraine (during captivity of her husband, René d'Anjou)
1436–80 René d'Anjou
1480–81 Charles III

Provence in the Kingdom of France

The House of Valois
1482–98 Charles VIII ('the Affable')
1498–1515 Louis XII ('Father of the People')
1515–47 François I
1547–59 Henri II
1559–60 Francois II
1560–74 Charles IX
1574–89 Henri III

The House of Bourbon
1589–1610 Henri IV ('the Great')
1610–43 Louis XIII ('the Just')
1643–1715 Louis XIV ('Le Roi Soleil')
1715–74 Louis XV
1774–92 Louis XVI
1792–99 The First Republic
1799–1804 The Consulate
1804–14 (and March–June 1815) The Empire of Napoleon I
1814–24 Louis XVIII
1824–30 Charles X

The House of Orléans
1830–48 Louis-Philippe
1848–51 The Second Republic
1851–71 The Second Empire
(Napoleon III)

Presidents of the Third Republic (1871–1940)
1871–73 Adolphe Thiers
1873–79 Maréchal MacMahon
1879–87 Jules Grévy
1887–94 Sadi Carnot
1894–95 Jean Casimir-Périer
1895–99 Félix Faure
1899–1906 Emile Loubet
1906–13 Armand Fallières
1913–20 Raymond Poincaré
1920 Paul Deschanel
1920–24 Alexandre Millerand
1924–31 Gaston Doumergue
1931–32 Paul Doumer
1932–40 Albert Lebrun
1940–45 Occupation
1942–44 Vichy Government under Maréchal Pétain

Presidents of the Fourth Republic (1946–58)
1947–54 Vincent Auriol
1954–58 René Coty

Presidents of the Fifth Republic (1958–)
1958–69 Général Charles de Gaulle
1969–74 Georges Pompidou
1974–81 Valéry Giscard d'Estaing
1981–95 François Mitterrand
1995– Jacques Chirac

Architecture in Provence

The Classical tradition

There are traces of prehistoric and Bronze Age building throughout southern France and a fascinating range of **vernacular building types** such as the dry-stone *bories* of the Lubéron, the *cabanes* of the *gardians* in the Camargue or the great stone-built *mas* (farmhouses) which can be found in most rural parts of the region. But it is the unbroken tradition of high-quality monumental architecture and public building established by the Romans that gives Provence such a distinguished place in European architecture.

The Romans established towns and trading colonies in southern Gaul in the 2C BC but it was not until the arrival of Julius Caesar and above all Augustus that the province of Narbonensis assumed the position of a new Rome. With the settlement of veterans in Arles, Nîmes and Orange these new cities were equipped with the principal building types on which Roman architects and engineers could display their skill. The best example is probably the Maison Carrée in Nimes, the finest **Roman temple** to have survived in any part of the ancient world. Raised on a podium and with one principal façade this building demonstrates the subtlety with which the Romans could deploy Greek architectural forms yet create from them something that is distinctively Roman. Another type of ceremonial architecture is seen in Les Antiques, two monuments erected at the entrance to the ruined town of Glanum near St-Rémy. The **triumphal arch** is hardly unique—there are better examples in Provence, notably the huge arch at Orange—but the so-called mausoleum is less common and offers an indication of the Roman sense of order and harmony in the relationship of simple geometric forms. It is, however, the combination of these two monuments in a deserted landscape that reveals both the beauty of their intrinsic form and the abiding romance of ruins.

Among the larger exercises in public building, there are the great **arenas** or amphitheatres at Arles and Nîmes, both built in the 1C and employing the massive forms and simple rhythms that distinguish Roman architecture and make it such a powerful influence on subsequent periods. These two buildings are still in use for bullfights, which may be regarded as a modern equivalent of their original function. The huge Roman **theatre** at Orange is also one of the finest surviving examples of its type and still in use for public performances. When critics have questioned the originality of Roman architecture they have invariably pointed to engineering as a field in which the Romans were unparalleled. There is no better example of this than the Pont du Gard, an **aqueduct** spanning the valley of the river Gard to carry water to Nîmes. Not only is this triple arcade efficient in a way that is deceptively subtle, it presents an orderly rhythm across the landscape that seems in complete harmony with its surroundings. This alone would seem to prove the view that engineering, when undertaken to such perfection, has its own intrinsic beauty equivalent to architecture in the pure sense.

The Middle Ages

The Romans left such an impressive legacy of building that it is understandable their influence should have loomed over all monumental building in this region for centuries and even millennia. The early Christians could do little more than appropriate the forms and materials of Roman buildings since they were so obviously imbued with a sophistication and prestige that was unparalleled. To visit the two great **baptisteries** at Fréjus and Aix-en-Provence is to recognise the authority that Roman fragments retained and which could be somehow preserved when columns and capitals from pagan temples were redeployed in a new Christian setting.

It is the Roman heritage which lies behind the distinctive character of **Provençal Romanesque**, the round-arched style of the 10C–13C which is to many people the great glory of French medieval architecture. St-Trophîme in Arles, St-Gilles-du-Gard at St-Gilles, St-Gabriel at Ganagobie, and a host of minor chapels throughout the region demonstrate the beauty of simple, repeated forms and spaces when applied to the ground plan of a Christian church. It is a lesson in pure architecture where the decoration is rarely allowed to interrupt the rhythms of the building or disguise the texture of the rough dressed stonework. In the great abbey complexes of Sénanque, Le Thoronet or Silvacane you are reminded of why the Romanesque was described as 'an architecture of equilibrium and humility', expressing the spirit of the monastic life that it enclosed.

The **Gothic** did not take hold in southern France to the same extent that it did in the north, possibly due to the strength of Provençal Romanesque and the abiding presence of Classical remains on which to draw. There are no breath-taking cathedrals, no soaring interiors such as one sees in Reims, Amiens or Notre-Dame-de-Paris, but the style did make some headway in a more modest fashion. The cathedral at Carpentras, the basilica at St-Maximin-de-la-Ste-Baume and the church of St-Jean-de-Malte in Aix are good examples of the fine structural qualities of the Gothic manner and of its elaborate decorative features. There is also, in the Palais des Papes in Avignon, an example of the Gothic style applied to a unique building; part palace, part fortress and the seat of God's vicar on earth, this formidable structure is in many respects the most important medieval building in Provence.

Another strand in the medieval building tradition is the **château** which, by the 14C–15C, had come to assume the role of cultural centre and home of the court as well as a defensive bastion. The castle at Tarascon has all the appear-ance of a late medieval fantasy, its sheer walls rising up almost 50m to the battlements, but it was actually a rather elegant home for Good King René and his retinue in the 1440s and '50s.

Renaissance to Neo-Classicism

If René d'Anjou was the last of the troubadours, François I saw himself as a Renaissance monarch and sought to introduce the new learning and the design of the Italians to the French court. Examples of this in the south can be found at Uzès, Lourmarin and Gordes, all of which seem to strike a balance between the continuing need to defend while demonstrating the Italianate taste of the seigneur. The greatest example of the **French Renaissance style** in Provence, however, was La Tour d'Aigues, a huge, symmetrical complex of rectilinear forms with distinctive French rooflines, built in the mid-16C. During the Revolution it was pillaged and set on fire, leaving a gaunt ruin in which the elegant Classical gateway is perhaps the finest monument to the wealth and sophistication of its owner.

The 17C and 18C were the great age of **French Classicism** as demonstrated in such restrained and orderly mansions as the Château Borély in Marseille or the Pavillon de Vendôme at Aix. There are a few notable churches in this rather academic manner, such as the unexpectedly grand parish church at Lambesc or the Vieille Charité in Marseille, but as a style high Classicism was more appro-priate for domestic buildings. It is seen at its best in the Mazarin district of Aix where the rational grid plan of streets and squares provides a perfect context for the sequence of elegant façades. This, more than any other part of Provence, seems to embody the Age of Enlightenment and provided the stage on which Mirabeau acted out his amorous adventures.

There is another side to the 17C which derives more from Italy and is there-fore better demonstrated in the towns of eastern Provence. This is the full-blown **Baroque** that you find in churches such as the Gesù and the cathedral of Ste-Réparate at Nice or St-Michel at Menton. In contrast to the restraint and order of Classical buildings, the Baroque makes an unashamed play for the emotions. Façades twist and swell like organic shapes and the rigid lines of the Classical orders seem to break or bend as a preamble to the religious ecstasy that was felt appropriate as one entered a church or chapel. These theatrical effects were even greater on the interior where different colours and fabrics as well as the piling up of paintings and sculpture gave an overwhelming impression of opulence and drama. In St-Michel at Menton this can still be experienced because the deep maroon damask hangings of the 18C interior have been preserved and are still occasionally displayed.

The modern era

The 19C is often regarded as an age of vulgarity and eclecticism in urban architecture and it is true that the French **Beaux-Arts tradition** instilled an approach to building that emphasised the monumental and the pompous, justified by the use of Classical motifs. To dismiss it in those terms, however, is to overlook the complexity of much 19C building and the excitement which some of it engendered at the time. Marseille, for example, has an excellent stock of public buildings from the last century though they still tend to be dismissed, like the city itself, as vulgar and trashy. But look at the great cathedral of La Major or the hotels and casinos of the coastal resorts and you cannot fail to sense the confidence and commitment that lay behind their gargantuan scale. Architecture has never been about form alone, and once we appreciate qualities like humour, drama and artifice the modern architecture of Provence becomes more interesting. No one could mistake the Moorish-style houses of Hyères and Toulon for the real thing; they are pastiches, riddled with errors and inappropriate juxtapositions, but they have a delightful quality that seems perfectly in keeping with their context. Similarly, the Scottish baronial houses such as the Château Scott at Cannes or the Anglo-Indian confection of the Château de l'Anglais at Nice, or the Russian cathedral in the same city, express something of the cosmopolitan character and exoticism of the Riviera.

The same is true of the 20C. There are many buildings that seem to define the high architectural values of their age. Le Corbusier's Unité d'Habitation at Marseille and Robert Mallet-Stevens' Villa Noailles at Hyères are outstanding examples of high **Modernism**, still visited like pilgrimage sites by architectural students and devotees. But they are only one aspect of the built environment in the south of France. Throughout this period there has been an eruption in building of all sorts from hotels to villas, churches, museums and civic centres, all of which play some role in defining the culture of Provence, and more especially the Riviera. Some of it is kitsch, some of it unselfconscious, some good and much bad, but it is definitely alive.

In the last two decades of the 20C there have been several attempts to revitalise the tradition of modern building in Provence, much of it undertaken by civic authorities anxious to promote their towns as centres of culture, quite separate and distinct from Paris. One may look cynically at such policies, but they have created a dynamic environment for architects and designers, and a number of interesting buildings have indeed been created. The new Carré d'Art at Nîmes, Le Grand Bleu civic headquarters at Marseille and the Musée d'Art Moderne at Nice all place Provence at the centre of the international design world.

Art in Provence and the Côte d'Azur

Early sculpture

Unlike the architecture of the region, painting and sculpture had a fitful development in the south of France and there were, arguably, only certain periods when they had more than local significance. Sculpture, it could be claimed, has only thrived in relation to architecture. This is true when one considers the decorative sculpture on Roman monuments like Les Antiques at Glanum or the triumphal arch at Orange. In both cases the reliefs are badly weathered but enough survives to suggest the qualities that were once a highlight of Roman public art. A better indication of **Roman marble carving** is that on the numerous sarcophagi found at Arles and now exhibited in the Musée de l'Arles Antique. The Hippolytus sarcophagus is perhaps the finest or at least the most Classical in its rendering of the figures but there are many others to suggest the range and quality of relief sculpture in both the late Roman and early Christian periods.

Romanesque sculpture was even more closely associated with buildings, the style relying on concentrations of carved decoration to relieve the essentially abstract articulation of space using piers and arches. At St-Trophîme in Arles and at St-Gilles-du-Gard it is the west doorway that supports the principal relief sculpture; two great cycles which reveal both the narrative skill of their masters and a grandeur of overall conception that evokes their Classical sources. For sensitive rendering of figures, the storiated capitals in the cloister of St-Trophîme and at St-Sauveur in Aix demonstrate the freshness of vision that Romanesque craftsmen could bring to familiar stories from the Bible.

From the Middle Ages to the 18th century

There were small local schools associated with the various courts in Provence in the Middle Ages, but they did not flourish or last. The establishment of a major school of painting can be dated to the arrival of the popes in Avignon in the 14C. There was a long tradition of **papal patronage** of the visual arts in Rome and it seemed only natural that this should continue in the papacy's new home. What gave this policy a distinctive character was the presence of leading Italian artists in the train of the curia. The central figure was Simone Martini (c 1284–1344) who brought the delicacy of line, elegance of figural description and richness of colour that were already characteristics of the Sienese school. Given the glamour and prestige associated with the papal court it is hardly surprising that this style should have been widely imitated but it also established a pattern of workshop training that led to an independent school. By the later 14C it is possible to talk of a **School of Avignon** which continued as a major force in European art long after the popes had returned to Rome. A cursory stroll through the Petit Palais is perhaps sufficient to see the full range and quality of artists such as Josse Lieferinxe (active late 15C) and numerous other anonymous masters.

There is, however, one enigmatic figure who towers over this. **Enguerrand Quarton** or Charenton (c 1410–c 1461) is the name most often linked to a group of pictures which are undoubtedly the greatest panel paintings produced in France during the 15C. The tragic *Pietà* now in the Louvre is perhaps the best known of this artist's works but one major painting by him survives in Provence in the municipal museum in Villeneuve-Lès-Avignon. The *Coronation of the Virgin* is an astonishing work by any standards but its clear and distinct character makes it stand out from a period of crisis in French painting.

Royal patronage in the greater France which included Provence tends to have been centralised in Paris and in the palace complexes at Fontainebleau and Versailles. There were still local schools but, in general, it is fair to say that they were provincial. This is not to dismiss them. After all, the appeal of works by the so-called **School of Nice** in the 15C–16C is precisely because they are fresh and direct. Nice was part of the independent County of Savoy and looked more to Italian traditions than to anything in France. This is clear, for example, when you look at the numerous altarpieces by the Bréa family which hang in large and small churches around Nice, or the vivid cycle of frescoes at Notre-Dames-des-Fontaines in the Roya valley.

During the 17C and 18C several striking individuals emerged, such as **Pierre Puget** (1620–94), the sculptor from Marseille who trained as a carver of ships' prows and graduated to great marble groups such as the muscular atlantes that support the entrance to the Hôtel de Ville in Toulon. There are other similar examples of this type of architectural sculpture at Aix. The normal pattern for a promising painter or scuptor, however, was to leave the south and move to Paris or Versailles where the money was and where there was real hope of improvement. **Jean-Honoré Fragonard** (1732–1806), for example, was from Grasse but made his career in Paris.

The golden age

It was not until the late 19C that Provence became a centre for art, a place that artists from other regions would visit and depict. **Paul Cézanne** (1839–1906) came from Aix-en-Provence and he chose to retreat from the Paris art world and concentrate on his singular view of landscape. The sense of form and structure that he felt was lacking in Impressionist paintings was somehow embodied in the colossal limestone Montagne Ste-Victoire looming over his native city. In all, he painted some 80 oils of the mountain, constantly returning to this powerful motif to reinforce his belief that a painting should have the underlying structure that palpably operates in nature.

In February 1888 **Vincent van Gogh** (1853–90) also left Paris seeking new inspiration in the warmth of the south. In fact he aimed to set up an 'Academie du Midi', a colony of artists who would escape from the stifling atmosphere of Paris and find a new art based on colour and emotion, inspired by the twin sources of Japan and the antique. Several artists were supposed to join him in Arles but only Paul Gauguin (1848–1903) did, pressed into going by Vincent's brother Theo with the inducement of some cash. The academy may have been a bad idea, at least with Gauguin as a member, but it set a pattern of living and working in the brilliant light of the south that others took up.

In 1892 the Pointillist painter **Paul Signac** (1863–1935) visited St-Tropez and was so impressed by the light that he bought a house there and invited many of his younger followers to join him. Among this group, Pierre-Albert Marquet (1875–1944), André Derain (1880–1954) and **Henri Matisse** (1859–1954) spent some time on the Mediterranean and the sheer brilliance of the colour and the surroundings helped them to break free of the normal constraints. Soon the

Mediterranean coast was seen as the very epitome of sensuality, beauty and colour. Matisse produced some of his greatest early works here and from 1916 onwards made Nice his home. 'In order to paint my pictures', he remarked, 'I need to remain for several days in the same state of mind, and I do not find this in any atmosphere but that of the Côte d'Azur.' To the end of his life he continued to work in and around Nice painting views out of his studio window, or the series of odalisques, half-naked women in oriental costume posed against sensual, exotic backgrounds. When he could no longer paint, Matisse turned to coloured paper cut-outs that seemed to simplify his ideas and keep him in touch with the ideals of his earlier art. His last and greatest work in this vein was the decoration of the Dominican chapel at Vence.

The other great 20C master who lived and worked along this coast was, of course, **Pablo Picasso** (1881–1973). He first came to Cannes after the First World War and was immediately impressed by the sensuality of the area and the sense of a tradition stretching back to the ancient world. Many of his paintings treat Classical myths or the ancient bull cults of the Mediterranean basin but they are animated by a kind of sensual immediacy or eroticism that was based on his personal feelings. In 1946 he returned to Antibes, Cannes and Vallauris to rediscover the spirit of his earlier work, which had been smothered by the experiences of Paris during the Occupation. It was a completely successful visit and he embarked on a vibrant and prolific new phase that restored his position as the greatest artist of the century.

There were many others of Picasso's generation who found the south conducive to their art. Derain, Raoul Dufy (1877–1953), Kees Van Dongen (1877–1968), Marc Chagall (1887–1985), Georges Rouault (1871–1958) and Fernand Léger (1881–1955) all chose to work along the Côte d'Azur. Perhaps the greatest figure to celebrate the Côte was **Pierre Bonnard** (1867–1947), who lived at Le Cannet for over 20 years until his death in 1947. Bonnard depicted the simple pleasures of domestic life—picnics, views over the garden, meals with friends and, above all, Marthe, his wife—and set out to develop a manner of painting that would communicate the union of colour, light and feeling that the south of France seems to evoke. In pictures of shimmering pink and orange we see Marthe bathing, resting or drying herself in the strong sunlight of a Riviera summer. There can be few better examples of the way in which a place has created a whole aesthetic.

Later generations of painters have continued to visit the south of France but, perhaps intimidated by the sheer range and fecundity, not to say reputations, of Matisse and Picasso, the bulk of the work produced has been very derivative. This problem was exemplified in the tragic life of **Nicolas de Staël** (1914–55), for many the great hope of French painting in the period after the Second World War. Settled in Ménerbes and looking to provide a bridge between the great achievements of the School of Paris and the recent eruption of Abstract Expressionism in New York, de Staël found many supporters among the French literary and critical establishment. Whatever the personal problems he may have had, the burden of hope and expectation in his work was too much for him to bear. In 1955, feeling that he had reached a dead end, he moved to Antibes, to the very building where Picasso had rejuvenated his own art, and shot himself.

The coastal region did, however, see the development of one group of artists who have adopted the title of the **School of Nice**. Rejecting the landscape of pleasure that has dominated French painting, they looked to a more witty and lighthearted play on found materials. Armand-Pierre Arman (1928–), Martial Raysse (1936–) and César (1921–) use the same motifs and even the same specific objects, such as violins or car parts, but their visual jokes wear rather thin after a while.

One artist who is often included in the group is **Yves Klein** (1928–62) but in fact he is quite individual. Born in Nice he was arguably the most important French painter of the later 20C but his reputation is based on a genuine subversiveness due to his early association with the Situationist Movement of the 1950s. Concentrating on one pure colour, a special shade of blue known as YKB (Yves Klein Bleu), he applied this to hosts of different objects but mostly to uniform blank canvases. In some respects this seems appropriate to his Nice background: after all, the blue sea and sky are the very features which have defined the Côte d'Azur. Klein was more than that, however, and his witty and challenging art offered a route into the mainstream of international art exhibitions and debate. Unfortunately, Klein died in 1962 and in many respects that French preoccupation with colour and sensuality which characterised the art of the Riviera went out of fashion. Since the 1970s it is the angst-ridden art of the British and Germans or the theory-driven obsessions of the Americans which have taken centre stage in the contemporary art market. Despite this change in taste, art lovers and the general public flock to galleries to see a great tradition of modern painting that reflects the warmth and life of the south of France in countless paintings of food, light, love and the joy of being alive.

Flora and fauna

 The temperate climate and the geological composition of the land were the defining forces that shaped the landscape of Provence. The Mediterranean climate may be generally warm and mild but it is prone to marked variations and localised microclimates due to the rock base that forms much of central Provence. The great limestone chains running like corrugations across the region have deep, sheltered valleys watered by rivers, producing areas of rich vegetation like La Montagnette contrasted with semi-arid deserts like La Crau, only 20km apart. These elements have distinguished Provence and the Côte from its neigbours such as the Languedoc to the west, Savoy and Piedmont to the east and the Cevennes or Massif Central to the north. Most guidebooks to the region remark on the palpable change in the air as you descend from the higher country of the massif into the drier, warm surroundings of upper Provence.

To accompany this change in temperature and atmosphere there is a corresponding change in the vegetation. After the mulberry bushes and deciduous trees of a northern climate you start to see the olive trees and herbs that are associated with the Midi and which evoke the spirit of Provence even to people who have never visited the area. **Olive trees** were introduced here by the Greeks around 600 BC and they have become an important element in the local economy. Long-lived and hardy, many individual trees date back to the Middle Ages, their trunks gnarled and twisted but still bearing fruit and sprouting their distinctive silvery green leaves. The olives are harvested every two years in the winter after which they are either prepared for the table or pressed to produce various grades of oil.

The other distinctive trees of the region do much to create the colour and overall texture of the landscape. There are three types of **pine tree**, maritime, Aleppo and umbrella, all of which thrive on the limestone soil along the Mediterranean coast. The umbrella pine, or *pin parasol*, is perhaps the most striking and, as its name suggests, can be found offering shade in open areas of the countryside. However, it is the Aleppo pine which is in the ascendant and covers large areas of the rough terrain. It was reputed to have been introduced from the Levant by the crusaders but there are traces of this species in the western Mediterranean dating back millions of years. Its powers of recovery are particularly important since the dry, rocky areas of the Maures and the *garrigue* are frequently ravaged by forest fires. The **evergreen oaks** which grow in most parts of Provence are similarly threatened by bush fires and they also show phoenix-like powers of rejuvenation. The cork and holm oaks are small and hardy, not at all like the great oaks of northern climes, and the even smaller Kermès oak is really a bush. Of the other trees, the most noticeable are planted for specific purposes. The tapering profile of the **cypress** can often be seen in rows acting as a windbreak against the Mistral while the large, spreading **plane trees** offer shade along the side of old roads or around the edge of village squares where the men play *boules*. The Riviera is the principal district for **citrus fruits** and there are considerable stretches of orange and lemon groves in the hillsides behind Nice and Menton. Limes, chestnuts and almond trees are also grown for their fruit.

In open country it is the low-lying aromatic plants and bushes that are most characteristic. Rosemary, basil, tarragon, thyme, fennel and oregano, the collective constituents of **herbes de Provence**, can be found growing in the *garrigue* and are accompanied by a range of attractive wild flowers such as rock rose and dwarf iris. There is also a profusion of hard and prickly plants such as gorse, thistle and juniper; attractive to look at but uncomfortable on the bare legs. **Lavender** has been cultivated in Provence for centuries and the preparation of lavender essence was one of the principal industries in the early part of the 20C. Nowadays it is more likely to be a hybrid which is grown but in summer in the Vaucluse and Valensole plain you can still come across large fields striped with the dazzling blue of the lavender plants as they await harvest. Grasse is the perfume capital of the world, but only one of a number of perfume and scent-extraction centres in the area, and Ollioules is the largest market for cut flowers in Europe.

An extra element in the flora of Provence is the wide variety of exotic imports which have been able to thrive due to the warm climate. Bormes-les-Mimosas, for example, takes its sobriquet from a flower brought to Provence from Mexico. There are numerous botanical gardens in the coastal resorts but equatorial and temperate plants are not restricted to these controlled environments. Palm trees from the Canaries are found along many promenades, while the Mexican agave, the Barbary fig (prickly pear) and the Australian eucalyptus can be seen in the wild. A profusion of **exotic plants**, frequently introduced by British travellers from the outposts of the empire, is now central to the life of Provence.

The wildlife of Provence is as diverse as the landscape. From the flat alluvial plains of La Crau to the mountains of Mercantour, or the marshes of La Camargue to the dry *garrigue*, there are birds, mammals and insects that depend on each type of environment. Among the animals that make the fauna of Provence distinctive are the **Etruscan shrew**, one of the smallest land mammals in Europe, and the **Eyed lizard**, the largest European lizard.

There are several large animals, both wild and semi-domesticated, around which there is much traditional lore and ritual. **Wild boar** are still quite common in forested areas such as the Lubéron, where they are hunted for the rich stew known as *daube*. The **chamois** and **ibexes** of the Parc National du Mercantour are felt to symbolise this area, partly because it was previously the Italian royal hunting-grounds. In La Camargue great festivities are held in the spring to accompany the round-up (*ferrade*) of the **black bulls** which are bred for fighting as well as for meat. The other famous feature of La Camargue is the **white horses** which can be seen in small herds moving across the plain and wetlands. An ancient breed, the stallions are short and sturdy but well suited to this landscape. The foals are born brown and only become white after four or five years.

Of the farm animals, **sheep** still dominate throughout the region, partly because they can survive in dry open country grazing on the *coussous*, the tufts of hard grass growing around the stones. The herdsmen still leave their flocks to wander free for much of the year, bringing them together in late spring to move up to the high summer pastures. This famous transhumance has been enacted for millennia, although now it is done with the help of trucks.

The wetlands of La Camargue are one of the richest sites for **birdlife** in the whole of Europe. Over 400 varieties of bird are either resident or visit, including flamingoes, storks, herons, egrets, marsh harriers and a bewildering range of ducks, gulls, waders and warblers. Visitors with a specific interest are advised to buy one of the numerous books devoted to the birdlife of this protected area. In the uplands and wooded areas of Provence you can see the increasingly rare red-legged partridge and the hobby as well as the familiar kestrel.

Recent attempts to protect certain **endangered species** have given rise to much discussion over a policy of their re-introduction to Provence. If this is implemented we should see, in the next few years, the return of birds like the bearded vulture and golden eagle to the Parc National du Mercantour, and possibly the wolf and bear to the forests.

Further reading

Art and architecture
Borg, Alan, *Architectural Sculpture in Romanesque Provence* (Oxford, 1972).
Elderfield, John, *Henri Matisse. The Early Years in Nice* (Washington, 1986).
Hyman, Timothy, *Bonnard* (Thames and Hudson, 1998).
Hilton, Timothy, *Picasso* (Thames and Hudson, 1975.
Jean-Nemy, Claude, *Les Soeurs Provençales. Silvacane, Sénanque, Le Thoronet* (Zodiaque, 1991).
Laclotte, M. and Thiebaut, D., *L'Ecole d'Avignon* (Flammarion, 1983).
Pickvance, Ronald, *Van Gogh in Arles* (New York, 1984).

Richardson, John, *A Life of Picasso* (2 vols so far, London, 1991).
Roskill, Mark (ed), *The Letters of Van Gogh* (Fontana, 1963).
Rouquette, J.-M. and Barruol, *Provence Romane*, (2 vols, Zodiaque, 1974 and 1977).
Terrasse, M., *Bonnard at Le Cannet* (Thames and Hudson, 1988).
Verdi, Richard, *Cézanne* (Thames and Hudson, 1992).
Whitfield, Sarah, *Fauvism* (Thames and Hudson, 1991).

Food and wine
David, Elizabeth, *French Provincial Cooking* (Penguin, 1960).
Médecin, Jacques, *Cuisine Niçoise* (Penguin, 1983).
Roden, Claudia, *Mediterranean Food* (Penguin, 1987).
Verge, Roger, *Cuisine of the Sun* (Macmillan, 1979).

French literature in translation
Bonner, Anthony, *Songs of the Troubadours* (Allen and Unwin, 1973).
Char, René, *Dawnbreakers* (Bloodaxe, 1992).
Daudet, Alphonse, *Letters from my Windmill* (Penguin Classics, 1984).
Daudet, Alphonse, *Tartarin de Tarascon, Tartarin of the Alps* (Routledge, 1888).
Giono, Jean, *Two Riders of the Storm* (Peter Owen, 1988).
Hugo, Victor, *Les Miserables* (Penguin, 1982).
Mistral, Frédéric, *Mireille* (Macmillan, 1868).
Pagnol, Marcel, *The Water of the Hills*, containing the two novels *Jean de Florette* and *Manon des Sources* (Picador, 1988).
Petrarch, Francesco, *Selections from the Canzoniere and other works* (Oxford, 1985).
Sagan, Françoise, *Bonjour Tristesse* (Penguin, 1976).

In addition to French authors, Provence has attracted many foreigners who have written some of their finest work in and about the south of France. The greatest of these is F. Scott Fitzgerald's *Tender is the Night* (Penguin Books, 1986). Others of note include:
Arlen, Michael, *The Green Hat* (London, 1924).
Connolly, Cyril, *The Rock Pool* (Oxford University Press, 1981).
Durrell, Lawrence, *Monsieur*, the first and best of his Avignon Quintet (Faber and Faber, 1986).
Greene, Graham, *Loser Takes All* (Penguin, 1972).
Greene, Graham, *May we borrow your husband* (Penguin, 1969).
Mansfield, Katherine, *Collected Short Stories* (Penguin, 1989).
Süskind, Patrick, *Perfume* (Penguin, 1990).

History, culture and society
Ardagh, John, *France Today* (Penguin, 1990).
Braudel, Fernand, *The Identity of France* (2 vols, Fontana, 1989 and 1990).
Greene, Graham, *J'Accuse. The Dark Side of Nice* (Bodley Head, 1982).
Howarth, Patrick, *When the Riviera was Ours* (Century, 1988).
Price, R., *A Concise History of France* (Cambridge, 1993).
Wylie, Lawrence, *Village in the Vaucluse* (Harrap, 1977).
Zeldin, Theodore, *The French* (Collins, 1983).

Travel writing

The best modern book on the whole of the south of France is Michael Jacobs' A Guide to Provence (Viking, 1988). Not only does this provide a selective survey of many of the main sites and their history, it offers a wry view of Provence that is a brilliant corrective to the more gushing appreciations. Its polar opposite is Peter Mayle's A Year in Provence (Hamish Hamilton, 1989), a publishing phenomenon that has proved to be the curse of the area that it described. Mayle's book and television series helped to perpetuate a myth about life in Provence that was already outdated in the 1930s. James Pope-Hennessy's Aspects of Provence (Penguin, 1988) is a sensitive appreciation despite the author's tone, which affects the snobbery of earlier British aristocratic visitors. Charles Graves' The Riviera Revisited (Evans Bros., 1948) is very lively while Marcel Brion's Provence (Kaye, 1956) and Pierre Borel's Côte d'Azur (Kaye, 1957) are translations of French guides with beautiful black-and-white photographs.

Of early accounts the following are distinguished by their views and their style:

Gould, S. Baring, A Book of the Riviera (Methuen, 1905).

Cook, Theodore, Old Provence (2 vols, London, 1905).

Hare, Augustus, The Rivieras (London, 1897).

James, Henry, A Little Tour in France (Boston, 1885 and many later editions).

Maupassant, Guy de, Afloat (London, 1889).

Smollett, Tobias, Travels through France and Italy (London, 1776).

Stendhal, Travels in the South of France (London, 1971).

Young, Arthur, Travels in France and Italy (Dent Everyman, 1915 and later editions).

There are several very detailed guides in French for which there is no English equivalent:

Guide Bleu, Provence, Alpes, Côte d'Azur (Hachette, 1987).

Bernard, Yves, L'Annuaire Touristique du Var (Edisud, 1989).

Bernard, Yves, L'Annuaire Touristique and Culturel des Alpes Maritimes (Edisud, 1991).

Clebert, Jean-Paul, Guide de la Provence Mysterieuse (Editions Sand, 1986).

For the more ambitious walker,

Robin Marsack's Walks in Provence (Robertson McCarta Ltd, 1989) gives detailed descriptions and itinerary for the Grande Randonnée routes prepared by the French ramblers' association.

The western coast

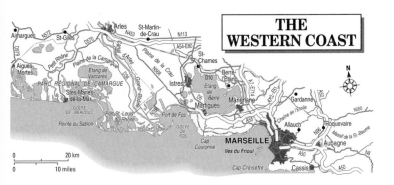

1 · Marseille

Of all the cities of France, Marseille is perhaps the only one with an international identity separate from that of Paris. It is simply too large and too important in French history and culture even to be regarded as just Provençal. In a sense, it is one of the capitals of the Mediterranean and should be compared with Venice, Barcelona or Alexandria. The principal port of France and the gateway to the colonies, Marseille has a dual nature; one looking inland to where it sends the cargoes and immigrants, and the other looking out to North Africa and the Levant, where it seems to spew out exports, colonists and travellers. For this reason, Marseille has often been regarded as a point of transit, a staging-post on journeys to or from the outside world, but this is misleading. Marseille is still the most vibrant centre along the whole coast and a city with its own secretive society that does little to ingratiate itself with the casual visitor or tourist. Notorious as a capital of vice, distinctive for its brashness and even vulgarity, it nevertheless has a huge amount to offer.

History of Marseille

The natural configuration of the landscape makes this an obvious site for a seafaring settlement. Described as a 'broken bowl' or an 'amphitheatre facing out to sea', the city is enclosed on three sides by tall limestone crags. The first people to appreciate this were the Greeks from Phocis who established the trading community of Massalia on the Lacydon creek (the site of the Vieux Port) around 600 BC. This thrived during the following centuries until a political miscalculation led the populace to align themselves with Pompey in his war with Julius Caesar in 49 BC. Caesar was victorious and, having taken Massalia (Roman Massilia), by siege, he set about breaking its power and privilege. Arles became the principal political and trading centre of Roman Provence but Massilia did more than survive. The remains which have been uncovered around the northern side of the Vieux Port suggest that the city continued to prosper from trade with the great centres in the east. Massilia also supported one of the leading universities in the ancient world, maintaining Greek language and culture in what must have been something of an outpost by the 3C and 4C. This may explain the early arrival of Christianity in Massilia, the first signs appearing from the 3C and the full impact felt in the 5C with the foundation of the abbey of St-Victor by St John Cassian. That the abbey buildings are well fortified sums up the history of the town in the period of Barbarian and Saracen incursions.

The key to economic revival in the 12C–15C was again expansion of maritime trade. The crusades and the scramble for trade with the east led Marseille into competition with the city states of Genoa, Pisa and Venice for the great wealth to be accrued. This prosperity continued after the city was absorbed into France with the rest of Provence in 1481, and Marseille became even more important as the principal port of the enlarged kingdom. Louis XIV expanded and rebuilt the great harbour to cope with increasingly large vessels and added a series of forts to protect the sea lanes to and from Marseille.

It was one of the many merchant ships plying the Mediterranean trade that brought the greatest disaster in the city's history. In May 1720 the *Grand St-Antoine*, bringing textiles from Smyrna (now Izmir, Turkey) to Marseille, was held up for quarantine at the Ile de Jarre due to reports of illness on the voyage. Fearing for the loss of their cargo, the crew made contact with shore smugglers who took off some of the cloth and, in doing so, transmitted a virulent plague to the mainland. Within weeks, this plague had gripped the populace and all medical and emergency measures had broken down. Houses were sealed off, corpses piled up in the streets and riots broke out in various districts. The city as a whole was closed to outside contact but some individuals managed to get through, only to carry the plague to many of the neighbouring towns and villages. It was two years before the epidemic ran its course, by which time it had taken the lives of 100,000 people, half of them in Marseille. Still regarded as the most momentous event in the city's history, the plague is recorded in numerous books, paintings and monuments. The heroes of the plague, Bishop Xavier de Belsunce, the Chevalier de Roze and the military commander Langeron, are commemorated in the names of some of the principal streets and there are many surviving symbols of the disaster, notably the remains of the plague wall, some 17km long, built to keep the victims inside the contaminated area. As recently as 1994, a mass grave of victims was discovered in the Panier district near the Vieille Charité.

Marseille quickly recovered from the plague to resume its position as the principal port of France. During the Revolution it played an active role in establishing the new order and in 1792 it replaced Aix as the capital of Provence. This ushered in its greatest period. Napoleon's campaign in Egypt pointed the way for French colonial expansion into North Africa, and Marseille became the gateway to the greater France that incorporated Algeria and Morocco. Marseille was further enhanced by the opening of the Suez Canal in 1869 which brought even more maritime traffic. This prompted the development of many new industries in the area and the huge expansion of the city out beyond the old limits and into the surrounding towns. Even as the docks expanded, however, they were unable to cope with the volume of trade and in 1844 it was decided to develop new port facilities along the coast to the north. Based on an English design, La Joliette became the largest port in Europe, handling goods from every part of the world.

It was this period, the late 19C and early 20C, that saw the creation of the Marseille that we mostly see today. Alongside the new districts built to house dock workers and a large industrial proletariat, Marseille attracted immigrants from the Mediterranean colonies who set up their own communities and ghettoes in the rapidly expanding metropolis. The new industrial city had its own culture laid over the traditional one of fishing and craft trades like rope-making. It is described by writers like Marcel Pagnol, and depicted in films by Julien Duvivier recounting the lives of poor workers and petty thieves in the Panier district. For others, Marseille was the exotic and dangerous city they passed through as they embarked on journeys to far-off lands. Céline's *Voyage au bout de la Nuit* begins in Marseille, André Gide's *Immoralist* passes through *en route* to Tunis, Blaise Cendrars leaves and arrives here in several tales, and Arthur Rimbaud returned to Marseille in real life to die after his expedition to Africa as a slave-trader. In 1940 Marseille was, for many, the last point of escape from the Nazis in Europe: it was here that the cultural theorists Walter Benjamin and Siegfried Kracauer stayed, the latter eventually reaching America while Benjamin committed suicide after a failed bid to cross the Pyrenees.

The Germans destroyed much of the old, densely populated area round the port in 1943 and the gradual loss of the French colonies has seen a

❖ Information, accommodation and food

🛈 3 La Canebière (☎ 04 91 13 89 00) and Gare St-Charles (☎ 04 91 50 59 18).

Finding **accommodation** in Marseille can be something of a problem, not because there is any shortage but because of the huge range and the fact that many of the lower-priced pensions/hotels are neither clean nor reliable. It is best to avoid the Belsunce area and be careful in the districts off La Canebière.

The cheaper hotels which can be recommended are **Le Bearn**, 63 rue Sylvabelle (☎ 04 91 37 75 83); the **Edmond-Rostand** at 31 rue Dragon (☎ 04 91 37 74 95); and the **Lutetia** at 38 allées Léon Gambetta (☎ 04 91 50 81 78).

Of the more expensive, Le St-Ferréol at 19 rue Pisançon (☎ 04 91 33 12 21), a pedestrianised area south of La Canebière, is one of the most charming while the **Athènes**, at 37 boulevard d'Athènes (☎ 04 91 90 12 93) by the Gare St-Charles, and the **Alize**, at 35 quai des Belges (☎ 04 91 33 66 97) facing the Vieux Port, are also good.

Around La Canebière the **Moderne** (☎ 04 91 53 29 93) at 30 rue Breteuil is very good and, slightly cheaper, the **Hôtel Azur** (☎ 04 91 42 74 38) at 24 cours F. Roosevelt or the **Montgrand** (☎ 04 91 33 33 81) near the Opera at 50 rue Montgrand are good value. The *Le Corbusier* has a specific appeal for some since it is within the architect's Unité d'Habitation at 280 boulevard Michelet (☎ 04 91 77 18 15).

At the top end, several international chains have hotels in Marseille but *Le Petit Nice*, in a 19C villa at 16 rue des Braves by the Corniche President J.F. Kennedy, is regarded as the finest, partly due to its outlook but also because of the modern interior design.

Marseille can offer a bewildering range of **restaurants** and types of cuisine thanks to the different populations which have settled here over the centuries. There is probably nowhere outside Paris where you can find such a range of African and oriental cuisine and many would claim that it is both more diverse and of better quality than in the capital. Marseille is also one of the centres of Provençal cooking, claiming several famous dishes such as *bouillabaisse* as local specialities.

Restaurants tend to reflect the character of the district: thus the cours Julien has the most international and exotic food; the pedestrianised cours d'Estienne-d'Orves to the south of the Vieux Port is best for seafood; while the more expensive traditional restaurants are along the Corniche. If you only have time for one meal you should perhaps try *Les Mets de Provence* at 18 quai de Rive-Neuve (☎ 04 91 33 35 38), a local institution specialising in traditional seafood dishes. *Chez Angele* at 50 rue Caisserie (☎ 04 91 90 63 35) to the north of the Vieux Port, *Chez Fonfon* (☎ 04 91 52 14 38) at rue du Vallon des Auffes, *La Chaudron Provençal* (☎ 04 91 91 02 37) at 48 rue Caisserie and *Miramar* (☎ 04 91 91 10 40) at 12 quai du Port are also very good seafood specialists and reasonably priced.

For a wider range of Provançal cuisine, *Possédat* (☎ 04 91 59 25 92) is rather good; *Chez Madie* (☎ 04 91 90 40 87) is also excellent. *La Patalain* (☎ 04 91 55 02 78) at 49 rue Saite is more reasonable and *Le Panier des Arts* (☎ 04 91 56 02 32) at 3 rue de Petit-Puits near the Vieille Charité or *La Garbure* (☎ 04 91 47 18 01) at 9 cours Julien are also reliable.

decline in trade and a change in the overall character of the city. The port continues to dominate but now it has spread far from the city along the coast to the huge industrial complex at Fos. Many of the old docks lie crumbling and empty, hulking monuments to urban decay and changed circumstances. Yet Marseille remains a lively place, remaking itself while preserving a certain defiance and mistrust of Parisian values. This hostility to Paris and the north, as well as the continuing presence of corruption and deep racial tension, partly explains why right-wing politics thrive in the industrial centres of Provence. On a more positive note, however, this independence is frequently expressed in civic values and monuments. In 1994 a new regional headquarters—designed by the British architect Will Alsop—was opened at St-Just in the north of the city. Known as Le Grand Bleu (it uses Yves Klein Blue, developed by the painter) this huge and exciting hi-tech building may go some way to embodying the new Marseille.

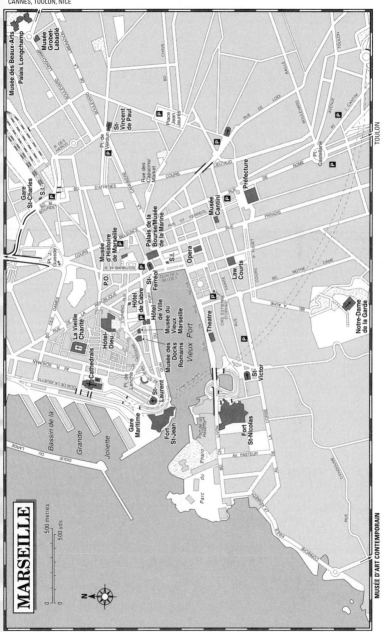

CANNES, TOULON, NICE

TOULON

CHÂTEAU D'IF

MUSÉE D'ART CONTEMPORAIN

MARSEILLE

N

0   500 metres

0   500 yds

Musée des Beaux-Arts
Palais Longchamp

Musée
Grobet-
Labadié

St-
Vincent
de Paul

Place
Jean
Jaurès

Pl.
Castellane

Gare
St-Charles

S.I.

Pl. de
Verdun

Rue des
Capucins/
Market

Préfecture

Musée
Cantini

Musée
d'Histoire
de Marseille

P.O.

Pl. Jn.
Guesde

Palais de la
Bourse/Musée
de la Marine

Musée du
Vieux
Marseille

Hôtel
de Cabre

Hôtel
Dieu

St-
Ferréol

Opera

S.I.

La Vieille
Charité

Hôtel
de Ville

Law
Courts

Notre-Dame
de la Garde

Cathédrals

Musée des
Docks
Romains

Theatre

Vieux Port

St-
Laurent

St-
Victor

Gare
Maritime

Fort
St-Jean

Fort
St-Nicolas

Bassin de la
Grande

Joliette

Parc
du
Pharo

The Vieux Port, the Panier district and La Major

A convenient spot to start any tour of old Marseille is the junction of La Canebière and the quai des Belges, beside the *office du tourisme*. This is the very hub of the whole city where the principal street meets the centre of its ancient and modern life, the port itself. From this point one can look down the great basin of the **Vieux Port** (Old Port) towards the Fort St-Jean and Fort St-Nicolas which guard the narrow opening to the sea.

History of the Vieux Port

Originally a sheltered creek, it was here that successive expeditions found a safe anchorage and, beginning with the Phocaean Greeks in the 7C BC, established a harbour for trade. The surviving arrangement of the basin and its perimeter dates from the massive reconstruction undertaken by Louis XIV, which was completed in 1666. The 18C English traveller Arthur Young described it, somewhat uncharitably, as a 'horse pond' but it is difficult to see why. Nowadays the port is crammed with yachts and various types of pleasure craft but the surroundings are too impressive for it to be mistaken for a mere marina.

The quai des Belges at the head of the basin is perhaps the busiest point in the city. From here boats leave for the Iles du Frioul or the Château d'If and there is generally a regular traffic of lighters or liberty boats ferrying sailors from foreign vessels lying offshore. A famous **fish market** is held here every morning, a reminder of the traditional life of this district which was once dominated by fishermen and other seafarers.

At the north end of the *quai* and facing the port is the **Eglise St-Ferréol**, otherwise known as the church of the Augustinians. This is all that survives of a convent built in the 14C–16C and originally one of the principal religious foundations in Marseille. Behind the rather dull façade, which dates from 1875, there is an interesting Gothic nave and a range of furnishings and pictures from the 17C and 18C. The traditional Offering of the Fish is maintained here at the midnight mass on Christmas Eve when fishermen in local costume recite a prayer in the Provençal language.

To the rear of the church, on the opposite side of the rue Reine-Elisabeth, is the pleasant and relaxed **Jardin des Vestiges** (entrance a few yards to the right on the rue Henri-Barbusse). This is the site of the ancient Greek port and township named Massalia. The location of the ancient port had been known for some time but it was not until the demolition of this area for redevelopment in 1913 that the full extent of the remains was recognised. Further destruction in the Second World War revealed even more and by the 1960s the site had been sufficiently excavated for the vestiges to be incorporated into this complex of shops and offices. The principal remains are the fortifications of the Hellenistic town dating from the 3C–2C BC, the wall known as *Le mur de Crinas* and a road and gateway which marked one of the main entrances to the town in the 3C and 4C AD. The materials for these ramparts, mostly pink limestone from La Couronne (see p 66), and the method of construction, using dressed stone without mortar, emphasise the lasting influence of Greek craftsmanship. The garden also reveals the ingenuity of the ancient engineers. This area was once a swamp and the site was stabilised and made more habitable by installing an elaborate drainage system with a network of pipes and cisterns which brought fresh water to the town.

The other major remains in the garden are those of the Roman port built in the 1C–2C AD and originally stretching along much of what is now the north side of the main port basin. The outstanding item related to that period is displayed in the adjacent **Musée d'Histoire de Marseille** (☎ 04 91 90 42 22: **open** Mon–Sat 12.00–19.00; closed Sun) at the eastern end of the Jardin de Vestiges. This museum is incorporated into the large and soulless shopping centre, the Centre Bourse, but it should not put you off. The collections offer a history of Marseille from prehistory to the Middle Ages using architectural fragments, ceramics, metalwork and several informative models and audio-visual displays explaining the layout of the ancient settlements. The centrepiece is a 3C Roman ship, a substantial merchant vessel 8 x 20m, discovered nearby in 1974. The fragile remains have been freeze-dried and are now exhibited in a controlled atmosphere to preserve the remaining timbers.

Returning to the rue Henri-Barbusse, cross to take the rue Henri-Fiocca leading to the rue de la République, a broad boulevard built in the 1860s on the lines of Baron Haussman's designs for Paris and entailing the demolition of one of the oldest quarters of the city. Cross to take the Grand Rue. At the junction of the rue Bonneterie (200m) is the **Hôtel de Cabre**, the oldest house in Marseille. Built in 1535 for the bourgeois Louis de Cabre and supporting a range of decorative sculpture, it shows a distinctive Provençal blend of Gothic and Renaissance elements. In 1954 the whole building was moved to accommodate the widening of the street.

Follow the rue Bonneterie to regain the Vieux Port on the quai du Port. This north side of the Vieux Port is the poorest and the most traditional. The surviving fishing boats are berthed here and the quayside is punctuated by cabins and landing areas reserved for the fishermen's societies. It was this stretch of the harbour that was used for the memorable last scenes of *The French Connection II*, a film which helped to perpetuate the area's reputation as a centre for drugs and gangsterism.

Between the Vieux Port and the cathedral of La Major is **Le Panier**, the quarter which housed the successive waves of immigrants to Marseille. Poor French peasants, Genoese and Neapolitan fishermen, exiled Armenians and Jews, and now Arabs have occupied this complex of narrow streets and tall crumbling buildings, giving Le Panier its reputation as an exotic if occasionally dangerous district. In this it resembles other Mediterranean ports, notably Naples, Genoa and Barcelona.

History of Le Panier

The principal industry of Le Panier was fishing although it was better known for vice and crime conducted by the Mafia-like underworld called the *milieu*. Attendant on this was a strong sense of community identity which the established forces of law and order always had difficulty in controlling. During the Second World War the German occupying forces found this to be a constant source of irritation, since Le Panier contained a number of undesirable elements and was a base for Resistance activities. In January 1943 the commanding officer implemented orders from Berlin to 'cleanse and purify' the area by blowing up all the buildings between rue Caisserie and the Vieux Port. As well as displacing some 40,000 people this provided an opportunity to detain and ultimately deport the surviving community of Jews and Gypsies. After the war the devastated area was rebuilt in a rather bland style by the architect and planner Fernand Pouillon, but the original character of Le Panier can still be found in the narrow streets up the hill to the north.

The only building on the Quai du Port to survive the destruction of 1943 was the elegant **Hôtel de Ville**, designed by Gaspard Puget and Mathieu Portal in the Genoese Baroque style and built between 1656 and 1674. The curious arrangement of this building meant that it had no internal stairway between the ground and first floor, access being gained only by means of a wooden bridge to the rear. This is still essentially the case although there is now a covered arcade from the building at the rear. The impressive crest on the façade is a cast of the original carved by Pierre Puget and now in the chapel of the Vieille Charité.

The area behind the Hôtel de Ville has two important museums. To the left or west on the rue du Lacydon (place de Vivaux) is the **Musée des Docks Romains** (☎ 04 91 56 28 38: **open** Tues–Fri 10.00–18.00, Sat, Sun 12.00–19.00 in summer; Tues–Sun 10.00–17.00 in winter; closed Mon). Housed in the ground floor of a modern block, the museum displays the remains of the 1C Roman docks and warehouses uncovered by the destruction of the area and preserved as they were found. Originally the buildings would have been on two or three storeys, opening onto the quay itself and up to the main street at the rear, now the rue Caisserie. The remains include a number of large ceramic vessels set into the masonry for storing wine, grain and oils. In addition to models and maps outlining the Roman town there are display cases with a selection of Greek and Roman artefacts (ceramics, metalwork, jewellery and small sculpture) discovered on the site and at sea. There is also a fine mosaic of a nude female bather from the 3C AD.

On the rue de la Prison directly behind the Hôtel de Ville is the **Maison Diamantée**, a 16C townhouse so named because of the diamond-faceted masonry of the façade. Built by the merchant Pierre Gardiolle in 1570, it was altered in 1593 by the soldier Nicola de Robbio, which may account for its military appearance. The interior, however, must have been in the finest Renaissance style if the surviving staircase on the first floor is any indication. The combination of Classical references and exceptional craftsmanship displays a very sophisticated knowledge of contemporary Italian decoration. This building houses an excellent museum of local crafts and traditions, the **Musée du Vieux-Marseille** (☎ 04 91 55 10 19: **open** Tues–Fri 10.00–18.00, Sat, Sun 12.00–19.00 in summer; Tues–Sun 10.00–17.00 in winter; closed Mon). Galleries and period rooms on the three floors display the collection of Provençal furniture, ceramics, textiles and prints and include a large model of old Marseille that records the appearance of the town during the riots of 1848. On the top floor there are examples of local lace and needlework, including items such as bonnets which formed part of traditional Provençal costume, and a display related to the manufacture of playing-cards, a small industry which flourished in Marseille from the 17C.

Continue up the rue de la Prison to join the rue Caisserie. At the junction to the right is the Palais Daviel, once the Palais de Justice and now an annexe of the Hôtel de Ville. Built in 1743 by the Gerard brothers, this handsome building has some fine architectural sculpture and fittings. Further along the rue Caisserie on the opposite side is the impressive **Hôtel-Dieu**, now the central hospital for the region. This foundation originates from the 12C although the present building, designed by Jules Hardouin Mansart, a descendant of the great 17C French architect François Mansart, dates from 1782. In front of the Hôtel-Dieu is a monument to the satirical artist Honoré Daumier (1808–79) who was born near this spot. The striking bronze head was made by the sculptor A. Bourdelle (1861–1929), although left incomplete at his death.

Beside the Hôtel-Dieu is the montée St-Esprit, a pathway leading up into Le Panier. A better route, however, is to take the montée des Accoules from the rue Caisserie opposite the rue de la Prison. This path passes below the **Clocher des Accoules**, the surviving belltower of an important 12C church and now a popular landmark, and into the warren of narrow streets that is the true Panier district. Some of the tenements are seven and eight storeys high, rambling, dilapidated and festooned with washing but probably destined to be chic within the next few years as renovation programmes take over.

Turn right at the rue des Moulins leading to the place des Moulins, one of the most attractive spots in the whole of Marseille. This upper section of the old town was dominated by convents and as late as the mid-19C still had the crowd of windmills from which it takes its name. One of the towers survives, at No. 28 rue des Moulins.

Take the rue des Muettes and turn right into the rue Michel-Salvarelli leading to the rue du Refuge, named after the convent of La Refuge which once covered a large part of this area. Many of the streets have names with a strong religious flavour—La Madeleine, La Repente, etc. The convent was built up during the 18C but suffered during the Revolution and was turned into a hospital for imbeciles and the poor. The remains of the convent buildings, constituting one side of the rue du Refuge, were converted into tenement housing in the 19C and are undergoing a further series of renovations to raise the tone of the district today. At the bottom of the rue du Refuge, turn left into the rue du Panier, from which the district takes its name, and then right into the rue Rodillat to face the **Centre de la Vieille Charité** (☎ 04 91 56 28 38: **open** Tues–Sun 10.00–18.00, Sat, Sun 12.00–19.00 in summer; Tues–Sun 10.00–17.00 in winter; closed Mon).

History of the Centre de la Vieille Charité

The Hospice de la Charité was designed by Pierre Puget in 1670 as a refuge and hospital in the wake of a royal edict which insisted on 'the locking up of the poor and the beggars'. Financed by local subscriptions it took over 70 years to build and work finally ground to a halt in 1745—before the chapel was complete—due to shortage of funds. By the time of the Revolution it was already falling into ruin and, after several failed attempts, a concerted programme of renovation was undertaken during the Second Empire. The problems of how to use a building of this scale have continued in the 20C and it has been successively employed as a barracks, a military hospital and a dormitory for people displaced by the wartime destruction. In the 1940s Le Corbusier took an interest, admiring its simple clear lines, and from this time its fortunes rose. Classified as a historic monument in 1951 it was eventually renovated and opened as an arts centre in 1989.

Despite its confused history the building is surprisingly unified and it survives today as one of the finest monuments of its type in Europe. The immense barrack-like blocks which enclose the whole foundation are perhaps appropriate for an alms house but the warm pink granite helps to soften their geometric regularity. Severe on the outside, they present an orderly series of three-tiered arcades to the inner courtyard which, in turn, contrast sharply with the elegant Baroque chapel at the centre. The oval plan of the chapel surmounted by an oval dome is itself unusual in French architecture and emphasises the strong Italianate character of that building, whose severe neo-Classical façade was only erected in 1863.

In its new role as an arts centre, the Vieille Charité houses a range of departments including the Institut National de l'Audiovisuel, the Ecole des Hautes Etudes en Sciences Sociales, and the Institut and Musée d'Archéologie Méditerranéene. It displays an important collection of ancient and tribal art including masks, reliquaries, painted and sculpted skulls, sculptures and textiles from Africa, Oceania and Latin America: the Egyptian collections are particularly important. It is also the headquarters of Le Fonds Regional d'Art Contemporain (FRAC) and the principal venue for exhibitions of contemporary arts and crafts in Marseille. To complement this there is a programme of concerts, lectures and events throughout the year.

Leave Vieille Charité by the rue du Petit-Puits where, at No. 3, the architect Pierre Puget was born, just a few yards from one of his greatest buildings. From the place des 13 Cantons, the rue Ste-Françoise and the rue Four-de-Chapitre lead out of Le Panier and into the open space of place de la Major before the cathedral. To the right on the rue de l'Eveche is the old bishop's palace, built between 1648 and 1671 and now the police headquarters.

Marseille has two cathedrals alongside one another, La Major, a small Romanesque building on a much older Christian site, and La Nouvelle Major, a colossal edifice built in the 19C to replace its neighbour. The original intention had been to pull down the older **La Major** to make way for La Nouvelle Major but the outcry of local people and antiquarians ensured that this historic church was preserved, albeit in a slightly truncated form. It can be visited, but only in guided tours by appointment (☎ 04 91 90 53 57).

History of La Major

The first church on this site was founded by Bishop Proculus in 381. Damaged and finally destroyed by Saracen raiders in the 8C–10C, it was rebuilt in the 11C and extended in the 12C and 15C to include fortifications. Therefore, despite its small size, it is still a combination of different periods and styles. The small nave is pure 12C Romanesque with plain piers, semi-circular arches and tall, narrow window openings. The most interesting section is the crossing and dome with its elaborate octagonal cupola, a feature which is distinctive of Provençal Romanesque. There are several important monuments in the apsidal chapels, including an early medieval relief carving of Christ with two bishops and a glazed terracotta relief by the Della Robbia studio in the chapel of St Serenus. The marble chapel of St-Lazare (1477–81) by the Dalmatian-born sculptor F. Laurana is the earliest example of Italian Renaissance art on French soil. There is also a very early baptistery with traces of the temple of Diana which preceded the church.

La Nouvelle Major, or Cathédrale Ste-Marie-Majeure, begun in 1852 and consecrated in 1893, is the largest cathedral built in France since the Middle Ages. Designed by Léon Vaudoyer and Henri Espérandieu, ostensibly in the neo-Byzantine style, it is actually a hybrid of various styles and periods. The exterior employs the alternate courses of light and dark stone so admired by the advocate of the Gothic Revival E.E. Viollet-le-Duc and the English art theorist John Ruskin and, in this case, seems to chart the progressive construction of the whole edifice.

This effect of scale above all is carried on into the interior where the single large nave with narrow side aisles emphasises the huge space enclosed by the walls and domes. Information about the building tends to underscore its size; 141m long, 60m high to the cross on the cupola, 444 marble columns, seating for 3000, and so on. Much maligned as a piece of architecture, it nevertheless has certain qualities. The sheer scale of the interior is impressive and the effect is enhanced by the simple rhythm of repeated arches and marble or porphyry columns. The banded masonry is also carried through to the interior, helping to give the effect of sumptuous ornament appropriate to the Byzantine style. The weakest aspect is the decoration. The mosaics, statues and stained glass which were designed for the building are largely of indifferent quality, as are the various altarpieces and religious paintings in the chapels.

From the esplanade in front of La Major there are good views over the new port district of La Joliette. Begun in 1844 to relieve the pressure on the Vieux Port, new docks were added throughout the late 19C and early 20C in response to the expansion of French trade with the East. Destroyed by the retreating German garrison in 1944 they were almost entirely rebuilt and expanded in the post-war period until they now extend along 12 miles of coastline to the north of the city. There is also a passenger-ship terminal and ferries operate between La Joliette and the ports of North Africa and the islands of the Mediterranean.

Take the rue de la Cathédrale leading from the front of La Major at the left to the place de Lenche, once an aristocratic district and still a lively residential square on the site of the ancient Greek agora and Roman forum. At the bottom, turn right into the rue St-Laurent, which passes the remains of the Greek theatre amid a large modern housing complex. At the end are the church of St-Laurent and the chapel of Ste-Catherine.

The 12C Romanesque **Eglise St-Laurent**, although closed, has a particular significance for the people of the quartier St-Jean, the 'fisherman's district'. The plain octagonal belltower (17C) is a famous and much-loved landmark and the church is still the focus of various local festivals and processions. The events of January 1943, when the Abbé Caillol rang the bells as a protest and warning while German troops evacuated the area prior to its demolition, are still talked about. The adjoining **Chapelle Ste-Catherine** is unfortunately rather dull but it has some interesting furniture and fittings, including a few fanciful Mannerist carvings.

Opposite the church is the parvis de St-Laurent, an open platform with good views over the Vieux Port, the two forts, and across to the Palais du Pharo. Steps from here lead back down to the quai du Port, from which one can cross to follow a path round the Fort St-Jean or return to the quai des Belges at the head of the basin.

Guarding the entrance to the Vieux Port on its northern bank, the **Fort St-Jean** was begun in the 12C by the Hospitalliers of St John of Jerusalem. After the suppression of the order, the fort was gradually extended by the authorities until, by the 17C, it had grown into this tight complex of towers and courtyards enclosed by ramparts. The tower of King René, dating from the 15C, is the most important part. These buildings are occasionally open to the public when temporary exhibitions or events are held inside. A path follows the walls round to the water's edge where a chain was once stretched across the harbour mouth as a barrier to enemy ships. Another interesting feature that once dominated this site was the tall transporter bridge (1905) which spanned the harbour, allowing ships to pass beneath. It was destroyed in 1945 but can be seen in old postcards or in the photographs of the Bauhaus designer László Moholy-Nagy, who was fascinated by its steel structure.

La Canebière to the Palais Longchamps

La Canebière is the most famous and traditionally the grandest street in Marseille. A broad boulevard stretching from the quai des Belges back into the principal commercial and shopping areas of the town, it was created when the centre of Marseille was redesigned in 1666. Taking its name from the hempfields (*chenevières* or 'canèbe') which were used in the manufacture of rope, its association with maritime industry gave way by the 19C to a more sophisticated and elegant lifestyle of cafés, theatres and luxury hotels. When Marseille was the gateway to the Orient this street was the haunt of European aristocrats, Levantine potentates and the full panoply of international traders, colonial servants and the military. All that has virtually disappeared and it is now a noisy thoroughfare with just a few buildings to remind the spectator of its golden age. One of these is the tourist office at the bottom of La Canebière (No. 3) which stands on the site of the *Café Turc*, one of several 19C *grandes cafés*, once famed for its orchestra and its chocolate.

Opposite this and to the right is the Palais de la Bourse (Stock Exchange), designed by Pascal Coste in the pompous Second Empire style and opened in 1860 by the 'Second Emperor', Napoleon III. On 9 October 1934 King Alexander of Yugoslavia and the French foreign minister were assassinated by a Croatian nationalist in front of this building. There is a monument at the Préfecture nearby but the most poignant record is a curious film of the outrage taken by a watching cameraman. The event seems almost calm, not at all what one would expect from a violent murder in a procession. The Bourse has an impressive interior, the main hall being decorated with a series of fine reliefs by F. Gilbert in the cove of the ceiling. Given this context and Marseille's history, it is all the more surprising that the **Musée de la Marine et de l'Economie de Marseille** (☎ 04 91 39 33 33: open Wed–Mon 10.00–12.00 and 14.00–18.00; closed Tues) on the ground floor should be so dull. The display comprises ship models, prints, paintings and miscellaneous artefacts associated with the sea, and one could reasonably expect something more ambitious. The building is also used for occasional temporary exhibitions of art and design but you can usually find something better in the fashion museum, the **Musée de la Mode**, a few doors up at No. 11 (☎ 04 91 14 92 00: open Tues–Sun 12.00–17.00; closed Mon). The permanent collection here is limited but the museum does hold interesting exhibitions drawn from other sources.

Facing the Bourse is the place Général-de-Gaulle, an open pedestrian area with fountains and some recent sculptural monuments. On the same side, two blocks up La Canebière, is the rue St-Ferréol which leads to the Préfecture, a huge public building of 1861–66 in the Classical style of the 17C. It was reputedly inspired by the Palazzo Vecchio in Florence although there is little evidence of this. Proceeding up La Canebière you can see the traces of its earlier, more elegant, existence within the shops and fast-food bars which now occupy the street front. At Nos 49–57 is the *Hôtel Louvre et Paix*, built in 1870, which has a range of interesting decorative sculpture including symbolic representations of the four continents on the façade.

For a greater sense of the surviving local character you can visit the fruit and vegetable market which takes over the narrow streets around the rue des Capucins to the south of La Canebière. The metro station Noailles, in the heart of the **Marché des Capucins** and on the site of the old Gare de l'Est, has a museum of local transport displaying models, prints and photographs. Behind the north side of La Canebière is the seedy rue Vincent-Scotto, named after a famous music-hall artist who performed in this area, and beyond that the rue Thubaneau where, at No. 25, the *Marseillaise* or *Song of the Army of the Rhine* was first played to the Jacobin Club on 22 June 1792.

Further north along the boulevard Dugommier/boulevard d'Athènes you will see the imposing white stone steps that lead up to the main railway station, the gare St-Charles. Flanking the stairs are two large allegorical groups from 1925, the monumental figures symbolising Marseille as the Greek port and as the gateway to the Orient. After this dramatic preamble, the station itself, built in 1848, is something of a disappointment but the esplanade at the front offers an excellent view over the city towards the church of Notre-Dame-de-la-Garde.

At the top or eastern end of La Canebière is the tree-lined square de Verdun where, on Sundays in December and January, the *santon* market is held. This area is dominated by the neo-Gothic **Eglise St-Vincent-de-Paul**, otherwise known as 'Les Reformes'. Built in the late 19C on the site of a reformed Augustinian convent, the architectural style of the church seems out of character for this region but it does provide a notable landmark in the city. Adolphe Thiers, the prime minister responsible for the brutal suppression of the Paris Commune in 1871, was born at No. 40 in the adjoining street named after him. His house is now occupied by the Académie de Marseille, an institution founded in 1726 by Louis XV.

From the square de Stalingrad, just to the north, the cours Joseph Thierry and the boulevard Longchamp lead up to the striking and elaborate **Palais de Longchamp**. Built in 1862–69 by the local architect, Henri Espérandieu, who was also responsible for La Nouvelle Major and Notre-Dame-de-la-Garde, the Palais de Longchamp is an ingenious structure, reviled by architecture critics but loved by the local people. The main pavilion in the centre is actually a water tower marking the end of the Canal de Marseille. This has been cleverly turned into a spectacular piece of architectural theatre, exploiting the elevated site to create a huge cascade of water in front of the building. The effect is further dramatised by the addition of two flanking colonnades which sweep forward in a semi-circle above the cascade to terminate in the buildings which now house, on the left, the Musée des Beaux-Arts and, on the right, the Musée d'Histoire Naturelle. The façade of this whole complex has some elaborate decorative sculpture, including the allegorical group *La Durance* by Cavalier, although the finest works are the wild animals by A.-L. Barye. To the left of the Palais is an observatory, also designed by Espérandieu, and at the rear there is a public garden with a number of monuments and a zoological park.

The **Musée des Beaux-Arts** (☎ 04 91 62 21 17: **open** Tues–Sun 10.00–17.00, Sat, Sun 12.00–19.00 in summer; closed Mon) was first established in 1800 using the plunder from Napoleon's campaigns and has been supplemented by numerous gifts, bequests and purchases to create a distinctive and important collection. There is a substantial group of Italian paintings from the 16C–18C including Annibale Carracci's *Village Wedding* which once belonged to Louis XIV. Of the Flemish and Dutch schools, Peter Paul Rubens' *Adoration of the Shepherds* is probably the most important. The main strengths of the collection, however, lie in the French School of the 17C–19C and include works by Jean-Antoine Watteau (1684–1721), Jacques-Louis David (1748–1825), Jean-Auguste-Dominique Ingres (1780–1867), Gustave Courbet (1819–77) and Jean-François Millet (1814–75). Despite these major figures, it is the local-born artists who provide the most distinctive and memorable works.

The enormous canvases of *The Plague of Marseille* by Michel Serre (1658–1733) are at least impressive, but the special display of models, fragments and finished pieces by the sculptor Pierre Puget is outstanding. On the top floor there is a large collection of bronze caricature figures by Honoré Daumier, also a local man, who is probably best known for his satirical lithographs. Finally, you should not overlook the large murals on the staircase by Pierre Puvis de Chavannes (1824–98) depicting Marseille as a Greek colony and as the gateway to the East. On first sight these may seem like dry academic decorations but Puvis' dreamlike figure scenes were an important landmark in the development of Symbolist art, and were much admired by Gauguin and Van Gogh.

On the opposite corner of the place H.-Dunant from the Palais Longchamp is a 19C townhouse built by a prosperous local merchant, Alexandre Labadié, to house his collection of fine and decorative art. Preserved and extended by his daughter, Marie-Louise Grobet, the house and contents were donated to the city in 1919 to create the **Musée Grobet-Labadié** (☎ 91 62 21 82: **open** Tues–Sun 10.00–18.00, Sat, Sun 12.00–19.00 in summer, closed Mon). There are good examples of Provençal ceramics, a fine collection of tapestries, furniture, drawings, paintings and bronzes, and a range of early musical instruments, but it is the ensemble of a well-preserved bourgeois interior from the late 19C that makes this museum a particular delight.

South of the Vieux Port and the Corniche

From the southeastern corner of the quai des Belges take the rue Pythéas, turning right into the rue Beauvau to face the **Opéra**, a good example of French Art Deco. Dating originally from the late 18C, the building was entirely remodelled in 1924 and has some fine bronze reliefs of Greek mythological figures by Antoine Sartorio on the façade and railings. There is other sculpture by Bourdelle on the interior.

Directly behind the Opéra, follow the short rue Lulli or the inppropriately named rue Paradis to rue Grignan, where at No. 19 is the **Musée Cantini** (☎ 04 91 54 77 75: **open** Tues–Sun 10.00–17.00, Sat, Sun 12.00–19.00 in summer; closed Mon) occupying the mansion built in 1694 for a fishing and trading corporation, the Compagnie du Cap Nègre. The last owner was the sculptor Jules Cantini who in 1916 bequeathed the house and furnishings to the city. The museum has an important collection of Provençal ceramics, particularly faience from Marseille and Moustières-Ste-Marie, and good holdings of 20C and contemporary art including works by Francis Bacon (1909–92), Balthus (1908–), Georg Baselitz (1938–), Georges Braque (1882–1963), Christo (1935–), Jean Dubuffet (1901–85), Wassily Kandinsky (1866–1944), Joan Miró (1893–1983) and Arman, Klein, Léger and Picasso. The museum also organises temporary exhibitions throughout the year.

Return to the rear of the Opéra and take rue Francis-Davso, leading west into the cours d'Estienne-d'Orves, an open pedestrian area in which many of the older buildings, notably the 17C Arsenale des Galères, have been converted into fashionable shops, restaurants and bars. Follow the *cours* or any of the streets to the north which lead down to the Vieux Port at the quai de Rive-Neuve.

This side of the Vieux Port, in contrast to the quai du Port opposite, is taken up with pleasure boats and with the various suppliers of equipment for yachts, diving and other maritime sports. The district takes its name, **Criée**, from the old fish market on the *quai* which was recently converted into the Théâtre Nationale de Marseille. A ferry operates throughout the day between the middle of the quai de Rive-Neuve and the quai du Port.

From the theatre and the *quai* take the rue du Chantier, turning right into the rue Neuve Ste-Catherine which overlooks the small basin and the entrance to the tunnel (1967) under the Vieux Port. This leads to the fortified basilica or **Abbaye St-Victor** (open daily 08.00–12.00 and 14.00–18.00), one of the oldest and most important religious establishments in Marseille.

History of the Abbaye St-Victor

The present building dates largely from the 12C although there are traces of earlier buildings throughout the interior, particularly the crypt, which chart the history of Christianity in this area from as early as the 3C. Much of the early history is clouded by legend but the origins of this church are often associated with Proculus, the Bishop of Marseille, who, in the 4C, brought the anchorite St John Cassian from Egypt to found a monastic order. What is certain is that by the late 5C some form of worship was conducted here around the relics of St Victor. Thereafter the foundation was the victim of repeated attacks by Saracens until in 1020 the Catalan monk Isarn began the extensive rebuilding and fortification which carried on for the next 300 years, and which you see today. Indeed, the fortifications themselves were still being extended and modified as late as the 15C. Throughout this period the abbey enjoyed a position as the most important Christian monastic foundation in the western Mediterranean but its significance declined in the 18C and it was badly damaged during the Revolution.

The 12C–13C upper church is a good example of late Romanesque in which the pointed arches and the cross-vaulting in the side aisles indicate the emergence of the Gothic style. A stair near the door leads down to the crypt, a network of arcaded chambers with early Christian sculpture and sarcophagi set into the walls or laid out in bare stone alcoves. The most important pieces are the 3C Twin Tombs of the Martyrs, the inscription of Lazarus, and the sarcophagi of SS Eusebius (4C), Maurice (4C) and John Cassian (5C). The 11C sarcophagus of Isarn also survives, his carved head and feet protruding from behind an inscription, and there are a few traces of decorative mural painting from the late medieval period. Above the main altar is a 13C painted statue of the Madonna, the 'Black Virgin', which is carried in a candlelit procession on 2 February to the old abbey bakery, the Four des Navettes, at the end of the road. This bakery makes special boat-shaped biscuits called *navettes* which are eaten at this festival to commemorate the arrival in Provence of the Stes-Maries (see p 84).

A detour to Notre-Dame-de-la-Garde

At 140 rue Sainte, opposite St-Victor, is a house where the poet Paul Valéry once lived. Behind the abbey is the rue d'Endoume and the chemin du Roucas-Blancs, an interesting 19C residential district with impressive villas and gardens. At the top there is a stairway leading up to Notre-Dame-de-la-Garde. Another pedestrian route ascends from the Jardin de la Colonne at the top of the cours Pierre-Puget. By car the best route up to the church follows the rue Breteuil and the boulevard Vauban.

History of Notre-Dame-de-la Garde

The strategic importance of the Garde hill was recognised in ancient times and it has served as a lookout-post ever since. François I built a fort there in 1524 to complement the Chateau d'If. It has also been a religious site since 1241, when the first church was built by the hermit Maître Pierre. Its real significance as a pilgrimage centre, however, dates from the 16C when it assumed a particular importance to mariners. The present church, built in 1853–64, has long been a byword for the tasteless design of the Second Empire, a reputation that is difficult to revise on closer inspection.

Like the cathedral of La Major, the Eglise de Notre-Dame-de-la-Garde (**open** daily 07.00–19.30 in summer; 07.30–17.30 in winter) was designed by H. Espérandieu in the Romanesque-Byzantine style, deploying alternate bands of dark and light stone as a decorative feature throughout. The tower is an unfortunate combination of awkward shapes and proportions but it does support the colossal gilded Madonna by E.-L. Lequesnes (1815–87) that has become the most famous landmark in Marseille. It goes without saying that the view from the top or from the esplanade in front is breathtaking. The interior has a simple nave of three bays with round arches supporting domes with gilded decoration. On the walls there are numerous mosaics and murals although the collection of *ex-votos* left mainly by sailors is of greater interest. The lower church or crypt has a 16C crucifix and a *Mater Dolorosa* in marble by Jean-Baptiste Carpeaux (1827–75).

From the rue Sainte by St-Victor descend to the boulevard Charles-Livon, which runs between the upper and lower bastions of the **Fort St-Nicolas**. These formidable pieces of military architecture were built by Louis XIV in 1660, the period after the civil unrest known as the Fronde, with the primary purpose of subduing the local population. Only the upper bastion, the Fort d'Entrecasteaux, is open to the public, the lower one, Ganteaume, being occupied by the Foreign Legion.

Beyond the Port de la Reserve the boulevard Charles-Livon leads to the **Parc and Château du Pharo**. In 1856 this piece of land was offered by the city to Napoleon III, who had a palace built to the designs of Espérandieu. It remained unfinished during the Second Empire and was eventually given back to the city by the Empress Eugénie. It is now used by the local legislature. The gardens have a beautiful outlook over the entrance to the harbour and out to sea. On a raised point of the promontory is a monument to the *Heroes of the Sea* (1923) by André Verdilhan.

The boulevard Charles-Livon leads into the Corniche President J.F. Kennedy, a 5km route which follows the coastline giving excellent views over the sea to the offshore islands. The first landmark is the *Monument to the Dead of the Orient* by Sartorio, near which is the picturesque fishing village of Vallon des Auffes. Further south, at the Parc Balnéaire, where the Corniche gives access to the main beaches of Marseille, a poor copy of Michelangelo's *David* marks the junction of the coast road and the avenue du Prado. Turn left into the avenue and then right into the avenue du Parc Borély leading into the park.

At the end of the formal perspective on entering the park is the Château Borély, an Italianate villa designed by Charles Louis Clérisseau in 1767 for a wealthy family of merchants. The interior retains much of its original neo-Classical decoration including frescoes by a local painter, Louis Chaix, after Old Master paintings in Rome. Since the mid-19C the château has been a museum displaying the city's archaeological collections, notably the impressive Clot-Bley and Campana collections of Egyptology, but these were transferred to the Vieille Charité in 1989. The Château Borély still holds the Feuillet de Borsat collection of drawings but, in the future, it will be used mainly as a museum of the decorative arts. The large park has a botanical garden as well as the main racecourse and there is a small Russian chapel near the château.

To the rear of the park, at 16 avenue d'Haïfa, is the new **Musée d'Art Contemporain** or MAC (☎ 04 91 25 01 07: **open** Tues–Sun 11.00–18.00 in summer; Tues–Sun 10.00–17.00 in winter; closed Mon) a single storey hi-tech building of the sort that often gives modern architecture in the south a bad name. The museum is linked to the Musée Cantini but concentrates on the art of the last 30 or 40 years, and particularly on that with some link to Marseille. In fact, the galleries display a fair representation of French art of the last few decades, with a good selection of interesting or humorous work amid the broadly meretricious. The so-called School of Nice (Arman, Raysse, César) is well represented but there are also more substantial pieces by Klein, Daniel Buren (1938–) and Jean Tinguely (1925–91). The museum also stages exhibitions devoted to popular art such as cartoons, street art and fashion, which offer a different perspective on the more conventional fine art.

From the rond-point at the top of the avenue du Prado, turn right into the boulevard Michelet and after 1km you will see on the right the **Unité de Habitation** (1946–52), the large apartment block designed by the Modernist architect Charles-Edouard Jeanneret, known as Le Corbusier (1887–1965). Impressive as it may appear on its own, it was intended as only one part of a complex of six tower blocks to be called the Cité Radieuse. This was the first of the architect's 'anti-rational' buildings in which the heavy concrete grid of the main exterior is contrasted with the more sculptural form of the roofline. Le Corbusier's aim was social as much as architectural and he sought to create a model or 'laboratory' in which all the requirements for 20C life were incorporated in one building. There is provision for a shopping street on the fourth floor and a community centre on the roof. Even here, the model for many modern apartment blocks throughout Europe, the services proved to be inadequate and the building was for a time unpopular with residents, who christened it the 'Maison du Fada' or madhouse.

Returning down the boulevard Michelet, the main road continues straight into the city centre.

Château d'If and the islands

Boat trips to the Château d'If and the Iles du Frioul, one of the most popular excursions from Marseille, depart from the quai des Belges throughout the day during summer. The journey usually takes a minimum of 1–2hrs. There are three principal islands in the group; Ile d'If, Pomègues and Ratonneau, lying just over 3km. from the entrance to the Vieux Port.

Ile d'If, the smallest and most famous of the islands, is little more than a shelf of rock sticking out of the sea.

History of the Ile d'If

Uninhabited until the 16C, it was visited in 1516 by François I who had the bizarre experience of encountering a rhinoceros there. The animal had apparently been put ashore to graze while *en route* to the King of Portugal as a gift from a maharajah. Recognising the strategic importance of the island, François ordered the building of the château, a severe keep with three formidable towers, although it never served any military purpose.

Within a few years of its completion in 1531 it had become a prison and the source of numerous stories, true and fictional, of dreadful hardship and torture. In the early years of the prison, a certain Knight Anselme is known to have been strangled in his cell and many others rotted and died there for minor offences. Between 1545 and 1750, some 3500 Protestants were sent to the château, which often acted as a staging-post before the equally brutal galleys, and after the revolution of 1848 another cohort of political prisoners was sent there. In 1774–75 the young orator Mirabeau spent eight months in the prison on the instructions of his father, to curb his excessive debts. He is reported to have praised the comfort of his lodgings but, as he was well-aired and fed, we can assume his was a special case.

The two most famous prisoners did not, in fact, spend any time in the Château d'If. If the Man in the Iron Mask ever did exist, there is no record of him here. Similarly, Edmond Dantès, the Count of Monte Cristo, was an invention of Alexandre Dumas (Père). The guides, however, continue to show 'their' cells to visitors.

The two larger islands in the group, **Pomègues** and **Ratonneau**, are joined by a breakwater which shelters a marina and holiday complex known as Port du Frioul. In the past these islands were used to quarantine those with infectious diseases of which the ruins of the **Caroline Hospital** on Ratonneau are a touching reminder in the face of rising seaside developments. This large neo-Classical hospital was built in 1821 in response to an outbreak of yellow fever which had recently been brought to Europe from America.

An excursion to La Sainte-Baume via Aubagne

The rocky heights that enclose Marseille also restrict movement back into the hinterland. A road (D908) runs through this difficult terrain via Allauch and the pass that divides the Chaîne de l'Etoile and leads to villages such as Mimet and to the farther industrial satellites like Gardanne. There is also a network of small roads and paths that ascend to the main peaks of the range from the city side. A good place to start the ascent by car is from **Château-Gombert**, a small village now at the edge of the city to the northeast. In the shaded main square, the place des Héros, you will find the **Musée des Arts et Traditions Populaires du Terroir Marseillais** (☎ 04 91 68 14 38: open Wed–Mon 14.30–18.30; closed Tues). This local history museum has an interesting collection of folk crafts, costumes and furniture, some of which is displayed in recreated period rooms.

The primary excursion from Marseille, however, is that to the **Massif de la Ste-Baume**, arguably the most sacred site in France and one that is certainly memorable for the wildness of the countryside and the spectacular views from the summit. The first part of the journey from Marseille can be a nightmare, since the main roads out to the east through the Huveaune valley (N8 or A50) are frequently congested.

Aubagne was once a fortified town well away from Marseille but the city's gradual spread has made it a suburb. Some of the walls have been preserved but industrial development and road-building have destroyed any sense of its past. This is ironic because Aubagne maintains many of its traditional industries, notably ceramics, and its surroundings were the inspiration for some of the most famous and evocative books about peasant life in Provence, those of Marcel Pagnol.

Marcel Pagnol

Aubagne was the birthplace of Marcel Pagnol (1895–1974) and it was in this area that he set the novels *Manon des Sources* and *Jean de Florette*, originally filmed by himself and later, in the 1980s, by Claude Berri with huge international success. The real heart of Pagnol's world, however, was the village of La Treille, some 5km to the west on the southern slopes of La Garlaban, where his family had a weekend home.

Later in life, Pagnol returned to this village where he wrote his autobiographical sequence *La Gloire de mon père*, *Le Château de ma mère* and *Le Temps de secrets*, describing an idyllic country childhood that has come to symbolise rural life in Provence as much as Peter Mayle's account of the Lubéron. Pagnol is buried in the cemetery at La Treille and you can obtain a map at the Tourist Office (☎ 04 42 03 49 98) on esplanade Charles-de-Gaulle which outlines several walks in the area taking in his grave and spots he described in books and films. For those with less energy, there is a display of santons and figurines derived from Pagnol's fictional characters in a gallery opposite the Tourist Office.

Aubagne is also the headquarters of the Légion Etrangère (Foreign Legion), best-known from countless books and films from P.C. Wren's *Beau Geste* (1924) to Laurel and Hardy's *Beau Chumps* (1933). A museum on the D44A towards La Treille gives the history of the regiment and a selection of mementoes from their campaigns in Africa, the Far East and Mexico.

From Aubagne, the most exhilarating route up to the shrine at La Ste-Baume is by the village of Gémenos and then on a twisting vertiginous road (D2) that ascends the face of the massif. Before the road steepens, a small side road to the right leads to the delightful park at **St-Pons** with the remains of an important 13C Cistercian abbey. This offers a gentle diversion before the rugged beauty of the mountains. From the top of the pass, the **Col de l'Espigoulier** (728m), there is a wonderful view down the funnel of the Huveaune valley to Marseille and the sea.

Continue down the north face on the D2, turning right onto the D80 at La Coutronne to Plan d'Aups. From here, two old pilgrimage routes lead up through the forest to the grotto and the summit at St-Pilon. The first begins at *La Hôtellerie*, on the site of the old pilgrim's hostel, just 3km beyond Plan d'Aups. This broad forest path is actually a section of the long national footpath, the GR9, which ultimately follows the full length of the Ste-Baume ridge. The other short pilgrim's path begins at the junction of the D80 and the D95, just 1km east of the *Hôtellerie*. Both paths converge at the oratory crossroads, from where there is a flight of 150 steps cut into the rock leading up above the treeline to the grotto of **La Sainte-Baume** itself.

History La Sainte-Baume

This magical spot was already a site of religious importance to the Ligurians and Romans and there are traces of prehistoric cave-paintings in the area. It is the cult of the Magdalene, however, which has made this one of the most sacred sites in Christian hagiography. According to the legend, Mary Magdalene was expelled from Palestine during the anti-Christian purges and she travelled to Provence with a party of saintly refugees in a boat with no sails. Landing at Stes-Maries-de-la-Mer at the mouth of the Petit Rhône (see p 84), she preached in Provence, helping to Christianise the region before retiring to this remote cave, spending her last 33 years here in prayer and contemplation.

She was not the first and certainly not the last to seek solitude and inspiration in high places. The Magdalene's remains were kept at St–Maximin to the north, but the cave attracted the more ambitious and devout pilgrims. St John Cassian, the founder of St-Victor at Marseille, carved the first steps up to the site in the 5C and this route was trodden by the great and the good of the Christian world including kings, popes and saints. Decoration and accretion in such places is almost invariably vulgar and the cave site is no exception. The early fittings were destroyed during the Revolution so the present furnishings, including a rather arresting, pure white marble statue, all date from the 19C.

Every day during her isolation, angels would transport the Magdalene to the highest point on the mountain at **St-Pilon**, where she could listen to the music of the heavens. The terrestrial route, however, starts back at the oratory where the GR9 leads up to the summit by the Chapelle des Parisiens. There is a small chapel here but it is the panoramic view that justifies the 45min walk. The novelist Stendhal struggled up here in 1838 but felt it was worth it when he reached the top, and the same is true today. On the cliff side to the south you can enjoy a huge vista over the sea, while on the landward side to the north the view extends across all the peaks of Provence to Ventoux over 100km away.

2 · Marseille to Arles via Martigues

The route from Marseille to Arles via L'Estaque and running to the north or south of the huge freshwater lagoon called the Etang de Berre shows you an aspect of Provence that rarely appears in the brochures or escapist memoirs of the region. To begin with, it passes some of the largest industrial complexes of southern France, in particular the great decaying dock developments at La Joliette to the north of Marseille and the huge petrochemical works around Fos. Beyond this, the flat plain of La Crau offers a landscape in marked contrast to the verdant hilly terrain of central Provence. Near the middle of this route, however, is the picturesque village of Martigues, once an artists' colony but now seemingly marooned in an alien environment.

Marseille's northern suburbs and the Chaîne de l'Estaque

Several major roads lead out of Marseille to the north. The N113 is the old road and is closely followed by the A7 motorway: both lead out to the airport at Marignane or to Aix-en-Provence. The suburban landscape is a sort of aromatic desert that once marked the sudden end to the city. Even in the 20C it was often remarked how Marseille seemed hemmed in by its climate as much as by the series of rocky hills, and that wild animals roamed in sight of the peripheral houses. All this has changed now and the surrounding countryside has been invaded by air-conditioned modern buildings and irrigation which has permitted an industrial sprawl over much of the area. Many of the towns and villages along the eastern fringe of the Etang de Berre, notably Vitrolles, Rognac and Berre itself, have expanded with the introduction of new industries but they are hardly an attraction to travellers. In recent years they have become best known for the strength of their political feelings, electing Front National representatives at local and national elections. **Marignane** will probably be just a point of passage to or from the airport although it has a pleasant town centre if you ever have to spend some time waiting on the arrival or departure of a plane. At the centre of the old town is the Hôtel de Ville, housed in the 17C château of the Mirabeau family, which still contains some original decoration including frescoes by the Aixois painter Jean Daret (1615–68).

A much more interesting journey out of Marseille is by the coast road, either the A55 autoroute or, preferably, the Chemin de Littoral, which becomes the N568. This passes the great port developments of **La Joliette**, begun in the 19C and expanded along the coast for some 6km during the 20C. The decline in sea trade, however, has left much of this area depressed and many of the huge dock installations loom over the streets as hulking ruins encrusted with decades of pollution. It may not be pretty but as a symbol of mercantile power and of post-industrial decay it could be described as sublime.

The depressed, industrial atmosphere extends to **L'Estaque**, a suburb which was once a picturesque fishing-village. Many leading French painters worked here, notably Cézanne, Dufy and Derain, but its place in the history of art is assured by the period Georges Braque spent here in the summer of 1908, when he produced his first Cubist paintings. The authorities have succeeded in giving the town a separate identity from the oversized remains of the port and there is now a lively atmosphere along the harbour front and marina. The modest beaches are popular with day-trippers from Marseille.

Above the town and stretching out along the coast to the west is the steep face of the **Chaîne de l'Estaque**, the last of the rugged limestone ranges that characterise the coast of Provence; beyond this the coast is very flat right to the Spanish border. The Chaîne has always acted as something of a barrier and a number of tunnels have been dug through the rock for road and rail links. The most famous, however, is the Tunnel du Rove, cut in the 1920s to create a subterranean canal for large barges between the Etang de Berre and the sea. At 7km, it was the longest in the world but it is now closed due to a landslip in 1963. The road crosses over it before ascending the heights towards Martigues and offering a good view back over the Rade de Marseille.

This rocky strip between the lagoon to the north and the sea to the south is a semi-arid terrain of white limestone and dark pines with few signs of human occupation at its centre. The seaward side, known locally as the **Côte Bleue**, can be very impressive with steep cliffs descending to the sea, broken by *calanques* and small bays. Roads off the N568 to the left lead down to small fishing-villages such as Niolon and Méjean, clinging to the cracks in the coastline. The main resort on this coast is **Carry-le-Rouet**, site of an ancient settlement and, in modern times, well known in France as the birthplace of the film actor Fernandel (1903–71). Carry is also famous for a local delicacy, sea urchins, celebrated in the annual *fête* held in February. There is a good beach here which has attracted many visitors, giving the village and much of the coast a rash of *maisons secondaire*. At the extreme western point of the Côte Bleue, where there is a lighthouse, is Cap Couronne, which has traces of Neolithic settlements. The district has been extensively quarried since Roman times for the hard stone that was used for many of the major building and engineering projects of lower Provence, including much of Marseille. The large beach is popular with day-trippers from the cities and towns nearby.

Martigues

To the north of the Chaîne, the N568 approaches the edge of the Etang de Berre, before arriving at the curious and improbably picturesque town of Martigues. Sitting astride the Chenal de Caronte, along which the lagoon drains into the sea, Martigues has inevitably been dubbed the Venice of Provence.

History of Martigues

In fact, the town is the result of a union in 1581 of three separate villages, Jonquières, L'Ile Brescon and Ferrières, whose boats had fished both the sea and the lagoon since the Middle Ages. In recent decades Martigues has expanded with the influx of workers for the various industries in the area. This has led to widespread development, signalled by the motorway flyover which passes the town at a considerable height. It is, therefore, remarkable that Martigues has been able to maintain a lively and pleasant atmosphere in contrast to the more fashionable resorts to the east. The best time to visit is during July and August for the Sardinades seafood festival, and especially on the first Saturday in July when the *Fête Venitienne* takes up many of the streets and canals with water sports, performances and an excellent array of fish and seafood stalls.

❖ *Information, accommodation and food*

🛈 2 quai Paul-Doumier, Ferrières (☎ 04 42 80 30 72).

Hotels. Places to stay in and around Martigues are taken up by tourists so it is best to book in advance, especially during July and August when the **Sardinade** festival is held. The **St-Roch** on the allée Paul-Signac in Ferrières (☎ 04 42 80 19 73) is regarded as the best hotel but there is an exceptional if expensive alternative, the **Abbaye de Ste-Croix** (☎ 04 90 56 24 55), 5km out on the D17 towards Val de Cuech. **Le Provençal** at 35 boulevard du 14 juillet (☎ 04 42 80 49 16) in Ferrières is a lot cheaper.

Restaurants. Of Martigues' many restaurants, **Berjac** at 19 quai Toulmond (☎ 04 42 80 36 80), **Le Miroir** on the quai Brescon (☎ 42 80 50 45) and **Chez Marraine** at 6 rue des Cordonniers (☎ 04 42 49 37 48) all have good seafood menus.

Given its location on water and the richness of the reflected light and colour, it is not surprising that Martigues should have appealed to painters. Camille Corot (1796–1875), Pierre-Auguste Renoir (1841–1919) and Augustus John (1878–1961) are among the artists who have worked here but the figure most closely associated with Martigues is Felix Ziem (1821–1911). He made his name in the 1850s from richly coloured views of Venice, so there was not a great leap of the imagination when he transposed his style to this smaller retreat. The **Musée Ziem** (☎ 04 42 80 66 06: **open** Wed–Mon 10.00–12.00 and 14.30–18.30 July, Aug; 14.30–18.30 only in other months; closed Tues) in Ferrières has a collection of his work and of other local artists as well as displays on the ethnology and archaeology of the area. Martigues has a few buildings of historic interest, such as the 17C **Eglise St-Genies** at Jonquières, which has a statue of Gerard Tenque, a local figure who in 1089 founded the Order of the Knights of St John. The town's greatest appeal, however, is simply in the various views gained from walking around its streets and waterfronts. The best vantage-point is by the Pont St-Sebastien on the Ile Brescon, which offers views of the *quai* known as the 'Bird's Mirror' and, on the opposite side, the ornamental façade of the 17C church of Ste-Madeleine-de-l'Ile.

The Etang de Berre and La Crau

Martigues sits at the mouth of the **Etang de Berre**, a huge lagoon of some 155 square kilometres fed by the rivers Arc and Touloubre. The shores have been settled since Neolithic times and over the centuries it has supported a range of communities based on fishing, manufacturing and, most characteristically, salt-making. Since the 1920s, however, it has become the centre of the French petro-chemical industry, giving rise to the prolific industrial installations round the edge of the lagoon. What was once a placid fresh-water lake is now ringed with refineries, storage tanks and pumping stations as well as the related factories for synthetics and rubber. Despite this modern development, a tour round the 80km perimeter of the lagoon has some surprises: the medieval walled towns of St-

Mitre-les-Remparts and Miramas-le-Vieux, for example, or the Roman Pont Flavien at St-Chamas with its elegant triumphal arches at each end of the span.

The most important archaeological site is **St-Blaise**, between two small lagoons just off the main road (D5) beyond St-Mitre. The Hellenistic walls are perhaps the most impressive feature of the remains but there are traces of successive settlements from 5000 BC, through the Phocaean, Roman and early Christian periods until the final abandonment of the town in 1390.

For the full impact of modern technological development you should continue on the main N568 from Martigues, passing Port-de-Bouc with its 12C lighthouse tower and extraordinary Musée Morales, a garden of fantastic animals constructed from metal parts, to **Fos-sur-Mer**. Stretching out to the south of the road and along the coast towards the mouth of the Grand Rhône, Fos is the very incarnation of petrochemical glory—at once the newest and largest port on the coast and a huge complex of factories and processing plants producing steel, plastics, chemicals, petrol and natural gases. There is an information centre and bus tours of the whole complex, which suggests that a significant number of visitors wish to look round the new industrial landscape. It is not difficult to see why. At night this huge installation sparkles with arc lights and the lurid flames of gases being burnt off like some fantasy of technological expansion taking over the whole area.

Fos has been able to develop because of the physical character of this area. Not only does it have a deep-water channel into the Mediterranean allowing large vessels to use the port, but the hinterland stretches back into a flat plain with little agricultural potential. This is the unsettling rock-strewn wilderness of **La Crau**, stretching right up to the outskirts of Arles, one of the defining features of the region and much bound up with the character and identity of old Provence. Visitors to the area have been fascinated by this curious desolate landscape and the fact that it lies next to the Grande Rhône has made it even more of an enigma.

History of La Crau

The ancient geographer Strabo told of the mythical origins of La Crau in a battle between Hercules and the native Ligurians, who had run off with the hero's cattle. His supply of arrows being exhausted, he appealed to Jupiter who sent a shower of stones as ammunition against the thieves. In fact, the landscape is the bed of an old rivercourse, probably the Durance, which swept the stones down from the higher stretches. In ancient and medieval times this was a barrier to travellers since the heat and lack of water made the broad expanse as formidable as a desert. In 1554, however, the Canal de Craponne brought water to irrigate the upper Crau and this section at least has been cultivated and used for grazing sheep ever since. Despite this, La Crau continues to exert a fascination. Van Gogh liked to work on the plain because it reminded him of the flat landscapes in Millet's peasant pictures. The most famous treatment of La Crau, however, is in Frédéric Mistral's epic poem *Mirèio*, in which the heroine almost succumbs to heat and exhaustion as she makes her way to Stes-Maries-de-la-Mer.

From Fos-sur-Mer the N568 cuts across La Crau to within a few kilometres of Arles, before hitting the east–west road (N113) which leads straight to the city. There is a small museum devoted to the history and landscape of this unique area at St-Martin-de-Crau, just east of the junction.

3 · Arles

Of all the towns with pretensions to be the heart or true capital of Provence, Arles is the one with the strongest claim. This may seem odd given that it lies far over to the west on the banks of the Rhône, which traditionally marked the boundary with the Languedoc. But Arles was once the capital of the region, albeit over a thousand years ago, and it is in this harsh but beautiful town that the spirit of the Félibrige, that attempt to maintain the traditional language and culture of Provence, is kept alive. Arles also seems to have partaken of all the phases in the history of Provence and in some it has played a leading role.

History of Arles

Arelate, meaning 'town on the marshes', was established on an island in the Rhône by Greek traders in the 6C BC. This was a favourable position from where they could control the river traffic, and it was further enhanced in 104 BC when the Roman consul Marius opened a canal between the Rhône and the sea at Fos which greatly improved access and navigation. With these advantages Arelate or Arles was soon in competition with Massilia (Marseille) as the principal economic and trading centre of the region. The rivalry was brought to a head in 49 BC when Arles supported Caesar in his campaign against Pompey. Caesar triumphed and Arles was rewarded while Massilia, which had supported Pompey, was penalised and stripped of its privileges. Thereafter, Arles became Caesar's favourite town in the province. A bridge over the Rhône was built here for the Via Domitia between Italy and Spain, a colony of veterans from the 6th Legion was settled in the area, and a series of major building projects was undertaken. Indeed, Arles became one of the principal cities of the empire, as can be seen from the scale and importance of the Classical remains found in almost every district. Even the grid plan of the Roman town can be detected in the surviving arrangement of streets.

Roman Arles reached its zenith under Constantine and his sons in the 4C–5C AD when it was declared capital of the 'Four Gauls' (North and South Gaul, Spain and Britain). By this time, however, the empire was in sharp decline and during the succeeding centuries the area was overrun by a sequence of invaders from the Visigoths to the Franks.

At the same time as the empire was disintegrating, Arles became one of the principal centres of the early Church in the west. St Trophimus, who Christianised the area, was held in high esteem by the Church Fathers and the town was able to maintain its position throughout the Middle Ages by responding imaginatively, some would say opportunistically, to the changing religious climate. Arles was the setting for one of the first councils of Christian bishops and, by judicious advertising of their holy relics, Les Alyscamps became one of the great burial grounds for wealthy Christians from far beyond even Provence.

The greatest sign of the town's prestige was in 1179, when the Holy Roman Emperor Frederick Barbarossa was crowned in the newly completed cathedral of St-Trophîme. This, however, marked the beginning of a downturn in the city's fortunes. In 1239, when Arles became part of the county of Provence, political authority was transferred to Aix, and at the same time Marseille began to outstrip it as a port and commercial centre. Nevertheless, Arles continued to prosper, albeit on a more modest scale. It is still the principal market for a huge agricultural area stretching out across La Crau in the east and along the banks of the Rhône in the west.

During the last two centuries Arles has become the heartland of traditional culture in Provence to the extent that items such as its distinctive bread cages are now taken to be typical of the whole region. Many images of traditional Provençal costume are unique to this area and you can still see some of the townspeople wearing the characteristic dress and coif for important festivals and holidays. This rich folk heritage has attracted many writers and artists to the town, notably Frédéric Mistral whose statue looks

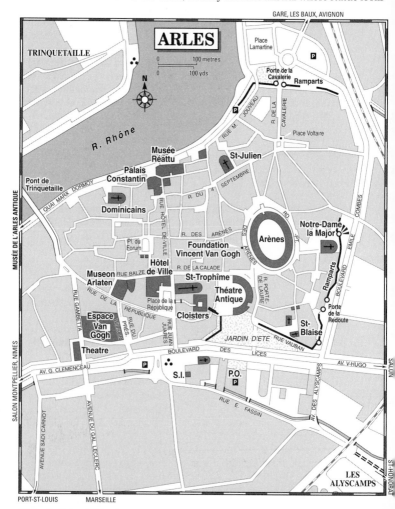

out over the place du Forum in the centre of town. Bizet's famous melody *L'Arlesienne* is in this spirit, although it also relates to a popular belief that the women of the town are among the most beautiful in Provence.

Vincent Van Gogh, who arrived in Arles in February 1888, was attracted by what he thought was an unspoiled, traditional community in touch with its Classical past. In fact, as he soon realised, it was a major railway junction with large marshalling yards and a garrison town for the 58th Infantry Division; soldiers, especially the exotic Zouaves, often appear in his paintings. Paul Gauguin, who spent a disastrous few months here later in the year, culminating in the famous ear-slashing incident, was appalled by the place and longed for the primitive atmosphere of Brittany.

In the 20C Arles has become something of a tourist centre on the basis of its Classical remains and its Provençal folk heritage, and the international popularity of Van Gogh's work has not been overlooked. But this has not eroded its essential identity. To some extent it has been bypassed in the wholesale modernisation of Provence; it is too far from the sea to be a resort and the bureaucracy of government is still concentrated in Aix and Marseille. Even the festivals which have sprung up (photography, folklore, music, etc.) have reinforced rather than corrupted the town and its native character. For these and many other reasons, it remains the most fascinating and distinctive of all the great centres in Provence.

❖ *Information, accommodation and food*

🗗 Esplanade Ch. de Gaulle by the boulevard des Lices (☎ 04 90 18 41 20) and at the train station.

Hotels. Leading hotels like the **Jules César** (☎ 04 90 93 43 20) are on the boulevard des Lices but there are two more distinctive establishments in the centre of the old town. The *Hôtel Arlatan*, 26 rue du Savage (☎ 04 90 93 56 66), in a 16C–17C mansion, is one of the most attractive hotels in Provence while the *Hôtel Nord-Pinus* at 14 place du Forum (☎ 04 90 93 44 44) has a curious bullfighting theme and an excellent position. Unfortunately, parking is a problem with both but it is worth persevering and the hotels will arrange to collect luggage from the town's main car parks. Of the middle-range hotels, the *Gauguin* at 5 place Voltaire (☎ 04 90 96 14 35), the *Diderot* at 5 rue Diderot (☎ 04 90 96 10 30) and the *Hôtel du Musée* by the Musée Reattu at 11 rue du Grand Prieuré (☎ 04 90 93 88 88) are all very good, while the cheaper hotels such as the *Hôtel de France et de la Gare* (☎ 04 90 96 90 87) or the *Hôtel Terminus et Van Gogh* (☎ 04 90 96 12 32) can be found at place Lamartine by the train station.

Restaurants. There are many bars and restaurants along the boulevard des Lices but very little to recommend them. The place du Forum, on the other hand, is quieter and more attractive with many mid-priced bars and bistros to choose from. The best restaurant in Arles is *Lou Marquès* in the

Hôtel Jules César (see above) but the prices do reflect its reputation. More reasonable is *Le Tambourin* at 65 rue Amedée-Pichot (☎ 04 90 93 13 32), best known for its seafood, *Le Médieval* at 9 rue Truchet (☎ 04 90 96 65 77), the *Hostellerie des Arènes* at 62 rue de Réfuge (☎ 04 90 96 13 05) and the excellent *Le Vaccarès* at 9 rue Favorin (☎ 04 90 96 06 17) overlooking the place du Forum.

The southern old town

The **boulevard des Lices**, a broad avenue lined with shops and cafés at the southern edge of the old town, is the best place to start a tour of Arles. There is a car park here although it is generally crowded and motorists may prefer to start at the place Lamartine to the north where parking is easier. On the southern side of the boulevard des Lices are several modern public service buildings such as the post office and police station as well as the *office du tourisme* overlooking the remains of an excavated Roman complex. On Saturday mornings there is a lively market here, filling the street with stalls selling local produce, Provençal and Arlesien specialities as well as old clothes, books and antiques.

Take the rue Jean-Jaurès north into the old town and leading to the place de la République. This is the principal square in the town with a number of important buildings including the Hôtel de Ville and the Cathédrale St-Trophîme. At the centre is an impressive **fountain** with a tall Egyptian obelisk which once adorned the Roman circus. Rediscovered in 1675, it was placed on a base designed by J.-B. Péru Péru with four fine heads of Hercules as water spouts.

Occupying the whole of the northern end of the square is the **Hôtel de Ville** (1673–75), a formal three-storey building designed by the local architect Jacques Peytret but following the plans of François Mansart. The ground floor, which is used as a passage to the street behind, has a good 'flattened' vault that was much admired in the 17C. The vestibule leads to the Plan de la Cour, a courtyard with some interesting medieval buildings such as the 12C–15C Hôtel des Podestats. This was where the magistrates pronounced sentence on civil matters and the remains of their 'bench' can still be seen. Rising above the roofline of the Hôtel de Ville is the elegant Renaissance belfry of 1555, originally part of the previous building. Reputedly based on the mausoleum of Les Antiques at Glanum, the cupola supports a statue of the god Mars.

To the right of the Hôtel de Ville, visible by its impressive sculpted west doorway, is the **Cathédrale St-Trophîme**, the finest example of Provençal Romanesque architecture and one of the greatest medieval monuments in the whole country.

History of the Cathédrale St-Trophîme

There was a Bishop Trophîme in this area in the early 3C but he has been confused in religious hagiography with Trophimus, a cousin and disciple of St Paul, who is reputed to have arrived in Provence in 46 AD. The earliest church on the site was founded by St Hilary in the first half of 5C and dedicated to St Stephen (Etienne). It was not until 972 that the remains of St Trophimus were installed and the cathedral assumed the name of this local saint. Another church was erected during the 10C but this was cleared in the 11C to make way for the present building. The great quality of St-Trophîme in Arles is that the bulk was completed in one campaign which gives the building a unity of style in both architecture and sculpture which is rare in the Middle Ages. The transept was completed by the end of the 11C, the nave by the mid-12C and the façade and portal were added in the later 12C. The culmination of this building programme came on 30 July 1178 when Frederick Barbarossa was crowned king of Arles in the new cathedral. By this time the church had become one of the principal staging-posts on the Via Tolosona, the lower route to the shrine of St James at Santiago de Compostela in Spain. Thousands of pilgrims travelled through Arles, worshipping at the altar of St-Trophîme as part of the sequence of their devotions on the way to Santiago. After the wedding of King René and Jeanne de Laval in 1456 it was felt appropriate to extend and rebuild the apse, by this time in the lighter and more slender Gothic style, but it hardly disrupts the coherence of the building as a whole.

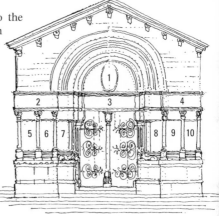

The main doorway, facing out on to the Place, is reminiscent of the simpler form of Roman triumphal arch, such as the one at Glanum outside St-Remy-de-Provence. It is the sculptural decoration, however, rather than the architectural conception, that is most engrossing. The main theme of the façade is the Last Judgement set off powerfully by the tympanum (1). Beneath this, in a long frieze strtching across the whole width of the portal, is a procession of the saved to the left (4) and the damned to the right (2) culminating in a vision of Hell on the side wall. In the centre, over the doors, is a group of seated apostles with the closed book of souls (3). The main tier is the life-size reliefs of saints flanked by columns which, reading from left to right, follow this sequence: St Bartholomew (5), St James the Greater (6), St Trophime (7), St John, St Peter, St Paul, St Andrew, St Stephen being stoned (8), St James the Lesser (9) and St Philip (10). Around this main register, there are two series of smaller reliefs. Along the top, at the level of the capitals, are scenes from the birth of Christ, while at the column bases is a group of reliefs on the theme of lions. Linked to the medieval tradition of beastiaries, the lion series contains both Samson and Hercules, a juxtaposition of the biblical and the pagan.

The **interior** of St-Trophîme, like most Romanesque churches, has a rather dark and gloomy aspect on first sight. Lit by a high, rounded clerestory, there is very little sculptural decoration on the fabric, and the bare stone walls provide a generally dull grey tone. It is nevertheless this sparseness which focuses attention on the basic lines of the interior, allowing the architectural members to provide an orchestrated rhythm of simple geometric shapes. The tall nave (20m) has five bays of plain rectangular piers supporting a slightly pointed barrel vault. But perhaps the purest Romanesque is found in the side aisles where the narrow openings are surmounted by perfect semi-circular arches. The order and

Cathédrale St-Trophîme façade

severity of the nave noticeably gives way after the crossing to be replaced by lighter and more elaborate Gothic tracery in the ambulatory and chancel dating from the 15C.

Among the most notable works decorating the interior are (a) an **early Christian sarcophagus** of the 5C, in the second bay of the north (left) aisle. It served as the baptismal font and was thought to contain the remains of St Honoratus who died in 429 AD. The two registers of relief decoration depict scenes from the lives of the Evangelists. On the north wall at the fifth bay there is (b) an 11C inscription describing events in the life of St Trophimus. At the crossing on the left there is (c) an *Annunciation* by the painter Louis Finsonius (c 1580–1617), dating from 1614. The first chapel in the north transept contains (d) a 4C sarcophagus with reliefs depicting the Crossing of the Red Sea. The central or extreme eastern chapel of the apse has (e) a statue of the Virgin by the Italian sculptor L. Murano, of 1619. In the adjacent chapel of the Holy Sepulchre to the right is (f) the **tomb of Geminius**, a 7C sarcophagus surmounted by a 16C marble group of the Entombment. On the west wall of the south transept there is (g) a painting of the *Madonna and Child with Saints*, c 1500. This actually records a notorious council of bishops called at Arles by St Césaire during which the Bishop of Riez was accused of stealing church treasures. Above the nave facing the west door is (h) a painting of the *Stoning of St Stephen*, the original patron saint of the town, by Finsonius from 1614 and in the King's Chapel on the south aisle there is another picture by him of the same date, (i) an *Adoration of the Magi*. Around the nave is a series of (j) **Aubusson tapestries** depicting scenes from the life of the Virgin.

Entrance to the cloisters is obtained through the courtyard of the 18C Bishop's Palace, to the right or south of St-Trophîme in the place de la République. From here there is a good view of the south side of the church and of the square **belltower** over the crossing. This tower, replacing an earlier dome, was built in the late 12C and remodelled again in the 17C, although it preserves its solid Romanesque character. The distinctive profile of progressively narrowing tiers surmounted by a squat pyramid roof is one of the most familiar features on the skyline of Arles and appears in several paintings of the town by Van Gogh. A stairway at the far right of the courtyard leads up to the cloisters.

Built in two distinct campaigns, the **cloisters** at St-Trophîme (**open** daily 09.00–19.00 in summer; 10.00–16.30 in winter) contain some outstanding examples from two phases of medieval sculpture. The north and east sides are the earliest, being completed in the later 12C in a pure Romanesque manner, while those of the south and west were undertaken in the early and mid-14C in the Gothic style. Perhaps the most interesting work is on the massive piers at each end of the north side (to the left on entering) in which full-size corner figures of saints in relief stand between scenes from the New Testament. Despite some weathering of the stone, these solemn figures reveal the full repertoire of stylisation and

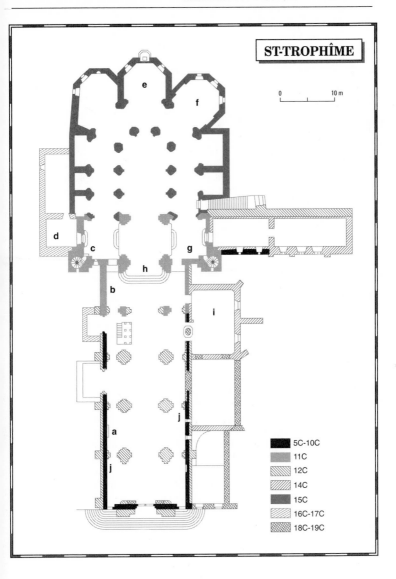

ST-TROPHÎME

0   10 m

■ 5C-10C
▨ 11C
▨ 12C
▨ 14C
■ 15C
▨ 16C-17C
▨ 18C-19C

human insight that is a feature of Romanesque art. There has been much speculation on the relationship between the sculptors of St-Trophîme and those of St-Gilles-du-Gard at St-Gilles, further west. Attempts to identify the work of individual masters have often picked out the figure of St Paul on the northeast pier, which does have a distinctive treatment of drapery similar to the figures on the central doorway at St-Gilles. The capitals on each side of the cloisters are the other main focus for figurative and decorative sculpture. On the north and east sides they

Detail of a carved capital in the cloister

depict scenes from the life and Passion of Christ, on the south episodes from the life of St Trophimus, and on the west from the lives of saints associated with this region such as Stephen and Martha. It is also worth noting the quality of the decorative foliated capitals. There is a walkway above the cloisters which leads into a series of monastic apartments used for temporary exhibitions.

Facing St-Trophîme is the dull 17C church of Ste-Anne which previously housed the collections of Roman art now displayed at the Musée de l'Arles Antique (see below). In their absence there is very little to see here although there are plans to use the space for exhibitions.

From the southern end of the place the rue de la République runs west towards the Rhône. Under its previous name of rue Royale it was the principal street in Arles and is still one of the main shopping streets, but there are several interesting 17C–18C façades and doorways which act as a reminder of its more elegant past. On the right after 100m is the **Museon Arlaten** (☎ 04 90 96 08 23: **open** Tues–Sun 09.00–12.00 and 14.00–19.00 in summer; earlier closing in winter; closed Mon) also known as the Palais du Félibrige, a regional and ethnographic museum founded in 1896 by the poet Frédéric Mistral. There are several mementoes of Mistral in the collection including his Nobel Prize citation from 1904. It was the money from the prize which enabled him to purchase this building, the 16C Hôtel de Laval-Castellane, and Mistral himself supervised the installation of the collection in 1906–09. The interior courtyard reveals an interesting architectural complex covering several periods and styles although the main part of the building is 16C. In an excavated area in the centre, however, you can see the remains of a Roman exedra with niches for sculpture which was uncovered in 1908.

In all there are some 30 rooms on three floors devoted to different aspects of the traditional life and customs of Provence. Furniture, costumes, ceramics, musical instruments, farm and domestic implements, prints, photographs and paintings are used to build up a picture of the folk traditions which Mistral and the supporters of the Félibrige tried to record and to preserve. One room is devoted to Mistral himself and to other members of the movement such as the painter Léo Lelée, who depicted many scenes of the everyday life and customs of Arles. As Mistral requested, the attendants in the museum wear the traditional costume of Arles, combining the full skirt with 'tail' pleat, shawl and distinctive coif round the hair.

A few metres down the rue Pres. Wilson, opposite the Museon Arlaten, and turning to the right is the renovated Hôtel-Dieu, a 16C hospital and almshouse, which has been renamed the **Espace Van Gogh**. The painter did spend some time here under the care of Dr Rey following his breakdown in December 1888 and this has been taken as the excuse to imitate one of his paintings of the hospital (Oskar Reinhardt Collection, Winterthur). Following attempts to save the building from dereliction it was decided to restore it as an art centre and to recreate on the walls the exaggerated colour scheme that Van Gogh used in his picture. It is now occupied by craft shops and postcard stalls.

From the front of the Museon Arlaten take the first street to the right along the edge of the building, the rue Mistral, then the rue Balze to the right along the rear of the museum. On the right is a 17C **Jesuit chapel**, once attached to the Hôtel Laval-Castellane and previously a museum of early Christian art. The interior of this chapel preserves some fine architectural details in the flanking arcades, a good panelled wooden ceiling and an elaborate High Baroque altarpiece and retable in the apse.

On the left side of the chapel there are stairs leading down to the **Cryptoporticus** (open daily 09.00–19.00 Apr–Sept; 10.00–16.30 Oct–Mar) a complex of underground chambers leading to two huge arcaded galleries which once supported the Roman forum. Begun in the time of Augustus (1C), the main galleries form a horseshoe stretching approximately 90m from the Hôtel de Ville to the chapel and on to the place du Forum to the north, where the remains of the temple supported by these foundations can be seen. There is still some uncertainty about the purpose of this vast complex: it appears that the underground corridors were well-ventilated, suggesting that they were used as passageways between different parts of the town. They do, however, give an immense amount of storage space and were later used as granaries.

Continue up the rue Balze, turning left into the **place du Forum**, one of the most attractive and relaxing squares in Arles. At its centre, shaded by plane trees, is a good statue of Mistral by Theodore Rivière (1909) enclosed by railings in the form of the tridents used by the cowboys of the Camargue, the *gardians*. Behind the statue and set into the wall of the *Hôtel Nord-Pinus* are two columns from the pediment of the 1C temple which stood here on the Roman forum. On the east side at the same corner was the subject of Van Gogh's *Café Terrace*, one of his finest paintings of Arles (now in the Kröller-Müller Museum, Otterlo). Like the Hôtel Dieu, this has been restored to look like the painting.

Along the Rhône

Continuing north from the place du Forum, by the rue de la Place and rue du Sauvage, you pass on the left the old townhouse of the Comtes d'Arlaten de Beaumont, dating from the 12C, 15C and 17C. Now a hotel, this well-preserved mansion with its own courtyard and garden evokes something of the grander lifestyle of the Arlesian nobility. Continue along the winding rue du Sauvage, turning left into the rue D. Maisto at the place Ste-Luce which leads down to the **Thermes et Palais de Constantine** (open daily 09.00–12.00 and 14.00–19.00 in summer; earlier closing in winter). This large Roman site is only partially excavated, the bulk of the ancient complex stretching south under the rue du Sauvage where it probably connected with a palace built by Constantine in the 4C. What can be seen are the ruined remains of the baths complex, the steam room (at the entrance), tepidarium on the left, caldarium in the centre and swimming pool at the bottom right, which produces the semicircular 'apsidal' protrusion on the exterior. These brick walls are quite impressive but there is very little to indicate the original character or function of the remains.

At the bottom of the rue D. Maisto, turn right into the rue du Grand Prieuré, a street of important medieval houses, on the left of which is the **Musée Réattu**

(☎ 04 90 49 37 58: **open** daily 09.00–12.30 and 14.00–19.00 June–Sept; 10.00–19.00 Mar–June). This museum occupies the Grand Priory of the Order of Hospitallers of St John of Jerusalem, which was built in the 14C and extended in the 16C. The complex includes a rambling series of domestic and religious apartments around two internal courtyards which create an attractively diverse ensemble. The ornamental sculpture on the stairways and arches is particularly fine. The outer wall to the north incorporates some of the old town walls, and the windows to that side offer good views over the Rhône.

The priory was pillaged during the Revolution and later bought by the painter Jacques Réattu (1760–1833) who bequeathed the building and collection to the town. Réattu, whose work occupies the first three galleries, was a fairly routine follower of David's neo-Classicism but there are interesting studies for some of his more important history paintings such as *The Death of Alcibiades*. During the Revolution Réattu undertook the decoration of the Temple of Rationalism in Marseille and there are grisaille studies for this on display.

The rest of the Old Master collection proceeds chronologically and includes works by Simon Vouet (1590–1649), Aelbert Cuyp (1620–91) and Antoine Coypel (1661–1722), as well as those by local artists of the 17C–19C. The collection's main strength, however, is in 20C French art. There are examples of the work of Ossip Zadkine (1890–1967), André Marchand (1907–) and Victor Vasarély (1908–97), drawings by Pierre-Albert Marquet (1875–1947) and Marcel Gromaire (1892–1971), and prints by Gauguin and Maurice de Vlaminck (1876–1958). There is also an interesting, if rather slight, group of 57 drawings by Picasso, all produced between 31 December 1970 and 4 February 1971 and given to the town in the same year. To this was added a portrait of the artist's mother painted in 1923, which Picasso's widow Jacqueline donated in 1985. On the second floor there are rooms devoted to the history of the Order of the Knights of Malta and, reflecting the town's association with photography, exhibitions of the work of leading photographers. The museum's collection includes prints by Man Ray, Henri Cartier-Bresson, Brassaï, Edward Weston and Cecil Beaton.

Of the other notable buildings in the rue du Grand Prieuré, directly opposite the museum is the 15C **Commanderie de Ste-Luce**, an extension to the Musée Reattu, which is also used for exhibitions. A combined ticket gives access to both.

To see the rear or river façade of the Grand Priory, return to the Thermes and join the bank of the Rhône to the right. This is the larger arm of the river, the Grand Rhône, which still carries a reasonable amount of water traffic. The quai Marx Dormoy to the west is backed by a number of old and picturesque buildings including the ruined 14C church of the Frères Prêcheurs and, before the **Pont de Trinquetaille**, some remains of the old town walls. The bridge itself, leading over to the district of Trinquetaille, was painted by Van Gogh several times in 1888, the stairway remaining much as it appeared then.

To the east of the Grand Priory the dull quai R.M. Jouveau follows a gentle curve round to the medieval ramparts and the fortified Porte de la Cavalerie. This area outside the old gate, now named the place de la Libération and the place Lamartine, was the site of Van Gogh's Yellow House but it was destroyed along with everything else by Allied bombing in 1944. From here you can see the surviving piers of the Pont de Lunel upriver, with their vigorously carved stone lions. This bridge was also destroyed in 1944 but not rebuilt, its replacement being the Nouveau Pont to the south which carries the main road out of Arles past Trinquetaille to the west.

Around the Arènes

Pass through the gateway into the rue de la Cavalerie and head back into the town, past the place Voltaire and straight ahead to the huge Roman arena or amphitheatre known as the **Arènes** (open daily 09.00–19.00 in summer; 10.00–16.30 in winter).

History of the Arènes

This, the largest of the amphitheatres in Roman Gaul, was built in the late 1C, probably in the reign of the emperor Flavius c 80 AD. At 136 x 107m it is slightly larger than its counterpart at Nîmes which was erected at approximately the same date. During the early Middle Ages it was turned into a fortress against Barbarian and Saracen attacks and gradually came to enclose a settlement of some 200 houses and two chapels. It was at this time that the four watchtowers were built using stone stripped from the main part of the structure. Indeed, throughout the Middle Ages the arena was a quarry for many buildings in Arles, resulting in the loss of the original third or attic storey. It was not until the 19C that many of the later additions and 'beggarly tenements' were cleared out and the building restored to something like its original appearance.

The outer wall rises to 21m on the two surviving tiers of 60 arches, the lower Doric and the upper Corinthian. The method of construction, however, is somewhat misleading since there are flat load-bearing slabs over each of the vaulted galleries suggesting a Greek trabeated as opposed to the Roman arcuated system of engineering. Access and egress (by exits known as *vomitaria*) for the 20,000 spectators was gained through a series of stairways and galleries which are still in operation today. In ancient times a canvas canopy could be pulled across the upper rim of the amphitheatre to protect the spectators from the sun in summer. The main entertainments were animal and gladiatorial contests, a solid wall acting as a barrier between the ranks of seating and the arena. Beneath this there was a series of passageways and cages where the animals and combatants were kept until their release into the open air. Nowadays the arena is used for a variety of spectacles including Spanish and Provençal bullfights. In 1909, however, it hosted a special performance of Gounod's opera *Mireille* based on the poem by Mistral. Visitors can ascend to the top of the towers from which there is an excellent view over the rooftops of the town towards Montmajour and Les Alpilles.

At 26 rond-point des Arènes, southwest of the arena itself, is the 17C Palais de Luppe which was once the residence of the bishop of Arles. Since 1984 this has been the location of the **Fondation Vincent Van Gogh** (☎ 04 90 49 94 04; open daily 10.00–19.00 in summer; 10.00–12.30 and 14.00–17.30 in winter), an arts centre which mounts temporary exhibitions. There are no paintings by Van Gogh himself in the collection but a number of eminent contemporary artists including Bacon, Roy Lichtenstein (1923–1998), David Hockney (1937–), Fernando Botero (1932–) and Arman have donated minor works on themes associated with the Dutch artist.

Continuing south, turn right into the rue de la Calade, where you will see the remains of the **Théâtre Antique** (open daily 09.00–19.00 in summer; 10.00–16.30 in winter), a Roman theatre greatly depleted from its original state but still impressive nevertheless. Built between 27 BC and 5 BC, during the reign of Augustus, this substantial theatre consisted of a proscenium stage and a semi-circular seating area which held up to 12,000 spectators. Like the arena, it was plundered as a quarry for building stone during the Middle Ages and had all but disappeared by the 17C. A full programme of excavation and renovation was not begun until 1825 and since then much has been done to at least suggest its scale.

The raked seating was supported by three tiers of arcades of which only one remains. The proscenium survives only in the two huge Corinthian columns, a testament to the monumentality of the whole complex whose remains are littered about the site. The Venus of Arles, now in the Musée du Louvre, Paris, was discovered here in 1651 as were several other important statues including that of Augustus now in the Musée de l'Arles Antique. In summer the theatre is often used for plays, concerts and performances of traditional dance.

The rue du Cloître along the western edge of the theatre leads to the Jardin d'Eté but a detour by the opposite side of the arena crosses a quieter part of town with several interesting sights. To the east of the arena is the place de la Major, an open esplanade in front of the Romanesque **Eglise de Notre-Dame-la-Major**. Built on the site of a Roman temple to Cybele and an early Christian shrine, the nave of the present church was begun in the 12C and additions were made in the 14C and 16C. The façade and tower are even later, having been completed in the 17C and 19C. Despite its rather dull appearance, inside and out, La Major has a traditional appeal to the people of Arles who regard it collectively as their local church.

Take the rue de la Madeleine south from the front of La Major to the place de la Redoute. This area is bounded by the ancient and medieval walls of the town and to the left is the old Porte de la Redoute. A few metres beyond the western corner of the place is a Renaissance archway leading to the ancient **Abbaye St-Césaire** and **Eglise St-Blaise**. This ancient abbey was one of the earliest Christian foundations in Provence and its first church was the original cathedral of Arles before it was supplanted in the 5C by St-Etienne (later St-Trophîme). It survived as an abbey until the Revolution and now serves as a hospital. The present church dates from the 12C although there have been numerous later additions and alterations and at one time it was reduced to being a warehouse and school. On the opposite corner to St-Blaise is the small and truncated chapel of St-Jean-de-Moustiers. Cut away in the centre, all that survives of this Romanesque church is the apsidal end which protrudes into the street.

The Alyscamps and the Musée de l'Arles Antique

From the rue Vauban opposite St-Blaise steps lead down into the Jardin d'Eté, with its inevitable bust of Van Gogh, and the boulevard des Lices. From this point it is worth making a short excursion to the Alyscamps. Turning left, follow the boulevard for 100m to the crossroads under the old town walls. Cross over to the other side and follow the avenue des Alyscamps by the police station, which bears left towards the entrance to **Les Alyscamps** (open 09.00–19.00 in summer; 10.00–16.30 in winter).

History of Les Alyscamps

The Alyscamps, like the Champs Elysées in Paris, take their name from the pagan paradise of the Elysian fields. In this case the name is entirely appropriate because the area has been a necropolis since Roman times. Its real fame, however, arose during the early Christian period when the faithful of the region wanted to be buried near the tomb of St Genesius, a 3C Roman scribe who had been beheaded for opposing the persecution of the Christians. Within a few years of his death miracles came to be associated with the saint's remains, making this site immensely popular as a burial place for the faithful. Its reputation was further enhanced by the legend that St Trophimus was also buried here and soon a major undertaking industry had been established in the town. Several chroniclers record the procedure whereby coffins were sent down the Rhône by barge or in barrels, with the appropriate payment, to be collected at the Pont de Trinquetaille and transported to the Alyscamps for interment. In the 10C a further legend, suggesting that the knights of Roncevaux (from the *Chanson de Roland*) were buried here, did even more to make the Alyscamps popular and pressure of space required the creation of two and even three separate layers of tombs.

Another indication of the site's popularity can be found in the reports of the monks of St-Victor in Marseille who, between the 11C and 15C, apparently maintained some 19 churches here. By this stage, however, the Alyscamps could be said to have been in decline. In 1152 the relics of St Trophimus were transferred to the cathedral in Arles, thus depriving the cemetery of one of its greatest attractions. Nevertheless, in the early 14C Dante refers to the Alyscamps in the *Inferno* (IX, 112) and it also appears in Ariosto's *Orlando Furioso* (1532). By then it had already begun to be broken up. Some of the old sarcophagi were being sold off or given as presents and many still rest in various museums throughout southern France and Italy.

Finally, the building of the railway line and canal in the 19C encroached on the ancient burial site, disturbing even more of the tombs and leading to the transfer of the most important to the museums in the town. What remains, although still extensive, is only a part of this huge city of the dead.

The Alyscamps are approached by a long avenue flanked by rows of excavated tombs and sarcophagi. The Greek sarcophagi generally have a pitched lid with raised corners whereas Roman lids are flat. This is one of the most pleasant and relaxing spots in Arles, much liked by both Van Gogh and Gauguin who often painted here. The arch near the entrance is the 16C gateway of the church of St-Césaire and, to the left, are the remains of the chapel of St-Accurse, built in 1520 by Quiquerin de Beaujeu in expiation for murdering Accurse de la Tour. Further on to the left is the 15C chapel of the Porcellet family and, finally, amid piles of partly excavated tombs, the **Eglise St-Honorat**. Originally dedicated to St Genesius, the church was rededicated to St Honoratus in 1040 when it came under the protection of the abbey of St-Victor at Marseille. During the 12C the monks built the present Romanesque church with its distinctive, arcaded tower and during the subsequent centuries a number of chapels in the Gothic style were added.

Alongside the Alyscamps is the old railway yard which once threatened the existence of the necropolis. Ironically, it is the marshalling yards that are abandoned although they have found a limited use. One of the sheds has been converted into a large exhibition hall for annual photographic conventions.

The new **Musée de l'Arles Antique** (☎ 04 90 18 88 89: **open** Wed–Mon 09.00–20.00 in summer; 10.00–18.00 in winter; closed Tues) is an important museum which should not be missed on a visit to Arles, although it is rather inconveniently placed at the southwest corner of the town, on the other side of a main road. Housed in a blue triangular building on a spur of land between the river and a canal, it brings together the vast array of antique artefacts that have been uncovered in and around the town. These collections were previously displayed in two separate churches in the town centre, an unconventional arrangement which nevertheless had its own charm. The new museum, however, offers an opportunity to see the full range of antique and early Christian pieces in a more coherent setting and with a range of models, diagrams and interpretive material.

The bulk of the collection consists of sarcophagi, statues, tombstones, mosaics and architectural fragments excavated from the various sites of what was once the capital of the western Roman empire. The colossal **statue of Augustus** which once graced the theatre is given pride of place, as are several other free-standing figures including a cast of the Venus of Arles. (The original is now in the Louvre.) The real treasures, however, are the carved sarcophagi. The most important of these is the 2C–3C BC **sarcophagus of Hippolytus and Phaedra**, a piece which has all the qualities of a metropolitan Roman work imported to Provence. Most of the other sarcophagi are the work of the local school of marble sculptors active in Arles between the 1C and 4C. The finest of the local work is the 2C **sarcophagus of Apollo and the Muses**.

The early Christians adopted Roman burial customs and adhered to the hierarchy which led rich families to decorate their tomb chests. It is hardly surprising that since Arles was the great necropolis of the west there should be a great range of **Christian sarcophagi**. There are good examples of various types of decoration from the foliated patterns of the 'Olivaison' sarcophagus to portrait reliefs and tiers of narrative scenes from the Old and New Testaments. A recurring feature of the gravestones and cineraria (urns) is the inscription 'D M' with a leaf alongside. The letters refer to the Latin *Dei Manus* ('into the hands of God') and the falling leaf symbolises death.

From the terrace of the museum you can see the excavations of the Roman circus which once occupied this area. Looking north, however, there is a good view over the Rhône and across the rooftops of Arles to the tower of St-Trophîme, much as it was once observed by countless travellers and pilgrims including Van Gogh.

4 · La Camargue

Arles looks out over the Grand Rhône to the huge expanses to the west which have some of the most famous and distinctive countryside in southern France. The main attraction is the Camargue, a great alluvial flat of marsh, lagoon and farmland between the two branches of the Rhône. The area has assumed an identity of its own, quite distinct from either Provence or the Languedoc, and due to its unique character is now a national park in which the landscape and the wildlife are protected.

History of La Camargue

The historical geography of La Camargue is directly related to the action of the Rhône over millennia. Such is the power of the river, and so great the amount of sand, mud and gravel it propels downstream, that it has created a loosely balanced ecosystem in the flat delta where it meets the sea. This is not to suggest that this land is in any way static. In fact, it has been subject to dramatic changes even during the last few centuries. The coastline, for example, has altered considerably so that buildings which were once on the seafront are now either several kilometres inland, as at Aigues-Mortes, or permanently submerged in the sea like the lighthouse at Faraman. Over the last two centuries, however, there has been increasing awareness of the need to stabilise the action of the river and to monitor the chemical balance of the soil and water, as much for the sake of agriculture as for the topography or wildlife. As a result, the impression of wilderness in La Camargue is largely a false one. It is a landscape that depends entirely on human intervention.

The closer scientific management of the region has meant that more of La Camargue is now cultivated than at any time in the past and this has created three distinct areas: the wetlands to the south with the pools and lagoons that drain into the sea, the salt marshes in the west, unsuitable for agriculture but rich in flora and fauna, and the upper Camargue where most of the farmland and cattle rearing is located. All of these areas can be visited by a network of paths or water channels but it is possible to get a flavour of the whole area by driving along the D570 from Arles to Stes-Maries-de-la-Mer.

Leave Arles by the new bridge (N113), taking the D570 to the left at the junction. It is not long before you enter the open flat countryside of La Camargue with its distinctive features such as the thatched *cabanes* of the *gardians*, the herds of black bulls or the famous small white horses. A good introduction to the history and traditions of the region can be gained at the **Musée Camarguais** (☎ 04 90 97 10 82: **open** daily 10.15–16.45 in summer; closed Tues in winter) at Pont de Rousty by the main road. Housed in an old sheepfold belonging to a *mas* or farmhouse are displays covering the different periods and activities of the region. The 19C is best served, for that is the period when the pattern of *gardian* life—bull-breeding, sheep-farming, horsemanship, fishing and the other activities that have gone to make up the popular image of La Camargue—was established. There is also a signposted path from the museum offering a taste of the marshland to the south.

After the Mas d'Avignon, one of the larger farmhouses, the road turns south through the wetlands where you can usually see some of the huge numbers of resident and migrant birds that depend on the marshes. The most spectacular are the flamingoes, but there are also various storks, herons, egrets and many others. For a closer look, visit the **Parc ornithologique** by the Etang de Gines on the east side of the main road and the information centre nearby.

Saintes-Maries-de-la-Mer

Continuing south, the D570 reaches the sea at Saintes-Maries-de-la-Mer one of the most unusual and fascinating places on the coast but becoming increasingly popular and commercialised by the year.

History of Saintes-Maries-de-la-Mer

According to local legend it was here that the boat carrying Mary Magdalene, Mary Salome, Mary Jacobea (the mother of James), their black servant Sarah, Martha and her brother Lazarus, Maximinus and Cedonius landed after a miraculous journey from Palestine. From here they set about their mission to Christianise Provence, the Magdalene settling at La-Ste-Baume while Martha became associated with Tarascon. The other two Marys (Salome and Jacobea) and Sarah remained in this area and were buried in an oratory by the shore. As a result, the village became an important pilgrimage centre, especially after the discovery of the saints' remains in 1448.

A separate cult has developed around St Sarah, who was adopted by Gypsies as their patron saint and is the focus of a festival in May. Thousands of Gypsies from all over Europe gather for the festival, a particularly lively affair with singing, dancing, horse-trading and the full panoply of folk activities much loved by ethnographers. Bob Dylan attended the festival in 1975 and was inspired to write the lyrical song *One More Cup of Coffee* on the album *Desire*.

❖ *Information, accommodation and food*

𝐳 5 avenue Van Gogh (☎ 04 90 97 82 55).

Hotels and restaurants. It can be difficult and expensive finding somewhere to stay at Stes-Maries-de-la-Mer and it is often best to take something out of town, such as the *Hostellerie du Pont du Gau* on the D570 (☎ 04 90 97 81 53), which has a good restaurant. *Les Vagues* (☎ 04 90 97 84 40) and the *Hôtel de la Plage* (☎ 04 90 97 85 09) are the most reasonable in town.

The focus for the cult of the Stes-Maries is the striking fortified **Eglise**, begun in the 12C but extended to cope with the processions of pilgrims in the 15C. Earlier churches on this site had suffered at the hands of Saracen raiders, which explains the fortress-like character of this remarkable building. The interior is a rugged Romanesque with some fine carved capitals in the nave. You can also see the various relics associated with the cult of the Stes-Maries, including the boat and a marble 'pillow' discovered 'in a column' when the saints' remains were uncovered. This church has a special significance in traditional Provençal culture and it is here that the final dramatic scenes in Mistral's poem *Mirèio*—when the heroine expires after her ordeal—are set. The relics of the Gypsies' saint, Sarah, are displayed in the crypt and every year on 24–25 May there is a pilgrimage and festival in which her statue is carried to the sea.

The Gypsy festival is actually quite recent, having been encouraged by Baron Folco de Baroncelli-Javon (1869–1943), a colourful figure closely associated with the town. Born in Avignon to an Italian noble family, in 1890 he decided to become a cowboy in La Camargue and spent the rest of his life celebrating the culture and freedom of the *gardians'* way of life. Linked to the Félibrige movement, he wrote stories about La Camargue and helped to celebrate and preserve many of the traditional activities associated with this region. There is an interesting display devoted to his life and work in the **Musée Baroncelli** on rue Victor-Hugo (☎ 90 97 87 60: **open** daily 10.00–12.00 and 14.00–18.00; closed Tues in winter) including some of the 'traditional' costumes that he himself designed. Another adopted son mentioned in the museum displays is Van Gogh, who painted a famous picture of boats on the beach at Stes-Maries while on a visit here in 1888. He was very drawn to the area, writing to his brother that the flat landscape reminded him of his native Holland. There is a lookout-point from the tower and terrace at the top of the building which gives a good view over the town and along the beaches stretching in both directions.

Stes-Maries-de-la-Mer is at the bottom of a strip of land between lagoons and once you have completed your visit there is little alternative but to turn back up the main road. While here, however, you might follow some of the good walks along the windswept beach and into the surrounding area. There are also boat trips up the Petit Rhône from the mouth of the river 2km to the west. Baroncelli-Javon was buried here, his grave marked by a flat slab, in what was, at the time, an isolated spot frequented only by *gardians* and wild horses.

Aigues-Mortes

One extraordinary site further west (accessible by the D58 off the D570) is **Aigues-Mortes** (Dead Waters), the town built by the French king Louis IX, later St Louis, when preparing for his crusade to the Holy Land in 1248. This is a remarkable place, made all the more fascinating by its solitary position and the melancholy atmosphere that most travellers have detected. Advance warning of what to expect is given by the 14C **Tour Carbonnière** at the turning on the D58. This is an outlying barbican of Aigues-Mortes, whose main fortifications gradually appear across the plain of the western Camargue.

History of Aigues-Mortes

In the early 13C the French lacked a seaport on the Mediterranean, so in 1240 Louis IX purchased a tract of land from the abbot of Psalmody which would allow him to build up his fleet and to embark for the Holy Land from native soil. Beginning with the powerful Tour de Constance in one corner, Louis had his new town laid out on a regular grid plan with a strong wall round the outside for protection. With various financial inducements and the promise of royal favour the families of tradesmen employed on the preparations quickly filled up the new town. Eventually in 1248 the fleet of some 1500 ships assembled off Aigues-Mortes and embarked for what proved to be a disastrous crusade. Within a year the army had been defeated and in 1250 the king was captured.

Aigues-Mortes, however, had a life beyond this escapade and it continued to prosper during the succeeding three centuries, albeit with regular outbreaks of war and invasion. During the Hundred Years War it was taken by the Burgundians but their enemies, the Armagnacs, led the most famous assault on the town to retake it in 1418. Using their own supporters inside to overpower the guards at one of the gates, the main Armagnac army entered the town at night and set about butchering the Burgundian garrison. The west tower, where the salted bodies of the victims were piled up before burial, is still known as the Tour des Bourguignons.

By the 15C the principal problem with Aigues-Mortes' location was becoming increasingly obvious. The coast was moving southwards, the harbour silting up and the town, which had begun as a port, was becoming landlocked in a marsh of brackish water. Nowadays it is some 5km from the sea and the channels around it are only suitable for small craft. The town has diversified into fishing, salt-extraction and wine-growing, but it remains a most curious place. Here, in a desolate flat landscape, is a substantial community living in a medieval walled town miles from the sort of ancillary industries and services that you would expect. Yet it remains one of the best-preserved medieval complexes anywhere.

Z By the Porte de la Gardette (☎ 04 66 53 73 00).

The main sight is the perimeter walls, punctuated by gates on each side and towers at the corners. You can walk around most of the ramparts, peering through the battlements to the flat marshland on all sides, a view marred only by the rash of new houses to the north. The **Tour de Constance** is the most impressive, a massive circular keep with walls up to 6m thick, which was later used as a prison. There is a display of documents and pictures inside with details of famous prisoners, who seem to have been drawn from all shades of opinion unacceptable to the French Crown. The Protestants fared the worst, one woman, Marie Durand, spending 38 years here after being imprisoned at the age of eight. Another Protestant, Abraham Mazel, succeeded in escaping by the old ruse of tying bedclothes together but, from the look of the buildings, this must have been very rare.

St-Gilles-du-Gard

Another detour from the direct route back to Arles from Stes-Maries-de-la-Mer takes you to **Saint-Gilles**, a rather depressing market town with heavy traffic running through it, but also the site of one of the greatest monuments of the Romanesque. This is the **Eglise St-Gilles-du-Gard**, a victim of periodic outbursts of vandalism, although the magisterial west front survives, displaying the finest examples of the Classical spirit in Romanesque sculpture.

History of St-Gilles-du-Gard

St Giles was a hermit living in this area in the 8C, around whom many unlikely stories have been woven. His most famous miracle involved saving a hind being pursued by the Visigoth king Wamba but, as with most local saints, he also had to spend some time in a boat without sails drifting around the Mediterranean before landing in Provence. He was venerated in this area for several centuries before the great abbey church was erected in the 11C–12C. The prime mover in the foundation was Raymond IV, Count of Toulouse and one of the most powerful nobles in Europe. Having supported the building programme, in 1096 he persuaded Pope Urban II to consecrate the main altar of the abbey church. Soon after this Raymond embarked on a crusade to the Holy Land, dying in the colony he had established at Tripoli. The crusades were one of the main sources of revenue for St-Gilles since the abbey controlled much of the trade with the eastern

Mediterranean. Furthermore, the use of the nearby ports carried a tax that brought more wealth from the constant movement of ships taking men and supplies to the armies in the east.

The abbey also benefited from its location on one of the main pilgrimage routes to Santiago de Compostela in Spain. St-Gilles was one of the principal staging-posts for pilgrims, who paid dearly in cash for their salvation. This helps to explain the scale of the original foundation, which was much larger than that which can be seen today. During the 16C–17C Wars of Religion it was badly damaged and at one time set on fire. Much of the vaulting collapsed and the overall scale of the building was dramatically truncated to form a local parish church. If we consider in addition the attacks of the Revolution we should perhaps be grateful for the survival of the west front, which supports the great cycle of relief sculpture.

ℹ Place Frédéric Mistral (**☎** 66 87 33 75).

The overall shape of the façade with its three openings recalls a Roman triumphal arch which is entirely in keeping with the style of the carving. The sculpture seems to have been undertaken in a single campaign during the mid-1140s and, although the hands of five separate masters have been identified, there is a remarkable unity to the scheme. The cycle begins in the lowest register with a series of life-size reliefs of the twelve Apostles and two archangels flanked by Classical columns. Above this a frieze running across the whole façade recounts the Passion of Christ in a manner reminiscent of Roman sarcophagus reliefs. The programme is completed with the three tympani above the portals which depict the *Adoration of the Magi*, the *Dream of Joseph* and the *Virgin Enthroned* on the left, *Christ in Majesty* in the centre, and finally, in an unusual arrangement, the *Crucifixion* flanked by personifications of the Church and the Synagogue on the left. The central tympanum is modern and noticeably weaker but the Crucifixion on the right is an very rare subject for this position. It may have been planned to

Eglise St-Gilles-du -Gard

emphasise the clergy's opposition to a local group of heretics led by Peter de Bruys who had denied the validity of the Mass. At Easter 1136 de Bruys and his colleagues removed wooden crosses from the church and built a fire in front of the abbey, over which they proceded to roast some pork. Several days later Peter and his associates were burned as heretics on the same spot.

The interior (**open** Mon–Sat 09.00–13.00 and 15.00–19.00, Sun 10.00–

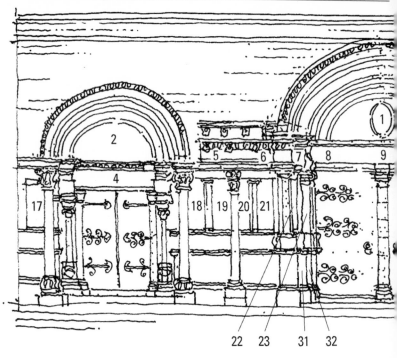

Key to the relief sculptures on the façade of St-Gilles

The Tympanums

1 *Christ in Majesty surrounded by the symbols of the four Evangelists*
2 *The Adoration of the Magi*
3 *The Crucifixion*

The lintels and frieze

4 *Christ's entry to Jerusalem*
5 *Judas returning the 30 pieces of silver*
6 *Christ driving the money changers from the Temple*
7 *Christ foretells Peter's denial*
8 *Christ washing the feet of the disciples*
9 *The Last Supper*
10 *The kiss of Judas*
11 *The Flagellation*
12 *Christ carrying the Cross*
13 *Mary Magdalene before Christ*
14 *The Holy Women buying spices*
15 *The Holy Women at the sepulchre*
16 *Christ appearing to his disciples*

13.00 July–Aug; 09.00–12.00 and 14.00–18.00 Apr–June and Sept; closes at 17.00 in winter) presents a completely different aspect, since all that survives of the original church is the huge and rather dark crypt that once had to accommodate thousands of pilgrims as they processed around the tomb of the saint. The rest of the church is in ruins except for the curious belltower with its covered spiral staircase known as *le Vis* (the Screw). This structure was much admired by stonemasons from all over France who were often required to make models and drawings of it as part of their training.

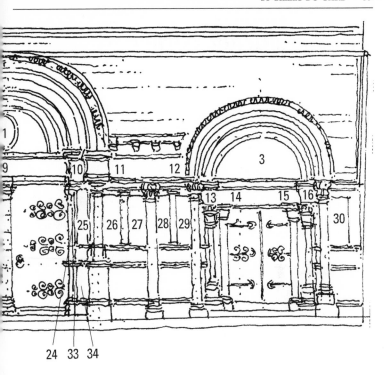

Saints and Apostles

17 *Archangel Michael*
18 *St Matthew*
19 *St Bartholomew*
20 *St Thomas*
21 *St James the Less*
22 *St John the Evangelist*
23 *St Peter*
24 *St James the Greater*
25 *St Paul*
26 *Apostle?*
27 *Apostle?*
28 *Apostle?*
29 *Apostle?*

Scenes flanking the main doorway

30 *Angels and Rebel Angels*
31 *Cain murders Abel*
32 *Cain and Abel making sacrifices to the Lord*
33 *Centaur shooting an arrow at a stag*
34 *Balaam and his ass*

There is another Romanesque monument not far from the church in the medieval quarter on the opposite side of the place de la République. The **Maison Romane** (☎ 04 66 87 40 42: **open** Mon–Sat 09.00–12.00 and 15.00–18.00; closed Sun and at 17.00 in winter) is a 12C townhouse where Guy Foulque, later Pope Clement IV, was born. It now contains a museum of local history and archaeology. This part of town is unassuming but presents a more relaxed aspect than the rue Gambetta, the busy main street which leads directly out on the N572 to Arles.

The Languedoc border

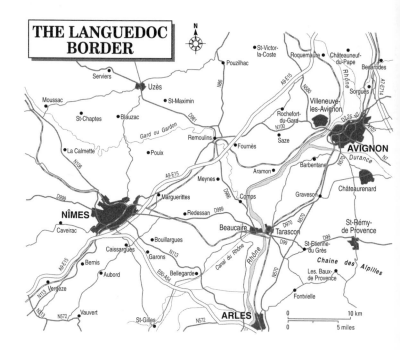

5 · Arles to Avignon: Les Baux and St-Rémy

This route, which covers a total distance of 51km, is by no means the most direct between Arles and Avignon but it takes in several of the most important historic sites in Provence. It follows an ancient drove-road through the only gap in the rugged Chaîne des Alpilles, traverses the flat plain to the east of Arles and moves through some fairly rough terrain. Les Baux-de-Provence is perhaps the most famous of its attractions, but the itinerary also visits the two Roman monuments known as Les Antiques, the remains of the ancient town of Glanum, and St-Rémy-de-Provence, a medieval town where Van Gogh spent much of 1889 as a patient in the hospital of St-Paul.

The ruins of Montmajour and Fontvieille

The first monument is the fortified tower and ruined churches of **Montmajour** (☎ 04 90 54 64 17; **open** daily 09.00–19.00 Apr–Sept; 09.00–12.00 and 14.00–17.00 Oct–Mar), a great Benedictine abbey just 4km northeast of Arles on the N570 and D17.

History of Montmajour

Despite the claims of an inscription that the abbey was established by Charlemagne, this foundation actually grew from a small community of monks who retreated here in the 10C. At that time the site was an island of limestone in the surrounding swamp, accessible only by boat and therefore offering security and isolation. The site already had early Christian associations. St Trophimus was reputed to have found refuge from the Romans here and there are a number of palaeo-Christian tombs cut into the rock itself. It seems that the earliest church was actually hewn out of this rock but it was replaced in the 12C by the surviving church of St-Pierre. It was in 1030 that the abbot instituted the annual pilgrimage to this site which became hugely popular and proved to be the main source of the abbey's wealth. At one stage it was estimated that 150,000 pilgrims had visited Montmajour in a single year. The revenue from this enabled the monks to expand their building programme and to begin the colossal task of draining the marshland for cultivation.

As is often the case with successful monasteries, the increasing wealth of the foundation led to a weakening of the rule and by the 17C Montmajour was attracting criticism from religious and royal sources about the decline in standards and the ostentatiousness of the community. In 1639 a group of monks from St-Maur was sent to reform it but they succeeded only in causing a minor civil war. The disgraced monks, who had been turned out, found support from a band of soldiers who proceeded to loot the abbey of everything they could find. Such disturbances continued into the following century and when the abbot, the Cardinal of Rohan, was accused of bribing the queen with a diamond necklace (*l'affaire de collier*) in 1786, Louis XVI ordered the abbey to be closed. From here on it was an unhappy history of destruction and vandalism. In 1791 the abbey was sold to a merchant who began dismantling the buildings for the stone which was then used in many engineering projects in the region. Sold again in 1793, it was divided up and used for cheap accommodation. The painter Jacques Réattu, who rescued the priory in Arles, was able to save the tower from destruction but the abbey continued to be broken up and cannibalised throughout the 19C.

It was not until 1862 that the authorities in Arles acquired the bulk of the abbey and began a programme of restoration. It is now a state property but the effects of those years of neglect are still evident. Of all the great monastic foundations in Provence this one has the least spiritual atmosphere and the sense of ruination still pervades the complex. When Van Gogh worked here in 1888 he was struck by its desolation and the absence of human life.

Of the three principal buildings at Montmajour, the small **Eglise St-Pierre** at the extreme south is the oldest. Begun in the 12C, it incorporates some of the

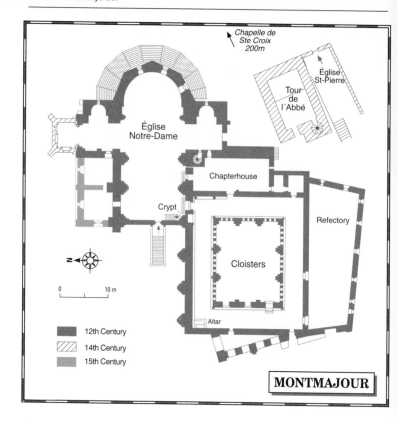

Chapelle de
Ste Croix
200m

Église
St-Pierre

Tour
de
l'Abbé

Église
Notre-Dame

Chapterhouse

Crypt

Refectory

N

Cloisters

0   10 m

Altar

12th Century

14th Century

15th Century

MONTMAJOUR

earlier shrine hewn from the rock but was itself superceded by the larger abbey church. It is built in a pure and plain Romanesque style but there are a few foliated capitals and geometric carvings in the interior and a crude relief of St Peter in the wall by the entrance. Special permission is now required to visit this church.

In marked contrast to St-Pierre, the monumental abbey church or **Eglise de Notre-Dame** is a weighty structure of finely dressed masonry. It is actually two churches, one above the other, both dating from the mid- to late 12C. The upper church was originally intended to be much larger which explains the rather ungainly proportions. The single nave should have contained five bays but a temporary wall was erected after only two, when work stopped in the late 12C. The solid piers for the remaining three bays can be seen on the exterior of the cloister wall. Another irregularity is the openings in the generous semi-circular apse which break the simple rhythms of the symmetrical design. Decoration is kept to a minimum, noticeable only in the Classical capitals on the half-columns of the apse. Alterations in the 13C–14C led to the cross-vaulting in the transept and to the construction of two Gothic chapels in the north wall.

A staircase outside the western end of the church leads down to the lower church. Built into the hillside as a foundation for the upper church this also served as the crypt where the holy relics were stored. At the heart of this is a circular chapel with a carved altar and, surrounding it, a narrow ambulatory with a series of five radiating chapels. Processions of pilgrims must have filed through these corridors, enclosed by massive walls and simple arched openings, to pray near the sacred relics.

To the south of the church is the cloister and abbey buildings, of which the chapterhouse and the refectory are the principal survivors. The rectangular cloister was built in the late 12C but only the east side has retained its original Romanesque character. Each of the other sides was rebuilt between the 14C and 19C. Nevertheless, the later additions have preserved the basic arrangement of three bays each enclosing a recessed triple arcade supported by small paired columns. The capitals on the original east side have some fine Romanesque carving and there is further decorative sculpture on the corbels inside the cloister and at the massive corner piers. Also on the east gallery is the wall tomb of the Counts of Provence. Overlooking this cloister is the belltower and, beyond, the huge fortified **keep** that dominates the whole site. Built in 1369, this tall tower was the abbey's principal defence against marauders and you can still get some impression of its original function when looking out over the surrounding plain from the viewing platform at the top.

Slightly apart from the main abbey complex to the northeast is the 12C **Chapelle de Ste-Croix**, a beautifully proportioned Romanesque building that would do justice to the Renaissance were the forms not so austere. The belltower has some restrained Classical decoration and there is a carved cornice or string-course marking the top of the semi-cylindrical apses. An inscription on the interior, claiming the legendary foundation of the abbey by Charlemagne, is apocryphal and dates from the 14C.

Continuing on the D17 for 4.5km you arrive at the small town of **Fontvieille** whose quarrymen and merchants prospered from Montmajour. The town has several interesting streets and the 14C **Tour de Guet** (Watchtower) but it is most famous for its association with Alphonse Daudet, who regularly visited friends at the 19C Château de Montauban on the eastern side.

Just south of Fontvieille on the D33 is the **Moulin de Daudet**, one of a group of windmills which inspired the short stories in *Lettres de mon Moulin* (1869), the author's most famous and enduring work. Daudet never actually lived in the windmill but came here to 'cure' himself of Paris and to write down some of the tales which were told by the peasant families that he met. The windmill, which has been restored with working machinery, houses a small Daudet museum (☎ 04 90 54 67 49: **open** daily 09.00–12.00 and 14.00–19.00 June–Sept; 10.00–12.00 and 14.00–17.00 Oct–May; closed Jan) with prints and mementoes as well as some illustrations to the letters by José Roy.

Continue down the D33 for 3km: the crossroads with the D78E marks the line of a Roman aqueduct. To the east and south there are several ruined mills, one of which, the Meuneries de Barbegal, is a rare surviving Roman flour mill dating from the 3C.

Les Baux-de-Provence

Leave Fontvieille by the D17 east, turning left after 4km onto the D78 which ascends through the rocky **Chaîne des Alpilles** to the formidable redoubt of

Les Baux. The mineral bauxite was discovered here in 1822 and takes its name from the village, but the site is notable primarily as one of the most spectacular and dramatic ruins in Provence.

History of Les Baux-de-Provence

It is easy to understand why Les Baux, situated on a tall spur of rock measuring some 900 x 200m and with sheer cliffs on three sides, should have been the impregnable centre of a feudal empire. Its history and legends have also caught the public imagination like few other places. In *The Pleasure of Ruins* (1953), the novelist Rose Macaulay described how it had everything that 'ruin tasters' could desire: antiquity, abandonment, decay, as well as a magnificent and forbidding site. It was indeed 'an awful pile ... Waste, desolate, where Ruin dreary dwells'.

In addition to this, it had romantic associations with troubadour Provence and as a Court of Love in the 11C–12C, although most of the romantic stories of knights and their ladies were invented in the 19C. More justified is the reputation for brutality and the single-minded pursuit of power that the lords of Les Baux maintained over several generations. When the 19C English poet John Addington Symonds wrote 'There is nothing terrible and savage belonging to feudal history of which an example may not be found in the annals of Les Baux', he was not exaggerating. In the Middle Ages the lords of Les Baux ruled the surrounding area and beyond as absolute monarchs within their own fiefdom. At one stage during the 14C they controlled much of Provence, vying with the neighbouring rulers of France, Barcelona and Savoy for dominance of the Mediterranean coast. The family, who claimed descent from Balthazar, one of the Magi of the Christmas story, saw to it that they were connected to most of the royal families of Europe. From this position they were able to press home their interests when political disturbances created opportunities in Provence. One member, Marie of Anjou, was widowed three times, each following a dynastic marriage, before she herself was murdered in 1382 by an ambitious cousin. The most notorious lord, however, was Raymond de Turenne, the Scourge of Provence, who waged war throughout the region with a band of brigands. A devious politician when dealing with the pope or the duke of Provence and a ruthless tyrant to his own subjects, he ruled from 1372 until forced to flee in 1399. He is reputed to have had fits of laughter while forcing prisoners to jump to their deaths from the cliffs at Les Baux. Raymond's niece, Alix, was the last of the independent rulers of Les Baux and in 1426 the lands and title were absorbed into the Duchy of Provence.

In the 16C Les Baux was a wealthy Protestant centre governed by the Manville family but Louis XIII's first minister, Cardinal Richelieu, would not tolerate such a fortified enclave. On his orders it was largely demolished in 1632 leaving only the spectacular outer walls of the castle. Thereafter it was a pathetic sight, the ruined mansions inhabited by beggars and a few refugees, until in the 19C it was rediscovered as a picturesque ruin. Daudet described it as 'That dusty pile of ruins, sharp rocks and old emblazoned palaces, crumbling, quivering in the wind like high eagles' nests', and Henry James relished the pleasure of 'climbing into this queerest of cities on foot ... Then you appreciate its extraordinary position, its picturesqueness, its steepness, its desolation and decay.' Nowadays it is one of the most popular tourist sights in Provence and the village of narrow streets and empty mansions is devoted to tourist shops, souvenirs and tacky craftwork. The upper part of the rock with the citadel, however, is preserved in its ruinous state.

❖ *Information, accommodation and food*

🛈 Grande Rue (☎ 04 90 54 34 39).

Hotels. The *Mas d'Aigret* (☎ 04 90 54 33 54) is one of very few reliable places in Les Baux.

Restaurants. The Val d'Enfer has one of the finest restaurants in Provence: *L'Oustaù de Baumanière* (☎ 04 90 54 33 07) is outstanding if expensive. For something less ambitious you could eat at the *Mas d'Aigret* (see above).

From the car and coach parks you ascend into the town through the 19C Porte Mage, where a large plaque records the visit of Charles de Gaulle. There are two principal streets running parallel to one another and to see most of the buildings it is probably better to take the lower one, Grand Rue, turning to the right into the place Louis-Jou. At the edge of the place and hanging over a precipice is the 17C **Hôtel de Ville** which has a museum of *santons*. Continuing south along the line of the parapet, a street to the right leads down to the Porte Eyguière, once the only entrance to the town. The rue de la Calade (or rue de l'Eglise) continues to the place St-Vincent at the entrance of which is the 16C Hôtel des Porcelet, now housing the modern **Musée Yves Brayer** (☎ 04 90 54 36 99; **open** daily 10.00–12.30 and 14.00–17.30; closed Tues in winter and Jan). The core of the collection is Brayer's own rather insignificant work but the museum itself is very attractive, with a series of decorative frescoes from the 17C–18C in the ground-floor rooms.

The place St-Vincent is very picturesque and gives excellent views over the valley to the west towards the Pavillon de la Reine Jeanne (see below), and to the north the Val d'Enfer. Of the two churches flanking the square the most important is the **Eglise St-Vincent**, a plain 12C Romanesque building with a square belltower and crypt cut into the rock. There have also been considerable modifications since it was built including the addition of three Gothic chapels on the north side during the 16C and an extension to the nave in the 17C. There are also some interesting fittings such as the modern stained glass by M. Ingrand and various items related to the annual *Fête des Bergers* (Shepherds Festival), a Christmas midnight mass which is attended by local people in traditional costumes. Facing St-Vincent is the chapel of the Pénitents-Blancs, built in the 17C but restored in 1935 and decorated with some disagreeable frescoes by Yves Brayer in 1974.

Returning to the Hôtel des Porcelets, take the rue Neuve which passes the ruins of the old Protestant temple on the right. The most notable feature here is the decorated Renaissance window bearing the motto *Post Tenebras Lux* (After darkness, light) and the date 1571. Facing the top of the street on the Grande Rue is the Hôtel de Manville, a 16C Renaissance house which now serves as the Mairie. There is an interesting courtyard inside leading to the **Musée d'Art Contemporain** (☎ 04 90 54 34 39: **open** daily 09.00–19.00; closed Jan) which has a modest collection of 20C art. Before ascending to the castle ruins, it is worth going down Grande Rue to the left for 50m to see the early 16C **Hôtel de Brion** (☎ 04 90 54 34 17: **open** daily 10.00–13.00 and 14.00–19.00 Apr–Sept), the most attractive house in Les Baux. This was once occupied by the printer Louis Jou (1882–1964) and is now administered by a foundation which mounts exhibitions of prints and books. Jou's studio and workshop is directly opposite.

Returning to the Hôtel de Manville you can continue up rue des Fours (named for the old communal bread-ovens you pass on the left) and the rue du Trencat to the **Musée d'Histoire des Baux** (☎ 04 90 54 55 56: **open** daily 08.00–19.30 Mar–Nov; shorter hours in winter), which gives access to the upper part of the village and the castle ruins. The museum itself is housed in the 14C Tour de Brau, once the mansion of the Glandeves family, but it is now a bare vaulted interior with a number of display cases of ancient ceramics, stone and metalwork discovered in the immediate area. There is a small cemetery at the rear where the poet André Suarès (1866–1948) is buried.

As you ascend to the plateau of the rock, the first group of ruined buildings to the left comprise the old hospital complex dating from 1584 and, facing the path, the 12C chapel of St-Blaise. This small Romanesque chapel has a permanent display of items related to the olive-oil trade, the **Musée de l'Olivier** (**open** daily 08.00–19.30 Mar–Nov; **open** till 21.00 in summer). Most of the ruins stretch in a line from the rear of the hospital but it is worth taking a walk in the opposite direction out to the southern edge of the rock for the panoramic view over what was once the marshland of La Crau. Near this end of the rock is the isolated monument to the shepherd poet Charles Rieu (1846–1924) who composed many Provençal songs.

Skirting the eastern edge of the rock with its worrying precipice you will reach the **castle ruins** by the Tour Sarrazine and its counterpart, the Tour Bancs. From here the castle occupies a line along the eastern edge, where the cliff is at its highest. A number of buildings attract the attention, notably the vaulted Gothic chapel of St-Catherine dating from the 15C–16C and the series of chambers cut out of the solid rock, but the most spectacular remains are the 13C castle keep which can be visited at ground level and then climbed by various stairways. The best ascent is via the Tour Paravelle at the northern extremity of the ruins where a vertiginous series of steps and pathways leads up to the parapet from which, as well as a spectacular view over the surrounding landscape, you can peer down into the castle chambers and over the cliff edge where, presumably, Raymond de Turenne threw his unfortunate prisoners. This is an exhilarating and fitting climax to a visit to Les Baux and the experience that is likely to remain longest in the mind.

There are a few interesting sights in the immediate vicinity of Les Baux. At the base of the rock to the southeast is the Chapelle des Tremaies supporting a large

Gallo-Roman stone relief of three figures, possibly the Stes Mairies. On the opposite side of the rock, a path from the Porte Eyguière leads down to the old royal garden containing the exquisite Renaissance **Pavillon de la Reine Jeanne**, established in 1581 by a baroness of Les Baux, Jeanne de Quiqueran.

One kilometre to the north of this is the jagged gorge known as the **Val d'Enfer**. The fantastic shape of the rocks has attracted many artists including Jean Cocteau (1888–1963), who filmed parts of *Orphée* here in 1948. For an even more exaggerated view of this landscape, the **Cathédrale des Images** (☎ 04 90 54 38 65: **open** 10.00–19.00 mid Mar–mid Nov; 10.00–17.30 in winter; closed Feb) is a *son et lumière* show featuring slide projections onto the caves and chambers left over from the bauxite mines.

Les Antiques, Glanum and the approach to St-Rémy

Leave Les Baux by the D27a and head towards St-Rémy, joining the D5 which follows a gap through the Chaîne des Alpilles. On emerging from the rocks the road descends gently towards the town. Before reaching St-Rémy, however, you will pass between two of the most important Roman sites in Provence. On the left-hand side of the road are the two monuments known collectively as Les Antiques and slightly before them on the opposite side are the remains of the city of Glanum.

Les Antiques comprise a mausoleum and a triumphal arch, probably erected in the early Julio-Claudian period around the time of Christ. The more interesting of the two is undoubtedly the mausoleum, a commemorative monument some 18m high composed of three distinct elements. The lowest register is a cenotaph with relief sculptures of battle and hunting scenes which, although weathered, have a vigorous, linear quality in the description. The real authority of the piece, however, lies in the overall architectural organisation. Standing on the podium is an elegant tier of four arches with a naval frieze and, above that, a rotunda of Corinthian columns enclosing two statues under a conical roof. A pinecone finial which crowned the whole ensemble is lost but the harmony of the separate parts is still obvious. There is a dedicatory inscription on the frieze above the arch to the north side which reads *Sex. L.M. IVLIEI C.F. PARENTIBUS SUEIS* (Sextius, Lucius, Marcus, sons of Gaius of the Julii family, to their parents). This has been linked to the two adopted sons of the emperor Augustus who died young and for whom the Maison Carrée at Nîmes was built.

Alongside the mausoleum and erected at roughly the same time is the triumphal or municipal arch, the earliest arch in the Roman region of Narbonensis and similar to

The mausoleum to Caius and Lucius Caesar, sons of the Emperor Augustus

others at Cavaillon and Carpentras. The principal decoration is the sculpted reliefs of slaves and trophies celebrating Caesar's victorious campaign in Gaul. Originally the arch would have been topped off with an attic storey but this was dismantled, probably for building stone, and in the 18C the tiled roof was added for protection.

Les Antiques have been a popular antiquarian sight for centuries, painted by Robert and Fragonard and visited by many travellers on the Grand Tour. But it was not until quite recently that they were linked to the major Gallo-Roman town of Glanum. In fact these monuments were the formal entrance to the town from the Via Domitia, the major Roman road between Spain and the Alps. Bearing this in mind, you can more easily understand the orientation of **Glanum** (☎ 04 90 92 23 79: **open** daily 09.00–19.00 Apr–Sept; 09.00–12.00 and 14.00–17.00 Oct–Mar) stretching back to the south on the opposite side of the road.

The town of Glanum was founded by the Celts in the 6C BC, developed under the Hellenistic Greeks in the 3C BC and finally taken over by the Romans in the 2C–1C BC. There are traces of all these settlements in the ruins but without doubt it was the Romans who left the most substantial urban complex. In plan, the town was organised along a clear north–south axis with the open area of the forum near the centre. As you enter the site nowadays, you will see first to your left the series of domestic houses (the Greek Maison d'Atys from the 2C BC and the Roman Maison des Antes) and baths. Not much survives of this district and it requires considerable imagination to re-populate the ground plan that is apparent amid the ongoing excavation. Above this to the south is the forum which was built on earlier remains including a house with some very early Roman mosaics. This area also has the plan of a basilica or public hall which would have been used for markets, a court and civic or political meetings.

Stretching in a line from the forum to the south is the temple district, which is the most interesting and atmospheric part of the whole complex. In all there are the remains of some five temples here, several altars and the original Celtic sanctuary around which the settlement developed. Like the rest of the site, there is not a great deal to see above ground but the proximity of the buildings and the sense of the main route through it gives a good impression of the scale and pattern of ancient life in this provincial town. A small display in the entrance block gives some information on the history of the town from its inception in the 6C BC to its collapse in the 3C at the hands of Barbarian invaders, and you can see some of the more interesting discoveries in the museums in St-Rémy.

Looking north from Glanum towards St-Rémy you will notice the tower of **St-Paul-de-Mausole** just a couple of hundred metres away. This was the hospital or asylum which Vincent Van Gogh entered as a voluntary patient after his attempted suicide at Arles in December 1888. It is still an asylum and clinic although the wisdom of naming part of the hospital after its most famous patient may be questioned. What is less well known is that the complex contains an attractive group of Romanesque buildings which are the remains of a 12C Augustinian monastery (☎ 04 90 92 02 31: **open** daily 08.00–19.00).

Closed down during the Revolution the buildings of St-Paul-de-Mausole were bought in 1810 by a doctor who opened a hospital that increasingly concentrated on mental and nervous disorders. Van Gogh arrived here in

May 1889 on the recommendation of his friend and physician Dr Rey, following a campaign by the people of Arles to have him removed from their town. The artist stayed in the asylum for just over a year, enjoying a degree of freedom which allowed him to paint in the surrounding fields. This was an intensely prolific phase of Van Gogh's career and over 150 paintings were completed here, including several of his room and the hospital buildings. The most famous works, however, are undoubtedly *Starry Night* (Museum of Modern Art, New York) and various views of the cornfields and the twisted cypress trees in the immediate surrounding area. Walking in the fields today you can easily locate the positions from which Van Gogh painted and the local tourist office has set up several information boards with illustrations. On a less sympathetic note, the bronze bust of Van Gogh by Zadkine, which stood at the side of the driveway, was stolen and has not been recovered.

Both the chapel and tiny cloister have been sensitively restored, revealing on a small scale the simple rhythms of the pure Romanesque. The capitals in the cloister have some good 12C carving and the tower is one of the finest in Provence, bearing comparison with the similar structure at St-Trophîme in Arles.

One of the areas where Van Gogh worked was the ancient Roman stone quarries beside the asylum. The chambers cut into the rock here were occupied by local farmers who named their residence the **Mas de la Pyramide** after the tall column around which the quarriers had hewn the stone for Glanum. This has been turned into a museum of local agriculture (☎ 04 90 92 00 81; guided tours of 30min 09.00–19.00 in summer; 09.00–17.00 in winter).

Continuing on the D5 down into St-Rémy you come to the small 15C–17C chapel, **Notre-Dame-de-la-Pitié**, at a fork in the road. This now houses a collection of rather depressing pictures by Mario Prassinos (1916–85), a Greek-born artist and poet who lived in this area for much of his life. It seems that the people of St-Rémy adopted this artist when the nearby village of Eygalières where he lived turned down his offer of the paintings. The Prassinos Foundation now has four buildings in St-Rémy administered by the artist's widow, who will often show visitors around.

St-Rémy-de-Provence

St-Rémy is a charming medieval town but it is often passed by in the haste to reach Les Alpilles and Les Baux, partly due to the efficiency of the ring road which skirts the town, following the line of the medieval walls. In fact St-Rémy is one of the most interesting and attractive towns in an area already rich in historical sites and its appeal is made all the more special when you experience the relative calm of the shaded streets and alleys which make up the old interior.

History of St-Rémy-de-Provence

Founded after the destruction of Glanum in the late 3C, the new village was occupied successively by the Visigoths and the Franks until, as part of a treaty with Clovis, it was placed under the protection of the abbey of St-Rémi of Reims. Thereafter its strategic position at the gateway through the Alpilles meant that St-Rémy was disputed and exchanged between different families and factions. From the counts of Provence it passed to the Aragonaise in the 12C, to the Angevins in the 13C, to the papacy in the 14C and then to the kings of France who gave it to the Grimaldis of Monaco. It was only returned to France proper during the Revolution. These various allegiances brought with them privileges which assured the economic prosperity of the town and it remains to this day an important market for fruit and vegetables and a centre for horticultural research.

St-Rémy is also noted for its literary and artistic associations quite apart from those with Van Gogh. Michel Nostradamus (1503–66), the physician and astrologer whose predictions are regularly reprinted for the mystically inclined, was born in St-Rémy in 1503. The poet Joseph Roumanille (1818–91) was also born here and his friendship with Mistral ensured that the Félibrige had strong links with the town. The composer Charles François Gounod (1818–93) was introduced to Mistral in a house in St-Rémy and this meeting prompted him to write an opera based on the latter's poem *Mirèio*. Of more recent authors, Charles and Marie Mauron and Marcel Bonnet all lived in the town and the English novelist Angus Wilson was one of a large Anglo-Saxon community in the area.

❖ Information, accommodation and food

🛈 Place Jean-Jaurès (☎ 04 90 92 05 22).

Hotels and restaurants. Staying and eating in St-Rémy is generally better value than in the more popular centres but, to be safe, you should still book in advance. One of the most distinctive hotels in the area is *Les Antiques* (☎ 04 90 92 03 02), a 19C mansion with rather grand interiors at 15 ave Pasteur on the edge of town. Of the less expensive, *Le Castellet des Alpilles* (☎ 04 90 92 07 21) , also in a period house from the turn of the century at 6 place Mireille, is a good middle range choice, while the *Hôtel des Arts* (☎ 04 90 92 08 50) and *Le Provence* (☎ 04 90 92 06 27), both on boulevard Victor Hugo, are the best at the lower price range. All of these hotels have good restaurants, the cheaper ones having the liveliest atmosphere.

You can begin a tour of St-Rémy at the main car park on the place de la République. It is unfortunate that this square is overlooked by the clumsy neo-Classical façade of St-Martin, a frontage built in 1820 to replace the main part of the medieval church which had collapsed. The belltower is the only surviving part of the 14C building. Inside there is a particularly good organ which has given rise to a small music festival in the first half of July. To the right behind the church, rue Hoche has some vestiges of the old town walls and several early buildings including the 17C hospital of St-Jacques and the house where Nostradamus was born.

Much more interesting, however, is the complex of Renaissance mansions on the opposite side of the church around the attractive place Favier. On the left side of the place is the Hôtel Mistral de Mondragon, a large and beautiful house built in 1550 around a courtyard. The upper rooms now accommodate the **Musée des Alpilles** (☎ 04 90 92 08 10: **open** daily 10.00–12.00 and 15.00–20.00 July, Aug; closes 18.00 Apr–June and Sept–Oct; closes 17.00 Nov, Dec; closed

Jan–Mar) a local history museum with exhibits relating to the geology and traditions of the area. Slightly further down the rue Parage is the Hôtel de Sade, a 15C–16C mansion built by the notorious family which houses the **Musée d'Archéologique** (☎ 04 90 92 64 04: guided tour of 1hr 10.00–18.00; closed Jan–Mar). The main part of the collection consists of artefacts uncovered at Glanum and St-Blaise by an earlier archaeologist and curator, Henri Rolland. There is very little of real interest compared to the beauty of the site of Glanum just outside the town but the material is displayed in an atmospheric interior and various items may divert the casual visitor. Almost opposite this is another Renaissance mansion, the 17C Hôtel de Lagoy, which is now used as a contemporary art gallery.

The main street in the old part of St-Rémy is the rue Carnot, running west to east past the place Favier. Near the middle is a small 19C fountain dedicated to Nostradamus, with a portrait bust of the prophet. To the right at this point, on the rue Estrine, is the 18C Hôtel Estrine, now the **Centre d'Art Présence Van Gogh** (☎ 04 90 92 34 72: **open** daily 10.30–12.30 and 14.30–18.30; closed Mon and Jan–Mar). There is no collection to talk of, but the gallery has a programme of temporary exhibitions, usually of artists with some local connection. In marked contrast to this 18C elegance, the Hôtel de Ville on the nearby place J.-Pelissier has a more diverse background. This long building was an Augustinian monastery built in the 17C and taken over during the Revolution for civic functions. It is still somewhat dusty and awkward but it has an attractive, informal aspect in the heart of this old town.

During the 19C the old town of St-Rémy was felt to be too enclosed and constricting so the local bourgeoisie tended to build their new residences on the outskirts. As a result, there are numerous attractive villas around the edge of town, such as the Château de Roussan and the Château des Alpilles to the west, both of which are now hotels. Another example nearer the centre is the **Hôtel des Antiques** on the avenue Pasteur to the south. This 19C mansion in its own grounds has fine neo-Classical interiors which evoke a different way of life to the peasant culture that tends to dominate popular views of this area.

To the north of St-Rémy is the flat country known as **La Petite Crau** although it has none of the mystery or desolation of the real thing to the west. In fact this is good farming land watered by canals from the Durance. The main road (D571/D34) crosses it in a more or less straight line to Eyragues and **Châteaurenard**, the latter a major market town for the fruit and vegetables of the area. Châteaurenard is notable for the two towers overlooking the town, all that remains of a 14C castle which was once occupied by the 'anti-pope' Benedict XIII as a refuge from Avignon. The castle was largely demolished during the Revolution but the surviving Tour de Griffon houses a small museum (☎ 04 90 94 23 27: **open** Sun–Thur 10.00–12.00 and 15.00–18.30; closed Fri and Sat morning Sept–June) and offers excellent views of the surrounding area and over to Avignon.

Just 6km to the east on the D28 is **Noves**, a medieval town which retains some of its 14C walls and gateways, although it is best known as the home of Laura de Noves, the girl who is thought to have been the poet Petrarch's inspiration. The large Romanesque church of St-Bandile was originally built into the ramparts and its belfry used as a watchtower for defence. To continue on this route, cross the Durance at **Bonpas**, which takes its name from the fact that it was a 'good crossing'. It only became so in the 12C when a group of monks were given responsibility for the bridge replacing a notoriously treacherous ford controlled by brigands. To consolidate their position the monks built first a chapel and then, in the 14C, a larger *chartreuse* (charterhouse). This foundation expanded throughout the succeeding centuries but was finally abandoned during the Revolution. Nowadays, the remains form the centre of a wine domaine which can be visited. Enter by the old gateway to the charterhouse which leads to the courtyard and a beautiful hanging garden with good views over the Durance. From here the busy N7 follows the north side of the river leading directly to Avignon.

An alternative route across La Petite Crau from St-Rémy follows the D5 to **Maillane**, a pleasant but unremarkable village which has nevertheless become one of the key sites of Provençal culture and a place of pilgrimage. This is due entirely to its most famous son, Frédéric Mistral. During his lifetime he was visited at Maillane by many celebrated figures and his house is now a museum (☎ 04 90 95 74 06: **open** Tues–Sun 09.30–11.30 and 14.30–18.30 Apr–Sept; 10.00–11.30 and 14.00–16.30 Oct–Mar; closed Mon) dedicated to his memory and to his life's work, the preservation of Provençal language and culture as a living tradition in the modern world. The writer Mistral (1830–1914) was born in Maillane and spent much of his life in the village. He was educated at St-Michel-de-Frigolet and at Aix but returned to Maillane to help his father with the farm at Mas du Juge (1km to the south by the D5). On his father's death in 1855, he and his mother moved to the Maison du Lezard near the centre of the village, and when Mistral got married in 1876 he built a new house opposite this for himself and his wife. Throughout his life Mistral remained close to his village roots and he was buried in the cemetery at Maillane on his death in 1914. His tomb is a copy of the so-called Pavillon de la Reine Jeanne at Les Baux.

The Félibrige

In 1854 Mistral and six other poets (Joseph Roumanille (1818–91), Theodore Aubanel (1829–86), Paul Giera (1816–61), Jean Brunet (1823–94), Remy Marcellin (1832–1908 and Anselme Mathieu (1828–1925)) founded the Félibrige, a literary movement dedicated to the revival of the ancient Provencal language and the traditional culture of southern France. The name Félibrige was taken from the Occitan word *felibres* found in a traditional song about Jesus and his dispute with the doctors at the temple. From this simple beginning Mistral went on to establish a literary version from the various dialects of the Langue d'Oc and to write some of his best known and most successful works; above all the epic poem *Mireio* (1859) and the huge compendium of Provencal words and proverbs, *Lou Trésor du Félibrige* (1879–86). From Maillane, Mistral expanded the activities of the Félibrige to touch the other traditional cultures of southern Europe and in 1904 was awarded the Nobel Prize for Literature, the only writer in a minority language ever to do so. He used the prize money to endow the Museon Arlaten in Arles (see p 76), a museum of traditional culture which is also known as the Palais du Félibrige.

6 · Tarascon and Beaucaire

The route north from Arles along the east bank of the Rhône leads across fairly flat countryside overlooked by the rugged outcrops of the Chaîne des Alpilles. This is the most direct route to Avignon but there are several important and very interesting distractions along the way, including one of the finest Romanesque chapels, two fairy-tale castles and an elegant 17C–18C château with some of the best interiors and furnishings in Provence.

Leave Arles by the N570, crossing the plain towards Tarascon in the north until the junction with the D79 and D33. This is a confusing intersection of several roads: turn right onto the D33 whereupon you should be able to see the 12C **Chapelle St-Gabriel** by the edge of the road on the left. Somewhat surprisingly, there was once a fishing-village at this ancient crossroads but it—like the water—has disappeared leaving a masterpiece of Romanesque architecture isolated in the countryside. The sculptural decoration is interesting, particularly the reliefs of the *Expulsion of Adam and Eve* in the tympanum and the *Annunciation* and *Visitation* in the pediment above. However, it is the ensemble of the façade, a sequence of arches round the pedimented doorway, which commands attention and draws parallels with a Roman triumphal arch. There can be few medieval buildings which demonstrate such a sophisticated grasp of the Classical language of architecture or exemplify more effectively the continuing spirit of antiquity in the Christian world. Despite this magisterial façade, the chapel is actually very small and, in recent years, it has been used as an art centre for youth groups.

From the junction continue on the N570 directly to **Tarascon** (for practical information,see p 105), a town made famous by Daudet's fictional character Tartarin who, despite his idiocy, has been adopted as something of a civic symbol. This line of publicity is unnecessary, because Tarascon has an important position in the religio-mythical history of Provence and has one of the most spectacular medieval castles in the whole of France.

History of Tarascon

The town was established, like so many others on the Rhône, as a trading-post by the Greeks and Romans, helping to open up the inland areas to the more developed communities of the Mediterranean. According to local legend the river was terrorised by a monster known as the Tarasque, half-dragon half-lion, which emerged from its lair every year to consume its quota of the young people. Dealing with it was a task for an early Christian saint and it was Martha who came here to confront the beast soon after disembarking at Stes-Maries-de-la-Mer. Holding up the cross she tamed the Tarasque, fettered it with a silken cord and made the area safe for settlement.

Martha was buried here and the discovery of her remains in the 12C began a new phase in the town's history as a pilgrimage centre. The festival of the Tarasque, held every year at the end of June, involves an elaborate procession with floats and a re-enactment of the combat with a huge model of the monster.

The saint's relics are preserved in the Collegiale de Ste-Marthe which faces the river on the west side of the old town. This collegiate church was built in the 12C and later extended to cope with more pilgrims in the 15C–16C but it suffered considerable damage in both the Revolution and the Second World War. The south door, stripped of its sculptural decoration, is the only substantial survival of the Romanesque period and the nave is a good example of Provençal Gothic. There are also several interesting paintings in the side chapels, notably those by Carle Van Loo (1705–65), Pierre Mignard (1612– 95) and Joseph Parrocel (1646–1704), but the finest treasure is the Renaissance tomb of Jean de Cossa attributed to Francesco Laurana (c 1430–1502), on the stairs leading down to the crypt.

The principal building in Tarascon is the spectacular **château** (☎ 04 90 91 01 93: guided tours hourly 09.00–19.00 in summer) which towers over the town from the banks of the river. Built in the early 15C this tall, crenellated structure seems to have been translated from the pages of a medieval manuscript and, appropriately, it is closely associated with the life of René d'Anjou, who was himself a troubadour poet and painter. King René completed the main part of the building in 1449 and was responsible for the elegant decoration and arrangement of the rooms and courtyard on the interior. The guided tour takes you round the main complex and the principal apartments, including a reconstructed pharmacy, culminating in a visit to the terrace at the top which has a wonderful view of the river and Beaucaire on the opposite bank. The castle served as a prison for much of its later existence and has accommodated many British prisoners from various wars whose graffiti is preserved in several rooms. One sad inscription from the 18C reads 'Here be three Davids in one mess, prisoners we are in distress ...' The inmates of the Revolutionary period were less fortunate, many of them being hurled off the terrace to their deaths on the rock below.

Courtyard of the château

Despite the destruction of the Second World War, there are a few early buildings in the old part of Tarascon, such as the Cloître des Cordeliers, the remains of a 15C Franciscan convent, or the 17C town hall behind the church. There is also an interesting museum, the **Musée Charles Demery** or Musée Souleïado (☎ 04 90 91 01 08: **open** by appointment Mon–Fri 10.00–15.00; closed Sat, Sun), devoted to the printed cotton fabrics known as Souleïado that have become a popular symbol of Provençal traditional style. Another museum with a less historic background is the **Maison de Tartarin** (☎ 04 90 91 05 08: **open** 10.00–12.00 and 13.30–17.00 in summer; closed Sun) on the boulevard Itam. Neither Daudet nor his fictional creation Tartarin had any link with the house but there are displays related to the novels and an attempt to recreate the character's exotic garden.

Beaucaire

Beaucaire faces Tarascon across the Rhône. Its 11C castle was a stronghold of the French Crown in the Languedoc watching over the rival castle of the Holy Roman Emperor in Provence. The castle at Beaucaire, however, has lost much of its glamour and Henry James was moved to remark that it 'looks over with a melancholy expression at its better conditioned brother'.

History of Beaucaire

This is unfortunate because Beaucaire has a genuine troubadour link, being the home of Aucassin in the romance *Aucassin et Nicolette*. It was a formidable bastion in the Middle Ages, withstanding a notorious siege by Simon de Montfort during the Albigensian Crusade of 1216. To celebrate the lifting of the siege the Count of Toulouse sponsored a fair which, over the following centuries, grew into the largest of its type in the whole of Europe. Merchants, craftsmen, entertainers and thieves travelled from as far away as Italy and Turkey to participate and estimates of the numbers attending are put as high as 300,000. The fair was held in July on the open ground by the castle which is still named the Champ de Foire, although the event ceased during the 19C.

The decline of the castle was due to Cardinal Richelieu who saw it as a stronghold of the provincial nobility and, in 1632, had most of the fortifications dismantled.

❖ *Information, accommodation and food*

🛈 59 rue des Halles (☎ 04 90 91 03 52) and 24 cours Gambetta, Beaucaire (☎ 04 66 59 26 57).

Hotels. Most visitors do not stay in Tarascon and Beaucaire so finding an hotel is generally not a problem, but the choice is limited. *Les Echevins* at 26 boulevard Itam (☎ 04 90 91 01 70) and the *Hôtel de Provence* at 7 boulevard Victor-Hugo (☎ 04 90 91 06 43) are among the most reliable in Tarascon.

Restaurants. Eating out in the two towns is also straightforward if unexceptional but the restaurants at the *Hôtel de Provence* (see above) the *Hôtel St-Jean* at 24 boulevard Victor-Hugo (☎ 04 90 91 13 87) and the *Hôtel Terminus* on place Col-Berrurier (☎ 04 90 91 18 95) are all reasonable. Beaucaire has some good bistros and cafés along the quai Charles-de-Gaulle.

Unlike many Provençal market towns, Beaucaire has resisted the temptation to gentrify and restore, but there are one or two places of interest. Chief of these is the **château**, of which the main towers—one circular and the other triangular—and a wall that encloses a small Romanesque chapel survive. Also within the castle is the **Musée Auguste-Jacquet** (☎ 04 66 59 47 61: **open** Wed–Mon 10.00–12.00 and 14.15–18.45 in summer; closed Tues), a small archaeological and local history museum with some interesting material related to the medieval fair. The castle complex now stands in a beautiful park with pleasant views and a number of activities such as falconry displays in the summer. It is a pleasant spot in which the medieval remains offer a striking backdrop for walks and picnics.

The Hôtel de Ville occupies a mansion designed by François Mansart in the late 17C and the principal church, Notre-Dame-des-Pommiers dating from 1744, has a 12C Romanesque frieze on its exterior wall.

There is a curious site just 5km to the north of Beaucaire beside the D986. This is the **Abbaye St-Roman-d'Aiguille**, founded as early as the 5C and thriving in the later Middle Ages until it went into decline, finally being abandoned in the 18C. There is hardly anything of the buildings above ground but the original cells and tombs of the monks still exist in caves or else cut into the rock.

The main road from Tarascon to Avignon is the N570 but the smaller D53, D811 and D35 take a more interesting route along the richly cultivated north side of **La Montagnette** via Boulbon. In a sheltered valley at the heart of these hills to the south is the **Abbaye St-Michel-de-Frigolet**, still occupied by monks of the Premonstratensian order and once a powerful religious and political force in the region. The childless Anne of Austria came here in 1632 to pray for a son and was rewarded with the future Louis XIV. Mistral, born in the nearby village of Maillane (see p 102), attended the open school in the monastery.

Further along La Montagnette to the northeast is the village of **Barbentane**. The two gates are the only survivors from its medieval walls and there is a group of other early buildings such as the 15C Maison des Chevaliers and the earlier Tour Anglica, the keep from a 14C castle, on the hill above. The main attraction in Barbentane, however, is the elegant 17C–18C château of the marquis in its own formal garden overlooking the Rhône valley (guided tours of c 30min at 10.00–12.00 and 14.00–18.00 Easter–1 Nov; closed Wed in Apr–June, Oct). Built in 1674 by Paul François de Barbentane, first consul of Aix, it was furnished and decorated by a later member of the family, J.-P. Balthazar de Barbentane, royal ambassador to Tuscany between 1766 and 1793, which helps to explain the harmonious combination of Italian Baroque and native French styles in the interior.

The D35 from Barbentane rejoins the N570 at Rognonas before crossing the Durance to reach the unattractive southern suburbs of Avignon.

7 · Avignon

The historic cultural centre of Provence and scene of a cataclysmic period in European history, Avignon is one of the greatest of all medieval cities. It may be known popularly from the famous song about dancing on its bridge but as the seat of the papacy for almost 60 years it could once claim to have been the most important and powerful centre in Europe. As such it has attracted affection and contempt in equal measure. To the poet Petrarch (1304–74) it was 'an abode of sorrows', 'a sink of vice' and 'a sewer where all the filth of the universe has gathered', while for Rabelais it was 'la ville sonnante' on account of the number of church bells. Henry James found the Mistral wind intolerable in Avignon, although he had come round to its charms by his third visit. More recently the English novelist Lawrence Durrell found it 'rotten' and 'fly-blown with expired dignities', but went on to add 'there was not a corner of it we did not love'.

History of Avignon

The ancient origins of Avignon are explained by the natural configuration of the landscape. Just above the confluence with the Durance, the Rhône is forced round a tall outcrop of rock with a commanding view over the surrounding country. This is the Rocher des Doms, still dominating the old town and first settled in the Neolithic period (c 4000 BC). Somewhat later the Romans developed the site as a river trading-post and the community continued in this role throughout successive invasions and population movements.

In fact, little is known of Avignon in the Middle Ages until the sequence of events which propelled it to the centre of European affairs. In 1226, having taken the side of the unfortunate Albigensians in the religious wars, the town was razed by Louis VIII of France and placed under the control of the county of Venasque, the Comtat-Venaissin. In 1274 the territory was acquired by the papacy in a routine expansion of interests but within 40 years it had replaced Rome as the capital of Western Christendom.

In 1309, with Rome a virtual battlefield of rival factions, Pope Clement V (1305–14) decided to move the papal court to his native France. Avignon seemed the natural choice. It was safe from the warring families of Rome, conveniently situated for trade and transport on the Rhône, and protected by the ambitious Louis the Fair of France. At first this was seen as a brief interlude but the Italians had underestimated the strength of feeling in the College of Cardinals. In 1316 Clement's successor, Jacques Duèse, a former bishop of Avignon, was elected Pope. Taking the title John XXII (1316–34), Duèse confirmed his city as the new seat of papal authority, occupying the episcopal palace by the cathedral and establishing a pattern of building and aggrandisement that his successors would follow. Alongside this, the curia, that vast army of clerics, courtiers, legates, scribes, notaries, advisers and hangers-on (the apparatus of any international organisation) moved into the town and built palaces, churches, abbeys, retreats and private residences for themselves and their families. A parallel community of merchants, diplomats, petitioners, entertainers, managers, thieves, pimps and prostitutes also came to Avignon as the wealth of the city expanded exponentially through the traffic in ecclesiastical funds.

At the heart of this wholesale development, the popes themselves drove the building boom with the need to express their power through ever grander residences. Benedict XII (1334–42) began the large-scale building of a papal palace in the 1330s but even this huge development was dwarfed by the grandiose Palais Neuf of his successor, Clement VI (1342–52). Having purchased Avignon itself from Queen Jeanne, Clement initiated the greatest period in Avignon's history. What had been a modest provincial town was transformed into the wealthiest and most powerful city in Western Europe in less than two generations. There was a corresponding rise in conspicuous luxury, the flourishing of a school of painting under the Sienese artist Simone Martini (c 1284–1344), and, predictably, a spectacular increase in graft, corruption and immorality. Petrarch, who took minor orders in the papal entourage, railed against the moral degradation of this new Jerusalem. 'There God is held in contempt, money is worshipped, and the laws of God and man are trampled underfoot. Everything there breathes a lie: the air, the earth, the houses and above all the bedrooms.' He was, of course, an Italian and longed for the papal court to return to Rome. In vain, he retreated to Fontaine-de-Vaucluse to escape the filth and degradation of Avignon during what became known as the Babylonian Captivity.

In all, seven popes reigned from Avignon but the Italian faction and the instability of the papal court built up strength of feeling for a return to Italy. Finally in 1376 Gregory XI (1370–78) gave in to the exhortations of St Catherine of Siena and returned to Rome. Even this, however, did not settle the matter. Gregory's death two years later caused a split in the church as two rival popes were elected by the Italian and Avignon factions. Thus began the Great Schism of the West, further complicated at one stage by the election of a third pope. Threats and insults were hurled between the cities as each incumbent was excommunicated and condemned as an 'anti-pope' by his rival. It was not until 1417 that the Schism was ended, the rival factions reconciled, and the papal see confirmed in Rome.

Despite this loss, the succeeding centuries were remarkably successful for Avignon. The city continued to be part of the papal lands and enjoyed considerable freedom from interference by the powerful states on her borders. The various penitent brotherhoods which had been set up or relocated to gain papal support continued to operate from the city, contributing to the active and diverse religious life. These foundations and confraternities, each of which adopted different-coloured robes to distinguish themselves, had the support of leading political figures as well as the wealthy families of the area and the economy was still expanding. Numerous churches, convents and chapels were built, many of which can still be seen today dotted throughout the medieval quarters where the Pénitents Noirs, Gris or Blancs carried out their work.

By the 18C, however, this largely independent state administered by the papacy within France seemed something of an anomaly. In 1790 the Revolutionary spirit ripped through Avignon causing a series of massacres, most notoriously in the old papal palace which had become a prison. The following year the Constitutional Assembly voted for union and the Comtat-Venaissin became part of France.

In the aftermath of the Revolution, the Romantic fascination with the Middle Ages made Avignon a popular destination for scholars, artists and travellers throughout the 19C. Prosper Mérimée was drawn here, partly in his role as an inspector of ancient monuments, and it was he who brought Viollet-le-Duc to restore and rebuild the city walls. Corot, seeing a poetic link between the gaunt monumentality of the ancient papal buildings and the continuing spirit of Classical Rome, produced some of his finest early paintings at Avignon in the 1830s. Daudet set his affectionate story *La Mule du Pape* here, and a stream of other writers as diverse as Stendhal, Henry James, Rainer Maria Rilke, Joseph Roth and Lawrence Durrell have visited the city and recorded their impressions.

More recently, Avignon and its surrounding area have prospered with the rise of new light industries but this has created an urban sprawl, particularly to the south and east, that detracts from its traditional beauty. Within the walls, however, the layout and character of the medieval city have been preserved and now offer an outstanding backdrop for the theatre festival set up by Jean Vilar in 1947 and still held every year in July and August.

❖ Information, accommodation and food

🛈 41 cours Jean-Jaurès (☎ 04 90 82 65 11) with another branch at the Pont St-Bénézet.

Hotels. It is difficult to find accommodation in Avignon in summer, especially during the theatre festival in July and August, but there is a great range to choose from both in the city and in the surrounding towns and country areas.

Of those in the old town, at the top end there is the *Hôtel d'Europe* at 12 place Crillon (☎ 04 90 82 66 92), where Napoleon once stayed, or the *Cloître Saint-Louis* at 20 rue du Portail Boquier (☎ 04 90 27 55 55) near the station, a 16C Jesuit seminary that has recently been redesigned in a Post-Modern style.

More reasonable is the *Palais des Papes*, rue Gérard Philippe (☎ 04 90 82 47 31), with good views of the palace, or the *Hôtel d'Angleterre* on boulevard Raspail (☎ 04 90 86 34 31).

Cheaper still are the *Mignon*, 12 rue Joseph-Vernet (☎ 04 90 82 17 30) or the *Innova* at 100 rue Joseph-Vernet (☎ 04 90 82 54 10).

Restaurants. There is a wide choice of restaurants, bars and cafés in all parts of the town and at all price ranges. The most famous for *haut cuisine* is the *Hiély-Lucullus* at 5 rue de la République (☎ 04 90 86 17 07), but it has a sister establishment in *La Fourchette*, 17 rue Racine (☎ 04 90 85 20 93) which is less expensive albeit very popular with tourists. *Le Petit Bédon* at 70 rue Joseph-Vernet (☎ 04 90 82 33 98) and the *Brunel* at 46 rue Balance (☎ 04 90 85 24 83) are well known for local dishes.

La Tache d'Encre at 22 rue des Teinturiers (☎ 04 90 85 46 03) is better for the music than the food, while Nani on the rue Aubanel near the tourist office has very reasonable salads. The Café des Artistes on the place Crillon is a good bistro for lunch in the open air, as is L'Epicerie on the quiet place St-Pierre.

Avignon, like many of the old cities of Provence, is ideal for pedestrians and completely unsuitable for cars. Even public transport makes little headway in the network of narrow streets that are typical of earlier urban life. The streets of Avignon are overlayed with meaning and associations—anecdotal, literary or historical—that make even a casual walk in unfamiliar districts constantly diverting.

This apparent antiquity should not necessarily be taken at face value, however. The great defensive walls that encircle the old town and determine the medieval character of the city as a whole were largely rebuilt in the 19C by the French scholar-architect Viollet-le-Duc. This is far from unusual. Viollet-le-Duc was responsible for much rebuilding on Notre-Dame-de-Paris as well as almost completely redesigning the medieval walls at Carcassonne. Be that as it may, the walls at Avignon are still very attractive and at first sight give an appearance of theatricality that could be out of Walter Scott.

If possible, you should approach Avignon from across the river to the north and west, which offers the most impressive view of the old town. The main car parks are outside the walls on the west side, although the number of visitors in summer, especially during the theatre festival in July, often fills them to over-flowing. This is the finest section of the walls, dating mainly from the 14C and showing the fewest signs of 19C rebuilding. The ramparts were never envisaged as a complete defence but must have presented a formidable show to visitors arriving at the papal court.

The main axis of the town runs north to south from the place du Palais to the Porte de la République but this thoroughfare, even when pedestrianised, gives little indication of the town's true character. Many of the most interesting and distinctive sights are off to one side or the other amid the network of narrow streets.

Pont St-Bénézet, Place du Palais and Place de l'Horloge

Most visitors enter the old part of Avignon by the main gate, the Porte de la République in the south, but a more attractive and atmospheric approach can be taken from the car parks outside the walls to the northwest. Make first for the **Pont St-Bénézet**, the bridge which features in the famous song *Sur le Pont d'Avignon* although it is unlikely that the townspeople ever danced there. The island of Barthelasse which was once under the bridge (*sous le pont*) is a more likely spot for dancing. First built in the 12C following a vision by the young shepherd Bénézet, its long span of 22 stone arches must have seemed a miraculous engineering achievement in medieval times. For 500 years this was the main crossing between Avignon and the north bank of the Rhône until, in the early 17C, the greater part of the bridge was swept away in a flood. By that time other bridges were more secure so the old bridge was never replaced. What remains, therefore, are four arches reaching out over the river, and graced with the small **Chapelle St-Nicolas** over the second pier. This is actually two chapels, one above the other; the lower is a 13C Romanesque sanctuary while the upper is a Gothic addition of 1513, built when the roadway was heightened. Tickets to go out onto the bridge and to visit the chapel—alongside which groups of people can usually be seen attempting to dance in circles—can be purchased at the gate.

Entering the town by either of the two gates near the bridge brings you into the district of La Balance, once a run-down area of narrow streets but now restored and in some cases rebuilt with modern blocks. At the top you emerge onto the large open space of the **place du Palais** facing the Rocher des Doms and the Gothic façade of the palace itself on the east side.

On the left, closing off the north end of the square, is the **Petit Palais**, once the residence of the archbishops of Avignon and now a museum of medieval and Renaissance art (☎ 04 90 86 44 58: **open** Wed–Mon 10.30–18.00 July–Aug; 09.30–12.00 and 14.00–18.00; closed Tues). Built in 1317–20 as a private house it was sequestered by the papacy but suffered during various sieges before being restored by Cardinal della Rovere (later Pope Julius II) in the late 15C. In recent years it has been extensively renovated to create the museum which is the best place to see works by the School of Avignon. The core of the collection belonged to the Marquis G.P. Campana who, while managing the papal finances in Rome during the mid-19C, acquired a great many early Renaissance paintings. Unfortunately, he was found to have supported his activities with misappropriated funds and the collection was transferred to Napoleon III and the Louvre. Since 1976, when it was installed here, the museum has been strengthened by various bequests and now forms a very substantial collection displayed in an attractive series of period rooms. The paintings are uneven in quality but there are important works by Sandro Botticelli (c 1445–1510), Vittore Carpaccio (c 1460–c 1525), Carlo Crivelli (c 1430–95), Giovanni di Paolo and the anonymous artist who has been given the curious name of the Master of the Madonna of Buckingham Palace. Of the School of Avignon, there is a substantial altarpiece by Enguerrand Quarton (active 1444–66) and numerous works by anonymous masters, such as the delightful *Dream of Jacob* (c 1500) or the grave *Adoration of the Child* (c 1500) in which the infant Jesus sits on a cushion to bless a knight in armour and an astonished bishop who is pulling off his mitre. Also on display is a number of fragments of very fine medieval sculpture, most of which derive from the papal monuments and tombs destroyed during the Revolution.

Alongside this museum to the east is the **Rocher des Domes**, the spur of rock that was the site of the earliest settlements in the area. Seeing it from the elevated position of the square gives a misleading impression of its scale. In fact it rises in a sheer cliff from the edge of the river some 300m below. In the 19C it was laid out as a public park which is still a delightful escape from the relentless tour groups around the main sights. Amid the outcrops of rock, meandering paths lead past statues and monuments to the duck pond, the grotto, and an outlook point from which there are excellent views over the river to the surrounding countryside.

On an elevated position at the southern edge of the park is the **Cathédrale de Notre-Dame-des-Doms**, a 12C Romanesque church which has undergone numerous alterations over the centuries. Despite being overshadowed by the

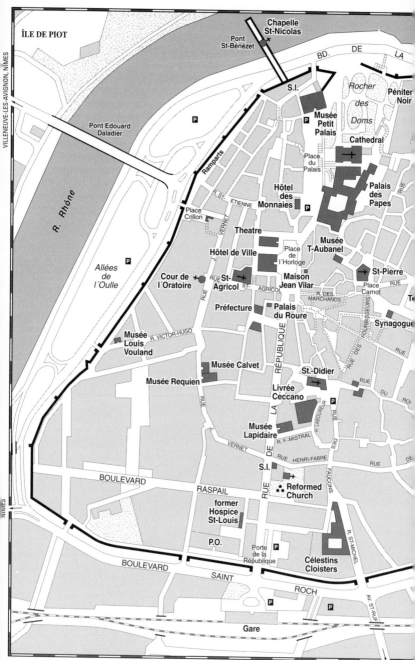

ÎLE DE PIOT

VILLENEUVE-LES-AVIGNON, NÎMES

R. Rhône

Pont Edouard Daladier

Allées de l'Oulle

NÎMES

Chapelle St-Nicolas

Pont St-Bénézet

S.I.

BD. DE LA

Rocher des Doms

Péniter Noir

Musée Petit Palais

Cathedral

Place du Palais

Palais des Papes

RUE

Ramparts

R. ST. ETIENNE

VERNET

Place Crillon

Hôtel des Monnaies

Theatre

Place de l'Horloge

Musée T-Aubanel

St-Pierre

Place Carnot

Cour de l'Oratoire

St-Agricol

RUE ST-

AGRICOL

Hôtel de Ville

Maison Jean Vilar

R. DES. MARCHANDS

RUE DES FOURBISSEURS

RUE

Préfecture

Palais du Roure

Synagogue

RUE

Musée Louis Vouland

R. VICTOR-HUGO

RÉPUBLIQUE

Musée Calvet

Musée Requien

St.-Didier

RUE

DU ROI

Livrée Ceccano

RUE DES

R. LABUREUR

Musée Lapidaire

VERNET

LA

DE

R. F.-MISTRAL

RUE HENRI-FABRE

RUE

FALCONS

RUE

DE

BOULEVARD

RASPAIL

S.I.

Reformed Church

former Hospice St-Louis

P.O.

Porte de la République

RUE DE

Célestins Cloisters

R. ST-MICHEL

BOULEVARD SAINT ROCH

AV. ST-RUF

Gare

ST-RUF, ARLES

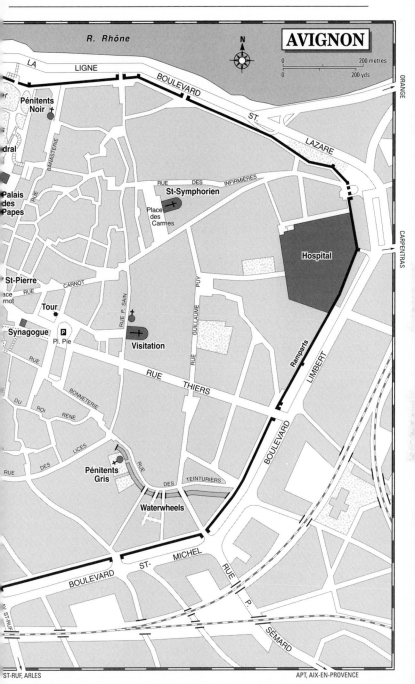

Palais des Papes, it has a very distinctive exterior, the best features of which are the handsome porch and square tower, the latter unfortunately disfigured by a statue of the Virgin that was added in 1859. The outline sketches of two frescoes by the Sienese artist Simone Martini survive in the entrance porch (the detached frescoes are displayed in the Palais des Papes) while the nave reveals a curious combination of the Romanesque and the high Baroque. The cupola is a particularly original feature surviving from the Romanesque church. Note the series of stepped arches mounting to an octagon which supports the dome on Corinthian columns. The principal treasure is the Flamboyant Gothic tomb of Pope John XXII in one of the side chapels, but also of note in the chancel is an interesting Romanesque throne with marble reliefs of an ox and a lion.

Alongside the cathedral, and dwarfing everything in the square, is the rather grim, Gothic bulk of the **Palais des Papes**. Mérimée compared it to an 'Asiatic tyrant's citadel' but to Henry James this was 'the dreariest of all historical buildings'. To be fair, at that point it was still being used as an army barracks. Nevertheless, the huge empty palace does require a considerable effort of the imagination to recreate the bustling activity and sumptuous colour that must have surrounded the medieval papacy. Furniture, textiles, paintings and all the other trappings of court life have disappeared leaving this immense building to echo with the sound of tour guides.

The ticket office is in the old guard room, just inside the main gateway, the Porte des Champeaux (☎ 04 90 27 50 74: **open** daily 09.00–19.00 Apr–Nov; 09.00–12.45 and 14.00–18.00 Dec–Mar; last ticket 45min before closing). Guided tours of the palace are available in most languages but you are free to follow the standard route through the main apartments at your own pace using the information panels or audio-guide.

History of the Palais des Papes

The Palais is actually two palaces, the product of separate building campaigns initiated by successive popes. The old palace was begun by Benedict XII in 1334 when he decided to clear away the original papal quarters to create a fortified residence round a central cloister. The result, seen in the wing to the north, is an impressive but hardly inviting edifice that served as a palace, chapel and fortress. In 1342 Benedict's successor Clement VI felt the need for something more courtly and engaged the architect Jean de Louvres to extend the palace to the south. In effect, he built a new palace, and it is the impressive doorway and heavy Gothic façade of this building that faces the main part of the square. After this major building campaign there was no substantial construction work on the palace. However, over the next 20 years an extensive programme of decoration was undertaken which made this one of the grandest and most influential buildings in Europe. Artists from Italy, particularly from the Sienese school, were attracted to Avignon to work on the interior while tapestries, sculpture, furniture and textiles were commissioned from the leading workshops of Europe. It is in this field that you comes to realise what has been lost. Walls that were once animated by elaborate fresco cycles or draped in sequences of Flemish tapestries are now reduced to bare masonry. Similarly, the great rooms which were once filled with a huge panoply of artefacts now seem almost barren.

Start your tour by crossing the Cour d'Honneur, the main courtyard between the old and new wings, and enter the Salle de Jésus, so called because it once displayed a series of monograms of Christ. This part of the building stands over the original treasury and the chambers below ground have some of the strongest masonry walls to protect the immense horde of gold, silver and precious goods that the popes kept on hand. The Salle de Jésus now holds a display of maps and prints of Avignon but it was originally for the papal accounts and a waiting-room for the Consistoire. The two small ante-rooms were related to this, one being the chamberlain's bedchamber, which has attractive 14C painted beams, and the other a small vestiary or dressing-room.

The next room is the large **Consistoire** (Consistory) or council room where the pope and his cardinals met, and where foreign delegations were received. As such this was one of the most lavish and highly decorated rooms in the palace but in 1413 it was destroyed in a fire. The main item of interest is the detached fresco of the *Virgin of Humility* by Simone Martini which was originally in the porch of the cathedral. Simone was the key figure in the development of the court style at this palace but only a few examples of his work have survived here. There is, however, a charming cycle of frescoes (1348) by Matteo Giovanetti (1300–69) of the *Lives of SS John the Baptist and John the Evangelist* in the small chapel off to one side of the main room. Matteo, who became Clement VI's court painter, was also from Tuscany, and exemplifies the strong Italian influence on the School of Avignon.

Upstairs on the first floor of the old palace, you enter the **Grand Tinel** or banqueting-hall, a huge room designed to accommodate the immense numbers of cardinals and courtiers who ate with the pope on formal occasions. This was also where the cardinals met to elect a new pope and, at one stage, it had to be expanded to accommodate the full college. The kitchen can be seen nearby at the Tour des Cuisines and Tour des Latrines. These latter towers are not open to the public but they were the scene of a notorious atrocity during the Revolution when 60 prisoners were massacred and their bodies thrown down a pit. The Grand Tinel is now hung with a series of 18C Gobelins tapestries but for a taste of the original decoration, the small chapel of St-Martial (currently under restoration) houses another cycle of frescoes by Matteo Giovanetti depicting scenes from the life of the saint.

From here the tour proceeds through a sequence of more private apartments (robing-room, study and dining-room) leading up to the papal bedchamber. This is decorated with an elaborate pattern of foliage inhabited by birds and animals, providing an attractive preamble to the **Chambre du Cerf** in the new palace, the most delightful room in the whole building. Originally Clement VI's study, this room was painted by the Frenchman Robin de Romans in 1343 with a series of frescoes depicting rural pursuits such as hunting, fishing and picking fruit. It is a lively sequence revealing the fascination with nature that is such a feature of the International Gothic style.

The next room is the sacristy which leads into the Great Chapel, a cavernous empty hall even larger than the Grand Tinel. The adjacent rooms have some fragments and casts of medieval tomb sculptures but this is a rather depressing display for a room which must have been at the very centre of the papal court in the 14C–15C. Downstairs, the equally large **Grande Audience** is broken up by its row of columns and it has retained some of the original frescoes of the *Prophets* by Giovanetti. This is the last major apartment but, as in every museum, there is a shop in the small audience room before the exit to the place du Palais by the main gate.

Facing the palace, and in marked contrast, is the elegant Baroque façade of the **Hôtel des Monnaies** which takes its names from the fact that it once served as the Papal mint. It was originally built, however, as a mansion for Cardinal Borghese in 1619, which explains the very Italianate character of the decoration, most obvious in the richly sculpted swags of fruit and coats of arms. In the 19C it was turned into a music conservatory and now bears the name of the French composer, Oliver Messiaen.

To the south of the place du Palais, alongside buildings painted with *trompe-l'oeil* scenes from the theatre, is the **place de l'Horloge**, one of the busiest and most animated parts of town. Occupying the site of the old Roman forum, this square is particularly lively during the summer festival period when it is filled with street entertainers and varied craft stalls. On the west side is the **Hôtel de Ville**, a 19C building which encloses a 14C belfry, all that survives of an earlier Gothic convent. Alongside this is the main theatre of the town, also from the 19C. A more interesting introduction to theatre in Avignon, however, can be found in the **Maison Jean Vilar** (☎ 04 90 86 59 64: **open** Tues–Fri 09.00–12.00 and 14.00–18.00, Sat 10.00–17.00), in the small rue de Mons opposite. Located in the 17C–18C Hôtel de Crochans, the house has displays of photographs, costumes and other memorabilia related to the *Arts du Spectacle*.

Jean Vilar and the Avignon Festival

When in 1947 the poet René Char and art critics Christian and Yvonne Zervos first proposed a festival, they invited Jean Vilar to devise new techniques and settings for the performance of drama. He was already well known for innovative productions of the Classics and it was in this field that he gave the festival a distinctive character. Rejecting the civic theatre in favour of the empty spaces of the Palais des Papes, Vilar put on several landmark productions which had a great influence on French drama in the years after the Second World War. For tickets and information on the festival contact the Bureau du Festival d'Avignon, also at 8 rue de Mons (☎ 04 90 82 67 08).

The rue de la République runs directly south from the place de l'Horloge to the railway station but it is little more than a thoroughfare with considerable traffic and few points of interest. Instead, you can set off into the network of streets on either side where there are many historic and attractive sights within a few yards.

St-Agricol and the museums of the western districts

The districts to the west of the rue de la République are the most compact of the old town, which means that they can be explored in an undemanding walk starting from the southwest corner of the place de l'Horloge.

Leaving the place by the small rue du Collège-du-Roure, you enter a warren of narrow streets and passageways with important 15C–18C mansions. Many of these houses are now occupied by civic offices and inaccessible but the finest, the **Palais du Roure**, contains a library and museum devoted to Provençal history and culture (☎ 04 90 80 80 88: guided tours Tues at 15.00 or by appointment). This townhouse, noticeable immediately for its Flamboyant Gothic portal, was built in 1469 for a family of Florentine bankers, the Baroncelli, who like the Medici controlled much of the international finance of the day. The last descendant was Baron Folco de Baroncelli-Javon, a poet, *gardian* (cowboy) and member of the Félibrige, who established the Provençal literary journal *Aïoli* from this house (see p 102). Most of the original interior has been lost but there is a beautiful courtyard in the heart of the house which alone makes the visit worthwhile. The most interesting parts of the museum collection are old Provençal folk items and some of the Baron's memorabilia. Nearby, on the rue St-Agricol, is **Roumanille's** bookshop and café where Baroncelli, Mistral and other members of the Félibrige used to meet. It is still one of the best bookshops for Provençal literature and the back room has been preserved as a sort of tribute to the movement's heyday in the 19C. Roumanille's imprint, under which many of the original literary works of the Félibrige were published, is still in existence.

On the other side of the street is the **Eglise St-Agricol**, one of the oldest religious foundations in Avignon. It was built on the site of earlier Roman remains but the present church dates mainly from the 15C and contains a number of paintings and sculptures, including a Provençal altarpiece from 1525 known as the *Doni Retable*. Alongside this is the rue de la Petite Fusterie leading to the rue St-Etienne, a residential district of old town houses, some dating from as early as the 15C. It was at No. 18 in 1782 that the Montgolfier brothers floated a piece of light material up their chimney, thus discovering the principle of aerostatics which led to their first ascent in a hot-air balloon the following year. Off the rue St-Etienne to the left is the rue Joseph-Vernet, a long and rather gracious street which curves along the line of the 13C ramparts.

Before going down this street, however, you can make a detour by the rue Baroncelli to the **place Crillon**, one of the most engaging spots in Avignon and the site of a popular flea market. The north side of the place is the façade of the 18C theatre La Comédie, which was abandoned to housing when the new theatre opened in 1824. At No. 12 was the **Hôtel Palais Royal** (now *Hôtel Europe*) which accommodated many distinguished visitors including Napoleon, Stendhal, Charles Dickens, George Eliot and, during their elopement, Robert Browning and Elizabeth Barrett. It is probably best known, however, for the vicious murder of Maréchal Brune, one of Napoleon's generals, who in 1815 was set upon by local Royalists who threw his body into the Rhône. In 1858 the British philosopher John Stuart Mill was staying here with his beloved wife Harriet when she fell ill and died. She was buried in the St-Véran cemetery, outside the walls to the east. Devastated by her death, Mill bought a house overlooking the cemetery and moved all his belongings there from the hotel to be near her grave. He spent much of the rest of his life in Avignon and on his death in 1873 was buried beside her. George Eliot remarked how he had written so much about her on the gravestone that there was no room left to mark his own death. He is given a few lines on the stone's edge.

Returning to the rue Joseph-Vernet, you can sense the change to a more bourgeois district as you proceed down this street of 17C–18C mansions. On the right, past the junction with rue St-Agricol, there is a large 18C oratory which is used for temporary exhibitions. There are also several museums in this area which are well worth visiting. Off to the right at 17 rue Victor-Hugo is the **Musée Louis Vouland** (☎ 04 90 86 03 79: **open** Tues–Sun 10.00–12.00 and 14.00–18.00 June–Sept; 14.00–18.00 Oct–May; closed Mon), a collection of

mainly French decorative arts from the 18C which was assembled by the eponymous wealthy industrialist in the earlier part of the 20C. This was Vouland's
own house but there is very little sense of character and, perhaps as a result, it
is one of the least visited museums in the city. The furniture is, nevertheless, of
a high standard and there is some good porcelain and a few interesting paintings, notably one by Joos van Cleve (c 1480–1540) of a *Child Eating Cherries*.

In marked contrast is the **Musée Calvet** (☎ 04 90 86 33 84: **open** Wed–Mon
10.00–19.00 Jun–Sept; 10.00–13.00 and 14.00–18.00 Oct–May; closed Tues) at
65 rue Joseph-Vernet, the principal civic art gallery and one of the most distinctive
collections in the whole of France. Visitors to this gallery before 1990 will
remember its richly evocative appearance, a combination of the beautiful building,
the casual layout of the paintings and the overwhelming sense of neglect, even
abandonment, which seemed to have overtaken the place. At that time it was very
easy to understand the reports of 19C writers like Stendhal who had visited the
gallery and emerged with a sense of having experienced something magical. In the
present age of museum technology and expansion this state of affairs could not be
allowed to continue. The museum is gradually emerging from several years of
renovation and, while it can never recapture its original atmosphere of dilapida-
tion, it is an enjoyable art gallery with a sensitive if pristine finish.

The origins of the museum lie in the collection of an 18C doctor, Esprit Calvet,
whose library and cabinet of curiosities were bequeathed to the city on his death
in 1810. Like many collectors from the age of the Encyclopaedists, Calvet
acquired a huge range of items including Stone Age implements, fossils, natural
history specimens, coins and metalwork, as well as the more predictable
Egyptian and Classical antiquities. The paintings owe more to subsequent collectors and, while several European schools are represented, the French works from
the 18C and 19C are the strongest. There are several landscapes by the local
born artist Joseph Vernet (1714–89), as well as fine works by Théodore
Géricault (1791–1824), Théodore Chasseriau (1819–56), Edouard Manet
(1832–83), Corot, Renoir and the early 20C Expressionist Chaim Soutine
(1894–1943). But the most famous and striking picture in the collection is
Jacques-Louis David's *Death of Barra*, one of this artist's series of Revolutionary
martyrs. Barra was a young drummer boy who was summarily executed for
refusing to shout 'Vive le Roi!' and instead shouted 'Vive la République!' In
David's textured, monochrome version of this scene, Barra is depicted as a curiously androgyne nude clutching the tricolour to his breast as he expires in
orgasmic rapture. Few paintings demonstrate more clearly that combination of
eroticism and morality that is such a strong undercurrent in neo-Classical art.

Next door to the Musée Calvet is the natural history museum, the **Musée
Requien** (☎ 04 90 82 43 51: **open** Tues–Sat 09.00–12.00 and 14.00–18.00;
closed Sun and Mon), which was founded by the botanist Esprit Requien
(1788–1851) who pioneered the recording and study of the flora of Provence.
His work drew many famous botanists and collectors to Avignon and to this day
the region is regarded as one of the great treasure troves for botanical studies.
One English visitor who came here for just such botanical study was John Stuart
Mill. So impressed was he with the collection and its director, J.-H. Fabre, that he
provided the finance to set up the museum. Unfortunately, the main exhibition
areas are rather dull but the museum's main role is as a research institute based
round the huge collection of specimens.

The rue Joseph-Vernet curves round to the east as it meets rue de la République, the main thoroughfare and shopping street. At this junction you can return directly to the place de l'Horloge by the rue de la République or embark on a tour through the eastern side of the old town.

If returning up the rue de la République, you should call into the **Musée Lapidaire** (☎ 04 90 85 75 38: **open** Wed–Mon 10.00–12.00 and 14.00–18.00; closed Tues) in the large 17C Jesuit chapel on the right at the junction with rue F.-Mistral. This is an outstation of the Musée Calvet devoted to Classical and medieval sculpture but on first sight it is somewhat bewildering. The most famous pieces are the *Venus of Pourrières* and the 2C BC *Tarasque de Noves*, a monster devouring a man. The gallery as a whole, however, is a reminder of Provençal museums of old: various sarcophagi, tomb fragments and assorted Classical, Egyptian, medieval and Renaissance items are littered across the floor and up the walls of the building. In one of the side chapels there is a very grand Renaissance fireplace which must have looked particularly impressive in its original location, a house in the impasse St-Pierre. From here you can rejoin the next walk half-way through its route at place St-Didier, along rue F.-Mistral and rue Laboureur, avoiding the southeastern part of town.

The old town east of rue de la République

Rue Joseph-Vernet becomes the rue Henri-Fabre, marked on the southeast corner by the *office du tourisme* and, in a garden beside the remains of a Gothic cloister, the 14C temple of St-Martial. To the rear of the church and accessible by a small alleyway is the place des Corps-Saints, a quiet area of rather grand houses, mostly from the 19C. This district is dominated by civic offices and the abandoned barracks and is not generally on the main tourist routes but it has a certain charm and can be quiet when most of Avignon is congested. On the south side of the *place* is the empty chapel of the Celestines, now used for a variety of performances and temporary exhibitions.

Take the rue des Lices, another long street following the line of the 13C town walls. On the left at No. 21 is a dilapidated building on four floors which was once an alms house and is now the Ecole des Beaux-Arts. A relic of its earlier role is the sign on the church of the Evangelique next door which urges passers-by to pray for the sick and destitute. Turn right into the cobbled **rue des Teinturiers** (Street of the Dyers), one of the most attractive streets in Avignon, which still has an exposed section of the river Sorgue flowing down one side. There are several pleasant shops and bistros along here and, at the bottom, a few waterwheels surviving from the time when textile dyeing was the main industry.

The principal monuments in this district, however, are the chapels amid the trees on the other side of the stream, accessible by a series of small bridges. The Gothic belltower near the top of the street is all that survives of the 14C Franciscan convent where Petrarch's Laura is thought to have been buried. Lower down is the 16C **Chapel des Pénitents Gris**, the earliest and longest lasting of the various penitent brotherhoods that were set up in Avignon under the papacy. Each group wore a distinctive coloured habit, hence the names Pénitents Gris, Noirs, Blancs or Rouges. Most of these orders were disbanded during the Revolution but their chapels and halls often survive under another name. This building is still a church and contains several paintings and sculptures from their heyday in the 16C and 17C. Idyllic as this spot is, it can suffer flooding. On the outside of the chapel, about 2.5m above the ground, is a line marking the height of the waters in the flood of 1840.

Retracing your steps up the rue des Teinturiers, turn left at the top into the rue de la Masse and on to the winding rue du Roi-René. This is another historic part of Avignon, studded with the town mansions of wealthy Provençal families of the 15C–17C. Note particularly the Hôtel de Berton de Crillon (1649) at No. 7, with its richly encrusted decoration, and opposite the Hôtel de Fortia de Montréal (1637), and at No. 11 the so-called Maison du Roi (1476), which is thought to have been owned by the king himself. Despite the associations with King René, however, the street is probably best known for a fleeting moment which formed the basis of a great literary tradition. A plaque at No. 22 records the site of the convent of Ste-Claire where on 6 April 1327 Petrarch first glimpsed Laura. The precise identification of this girl remains a mystery but she is often thought to be Laure de Noves, the married daughter of a noble family who, even if Petrarch could have got close to her, would hardly have been able to conduct a love affair with a poor scholar. In his isolation from her Petrarch created a cult of pure spiritual love and unrequited longing that produced some of the greatest lyric poetry of the late troubadour style and the early Renaissance.

At the western end of the street you can see the impressive forms of the 14C **Eglise St-Didier**, its pale stone walls and buttresses rising to dominate the surrounding square. The interior is similarly plain but well proportioned with good clear lines in its six bays. In 1953 a series of frescoes dating from the late 14C was uncovered in one chapel, and these have now been cleaned and restored. The principal attraction of the interior, however, is the coloured marble relief of *Christ Carrying the Cross* in the first chapel on the right. Commissioned in 1478 by King René from the Dalmatian-born sculptor Francesco Laurana, this is one of the earliest and finest pieces of Renaissance sculpture in Provence.

The large castellated tower to the south of the church on the rue Prévost was once part of the medieval palace of the cardinals but in the 16C it was taken over by the Jesuits who used it for star-gazing through telescopes. Ironically, it was the Jesuits who were Galileo's most virulent critics, regarding his theory on the movement of heavenly bodies round the sun as heresy. The tower is part of the old public library, housed in the mansion of Cardinal Ceccano, and recently converted into a *mediathèque* incorporating a reference library as well as other popular diversions.

Facing the entrance courtyard of the *mediathèque* at 5 rue Laboureur is the **Musée Angladon** (open Wed–Sun 13.00–19.00 in summer, 13.00–18.00 in winter), a new museum set up in their private home by two local artists and opened in Doucet, a famous collector of 18C art and later of contemporary work includingPicasso's *Demoiselles d'Avignon*. Most of Doucet's artworks were sold or bequeathed to the Louvre after his death in 1929 but some, including paintings by Manet, Cézanne, Van Gogh and Amadeo Modigliani (1884–1920) remain in the collection. Another feature of the museum is a recreation of Doucet's Art Deco studio at Neuilly and an 'art lovers' interior' combining various items of furniture and works of art from the 13C to the 18C.

From the place St-Didier, take the pedestrian rue des Fourbisseurs through the shopping district towards place Carnot in the north. This passes close by the old Jewish quarter of Avignon round the place Pie and, although the character of the area was altered with the building of a new bus station, street names like rue

Jacob and place Jérusalem are reminders of its earlier existence. Near the top of the rue des Fourbisseurs stand two of the earliest surviving townhouses, the Hôtel de Belli at the junction of the Vieux-Sextier, part of which dates from the 14C, and further up on the left, the 15C Hôtel de Rascas. Timber construction, as seen in both these houses, was widespread in Avignon but it was stopped in the 16C to avoid the fires that devastated many medieval towns.

Across the place Carnot to the left is the **Eglise St-Pierre**, founded in the 14C but notable more for its 16C Flamboyant Gothic façade and carved wooden doors. There is other fine woodwork on the interior, dating from the 17C. The place St-Pierre used to be a refuge from the bustle of the place de l'Horloge just up the hill but is now well known and it is often difficult to find space in the cafés. It is a pleasant shaded square, nevertheless, and in a narrow street behind the church there is one of the town's most enjoyable small museums. The **Musée Théodore Aubanel** (☎ 04 90 82 95 54: guided tours Mon–Fri 09.00–12.00 and 14.00–19.00; closed Sat, Sun and Aug), named after one member of a local press and publishing dynasty, is devoted to the history of publishing in Avignon from the 18C to the present. As founders of the *Courrier d'Avignon*, one of the leading newspapers of the Revolution, the Aubanels have been at the centre of this industry for over 200 years. The museum, near the printing-works, is still run by the family as is apparent from the intimate scale and thoughtful presentation of the exhibits. There are some early presses, examples of different types of printing, and a selection of interesting documents related to the town and the family firm. Théodore was a poet and one of the founders of the Félibrige, and a series of his manuscripts and personal items gives a further literary dimension to the museum.

To return to the place de l'Horloge, take any of the streets ascending to the west, such as the rue Peyronnerie along the edge of the Palais des Papes. As a final diversion, however, there is an interesting group of buildings out to the east of the old town, about 500m along the rue Carnot. On the left, off the rue Portail Matheron, is the place des Carmes, a shaded square that often seems in a different town to the more popular areas of Avignon. This area was once dominated by two great religious foundations, the Carmelites and the Augustinians. The convent chapel of the Carmelites survives as a parish church, the **Eglise St-Symphorien**, and retains its 15C Gothic façade. Just to the left of this is the cloister, a large Gothic arcade with fine details and gargoyles. The space is often used for theatre performances. The Augustinian monastery did not fare so well during the Revolution. All that remains of this huge establishment, founded in 1261, is the tall 14C clocktower standing on the main street at the southern end of the place des Carmes.

8 · Villeneuve, the Pont du Gard and Uzès

During the late medieval period the Rhône marked the border between the papal lands and the Languedoc, part of the French kingdom. This seems to explain why there should be such a complex of fortifications facing Avignon from the opposite bank of the river. It was not, however, a confrontation between two armed camps. In fact, the cardinals and members of the curia were allowed by

❖ Information, accommodation and food

🄸 1 place Charles-David (☎ 04 90 25 61 33) with an annexe in the Chartreuse in summer. A combined ticket, the Passeport pour l'Art, can be purchased here (45Fr) which allows access to all the sites listed. The Passeport is also available at each site or monument,

Hotels. Villeneuve can be a quieter alternative to Avignon itself but at the busiest times there is considerable overspill of visitors to the hotels and restaurants across the river. *Le Prieuré* (☎ 04 90 25 18 20), a 16C priory at 7 place du Chapitre, is probably the best and most expensive but *L'Atelier* at 5 rue de la Foire (☎ 04 90 25 01 84) and *Residence Les Cèdres* at 39 boulevard Pasteur (☎ 04 90 25 14 66) are both reasonable while the *Beauséjour* is among the cheapest.

Further out of the way, the **Château de Cubières**, an 18C mansion in its own grounds at Roquemaure to the north on route d'Avignon (☎ 04 66 82 64 28: closed mid-Nov–mid-Mar), is excellent.

Restaurants. *Le Prieuré* (see above) and *La Magnaneraie* at 37 Camp-de-Bataille (☎ 04 90 25 11 11) have the finest restaurants in Villeneuve, as is reflected in the prices. *Aubertin*, at rue de l'Hopital (☎ 04 90 25 94 84), is also very good while *La Mamma Lucia* at place Victor-Basch (☎ 04 90 25 00 71) and *La Maison* at 1 rue Montée du Fort St-André are both reasonable.

the French to build houses and take estates on the opposite side of the river in order to escape from the filth and disease of the metropolis. To this day the 'new town' of **Villeneuve-lès-Avignon** has a relaxed, quiet atmosphere that contrasts with the congestion of its larger neighbour. It also offers one of the best views of Avignon with its skyline of towers.

The impressive fortifications at Villeneuve predate the arrival of the papacy, reflecting the less cordial relations that existed between the kingdom of France and Provence—then linked to the Holy Roman Empire—in the 13C–14C. There was a real need to oversee this vital crossing-point on the Rhône and, in fact, the **Tour de Philippe-le-Bel** (☎ 04 90 27 49 68: **open** daily 10.00–12.30 and 15.00–19.00 Apr–Sept; Wed–Mon 10.00–12.00 and 14.00–17.30 Oct–Mar; closed Tues and Feb) stands on the spot where the Pont St-Bénézet once joined the west bank. Built between 1293 and 1307 it was further strengthened and heightened later in the century and, even after years of misuse, it still gives a sense of military strength as well as an excellent view.

The town centre is marked by the substantial 14C church of Notre-Dame with a well-preserved cloister which is open to the public, but the finest of the treasures have been installed in the **Musée Municipal Pierre de Luxembourg** (☎ 04 90 27 49 66: **open** daily 10.00–12.30 and 15.00–19.00 Apr–Sept; Wed–Mon 10.00–12.00 and 14.00–17.30 Oct–Mar; closed Tues and Feb) just a few yards away on the rue de la République. This museum has a good collection of paintings and sculpture but there are two items of outstanding importance. The first of these is a 14C ivory *Madonna and Child*, a particularly fine piece of

International Gothic art from the Ile de France. The other work, displayed in a gallery on the first floor, is the great *Coronation of the Virgin* (1454) by Enguerrand Quarton, one of the supreme masterpieces of 15C French painting. It would be difficult to overpraise this work since it seems to offer so many fascinating aspects, from the simple monumentality of its design, the unusual twinned representation of God and Christ, or the curiously unsettling features of the Madonna to the detailed landscape of Provençal mountains in the background. Some commentators seem to recognise the Montagne Ste-Victoire in this scene. It also repays close examination of the townscapes, where a swarm of tiny devils seems to have infested the buildings, one even proclaiming his defiance from the top of a tower.

This altarpiece once belonged to the **Chartreuse du Val de Bénédiction**, 200m further along the street, the largest and most important charterhouse in France (☎ 04 90 15 24 24: **open** daily 09.00–18.30 Apr–Sept; 09.30–17.30 Oct–Mar). Established in 1352 by Pope Innocent VI, in recognition of a Carthusian who had refused the papal tiara, the foundation was greatly enlarged and endowed by his successors until it spread over a major part of the estate. Such was its scale and importance that it became an immediate target of anticlerical attacks during the Revolution, after which it was sold off in parcels of land. What survives gives some indication of the original complex but the principal buildings are largely ruined. It is still, nevertheless, a fascinating place to visit and the walk through the remains on a quiet day is remarkably evocative. The Carthusians enforced a strict regime of hard work, modesty and silence but the elaborate Gothic tomb of Pope Innocent and the 18C circular well in the large cloister give an air of sophistication that seems slightly out of character. Of the other buildings, some have been given over to craft workshops and a cultural centre but, as is often the case with monastic remains, the more intimate small cloisters seem to retain more of the original spirit.

Tomb of Pope Innocent VI

The rear of the charterhouse is overlooked by the battlemented walls of the **Fort St-André** (☎ 04 90 25 45 35: **open** 09.00–19.00 July–Aug; 09.30–12.30 and 14.00–18.00 Apr–June and Sept; 10.00–12.00 and 14.00–17.00 Oct–Mar), the bastion on the summit of Mont Andaon. It is well worth walking up to this citadel if only to see the magnificent 14C fortifications, which are often used as a location for historical films. The remains of an important abbey and pilgrimage chapel can be visited within the fort but these were badly damaged in the 1790s. More worthwhile is the walk along the walls and through the formal Italian garden for the view out over the Rhône to Avignon on the opposite bank.

Pont du Gard

While on this side of the Rhône, it is possible to make the one short excursion by car that is essential for every visitor to the area, to the Pont du Gard, some 22km to the west. Take the N100 from the southern part of Villeneuve (or the D900 which leads into the N100) to Remoulins, from where there is a loop north (D19 or D981) to the site. There are car parks at both sides of the river and, except in high summer, cars can cross one way, north to south, on the roadway built alongside the lowest level.

History of the Pont du Gard

Built in 19 BC to bring fresh water from a spring near Uzès to the metropolis of Nemausus (Nîmes), this aqueduct was and still is one of the great monuments of Roman engineering. The water channel itself is a remarkable achievement. Precisely calculated to cover the 45km with a steady declivity of 34cm/km, the channel of solid stone blocks allowed consistent flow along its full length until it drained into the great cisterns in the town. To achieve this, however, the natural contours of the landscape had to be overcome by a series of tunnels and supports. Crossing the river Gardon was clearly the major problem. Not only was there a considerable distance to be spanned, the structure had to be sufficiently strong to withstand the river's seasonal floods. In the event Marcus Agrippa, son-in-law of the Emperor Augustus, devised a solution in which three ranks of dry-stone arches, using blocks as heavy as six tons, were combined in a structure that is as elegant as it was efficient. The two lower tiers are composed of successive arches over 20m tall while the top tier, which carried the channel, is a sequence of 35 smaller arches 7m high. The protruding blocks which stud the surface were employed in the initial construction and were left in that state to support scaffolding for repairs.

Its very success as a feat of engineering made the Pont du Gard vulnerable to sabotage. This vital source of water to Nîmes was an immediate target when the city was under siege, as it frequently was in the early Middle Ages. By the 9C it had been virtually abandoned, silted up, and the stone pilfered for building projects. In the 18C, however, it became a famous staging-post for travellers on the Grand Tour and its rising fame made it an object of historical importance and national pride. Accordingly, Napoleon III paid considerable amounts to have it restored to something approaching its original splendour.

One of the most remarkable features of a visit to this monument nowadays is that, like those 18C travellers who came across it deserted in the heart of a romantic landscape, you are still able to clamber over the great Roman masonry. The best approach is by a path to the north which not only gives a beautiful view of the aqueduct across the tranquil waters of the Gardon, but leads back to the water channel at the top. From here you can stumble along the dark enclosed tunnel, where a few openings allow you to see out over the river. Those of a more daring disposition or with a complete absence of vertigo may walk along the top exposed to the elements. Local stories do refer to unfortunate accidents and there is a sign warning the foolhardy of unexpected gusts of wind which could lift the innocent pedestrian from the top to the river bed some 50m below.

Uzès

Just 17km further on the D981 is Uzès, one of the most delightful medieval towns in this border area between Provence and the Languedoc.

History of Uzès

The Duchy of Uzès is very old, tracing its origins back to Charlemagne, and at one stage in the 17C this was the premier title in France. For centuries a stronghold of Protestants, the population of Uzès suffered during the religious wars of the 17C, creating a rivalry with and defiance of their neighbours which many commentators have detected even in recent times.

Uzès hosts a number of festivals including a garlic fair, the *Foire à l'Aïl*, on 24 June and a regular truffle market on Saturdays in winter. Given the setting, however, the most appropriate festival is the *Nuits Musicales*, a series of concerts of ancient music held throughout the town in the second half of July.

❖ *Information, accommodation and food*

🛈 Avenue de la Libération (☎ 04 66 22 68 88).

Hotels. The choice of hotels in Uzès is not extensive but the *Hôtel d'Entraigues* (☎ 04 66 22 32 68) in a 16C mansion at 8 rue de la Calade is one of the best while *La Taverne* at 7 rue Xavier-Sigalon (☎ 04 66 22 47 08) is less expensive.

Outside the town there is *Le Castellas* (☎ 04 66 22 88 88), a stylish hotel and restaurant at Grand Rue in Collias. For something special you could stay or dine at the *Hôtel d'Agoult* (☎ 04 66 22 14 48) closed mid Nov–mid Mar) in the 18C Château d'Arpaillargues 4km to the west of Uzès. Marie d'Agoult, who was Franz Liszt's lover, came from the family and often stayed here in the mid-19C.

Restaurants. You can dine at *Le Castellas* and at the *Hôtel d'Agoult* (see above) or, for a more modest meal, there is *La Taverne* (see above) or *l'Emeraude* (☎ 04 66 22 07 50) just outside Uzès on the road to Nîmes).

The old ruling family still live in the **Duché** or ducal palace (☎ 04 66 22 18 96: guided tours 45min 10.00–18.30 June–Sept; 10.00–12.00 and 14.00–18.00 Oct–May), an impressive ensemble of buildings topped by a polychrome tiled roof. There are elements in the palace from every period between the 11C and the 18C but the finest part is undoubtedly the Renaissance façade (c 1550), which is reputed to be based on designs by Philibert Delorme, the most original French architect of the period. The interiors are richly appointed with period furniture and elaborate plasterwork although the most memorable items are the dressed waxworks in 16C–17C costume.

The other principal monument in Uzès is the 12C **Tour Fénestrelle**, part of a complex of ecclesiastical buildings outside the old walls to the west, including the cathedral and the bishop's palace. The tower is the only surviving part of a

Romanesque cathedral destroyed in the Wars of Religion. Six tiers of subtly varied arcades rise some 42m to create a curious landmark visible from much of the surrounding area. The cathedral of St-Théodorit which replaced the older building dates from the 17C and, although there are some fine features such as the organ, the façade and many of the details show the hand of a very dull 19C renovation.

Beside the church, on a quiet terrace overlooking the old ducal gardens, there is a small pavilion that was occupied by the great Classical dramatist Jean Racine (1639–99) during his exile here in 1661. Racine had been sent to stay with his uncle, the vicar general of Uzès, in a vain attempt to dissuade him from a career in the theatre. The town has another literary association in André Gide (1869–1951), whose family came from here. The novelist and Nobel Prize-winner passed his childhood holidays in this area with his grandmother, as he recounts in his memoir *Si le grain ne meurt* (*If it die …*). There is some memorabilia of the author's life and work in the **Musée Georges-Borias** (☎ 04 66 72 95 99: **open** daily 15.00–18.00 Feb–Oct; 14.00–17.00 Nov–Jan), a modest local history museum in the rather grand bishop's palace.

Leaving these major buildings aside, one of the most attractive aspects of Uzès is the town itself; its winding streets, its 16C–18C mansions, and, above all, the place aux Herbes, a beautiful but not over-precious 17C market square fringed by a massive arcade. The successful film *Cyrano de Bergerac* was shot here in the late 1980s and it is not difficult to see why. There can be few towns anywhere in France able to recapture the spirit as well as the architectural fabric of the Ancien Régime in the provinces.

9 · Nîmes

Strictly speaking, Nîmes should not appear in a guide to Provence since it is one of the principal and most characteristic towns of the neighbouring Languedoc. It is, however, so clearly related to the outstanding group of Roman imperial centres in western Provence that it would be pedantic to leave it out of this guide. Indeed, Nîmes is in many respects the greatest of all the ancient sites in southern France, if for the Maison Carrée alone. The fact that there are many other Roman monuments in the town underscores its appeal and importance to the traveller. Add to this the recent attempts to dramatise the urban landscape by a series of bold architectural developments and it should be obvious why it is worth extending any tour of Provence across the Rhône.

History of Nîmes
The chained crocodile that is the symbol of Nîmes relates to the origins of the town as a settlement called Nemausus, built for the legions who had fought the victorious Egyptian campaign against Antony and Cleopatra. Augustus was generous to his troops and before long Nemausus became one of the largest and wealthiest towns in the province, with an array of public buildings that was among the finest outside Rome. The Maison Carrée, the amphitheatre and Temple of Diana are only the most celebrated survivors of a Roman town that, at its height in the 2C, had a population of

around 25,000. To support this metropolis much of the surrounding area was cultivated, trade links were established across the whole of the western empire and, on a more immediate level, the great channel and Pont du Gard were built to bring fresh water to the cisterns in the north of the town.

During the Middle Ages the town shrank to a fraction of its former size, to the extent that the bulk of the populace could live within the arena for defence against Barbarian invasion. It was not until the 12C and 13C, with the establishment of consular elections, that Nîmes began to regain a position of importance. This coincided with the first of the great religious disputes which have scarred the town's history right down to the 20C. Siding with the Albigensians, Nîmes suffered at the hands of Simon de Montfort in his brutal crusade to suppress the heretics in 1213.

In the 16C the town became a stronghold of the Huguenots who spent most of the next hundred years at war with the Catholic forces of the Crown. Indeed, much of this period is a story of successive massacres and reprisals by both the Catholics and Protestants of the Languedoc. It even spilled over into the Revolution, with the Protestants supporting the new order taking the opportunity to attack the Catholic population. On the Bourbon Restoration of 1814 the Catholic 'White Terror' was then directed against their Protestant neighbours.

Against this backdrop of religious warfare, the town actually underwent a period of expansion in commerce and industry. Silk- and cotton-weaving, trades which had been set up by the Protestants and supported by François I in the early 16C, had by the mid-18C expanded into a major industry employing upward of 10,000 people. The hard-wearing *serge de Nîmes* is perhaps the most popular clothing fabric in the world today under its shortened name of 'denim'. (The term 'blue jeans', incidentally, is derived from *Genes* or Genoa, the port through which Nîmes cloth was exported.) Like all the great European textile centres, however, Nîmes experienced the near total decline of the industry and its related activities in the 20C. Nowadays the local economy is supported primarily by electronics and light industries, a far cry from the grandeur of Nîmes' Roman past and perhaps the reason behind its recent facelift by modern architect-designers.

❖ *Information, accommodation and food*

🛈 6 rue Auguste, near the Maison Carrée (☎ 0466 67 29 11) and at the train station to the east of town.

Hotels. At the top end of the spectrum the *Hôtel Impérator Concorde* on quai de la Fontaine by the gardens (☎ 04 66 21 90 30, fax 04 66 67 70 25) has recently been rivalled by the new *Hôtel de la Baume*, closer to the centre at 21 rue Nationale (☎ 04 66 76 28 42).

In the middle range the *Hôtel Plazza* at 10 rue Roussy (☎ 04 66 76 16 20, fax 04 66 67 65 99) and the bullfighters' hotel *Le Lisita*, 2 boulevard des Arènes (☎ 04 66 67 66 20) are both recommended while, among the many cheaper hotels, the *Hôtel La Mairie* at 11 rue des Greffes (☎ 04 66

67 65 91) and *Hôtel La France* overlooking the amphitheatre at 4 boulevard des Arènes (☎ 04 66 67 23 05) are good.

Restaurants. The boulevard Victor-Hugo is the liveliest street for bars and
restaurants but for more subtle cuisine the top restaurant is *L'Enclos de la
Fontaine* in the *Hôtel Impérator* (see above). *La Belle Respire* in the old
town at 12 rue de l'Etoile (☎ 04 66 21 27 21) and the more rustic *Lou Mas*
at 5 rue de Sauve (☎ 04 66 23 24 71) are both good and distinctive.

The Maison Carrée and the 'designer' city

The centre of Nîmes is quite large but it can be difficult to negotiate in a car. It is
best to park and resign yourself to walking round the main monuments. Begin
with the Maison Carrée (Square House), widely regarded as the finest and most
beautiful surviving temple of the Roman empire. When Thomas Jefferson visited
Nîmes in the 1780s he was enraptured by it, spending hours contemplating the
façade and the fine carved detailing 'like a lover with his mistress'.

History of the Maison Carrée

The temple was built by Augustus around 20 BC and dedicated to his two
grandsons as part of a new cult elevating the imperial family to god-like
status. Even after the collapse of the Roman empire the building seems to
have been in constant use which may explain why, despite having served as
a church, residence, stables and town hall, it has survived in such good
condition. For many years it was used as a museum to display various
Classical remains. In 1990, however, it was decided to turn the space into
an art gallery and the much-reviled American painter Julian Schnabel
(1951–) was invited to decorate it. In the event, he produced one of his
finest works, a large decorative scheme of warm terracotta colours inspired
by the story of an audacious young bullfighter.

Like most Roman temples the Maison Carrée stands on a high base or podium
with access to the chamber by means of a triumphal staircase leading up from
the main forum. The well-proportioned Corinthian columns on the façade are
not continued round the building, as on Greek temples, but instead are represented by half-columns against the chamber wall. The inner chamber (cella)
would have housed the cult statue or altar but this has disappeared.

Schnabel's Maison Carrée murals were part of a larger cultural policy inaugurated by the mayor of Nîmes, Jean Bousquet. If these have generated some
controversy, they are probably the least public of his ventures. During the 1980s
Bousquet employed a string of glittering names in the world of contemporary
design to give the city a new image. Philippe Starck, at that time an *enfant
terrible*, was responsible for a bus stop and street furniture on the avenue Carnot
as well as the city's new logo. The Parisian decorator Andrée Putman designed
the public benches and Martial Raysse the fountains on the place du Marché and
place d'Assas; V. Gregotti produced the new sports stadium by the boulevard
péripherique Salvator Allende to the south and V. Kurokawa the vast shopping
and business complex, Rond-Point Nord, nearby; and, in a housing area at the

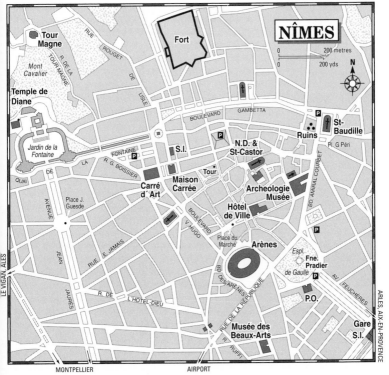

southeastern edge of the city, Jean Prouvé designed a bold hi-tech apartment block known as Nemausus.

By far the most prominent part of this grand scheme is the large *mediathèque*, the **Carré d'Art** (☎ 04 66 76 35 70: **open** Tues–Sun 10.00–19.00; closed Mon), an art gallery, library and resource centre just a few metres to the north of the Maison Carrée. Designed by Norman Foster and opened in 1993 it is clearly related to its neighbour as a sort of civic temple of contemporary culture. Despite the obvious use of new industrial materials (plastics as well as concrete, steel and glass), the huge canopy at the front supported on five slender columns suggests a Classical portico. The interior also has the sort of witty references to the antique characteristic of post-Modern design, notably in the use of a glass atrium running the whole height of the building. This device helps to reveal one of the most striking features of the building—that over half of it is underground. The library is in this lower area while the art galleries on the upper floors use natural lighting constantly reflected throughout the interior by the use of pale and transparent materials. On the roof terrace there is a café with excellent views over the town. Bousquet's aim was to create a southern equivalent of the Beaubourg (the area around the Pompidou centre in Paris). It is unlikely to have the same impact as its Parisian counterpart but in terms of the publicity generated by the architectural and design press, the Carré d'art has certainly given Nîmes a boost in its rivalry with Montpellier.

Paradoxically, this highly visible restyling has been made possible by declaring the entire city centre a conservation zone. Only by controlling development could the designers have been let loose on many of the most famous and popular sites. There is no doubt that the policy is questionable and it is unlikely to happen in British cities, for example, but it does provide novelty and entertainment for the pedestrian.

Other Roman remains and museums

You can start a convenient circuit of the town centre by leaving the place de la Maison Carrée and taking the boulevard Victor-Hugo towards the arena. Just off the boulevard by the rue E. Jamais to the right is the 19C Byzantine revival church of St-Paul, but there is very little else here to distract attention from the monument directly in front of you. The **Arènes** (open daily 09.00–18.30 in summer; 09.00–12.00 and 14.00–17.00 in winter; closed on days of bullfights) is unmistakable. It is one of the largest amphitheatres of its type, similar in scale and design to its counterpart in Arles but slightly better preserved. Here you can sense the solidity and grandeur of Roman public buildings, the two tiers of round arches interspersed with pilasters and Doric half-columns providing a simple rhythm that is carried round the entire oval perimeter. It was built at the end of the 1C to hold around 24,000 spectators who would have been protected from sun and rain by a canvas *velum* or awning pulled out over the open top. Recently, a modern covering was installed to allow concerts in the centre. The ancient audience came here to see either gladiatorial contests or combats with wild beasts, and the latter have carried on to the present day in the form of bull-fights.

Nîmes is the centre of bullfighting in France and throughout the summer there is a regular programme of fights, most in the Spanish style (i.e. the bull is killed). To further develop this as an indigenous or at least local sport, a Whitsun festival of bullfighting, the *Feria de la Pentecôte*, was established in 1952 and this has been joined by another festival in September to coincide with the grape harvest. As well as fights of different category in the arena, bulls are driven through the streets and stalls are set up with local wine, produce and *tapas*. There is a small museum devoted to bullfighting on the boulevard des Arènes with souvenirs and information on famous *torreros* from Nîmes.

The old town, stretching back to the north and east of the arena, offers a pleasant walk through streets which show the obvious signs of recent renovation. The place du Marché was once a market square but it is now the focal point of the old town with a decorative fountain of the city's arms. From here, the most pictures-que streets, the rue de l'Aspic, rue de Bernis, rue du Chapitre and rue de la Madeleine, all with interesting 17C–18C houses, are just to the north. At the centre

Fountain in place du Marché

dates from the 11C but was almost entirely rebuilt during the 19C in a dry Classical manner. The old episcopal palace at the side, however, houses the **Musée du Vieux Nîmes** (☎ 04 66 36 00 64; open Tues–Sun 11.100–18.00; closed Mon), a good local history museum with some recreated interiors and other items illustrating traditional crafts and activities of the region.

Two other museums, the **Musée d'Archéologie** (☎ 04 66 67 25 57; open Tues–Sun 11.00–18.00; close Mon) and the **Musée d'Histoire Naturelle** (☎ 04 66 67 39 14; open same times as Musée d'Archéologie), can be found in the 18C Jesuit College at Grande Rue and boulevard Amiral-Courbet. The building itself says a lot about the history of Nîmes. In the 17C it was divided into two separate parts, one Protestant and the other Catholic. On the Catholic side there is an ornate Jesuit chapel dating from the 18C with rich sculpted decoration. As you might expect, there is a good collection of Roman artefacts in the archaeological museum, including coins, inscriptions, pottery and sculpture, but much of it is rather specialised.

The **Musée des Beaux-Arts** (☎ 04 66 67 38 21: open Tues–Sun 11.00–18.00; closed Mon), some way to the south on the rue Cité Fulc, has no outstanding works but there are some interesting items in the collection. French and Dutch pictures of the 17C–18C are probably the strongest but there is a large painting of *Cromwell and the dead Charles I* by Paul Delaroche (1797–1856), the 19C specialist in scenes from English history. On the ground floor there is a large Roman mosaic of the *Marriage of Admetus*.

There is one other Classical site in Nîmes which should not be missed: the **Jardins de la Fontaine**, to the northwest beyond the Maison Carrée. The 'fontaine' was the spring around which a cluster of Roman sacred buildings was erected in the 1C–2C. To visit it now, however, is to enter an 18C garden in which the ruins at one side create a picturesque diversion as you walk along the formal paths and watercourses. The garden was created by J.-P. Mareschal, a military engineer who channelled the waters into basins surrounded by bridges, urns and elegant balustrades. Of the Roman remains, the so-called **Temple of Diana** is the most impressive, a cavernous ruin with some rich decorative mouldings and fragments. It is not known what the original function of the building was but it may have been some sort of public gallery or library for prominent citizens. Appropriately, it was depicted in 1787 by Hubert Robert (1733–1808), the French artist who specialised in antique ruins. He also produced one of the most Romantic views of the Pont du Gard from the same trip.

On the hill overlooking the gardens is a distinctive tower, known as the **Tour Magne**, which may have been part of the original outer defences of Nemausus built in 15 BC and consisting of some 30 towers in all. It may equally have been a signal- or lookout-tower built in the Middle Ages on a Roman base. What is certain is that it was originally much taller, although climbing the 140 steps on the interior staircase takes you sufficiently high to give a superb view over the town and surrounding countryside.

Northern Vaucluse and Alpes de Haute-Provence

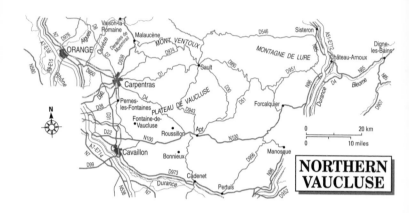

10 · Orange, Carpentras and Mont Ventoux

Orange

Orange has nothing to do with the fruit but that is only one paradox in a place with the most far-reaching and curious connections. This town of only 27,000 people has given its name to the Dutch royal house, the principal river in South Africa, the Protestant society in Northern Ireland and the Republican county in California that was once represented by Richard Nixon.

History of Orange

The name Orange derives from the Ligurian tribe Arausio who settled in this area around 1000 BC. The recorded history of Orange, however, begins in 36 BC when Julius Caesar presented this territory to a group of veterans from the 2nd Galician Legion. This policy of settlement was one of the most successful aspects of Roman imperial administration and within a few years the surrounding land had been allocated for cultivation and the population of Orange had expanded to over 100,000. Imagining a town of that size makes it easier to understand the scale of the monumental theatre and triumphal arch that survive today, but in the 1C AD there was also a temple, a huge sports stadium, a baths complex and an amphitheatre laid out in the regular plan that one associates with ancient towns. In fact, Roman Orange was probably larger even than Arles or Nîmes.

Its scale helped the town to survive the destructive incursions of the early Middle Ages and in the 12C Orange was declared an independent principality by the Holy Roman Emperor, Frederick Barbarossa. This period saw the city state evolve as one of the chief cultural centres of Provence, home of a troubadour court under Raimbaut d'Orange and the seat of a university. Eventually in the 16C it passed through inheritance to William the Silent, the architect of Dutch independence, who adopted the title Prince of Orange-Nassau. This, in turn, was passed on by descent to William III of Great Britain, popularly known as William of Orange.

Under William the Silent, Orange became a stronghold of Protestantism but it required extensive fortifications to survive during the religious wars of the 16C–17C. As a result, most of the Roman monuments were stripped of their masonry to create a ring of defensive walls and castles around the town. It is ironic that, having survived a millennium of Barbarian incursions, Roman Orange should have been destroyed by Europeans during the Renaissance, a period when elsewhere the Classical world was being rediscovered. The theatre and triumphal arch survived because they could be incorporated into the defences. The fortifications served their purpose—although they were breached on several occasions—and the town retained its independence. Finally, in 1713, the period of open warfare was ended when Orange was ceded to France by the Treaty of Utrecht. The authorities had the ramparts dismantled as a physical expression of the new regime but they also presided over the disintegration of the local economy. Traditional industries such as textiles went into decline as the Protestant community felt the effects of restrictive legislation. Orange never really recovered but it is now a thriving small town at the centre of the Côtes-du-Rhône wine-growing area.

❖ Information, accommodation and food

🛈 5 cours Aristide-Briand (☎ 04 90 34 70 88).

Hotels. It is relatively easy to find a hotel in Orange except at the time of the *Chorégies* festival in July. *Hôtel Arènes* at place des Langes (☎ 04 90 34 10 95) is the best in the centre but the *Hôtel Arcotel* at 8 place aux Herbes (☎ 04 90 34 09 23), the *Hôtel Fréau* at 3 rue Ancien-Collège (☎ 04 90 34 06 26) and especially *Le Glacier* at 46 cours Aristide-Briand (☎ 04 90 34 02 01) are all reasonable and can be recommended.

Restaurants. Eating out does not offer any surprises in Orange. *Trimalcion* at 12 rue Petite Fusterie (☎ 04 90 34 09 96) and *Le Yaca* at 24 place Sylvain (☎ 04 90 34 70 03; closed Tues eve and Wed) are both good if unexceptional.

If you approach the town from the north, the first landmark on entering Orange is the great **Arc de Triomphe**, once a feature of the Via Agrippa but now in the centre of a roundabout on the N7. Strictly speaking it is not a genuine triumphal arch in that it does not commemorate a particular victory but was probably built in 20 BC to celebrate the achievements of the 2nd Legion. It is nevertheless one of the largest of its type with three openings flanked by columns and a wealth of sculptural decoration, still discernible despite considerable weathering. The subjects are all military, including land and sea battles accompanied by trophies and other symbols of war.

The principal monument in Orange, however, and one of the most spectacular antique remains anywhere, is the **Théâtre Antique** (☎ 04 90 34 70 88: open daily Apr–Sept 09.00–18.30; 09.30–12.00 and 13.30–17.00 Oct–Mar), built into the hillside at the edge of the old town at place Frères-Mounet. Drawing near to this building for the first time one is impressed by the sheer scale of the outer wall, 103m long and 36m high. This cliff of deep ochre masonry dwarfs everything around it with an almost intimidating presence. It is actually the rear wall of the proscenium stage which, from the inside, forms a screen of arches and openings against which the dramatic action was played. There are still traces of the marble cladding which once covered the coarse stonework but it survives mainly as a gaunt backdrop with only the statue of Augustus in the upper niche as a remnant

The statue of Augustus

of its earlier grandeur. The holes in the upper storey originally held wooden beams to support a canopy that hung over the stage and part of the audience. The seating area, or cavea, follows the traditional semicircular plan but in this case the designers exploited the contour of the hillside to support the ranks of marble benches. In all, this theatre could hold some 9000–10,000 spectators, ranked in distance from the stage according to their social status, although the excellent acoustics ensured that everyone heard the play. This is still the case and you can test it in any of the numerous performances held throughout the year. The best time to attend, however, is during the festival of music and drama known as *Les Chorégies* held here in the latter half of July. The theatre was originally part of a larger complex of Roman public buildings including two or perhaps three temples alongside the main structure which are still being excavated by French archaeologists. The complex also included Roman baths and a gymnasium which extended over the hill to the rear, part of which is now turned over to a public park.

Directly opposite the outer wall of the theatre is the **Musée Municipale** (☎ 04 90 51 18 24: open daily 09.00–17.00 Apr–Sept; 08.30–12.00 and 13.30–17.30 Oct–Mar) which has extensive collections of Roman artefacts discovered in the antique sites in and around Orange. Statues, coins, ceramics and models are all displayed on the ground floor as is a number of inscribed marble tablets from a Roman cadastral land survey of 77 AD, the only one of its type to have survived. Less expected is the collection of works by the British artist Frank Brangwyn (1867–1956) on the upper floors. Brangwyn's friend and patron Albert de Belleroche, also an accomplished artist, spent his last years in Orange and bequeathed this collection of paintings and drawings to the town. There is also an interesting display devoted to the Nassau period and the printed textile industry which flourished here in the 18C and 19C. In recent decades there has been a revival of interest in these patterns, partly due to the British firm Laura Ashley, but equally, in France, as part of the creation of *le style Provençale*.

Behind the museum is the core of the old town, but despite its traditional plan of narrow streets and small squares the area lacks character. The same is true of the cathedral of Notre-Dame-de-Nazareth. Orange was an early bishopric and the present church dates from the 12C but it was badly damaged in the Wars of Religion and subsequent rebuilding was not sympathetic.

Carpentras

Carpentras, accessible from Orange via the N7 and D950, has a lively, work-manlike atmosphere which can be a pleasant relief from the more picturesque villages that depend on tourism. It is an important agricultural centre at the heart of a fertile fruit-growing area, the local produce being brought in for the busy market held on Friday mornings. Life in Carpentras was not always as prosaic as this, however. A number of elegant public buildings and some of the finest Rococo interiors in the region hark back to its position as the administrative capital of the Comtat-Venaissin.

History of Carpentras

In fact, Carpentras' prominence goes back even further to Ligurian and Roman times, best illustrated by the triumphal arch against the north wall of the cathedral. Despite its poor state of preservation, this was an important Roman monument rivalling those at Orange and Glanum, although the reliefs depicting two prisoners chained to a tree are so badly mutilated as to be almost unrecognisable. The early damage was probably at the hands of Barbarians because the town was an obvious target for tribal incursions from the north after the departure of the Romans. Like most major centres, Carpentras suffered during the later invasions and, despite being the seat of a bishopric, it was repeatedly attacked and weakened.

It was during the later Middle Ages that Carpentras emerged as the major town in this area. Benefitting from the patronage of several Avignon popes, notably Clement V who had a house here, it was declared the capital of the Comtat-Venaissin in 1320. During this period the whole town expanded and an impressive wall with some 32 towers was built to protect the community. Modern boulevards now mark the line of the medieval ramparts, which were only demolished in the 19C. Only one gate survives from the old walls, the Porte d'Orange at the northern edge.

The 18C was a period of great prosperity in Carpentras and throughout the old town there are numerous mansions with elegant façades looking out on to the street suggesting a sophisticated community in the Age of Enlightenment. To many it seemed that this prosperity had ended with the Revolution when the Comtat-Venaissin was incorporated into France. In fact, the 19C saw the introduction of new industries while the building of the Durance canal changed the character of the whole area, with irrigation of the land giving rise to an immense expansion in farming. The great 19C market halls still survive in the centre of the town but the bulk of the produce is now sent out to all parts of the country.

❖ *Information, accommodation and food*

🛈 170 avenue Jean-Jaurès (☎ 04 90 63 00 78).

Hotels. There is not a great range of hotels in or around Carpentras, probably because it is outside the normal tourist itinerary, but it is not difficult to find places to stay. *Le Fiacre*, an 18C house at 153 rue Vigne (☎ 04 90 63 03 15), is the best in the town centre while the *Hôtel du Théâtre* at 7 boulevard Albin-Durand is good for a lower budget.

Restaurants. The standard of restaurants is generally high: *L'Orangerie* at 26 rue Duplessis (☎ 04 90 67 27 23) and *Le Galant Vert* at rue des Clapiers (☎ 04 90 67 15 50) both have local specialities and seafood, while *Le Marijo* at 73 rue Raspail (☎ 04 90 60 42 65; closed Sun and Mon eve) is more popular.

The pedestrianised place Général-de-Gaulle, recently furnished with new fountains, is the best point at which to begin a tour of the old town. This attractive area is overlooked by the **Cathédrale St-Siffrein**, a somewhat uneven building begun in 1404 and showing signs of every other building campaign up to the 19C. The main part of the church is in the southern or 'Meridional' Gothic style but there are traces of an earlier Romanesque building in the choir and apse. The interior also has some interesting ecclesiastical treasures including the 'Sacred Bit', a piece of the true cross worked into a horse bit, a group of 15C wooden statues and, in a chapel to the left, a 15C altarpiece of the *Coronation of the Virgin* by an anonymous painter from the School of Avignon. The finest feature of the cathedral as a whole is the late Gothic south doorway with its flamboyant decorative carving. This is known as the Porte Juive (Jews' Gate), having been the entrance used by converts for baptism. It is also a reminder of the large Jewish ghetto in Carpentras, established in the 14C at a time when Jews were persecuted in France.

An even better indication of their prominence in the community is the **synagogue** (open Mon–Fri 10.00–12.00 and 15.00–17.00; closed Sat, Sun and Jewish festivals) in the rue d'Inguimbert to the north of the cathedral before the town hall. The first synagogue was established here in the 14C–15C but it was pulled down in the 18C to make way for the present building. It is rare to find the full-blown Rococo style applied to a liturgical purpose in Western Europe but this is one of the finest examples. Most of the elaborate *boiseries* and ironwork in the main room on the first floor have been restored recently and the synagogue is still in use although the Jewish community, once over 1000 strong, is now greatly depleted. It is perhaps not a coincidence that the extreme right-wing parties emerged in Provence at the same time as a notorious desecration of the Jewish cemetery in Carpentras.

The other major 18C building in Carpentras is the impressive **Hôtel-Dieu** founded by Bishop Inguimbert on the southern edge of the town. This is still a hospital and therefore public access is restricted but you can enter the old pharmacy with its original decoration and racks of Moustiers ceramic jars (open

Mon, Wed and Thur 09.00–11.00). The bishop, whose tomb is in the chapel, was an important civic benefactor who left his huge library of books and manuscripts to his native town. This, the **Bibliothèque Inguimbertine** (open Tues–Fri 09.30–18.30, Mon 14.00–18.30, Sat 09.30–12.00; closed July), is housed in an 18C mansion on the boulevard Albin-Durand, which also contains the **Musée Comtadin** and the **Musée Duplessis** (all museums ☎ 04 90 63 04 92: open 10.00–12.00 and 14.00–18.00 Apr–Oct; 10.00–12.00 and 14.00–16.00 Nov–Mar). The former is devoted to the traditional life and folklore of the Comtat-Venaissin while the latter, on the first floor, holds the civic collection of paintings. Most of the works are by local artists but there are pictures by Hyacinthe Rigaud (1659–1743), C.-J. Vernet and Pierre Parrocel. There are two other museums nearby; the **Musée Sobirats** on rue du Collège, an 18C house with a slightly seedy interior, although the decorative arts it displays are very good, and the **Musée Lapidaire** on the rue Stes-Maries, a collection of antiquities housed in a striking 18C convent.

The Dentelles de Montmirail and Vaison

The direct route from Carpentras to Mont Ventoux follows the main D9 38 via Le Barroux, with its massive 12C castle, and Malaucène, a beautiful medieval village encircled by an avenue of plain trees. It is, however, worth considering a detour to the north which takes you through the **Dentelles de Montmirail**, a range of steep jagged hills with isolated villages concealed within its network of woods and vineyards. It is a great area for walkers as well as for naturalists since the landscape offers such a range of impressive views. The name 'dentelles' is often thought to refer to the tooth-like rocks but in fact the metaphor is to lacework, suggested by the pale, eroded limestone. This longer route following the base of the Dentelles also takes in Vaison-La-Romaine, one of the most important Roman sites in Provence, before making the ascent of Mont Ventoux.

Virtually all the villages on the western fringe of the Dentelles are worth visiting but there are some highlights on the route up to Vaison which give the area a particular appeal. The first of these is **Beaumes-de-Venise** (leave Carpentras by the D7 and turn onto the D90 at Aubignan). Despite its position on the river Salette, the suggestive name of this village has nothing to do with Venice. Instead it relates to the many caves in the area of the Comtat-Venaissin. There are several medieval remains in the village but it is probably best known for its wine, a sweet muscat described by one noted *vigneron* as 'nectar of the gods'. Anne of Austria was so impressed by this wine on her pilgrimage to Provence in 1660 that she presented the village with a costly chasuble which is still on display in the 16C parish church.

To the northeast the D90 leads into the more rugged heart of the Dentelles, seen to their best advantage from the tiny village of Suzette (8km), but the main route follows the D81 and D7 towards Vacqueyras and Sablet. Just 1km outside Beaumes by this route is the 10C–12C Romanesque **Chapelle de Notre-Dame-d'Aubune**, with a particularly fine square tower at the foot of the Dentelles (the key is available from the farmhouse by Fontenouille). Following the D7 north to Vacqueyras and Gigondas you will pass **Montmirail** itself. The latter is now an isolated hamlet but its foul-smelling sulphurous spring was a popular cure in the late 19C, frequented by Mistral and the actress Sarah Bernhardt.

Gigondas, a village of only 648 inhabitants, has a ruined medieval castle and ramparts giving excellent views over the Comtat but, like Beaumes, it is noted more for its excellent wines, in this case mainly reds. Several of the villages in this area have the distinction of their own *appellation contrôlée*, a measure of the quality of the Dentelles vineyards, most of which are represented in the Caveau des Vignerons in the centre of Gigondas. There is also a Musée du Vigneron at Rasteau, further north on the opposite side of the river Ouvèze, with information on the whole of the Côtes-du-Rhône area and Chateauneuf-du-Pape.

From Gigondas, the D7 proceeds through Sablet and forks right on to the D23 leading to **Séguret**, the most famous and the prettiest of the villages fringing the Dentelles. Séguret has pretensions to being an art centre but it is really too picturesque in itself to be a serious painting motif. The village encloses several medieval monuments, such as the 12C church of St-Denis with its 14C belfry, and is set against a steep hill with a terrace at the summit offering a spectacular view over the vineyards of the Rhône valley. On Christmas Eve a famous nativity play is performed here by candle and torchlight, all the parts being played by the villagers.

Further north from Séguret, the D88 joins the main road (D977) to **Vaison-la-Romaine**, the Pompeii of France, which straddles both banks of the river Ouvèze.

History of Vaison la Romaine

The original settlement on the north bank was Ligurian but by the end of the 2C BC it had been incorporated into Roman Provence where it flourished as a wealthy residential town for government officials and their families. Vaison has few large public buildings such as one finds at Nîmes and Arles but the villas here were sufficiently grand and luxurious to suggest the top rung of Roman colonial society. This community was among the earliest to adopt Christianity and, by the 4C, Vaison was the seat of a bishopric which rivalled that of Arles and Marseille. A succession of Barbarian and Saracen incursions took their toll, however, and by the 12C Raymond de Toulouse took control of the area and built the castle on the rocky hill to the south of the river. Gradually the population gravitated to this defensible position, a tight medieval village grew up and the old Roman town was abandoned. Only in the 19C was the trend reversed and the population began to move back to the north bank, building the modern town over the Roman ruins while the medieval village was left to decline. Mérimée was one of the first to take a serious interest in the antiquities in the 1840s but the major excavations were all undertaken in the 20C and indeed are still in progress.

The Roman town centre and forum are largely concealed beneath the modern road network around the cours Taulignan but a complex of substantial villas has been unearthed in two major residential districts, the Quartier de la Villasse and, further north, the Quartier de Puymin. Between the two is the modern tourist office with information on all the ancient sites and, in the basement, a **Maison du Vin** where you can taste and buy wines from the whole of the Côtes-du-Rhône region. A combined ticket gives access to the major sites and museum.

❖ Information, accommodation and food

🛈 Place du Chanoine-Chautel (☎ 04 90 36 02 11).

Hotels. The Haute Ville has some of the best of the limited accommodation in Vaison. *Le Beffroi* at rue de l'Eveche (☎ 04 90 36 04 71), which occupies a 16C townhouse, and *Le Logis du Château* on the montée du Château (☎ 04 90 36 09 98) are both good and reasonably priced. *Hôtel Le Burrhus* at 2 place de Montfort (☎ 04 90 36 00 11) and *Hôtel des Lis* at 20 cours Henri-Fabre, owned by the same family, are both near the town centre to the north of the river.

Restaurants. The popularity of Vaison-la-Romaine among tourists has done little to stimulate interesting restaurateurs and pizzerias tend to dominate. Nevertheless, *La Fête en Provence* on place Vieux-Marché (☎ 04 90 36 36 43) and *Le Bateleur* at 1 place Théodore-Aubanel (☎ 04 90 36 28 04; closed Mon and Sun eve) are both distinctive and reasonably priced.

At the centre of the Quartier de Puymin is the partly underground **Musée Archéologique Théo Desplans** (☎ 04 90 36 02 11: **open** daily 10.00–13.00 and 14.30–19.00 June–Aug; closes at 18.00 Mar–May and Sept, Oct; 10.00–12.00 and 14.00–16.30 Nov–Feb) where there is a good display of items from the various villas in the area. Statues, mosaics, arms, jewellery, glassware, coins and all manner of items illustrating Roman life are displayed although the most famous pieces are the imperial statues of Claudius, Domitian, Hadrian and his wife Sabina which were found in the theatre. The theatre itself, cut directly into the hillside and accessible through a Roman tunnel to the north of the museum, has been substantially restored and now hosts a festival of music and drama in July and August. The main villas, particularly the large house of Messius, are south of the museum and the whole complex is continued over the main road in the Quartier de la Villasse. Here there are the remains of the baths, the Dolphin House and the large Maison du Buste en Argent, named after the 3C silver figurine found there and now in the museum.

Standing on its own to the west of the Quartier de la Villasse is the old **Cathédrale de Notre-Dame-de-Nazareth**, the last of a succession of buildings on this spot. One of the most interesting features is the base of the 'chevet' or east end where excavation has revealed the fragments of a Roman temple supporting the Romanesque walls. It is not certain when the Roman remains were first deployed here but they may have been used on the 6C church which was devastated by Frankish invaders. The present building dates mainly from the 11C–12C and, despite its rather stark appearance, displays many of the distinctive features of Provençal Romanesque. The most interesting section is the apse, at the centre of which is the bishop's throne and, in front of it, a sarcophagus with the relics of St Quenin, a 6C bishop of Vaison. There is also a selection of carved capitals in the cloisters, originally 13C but many restored in the 19C, and a small lapidary museum with early Christian sarcophagi and fragments (**open** daily 09.00–12.30 and 14.00–18.45 June–Aug; closes at 17.45 Mar–May and Sept, Oct).

A few hundred metres north of the old cathedral is the **Chapelle St-Quenin**, one of the most unusual Romanesque buildings in Provence, not least for its curious triangular apse decorated with a carved frieze and elegant half-columns. This part dates from the 12C but until recently it was thought to be early Christian and even antique.

In recent years the old town or Haute-Ville of Vaison on the opposite bank has been increasingly renovated but the castle at the top of the hill is still derelict. It is nevertheless worth the walk up the narrow streets for the excellent view over the valley and to Mont Ventoux.

Mont Ventoux

Leaving Vaison by the D938 towards Malaucène, it is worth taking a short detour by the D76 to visit the hilltop village of **Crestet** with its 12C church and old houses clustered round the tiny square. The narrow streets lead up to the 11C castle above the village but this is now a private residence. As a diversion there is an attractive art centre outside the village. None of the open-air sculptures are very distinguished but the wooded surroundings offer a pleasant walk with some striking views. By contrast, **Malaucène** is a substantial market town surrounded by a shaded avenue of plane trees. There are several attractions in the town itself such as the 14C fortified church and the picturesque old quarter but, since the time of Petrarch, Malaucène has been the gateway to Mont Ventoux and the starting-point for the various routes leading up to the mountain slopes.

Petrarch at Mont Ventoux

Petrarch was hardly the first person to seek solace or inspiration in high places but there can be little doubt that his ascent of Mont Ventoux in 1336 and the subsequent account he wrote about it has become one of the landmarks of European literature. Setting out from Malaucène at sunrise he climbed through a wild landscape of overgrown vegetation until he emerged into the clear mountain air above the treeline. Petrarch's route is thought to be the main footpath from Groseau, the GR4, which follows the north face of the mountain up to the summit. There are other routes on the southern slopes information on which, as well as the various outdoor activities of the Ventoux area, can be obtained from the Tourist Office at Bédoin (☎ 04 90 65 63 95).

Groseau was the site of a Benedictine abbey, the 12C chapel of Notre Dame being all that survives of the abbey church. The frescoes in this chapel actually date from the 14C having been executed for Pope Clement V who built a summer residence nearby as a retreat from Avignon. This has also disappeared but Clement is well known in the area. He had the original church in Malaucène, which was supposed to have been built by Charlemagne, pulled down and replaced it with the present fortified building as a refuge in case of trouble. What attracted Clement to Groseau was the spring which emerges from the rocks to the left of the road. This was the source of Vaison-la-Romaine's water in Roman times, carried to the town by an aqueduct.

The main road to the summit of Mont Ventoux may be less romantic than Petrarch's footpath but it can still be an exhilarating experience as the meandering route ascends through a series of hairpin bends over steep drops above the rocks below. The Tour de France still occasionally comes here in July although many feel it to be too demanding. A roadside memorial marks the spot where the English cyclist Tommy Simpson collapsed and died on the ascent in 1967.

At 1909m, **Mont Ventoux** is the tallest mountain in Provence but it is also rather enigmatic. The solid pyramidal shape looms large over much of the surrounding area and yet for all its sentimental associations it is loved more as a backdrop than as a place to visit. Climbers seem to enjoy it and it is a popular skiing resort in winter but the summit itself is rather disappointing. The shimmering white cap which appears as snow from a distance is actually an arid carpet of limestone gravel and at close quarters the effect is further spoiled by the ugly tourist complex and military radar mast. It can also be unhospitable when the Mistral is blowing. The name Ventoux (from 'vent') relates to this wind. The views are, of course, spectacular but they can only be appreciated on a clear day, so it is best to visit in the morning when there is less haze. There is a viewing table at the observatory and in the right conditions you can see from the Alps to the Pyrenees.

The descent of the eastern side, appropriately named the Col des Tempêtes, is even more dramatic than the west and leads on by the D164 to **Sault**, a small town in the rocks at the edge of the Plateau de Vaucluse. Sault is noted for its *charcuterie* and for the fields of lavender harvested in midsummer. It is an attractive town slightly off the main tourist routes but it is near the end of one of the gorge systems that cut through northern Provence, the **Gorges de la Nesque**, a spectacular rift through the white calcareous rock of the plateau. At its highest point there is a belvedere by the road looking across to the Rocher de Cire, a sheer cliff of 400m. The name Rock of Wax refers to the wild bee hives on the cliff which were harvested by the young men of Sault lowered on ropes over the chasm. The D942 follows the gorge back almost to Carpentras but before leaving Sault it is worth taking the D950 east for 7km to the tiny stone-built village of **Saint-Trinit**. The 12C church, once a priory of the Benedictine abbey of St-André at Villeneuve-Lès-Avignon, is a gem of Provençal Romanesque architecture.

Venasque and Pernes-les-Fontaines

The route back to Carpentras passes near two important medieval centres in the foothills of the Plateau de Vaucluse which should not be missed. The first of these is **Venasque**, a particularly attractive small village which belies its seminal role in the history of Provence. (Turn south onto the D1 at Mazan and after 5km turn left onto the D4.)

History of Venasque

During the Barbarian incursions of the 6C–10C the bishops of Carpentras retreated to this commanding position and made Venasque the effective capital of the region. In fact, Venasque gave its name to the Comtat-Venaissin. The presence of the bishopric accounts for the town's impressive series of early Christian and medieval buildings.

❖ *Information, accommodation and food*

🛈 Grand' Rue (☎ 04 90 66 11 66).

Hotel/restaurant. Les Ramparts (☎ 04 90 66 02 79) on rue Haute is a well recommended hotel and has a very good restaurant, while the *Auberge de la Fontaine* (☎ 04 90 66 02 96) on place de la Fontaine is excellent althgouh this is reflected in the prices of the rooms and the menu.

The most important of Venasque's medieval buildings is the so-called **baptistery** (☎ 04 90 66 11 41: guided tours of 15mins Thur–Tues 10.00–12.00 and 14.00–17.00 Mar–Nov; closed Wed). Built in the 6C on the site of an earlier pagan temple, this small cruciform structure is one of the earliest Christian buildings in France. There is considerable doubt, however, about its original function and appearance since it was substantially remodelled in the 11C to create a funerary chapel for one of the bishops. There was also an early 'cathedral' on the site but it was demolished at the same time (11C–12C) to create the church of Notre-Dame. The tomb of St Siffrein, the first 'Bishop of Carpentras and Venasque', is here, as are several other reminders of the great age of the bishopric, but the most interesting treasure is the altarpiece of the *Crucifixion* (1498) by a master of the School of Avignon.

If these early ecclesiastical remains are of interest, you should also visit the 17C **Chapelle de Notre-Dame-de-Vie**, just below the village by the D4, which houses the carved 7C tomb of Bishop Bohetius, a rare example of Merovingian art. Slightly further away to the south, past the fortified hamlet of Le Beaucet, is the **Oratoire de St-Gens**, a celebrated pilgrimage centre. On the nearest Saturday to 16 May a candlelit procession of farmers carries the saint's statue as a thanksgiving for rain.

Further west, **Pernes-les-Fontaines** is another charming town with an impressive history which is often overlooked by visitors to the region.

History of Pernes-les-Fontaines

It is said to have been founded by a 'Paternus' in Roman times but its greatest phase came in 1274 when the Comtat-Venaissin was handed over to the papacy. For almost 50 years Pernes was the capital of this wealthy region until in 1320 it was superseded by Carpentras. The remains of that period are still apparent in the towers and gateways of the old centre but another element was introduced to the townscape in the 18C. With the building of canals and irrigation schemes to open up the Comtat for agricultural development, Pernes and and its southern neighbour L'Isle-sur-la-Sorgue acquired water in abundance. This accounts for the numerous fountains which are spread throughout the town (36 in all) and which give it such a lyrical and relaxing atmosphere.

Pernes is best explored on foot so you should park at the cours Frizet on the north side of the river Nesque. Also on this side is the large **Collégiale de Notre-Dame-de-Nazareth**, an 11C–12C Romanesque building with some

❖ *Information and accommodation*

ℹ Place du Comtat-Venaissin (☎ 04 90 61 31 04).

Hotels. Places to stay in Pernes are limited to *La Margelle* at place Giraud (☎ 04 90 61 30 36) but there are better hotels in the surrounding area such as *Mas de la Bonoty* (☎ 04 90 61 61 09) by the D28 to St-Didier, or *Prato-Plage* (☎ 04 90 61 31 72) beside an artificial lake to the west.

refined architectural decoration on the interior. From the *parvis* or church grounds there is a good view across the bridge to the 16C **Porte Notre-Dame**, the finest of the old gates which once gave access through the town walls. Passing through here you will come immediately to the 18C Fontaine du Cormoran (Cormorant), one of the most beautiful of the many fountains that give Pernes its sobriquet.

The old quarter has many attractions that can be appreciated from even a casual walk around the narrow streets but you should look out for the crenellated **Tour Ferrande** at the end of the rue Victor-Hugo (guided tours arranged at the tourist office). This remnant of a palace built in the 13C by the Hospitallers of St John of Jerusalem has an important fresco cycle in the upstairs apartments depicting scenes from the conflict between Charles of Anjou and the Hohestaufens in southern Italy. There was also a substantial castle within the town belonging to the Counts of Toulouse but that was demolished leaving only part of the wall with the **Tour de l'Horloge**, from the top of which there is a beautiful view out over the surrounding country towards Carpentras and Avignon in the west.

11 · Fontaine, Roussillon and Apt

The road between Avignon and Fontaine-de-Vaucluse has been trodden by pilgrims for over 600 years. They were travelling not to see the site of a miracle or the relics of a saint, but because this was the route taken by the Renaissance poet Petrarch when he sought to escape the filth and corruption of Avignon. He found his refuge in the quiet valley where the river Sorgue rises and generations of scholars and devotees have followed him to Fontaine to recapture the love of nature and the spirit of lyricism that informed his art. This route, therefore, starts with the same journey but proceeds around the lower slopes of the Plateau de Vaucluse to Apt in the valley of the Calavon. This latter section enters the **Parc Naturel Régional du Luberon**, a protected area of great beauty and fascinating old villages. The itinerary visits a series of the most interesting villages, from the water channels of L'Isle-sur-la-Sorgue to the hilltop castle of Gordes and, even more unusual, the vivid red landscape of Roussillon. As a further contrast, the route also takes in the remote Val du Sénancole and the 12C Cistercian abbey of Sénanque.

Along the Sorgue

Leave Avignon by the N100, which passes some of the least attractive commercial suburbs of the city. This extensive industrial estate is the source of the city's modern prosperity but it is a wasteland of fenced-off factories and warehouses broken only by gaudy advertisements. Fortunately, it eases off after crossing the Autoroute du Soleil, giving way to pleasant rolling countryside with views over the plain towards Les Alpilles and the valley of the Durance. The first place of interest (13km) is **Châteauneuf-de-Gadagne**, an attractive village of old streets, fountains and some antiquities. The château, built in 1150 but abandoned even before the Revolution, survives only in its gateways and some fortifications. Other buildings of note are the 13C church and the 18C Tour de l'Horloge. The Félibrige poet Alphonse Tavan (1828–95) was born in Châteauneuf and the movement itself was founded at the château of Font-Ségugne nearby, where the seven members of the group were staying in 1854 (see p 102).

Continue on the N100 for 3.5km to **Le Thor**, one of the principal markets for the rich fruit production of the Sorgue valley and a village noted especially for its white dessert grapes. The 12C church of Notre-Dame-du-Lac is one of the finest in the region and has a particularly attractive setting in this medieval complex. The façade and the octagonal belltower are both unusual, as is the Classicising decoration on the doors. These elements are all in keeping with its overall character but the rather plain interior is lightened by some of the earliest examples of Gothic tracery over the Romanesque piers. Not much survives of the 12C castle and the same would have been true of the striking Porte Notre-Dame or Douzabas Gate, through which you enter the village from Avignon, had not this 'medieval' structure been almost entirely recreated in 1847.

In the Middle Ages the prominent hill Le Mourre-de-Diable, 3km north of the village on the D16, was a pilgrimage site with two chapels, both of which survived repeated sack and pillage. In 1902, as a result of some blasting for a quarry, a long cave was discovered at the foot of the hill which has interesting rock formations and stalactites. Since then a spurious legend has grown up that this cave had a secret entrance where a poor troubadour and his lover La Belle Noëlie found refuge in 1207 while escaping from Raymond VI.

Five kilometres further along the N100 is the fascinating market town of **l'Isle-sur-la-Sorgue**. Two branches of the Sorgue meet here creating the network of canals and water channels that surround the town centre and give it such a curious character. L'Isle is a convenient place from which to explore this area, especially when the more popular Fontaine-de-Vaucluse is busy.

History of l'Isle-sur-la-Sorgue

In ancient times this was a settlement of fishermen but by the late Middle Ages, when the community withdrew from the feudal control of the Venaissin, the Isle expanded as a commercial and manufacturing centre. In the 19C there were over 70 mills at work in the town. There are still waterwheels gently turning although they no longer have anything to do with weaving, olive oil, paper or any of the other milling industries which thrived here until quite recently. Despite this decline in manufacturing, the town retains a fairly prosperous and up-beat appearance, the highlight of local life being the lively antique and second-hand market which fills the streets on Sunday mornings throughout the year.

❖ *Information and accommodation*

🄸 Place de l'Eglise (☎ 04 90 38 04 78).

Hotels. Le Bassin (☎ 04 90 38 03 16) on avenue Ch. de Gaulle is a modest hotel by the river but, just outside town, the *Mas de Cure Bourse* (☎ 04 90 38 16 58), an 18C farmhouse with a good restaurant at Velorgues to the south, or *Le Pescador* (☎ 04 90 38 09 69) in Partages-des-Eaux to the north, are both more interesting.

There are several car parks at the perimeter of the old town from where you can walk to the place de l'Eglise and the tourist office in the centre. Overlooking this square is the large **Collégiale de Notre-Dame-des-Anges**, begun in the Gothic period but so extensively remodelled in the 17C by François Royer de la Valfrenière as to be one of the most impressive Baroque monuments in Provence. In its present form it was consecrated on 29 May 1672 by Jean-Baptiste de Sade, Bishop of Cavaillon. The interior is particularly opulent, combining rich architectural decoration with furniture, fittings and altarpieces by some of the leading artists from Avignon.

Behind the church at 20 rue du Dr-Tallet is the **Hôtel Donadeï de Campredon**, an 18C mansion which has been sensitively restored to house an art gallery (☎ 04 90 38 17 41: **open** Tues–Sun 10.00–13.00 and 15.00–19.00 July–Oct; 09.30–12.00 and 14.00–17.30 Nov–June; closed Mon). Some of the paintings in the collection belonged to René Char (1907–88), one of the greatest modern French poets and a member of the Surrealist group, who was born in L'Isle-sur-la-Sorgue. Char was an active Resistance leader in this area during the Second World War and he recounted some of his experiences in *Seuls demeurent* (1945), the collection of poems which made his reputation. There are a number of 16C–18C buildings in the town centre, one of the most important being the old hospital or **Hôtel-Dieu** (☎ 04 90 21 34 00: **open** Tues–Sat 09.00–12.00 and 14.00–17.00; closed Sun am and Mon) on the rue Jean-Théophile. Built in 1757 by two local architects, les Frères Brun, it has a handsome staircase in the entrance hall, some 17C–18C carved wooden figures and an old pharmacy laden with faience jars from Moustiers. The garden has an attractive 18C fountain.

Fontaine-de-Vaucluse

Leave L'Isle by the D938 to the north, turning right after 1km onto the D25 which leads directly to Fontaine-de-Vaucluse, one of the most famous sites in Provence due to its association with Petrarch. The 'fountain' is not exactly the source of the Sorgue but the point where the powerful underground river rises from a gaping grotto in the side of the mountain. Depending on the time of the year, this can either be a still dark pool within the cave or, in winter, a genuine torrent pouring out from the mouth of the cave into the river course. This natural phenomenon has attracted settlers and migrants since prehistoric times and was the base from which the hermit St Véran Christianised the region in the 6C. From that time onwards the site had strong religious associations and several churches and monasteries, as well as the village itself, were established in the area around the spring.

History of Fontaine-de-Vaucluse

Petrarch, who was attached to the papal court at Avignon, retired to Fontaine-de-Vaucluse in 1337 and stayed there intermittently for the next 15 years. During that time he composed the great *Canzonière* series of 366 sonnets inspired by Laura, the girl whom he had seen on 6 April 1327 in the convent of Ste-Claire in Avignon (see p 120). Such was the success and influence of these poems throughout Renaissance Europe that by the 16C many visitors to Provence would make the pilgrimage to Fontaine in homage to Petrarch. To this day it is solely a tourist centre with no industry or agriculture to talk of, and a population of only 604.

❖ *Information and accommodation*

🛈 Chemin de la Fontaine (☎ 04 90 20 32 22).

Hotels. Finding a place to stay in the village can be difficult, especially in summer, but the modest *Hostellerie Le Château* (☎ 04 90 20 31 54) is beautifully situated overlooking the river, while the *Hôtel du Parc* (☎ 04 90 20 31 57) at Les Bourgades, also by the river, has its own garden. Both these places also have very good restaurants.

At the edge of the village, not far from the car park, is a column erected in 1804 to commemorate the 500th anniversary of Petrarch's birth. Unfortunately, there is very little else in Fontaine to preserve the spirit of the place and none of the three museums succeeds in bringing its long history to life. The **Musée-bibliotèque Pétrarque** (☎ 04 90 20 37 20: **open** daily 09.30–12.00 and 14.00–18.30 June–Sept; 10.00–12.00 and 14.00–18.00 Oct–May; closed Tues in winter and Mon–Fri in April) was set up in 1927, reputedly on the site of the poet's house, and consists mainly of books related to Petrarch. The **Musée d'Histoire 1939–45** (☎ 04 90 20 24 00: **open** Wed–Mon 10.00–19.00 July–Aug; 10.00–12.00 and 14.00–18.00 Apr–June and Sept, Oct; shorter hours Nov, Dec, Mar; closed Tues and Jan, Feb) treats its subject in an interesting way reflecting the fact that the Vichy period is undergoing radical reconsideration in France.

Le Monde souterrain de Norbert Casteret (☎ 04 90 20 34 13; guided tours c 45min daily 10.00–12.00 and 14.00–18.30 June–Aug; closed Mon, Tues in Feb–May, Sept, Oct; closed Nov–Jan), is an underground gallery displaying a collection of rocks, crystals and other speleological samples assembled by France's famous cave explorer. Since the 19C the Fontaine has ' en the focus of much investigation to chart the various underwater channels and to establish the depth of the chasm. The most recent attempt was in 1985 when the Modexa, a remote-controlled submarine, reached 308m. Slightly beyond the museum is the **centre astisanal de Vallis Clausa**, a craft centre taking its title from the Latin name for the region. Occupying an old watermill, the centre was set up in 1976 to produce a range of hand-made papers using traditional methods.

Despite the varying interest of these museum and educational displays, the only palpable historic monument in Fontaine is the **Eglise Ste-Marie-et-St-Véran**, a 12C Romanesque church on the site of an earlier pagan shrine. There were several successive early Christian chapels here, one of which forms a crypt containing the tomb of St Véran, the first bishop of Cavaillon. Above this cramped and resonant space, the plain vaulted nave of the church is elaborated by fluted Roman columns and a number of interesting carvings of heads and masks at the cornice. Of the various furnishings, there is an interesting altar table remodelled from an antique marble, some good 15C polychrome sculpture and a copy of a painting by Pierre Mignard (1612–95) depicting *St Véran Driving out the Coulobre*, the monster who lived in the spring.

On the rock above the village you will see the ruined 13C castle of Philippe de Cabassole, the bishop of Cavaillon who first invited Petrarch to this area. There is a good view from this spot but the castle is probably better appreciated as a romantic ruin from the valley below. It does make for a reasonable walk, however, and there are several other good walks from Fontaine-de-Vaucluse into the plateau to the north and east. One in particular, along part of the GR6, leads across the lower slopes to the abbey of Sénanque.

East of Fontaine

Leave Fontaine by the D24, turning left onto the D99 and D100 by the villages of Lagnes and Cabrières-d'Avignon. There is not a great deal to see in either but the château at Lagnes has very early origins, being composed of two 12C baronial houses remodelled in the 16C to enclose a courtyard with the 12C chapel of St-Antoine. Cabrières suffered badly during the suppression of the Vaudois in 1545 but its castle and some of the ramparts have survived. Leave Cabrières by the D110, joining the D2 north to Gordes, a well known and very impressive hilltop village.

The approach to **Gordes** is one of the most spectacular in Provence since the village sits on a steep promontory of the plateau traversed on the ascent by olive terraces and crowned at the summit by the impressive Renaissance castle. The views across the Coulon valley to the Luberon are similarly outstanding.

History of Gordes

During the Wars of Religion in the 16C–17C Gordes was an important stronghold and at the time of the Revolution it was controlled by Louis de Bourbon, the Prince de Condé. The strength of its position and fortifications meant that Gordes was still a picturesque ensemble of 16C–17C houses grouped around the principal monuments when it was 'discovered' by the Cubist painter André Lhote (1885–1962) in 1938. It did not last for long. In reprisals for an attack by the Resistance in 1944, German troops destroyed much of the village, killing 13 people, and were only stopped from further destruction by the intervention of a monk from the nearby abbey of Sénanque. Since then the village has been largely rebuilt, albeit sensitively, but this has contributed to the overall impression of gentrification and outside colonisation. This effect is completed by the ubiquitous presence of Victor Vasarély, the Hungarian-born Op artist who bought the château in

1970 to establish a museum and study centre devoted to his own work and ideas. Following suit, other galleries and art studios have been opened in the last few years.

❖ Information and accommodation

🄵 Place du Château (☎ 04 90 72 02 75).

Hotels. There are several hotels and guest houses in the area although, like the village itself, they are fairly expensive. *La Bastide des Gordes* (☎ 04 90 72 12 12) on rue de la Combe is probably the best hotel and restaurant, but *La Mayanelle* (☎ 04 90 72 00 28) in a 17C mansion near the centre is very good.

The **château** at the highest point in the village was built in 1525 by Bertrand de Simiane on the remains of an earlier 12C fortress. The most impressive parts are the huge machicolated towers to the north but the whole complex encloses an interesting Renaissance courtyard. The finest room in the interior is the Great Hall which has an elaborate architectural chimneypiece from 1541. The **Musée Didactique Vasarély** (☎ 0490 72 02 89: **open** Wed–Mon 10.00–12.00 and 14.00–18.00; closed Tues) fills some five rooms with the abstract paintings, sculptures and prints that one has come to expect from this artist. There are one or two surprises, however, in the early figurative pieces, including two self-portraits.

Alongside the château, the 18C church of St-Firmin is the only other major building in Gordes. There are, however, several important monuments in the immediate vicinity about which you can find information at the tourist office.

A further 4km north of Gordes, in a desolate rocky valley, is the 12C **Abbaye de Sénanque** (☎ 04 90 72 05 72: **open** Mon–Sat 10.00–12.00 and 14.00–18.00 Mar–Oct; 14.00–17.00 Nov–Feb; closed Sun morning) one of the three Cistercian Sisters of Provence (see pp 177 and 195).

History of Abbaye de Sénanque

The abbey was founded in 1148 when a parcel of land in this remote valley of the Sénancole river was presented to a group of monks by the Simiane family, lords of the area. The remote location suited the ascetic life of prayer and solitude advocated by the Cistercians and over the next two centuries this large abbey complex gradually developed. The abbey appears to have thrived in its early years but this very success may have contributed to its decline. The accumulation of more land and the relaxing of the strict discipline led to disorder and corruption in the 14C and 15C. Then in 1544 the abbey was attacked by the Vaudois and the buildings badly damaged. Thereafter, various attempts to restore the abbey's position failed and it was eventually sold off by the Revolutionary government in 1792. During the 19C and 20C further attempts were made to re-establish the monastic community but they all failed. It is now operated indirectly by monks from St-Honorat and, to preserve something of the original spirit, is now used as a cultural centre with facilities for residential visitors seeking retreat.

In keeping with Bernard of Clairvaux's teaching the buildings are very plain with little decoration, a feature which makes them even more appealing to modern visitors who admire the purity of the forms and the simple clear lines of the architecture. The pale weathered stone likewise seems to present a certain ideal quality as well as merging beautifully with its natural surroundings.

The oldest part of the abbey buildings is the church itself, begun in 1160 and completed in the early 13C. The façade is interesting because it has no principal door. As if to discourage excessive pomp or grandeur, there are just two subsidiary portals which allow access to the side aisles of the five-bayed nave. Like its sister houses, the interior is a masterpiece of the Romanesque made more pure by the simplicity of its forms. A famous tribute in praise of medieval churches was to suggest that the proportions had a divine perfection and that if the building could sing 'it would sing in harmony'. This seems true here and, as if to confirm it, excellent concerts of choral and ancient music are held in the church during the summer. One item breaks the order of this bare interior: the 13C Gothic tomb of the Seigneur de Venasque against the wall in the transept. Attractive as this is, it is also an insight into the economics of salvation. The Seigneur would have paid a huge amount to have his tomb placed near the high altar, particularly in the church of such a devout community.

Alongside the church are the 12C cloisters, a beautiful ensemble of arches and decorated capitals, around which all the other abbey buildings are arranged. The refectory, the chapterhouse, the warming room and the dormitory can all be visited: there you will find a display on the history of the Cistercian order and, less predictably, a centre for studies into the nomadic peoples of the Sahara.

Two kilometres to the southwest of Gordes, off the D15, is the **Village des Bories** (☎ 04 90 72 03 48: open daily 09.00–sunset), a small settlement of dry-stone dwellings that have been restored as a museum of rural life. These *bories*, which were quite common in the Luberon area until the 19C, have prompted considerable controversy as to their origins. For many local chroniclers they bear a remarkable similarity to ancient Mediterranean tomb constructions although most other historians remain unconvinced. There has also been much speculation about the structure of ancient herdsmen's dwellings that may have been handed down through countless generations to the shepherds of upper Provence. The *bories* in this village are no older than the 17C and are not part of an unbroken ancient tradition. Nevertheless, as a pattern of vernacular building, possibly for livestock, they sit well in the landscape, reminding some visitors of certain types of contemporary 'land art'.

Dry stone 'borie' of the Luberon

Further down the D15 turn left into the D103 and again into the D148 towards St-Pantaléon to arrive at the **Musée de Vitrail** and the **Moulin des Bouillons** (☎ 04 90 72 22 11: open Wed–Mon 10.00–12.00 and 14.00–18.00 Apr–Oct; closed Tues and Dec–Feb). Both these establishments are run by the stained-glass artist Frédéric Duran, one to display his own work alongside examples of earlier stained glass, and the other, in a 16C–18C mill, to demonstrate aspects of the history of olive-oil culture. The latter is enriched by a splendid old oil-press made from a single oak tree and by the charming enthusiasm of the guide, Madame Duran.

Continuing on this road for 4km you arrive at the tiny village of **Saint-Pantaléon**, which has only 91 inhabitants. It is a pilgrimage centre with a small Romanesque chapel built into the rock over an even earlier necropolis. Around the chapel are numerous small tombs cut into the rock which have given rise to the suggestion that they were intended for children. Linked to this was a legend that infants who died before baptism could be revived during the mass so as to receive the sacrament. In an age of high infant mortality such a belief must have appealed to thousands of bereaved parents who brought their dead children to be interred here.

Leave St-Pantaléon by the D148 north, turning left after 2km into the D104 and then right into the D169. **Roussillon** is visible from some distance, standing on the most prominent hill in this relatively flat valley. It is also announced by the increasingly vivid red-ochre soil, from which the village takes its name. The impact of the various hues, which range from deep orange to pink and yellow, is further exaggerated by the stained and crumbling rock formations, suggesting a surreal or alien landscape. One of the best spots to see this effect is at the **Chaussée des Géants** (Giants' Pathway) leading out of the village to the southeast by the cemetery, where the erosion has created ravines and jagged points in the cliff face.

History of Roussillon

Roussillon has had a troubled history. It was besieged and ravaged in the 16C Wars of Religion and during the Revolution suffered the indignity of having its mayor executed at Orange. Samuel Beckett passed much of the Occupation here in hiding and was an active member of the local Resistance. Despite these occasional distractions, however, he found the boredom of village life unbearable and referred to it obliquely in *Waiting for Godot*.

Nowadays Roussillon is one of the most popular tourist sights in the Vaucluse and, in summer, the local authorities have to lay aside some of the surrounding fields for parking. All this is in marked contrast to the 'agricultural community' discovered by the American sociologist Laurence Wylie and recorded in his book *A Village in the Vaucluse*. In 1950, when he first visited the area, Roussillon was greatly depopulated and only held together by a few close families who worked the land and the ochre quarries. Nowadays it is dominated by second or holiday homes and the principal industry is tourism.

The best route into the village is by the place de la Mairie and through the mainly 19C Tour de l'Horloge leading to the **castrum** at the top. This was the fortified stronghold in the Middle Ages and is now a viewing-point from where you can see over the whole of the Coulon valley between the Plateau de Vaucluse and the Luberon. Nearby is the 12C Romanesque church which was originally the castle chapel and now overlooks the small village square. This area is noted for its *fêtes* in summer and that in Roussillon is one of the liveliest. Local bands, dancing, fireworks and copious amounts of drinking are a reminder of what village life could be but nowadays it is attended mostly by weekend house-owners.

Leave Roussillon by the D227 east which after 6km joins the D2 to **Saint-Saturnin-lès-Apt**.

History of Saint-Saturnon-lès-Apt

An ancient tradition suggests that St-Saturnin was the site of a battle between the Roman generals Sylla and Marius in the 1C BC but there is little evidence to support it. Instead, one can certainly point to very early settlements on the rocky escarpment behind the town and to the existence of a castle and a monastery at the top of the rock since the 10C. These were replaced by a Templars' priory devoted to St Maurice in 1176 and followed by further rebuilding of the church and fortifications in the following centuries. By the 17C the population had moved down to the gentler agricultural land below the rocks and there are several ornate doorways which testify to the wealth of the district in this period.

In the mid-19C St-Saturnin was the scene of a famous religious controversy when various visions and miracles were linked to a local girl, Rosette Tamisier. On one occasion blood flowed from a painting of the Crucifixion in the church after she had kissed the wounds of Christ. This and other events prompted a papal enquiry as a result of which Rosette was imprisoned in 1851. From this point onwards the miracles ceased and on her release nine months later she disappeared without trace.

The rather dull parish church of St-Etienne at the centre of St-Saturnin replaced an earlier Romanesque church which was demolished as recently as 1860. Not content with this, a Carolingian crypt was also filled in during the construction of the new building. Much more interesting are the chapel and fortifications of the **castrum**, access to which is gained by ascending the stairs to the left of the church. From here, a rock-strewn path leads up through the remains of the 13C–15C ramparts and alongside the dam to the 11C chapel of St-Saturnin. An inscription in the apse records the consecration in 1048 and 1055. The chapel has been recently restored but is unfortunately not open to the public.

From St-Saturnin the D943 leads directly to Apt, 9km due south.

Apt

Apt, the main town in the Parc Naturel Régional du Luberon, has an illustrious history. Its industries include an old tradition of faience manufacture and of ochre quarrying and there is also a substantial confectionary factory in the town supplemented by the local producers of fruit preserves. Indeed, jams and candied fruit are the town's most famous products and they are featured—alongside the rich local agricultural produce—at the busy market held throughout the town on Saturday mornings. This is one of the liveliest local markets in Provence, made even more interesting because it is still intended for, and supported by, local people. In an area much given over to tourism, Apt does not play the rustic village role expected of it by Anglo-Saxons.

History of Apt

Its ancient name, Apta Julia, was conferred in honour of Julius Caesar, possibly in the wake of his victorious campaign in Spain, but it had been settled by numerous peoples before that time. There is a legend that the Emperor Hadrian hunted in the area and that when Boristhenes, his favourite horse, was killed the Aptesians built a mausoleum for the animal. They were rewarded for their obsequiousness with further privileges. The town was already well situated on the Via Domitia and was quite a prosperous centre, which made it vulnerable to Barbarian incursions between the 3C and 6C, and to the Saracens in the 9C.

Christianity was established very early by St Auspice in the 3C and confirmed by SS Castor and John Cassian from Marseille but it was not until the cult of St Anne developed that Apt became a great centre for pilgrimage. There are in fact two legends associated with St Anne, the mother of the Virgin. The first, and more prosaic, relates to a cape, claimed to be that worn by the saint, which was brought to Provence in the 3C by a pilgrim from the Holy Land. This alone would have ensured considerable prestige for the cathedral but it was enhanced by a legend that St Anne had herself visited the region, her remains being miraculously discovered in the crypt during the service of consecration in 776. St Anne was invoked for fertility by childless women, which made Apt a very popular pilgrimage centre—all the more so after the visit of Anne of Austria, future mother of Louis XIV, in 1623. To confirm the celebrity of the town and the potency of the relics she returned in 1660 with her son, by this time the king. To this day the saint's feast is celebrated on 26 July by offerings of grapes, one of the fruits for which the area is justly celebrated.

Alongside its cathedral and bishopric, Apt was an important administrative and political capital during the later Middle Ages. The Holy Roman Emperor Frederick II convened a parliament here during the 13C, and the town enjoyed considerable privileges from the papacy at Avignon. There were, however, setbacks to this tale of success. The religious wars of the 16C and 17C wrought havoc here, as they did throughout the Luberon, and Apt was also prone to outbreaks of plague which at times seemed endemic to the town. During the Revolution, Lauze de Perret, the prefect for Apt, was guillotined for complicity with Charlotte Corday in the murder of Marat and this was followed up by a few more executions locally to press home the point. The town was similarly active in the revolution of 1848, and the *coup d'état* of 1851 prompted an insurrection following which several locals were exiled to Nice.

The best place to begin a visit to Apt, especially on market days, is the place de la Bouquerie which is fringed by cafés. From here the rue du Dr-Gros leads into the old town, at the centre of which is the former **Cathédrale Ste-Anne** (☎ 04 90 74 36 60: opening times can vary, but normally Tues–Sat 09.00–12.00 and 15.30–18.00; closed Mon; guided tours of treasury from 1 July–30 Sept at 11.00 and 17.00) with its 16C clocktower. The main part of this church,

❖ *Information, accommodation and food*

🛈 Avenue Philippe-de-Girard (☎ 04 90 74 03 18).

Hotels. The best and most reasonable hotel is the *Auberge du Luberon* (☎ 04 90 74 12 50) on the opposite bank of the river at 17 quai Léon-Sagy.
   In the surrounding area, the *Relais de Roquefure* (☎ 04 90 04 88 88), at Le Chêne 6km to the west, is very good as is the *Auberge de Presbytère* (☎ 04 90 74 11 50) in Saignon to the southeast on the road towards the Grand Luberon.

Restaurants. The *Auberge du Luberon* (see above) has a good restaurant specialising in local dishes.

notably the nave and south aisle, dates from the 12C with further additions of the 14C and 16C but there are foundations of earlier buildings stretching back to Roman times. This long history is amply demonstrated by the two crypts, placed one above the other. The upper crypt dates from the 11C but it stands over an early Christian shrine at the end of a narrow vaulted passage possibly marking the site of a 3C martyrdom. During the Middle Ages these chambers were opened to processions of pilgrims who had travelled from all over Provence to see and touch the holy relics. After the visit of Anne of Austria in 1660 a rather more grand royal chapel was built in the north aisle and the relics were placed there.

The **treasury** has an interesting collection including 12C manuscripts, medieval enamels from Limoges and a number of reliquaries. The most important item is the 'veil' of St Anne, an object fascinating not for its links with the mother of the Virgin but because it is actually an Egyptian or Coptic textile from the 11C. Among the other features of the church is a good 12C altar in the south apse with Classical decoration and some interesting Romanesque carvings of the signs of the Evangelists at the base of the cupola.

Nearby, in the rue de l'Amphithéâtre, is the **Musée Archéologique** (☎ 04 90 74 00 34; **open** Wed–Mon 10.00–12.00 and 14.00–17.00 June–Sept; 14.00–17.00 Oct–May; closed Tues) housed in a renovated 18C mansion. The collection consists of numerous Gallo-Roman antiquities, some ecclesiastical treasures from the former cathedral, various items of local history and some examples of the faïence ware produced in Apt since the 18C. For something more palatable, albeit sickly, you might try a tour of the Apt-Union factory (☎ 04 90 76 31 31) to the west of town where much of the local fruit is candied.

Apt is an excellent base from which to explore the Parc Naturel Régional du Luberon (see pp 154 and 160). Information on the area can found at the tourist office (see above) or at the **Maison du Parc Naturel Régional du Luberon** (☎ 04 90 04 42 00) at the place Jean-Jaurès. The latter, as well as covering all aspects of the flora and fauna, also has a small museum of palaeontology with interactive displays.

12 · Cavaillon and the Petit Luberon

The area round the long chain of mountains known as the Grand and the **Petit Luberon** has been designated a national park since 1977, which means that no new building or industrial developments are allowed to encroach on the traditional landscape within its boundary. It is not difficult to understand this policy, because the area has some of the most beautiful scenery in the south of France. Indeed, these wooded hillsides and tightly clustered villages have come to represent a sort of archetypal Provence in which patterns of life developed over centuries are expressed in the landscape.

History of the Petit Luberon

This was what the advertising executive Peter Mayle recognised when he wrote *A Year in Provence*, describing an idyllic rural life near Ménerbes. The book confirmed a notion of Provençal life that many had already sensed at second hand. But it was also a misleading fantasy that idealised an area riven with problems. The Luberon was chronically depopulated, with the land falling into disuse in some parts as the old farmhouses were taken over by wealthy townspeople from northern Europe and America.

This compounded a more deep-rooted problem going back to the 16C when the Luberon had been a largely Protestant area populated by Waldensians or Vaudois, followers of the sect of Pierre Valdo. On 18 April 1545 a campaign to suppress the Protestants was initiated by the burning of Merindol and the massacre of the entire community. Over the following months all the Protestant villages were attacked, thousands were killed in a form of religious 'cleansing' and the area was laid waste. The population levels never really recovered thereafter.

To travel through this area now is to be reminded constantly of the waves of brutality that have enveloped even the smallest communities and yet also to see a landscape of surpassing beauty bathed in warm southern light. It is a paradox that makes the Luberon one of the most sensual and arresting parts of Provence.

This route covers the sequence of villages along the northern slopes of the Petit Luberon, moving from Cavaillon eastwards towards Apt and taking in Oppède, Ménerbes, Lacoste and Bonnieux. It is a journey that must be taken by car or, for the more energetic, by bicycle, because public transport is all but non-existent.

Cavaillon

Cavaillon is a prosperous market town at the centre of one of the richest agricultural areas in France. It has enjoyed this prosperity for centuries but nowadays it is known principally for the sweet melons that are harvested in May and sold in the street markets during the summer. This succulent fruit so appealed to Alexandre Dumas that in 1864 he presented a set of his books to the local library on condition that the people of Cavaillon sent twelve melons to him in Paris every year. It is not a picturesque town, causing many visitors to pass it by, but it has several attractions, not least the sense that it has a purpose in life separate from the tourist industry. It is also well placed to begin any tour of the Luberon, because the main railway and bus stations in the area are located here. These are both situated in the place de la Gare at the eastern edge of the town.

History of Cavaillon

Even in ancient times Cavaillon, or Cabellio as it was known, had certain advantages. As well as the agricultural wealth of the area, the town levied tolls for the bridge at this crossing-point of the Durance. On one side of coins in the local museum you can see a horn of plenty, which must have been an appropriate symbol. In 396 St Genialis became one of the earliest Christian bishops in Provence and the prestige attached to his seat was maintained by close links to the papacy thereafter. In 1562, however, Cavaillon was sacked by Protestants under the Baron des Adrets. Restored to prosperity, largely through the development of canals for irrigation and the arrival of the railways for distribution of the local produce, Cavaillon is now the largest National Market in France.

❖ *Information and accommodation*

🛈 79 rue Saunerie (☎ 04 90 71 32 01).

Hotels. It should not be difficult to find a room in Cavaillon but there is not a great choice. *The Toppin* (☎ 04 90 71 30 42) on the cours Gambetta is probably the best hotel, but *Le Parc* (☎ 04 90 71 57 78) at place du Clos is reasonable. Two kilometres outside town, *Le Christel* (☎ 04 90 71 07 79) at Digues-des-Grands-Jardins is a more modern hotel with a swimming pool.

The hub of the town is the place Gambetta, a busy road junction with a fountain surrounded by anonymous buildings. The best place to start any tour, however, is the cours Bournissac and the tree-lined place du Clos to the south. At the bottom of the *place* and dwarfed by the huge cliff of the Colline St-Jacques is the so-called *arc de triomphe*, in fact two carved stone archways which were probably part of the 1C gateway to the Roman town. Behind this is a stepped pathway leading up the rock to the 12C **Chapelle St-Jacques** (45 mins). Half-way up an inscription to Frédéric Mistral is carved in the rockface and beyond it are a calvary and memorial tablet to the people of Cavaillon who died in the plague of 1630. The chapel itself has been heavily restored but there is an excellent view over the Luberon. If the prospect of the walk is too much, there is access by car via the D938 to the north of the town.

Returning to the place du Clos, it is worth looking into the *Café Fin-de-Siècle* at No. 42, one of several old cafés with some of their original fittings. Alongside this is the passage Vidau leading to the place P. de Cabassol, an attractive part of the old town with several interesting buildings and the 16C gateway. Straight ahead is the **Cathédrale St-Véran** but it is so crowded by other buildings that it is difficult to identify the full size or shape of this basilica. Furthermore, the main façade on the place Voltaire is a dull and crumbling 18C addition that does little to attract the passing visitor. This is unfortunate, because the cathedral is one of the most unusual in Provence. Begun in the late 12C, it was extended in the 13C and 14C to include a series of lateral chapels. Attacked and set on fire during the Wars of Religion, it required even more alterations in the 17C and 18C which overlayed much of its medieval origins. The best entrance is by the cloister, a delightful small courtyard with a plain arcade of crumbling, weathered stone. From here you can see the clock tower and the main octagonal tower with its fine Classical details. After this, the rich and gloomy interior comes as a complete contrast. In essence the nave is pure 12C Romanesque but the stonework is covered with painted decoration which, along with the gilded altarpieces and rich furnishings, glows in the dark like some Byzantine ensemble. Look out for the funerary monument of Monseigneur de Sade, a vigorous 18C marble group in which the figure of Death, consulting his book, reaches out to claim the prelate. There are also several good 17C altarpieces by Nicolas Mignard (1606–68) and Pierre Parrocel and fine woodwork on the organ and choir stalls.

On leaving the church it is worth taking rue Diderot along the north side to see something of the exterior. Much of it appears as a rambling assortment of different walls and variegated masonry but the five-sided choir at the east end is marked by elegant Romanesque pilasters. The rue Raspail leads to the place Castil-Blaze, 100m further on to the east, which marks the central point of the old town and is named after a local poet and folklorist. In rue Chabran to the right is the old **synagogue** of Cavaillon (☎ 0490 76 00 34; **open** Wed–Mon 09.30–12.00 and 14.00–18.00 June–Sept; 10.00–12.00 and 14.00–17.00 Oct–May; closed Tues), the entrance to which is under the arch leading into the cobbled rue Hebraïque. The lower part of this building is the oldest, dating from the 15C, but the principal attraction is the synagogue itself on the first floor. Built in 1774 in an elaborate Rococo style, the interior has a lightness of effect and a decorative quality that is not normally associated with religious buildings. The elaborate ironwork is by a local craftsman, François Isoire, and the glass chandelier is Venetian. The whole building was recently renovated and the lower part now houses a small museum of Jewish life and culture.

North of this on the corner of Grand Rue and the busy cours Gambetta is an 18C hospital or Hôtel-Dieu which now houses the **Musée Archéologique** (☎ 04 90 76 00 34; same ticket and times as the synagogue). The collection covers most periods in the history of the town but the most memorable feature is the interior of the building itself, a plain but harmonious chapel that has a number of architectural fragments displayed around the floor.

Villages of the Petit Luberon

From place Gambetta, the D2 leaves Cavaillon towards Apt via Robion 5.5km away. To avoid the main road, which is outside the national park at this point and therefore marked by new developments and factories, after 4km turn off to the right beside an old mill to **Les Taillades**. After 1km you will arrive at the old village with its narrow stone streets climbing up to the lower slopes of the Luberon. Some of the medieval walls survive and at the top of the village there is an 18C church and a castle dating from the 17C which is set within the rock. The most interesting building, however, is the Romanesque Chapelle Ste-Luce which is now part of the presbytery.

From here you can follow a meandering route through Robion and Maubec, each with some interesting features, before reaching the fascinating and somewhat ruinous settlement of **Oppède-le-Vieux**. This village was almost deserted until recent years, the population having abandoned it in 1910 for the gentler terrain of Oppède-les-Poulivets 2km to the north. Despite the current renovation of some of the houses round the main square and the gradual encroachment of tourism, this is still one of the most striking and evocative sites in the Luberon. Built on a steep rocky outcrop with a 12C castle at the most strategic point, it presents a formidable series of obstacles to the casual walker. The streets are littered with the masonry of collapsed walls and, in the upper reaches near the **castle**, there are perilous paths and walkways in which gaping holes open out over a sheer drop of 15m to the rocks below.

History of Oppède-la-Vieux

The castle of Oppède dates originally from the 12C but it was enlarged in the 15C–16C and came to play a notorious role in the history of the region. Controlled by the papacy and occupied successively by the Counts of Forcalquier, the Counts of Provence and the lords of Les Baux, it was given in 1501 to the Meynier family who, as barons of Oppède, established a rapacious control on the area. It was from Oppède that Jean Meynier directed the massacres of the Vaudois in 1545 and it is said that he and his allies from Aix gathered on the walls to witness the burning of the village of Cabrières across the valley. Meynier was put on trial in Aix for these atrocities but acquitted. He died in 1551, however, reputedly poisoned by a Protestant doctor.

During the Second World War, Consuelo de Saint-Exupéry, wife of the novelist Antoine, established a colony of artists and architects known as the Group of Oppède dedicated to preserving and rebuilding French culture in those dark times. After the war they dispersed but in recent years J.-B. Clébert, one of the leading collectors of Provençal folklore and history, has lived here.

Slightly higher up the hill from the castle is the **Eglise de Notre-Dame-d'Alydon**, dating originally from the 12C but largely rebuilt in the 16C and restored in the 19C.

Just over 4km to the east of Oppède-le-Vieux, the D188 climbs steeply to the ancient village and citadel of **Ménerbes**. The village occupies a long narrow outcrop of rock, often compared to a ship, which has been settled since Neolithic times.

History of Ménerbes

In the Middle Ages this village was known as Manencha, probably taken from the Roman Machovilla, suggesting a link with the ancient cult of Minerva. During the 16C it became the Protestant capital of the region, withstanding a five-year siege by the army of Henri de Vendôme before it eventually fell in 1579. During the Second World War and the Occupation Ménerbes resumed its role as the nerve centre of the area, becoming an important base for Resistance activities in the Vaucluse.

The principal building in the heart of the village is the castle or **citadel**, originating from the 13C although largely rebuilt in the 16C following the siege. For over 30 years this was the home of the American art historian John Rewald, author of pioneering books on the Impressionists. Beside the castle there is a bust of the Provençal poet Clovis Hugues (1851–1907) who was born in Ménerbes. Moving westwards through the place de l'Horloge you pass the Mairie, which has a 17C bell tower, before arriving at the small 14C **Eglise de l'Assomption**. This has an interesting cemetery and terrace with spectacular views over the plain and up to the Luberon itself.

Immediately below this, built into the original walls of the village, is the beautiful 15C fortified house of **Le Castellet**. In the late 18C Count Rantzau of Denmark took refuge here after a court scandal in Copenhagen when the queen's lover, Frederick Struensee, was murdered. Rantzau is buried near the house. The French abstract painter Nicolas de Staël bought Le Castellet in 1953, two years before his suicide at Antibes. His widow still lives here. Ménerbes has attracted many other distinguished artists. In July 1945 Picasso acquired a house in the ramparts in exchange for one of his paintings but he never lived there. Instead he gave it to his lover, the Yugoslavian artist and photographer Dora Maar, thereby indicating that he was about to leave her for Françoise Gilot.

The area between Ménerbes and Bonnieux is the setting for Peter Mayle's hugely popular accounts of expatriate life in Provence. So successful have these books been that many of the locals and most of the incomers who sought the simplicity that he described now find their idyll shattered by visitors clutching copies of *A Year in Provence*. Indeed, the effects of the book were so great that several of his neighbours launched a campaign against Mayle, one of them writing a rival book that refuted most of his descriptions of life in the area.

Six kilometres east of Ménerbes, past the 12C–13C abbey of St-Hilaire (private), is **Lacoste**, one of the most attractive of all the ancient villages of the Petit Luberon. Part of its appeal is undoubtedly due to its situation, which offers excellent views out over the valley, but Lacoste has a fascinating history and the old part has not yet been over-restored. The winding cobbled streets that climb the hill to the castle of the Marquis de Sade are still in picturesque disorder that contributes much to its atmospheric quality.

As a Protestant centre close to Catholic Bonnieux, Lacoste suffered greatly in the suppression of the Vaudois in 1545 which left the village chronically depopulated. The religious tradition was maintained, nevertheless, and the Mairie now occupies an abandoned Protestant church. The previous civic building is in a warren of narrow passages at the heart of the old village, recognisable only by its decorative wrought-iron belfry sticking up over the rooftops. The upper part of the village, until recently deserted, is now occupied by an American art school which runs classes throughout the year. The students can be seen sketching or hanging out at the two cafés, much to the fascination of the local youths.

At the very top of the hill is the **Château de Lacoste** (☎ 04 90 75 80 39; **open** by appointment), built originally in 1038 but repeatedly destroyed and rebuilt ever since. The early owners of this impressive pile were the Simiane family but in 1716 it was passed on to François Gaspard de Sade. His grandson, the 'Divine' Marquis de Sade, spent a considerable amount of time here between jail sentences, and the debaucheries described in *Justine* and *The 120 Days of Sodom* are often associated with this residence. It is now owned by M. Bouer whose mission to restore the building has detracted from its earlier character as a ruin, but it remains a striking landmark on the hilltop above the village. Behind the castle is an interesting plateau rarely visited by tourists but concealing some abandoned quarries with cavernous chambers cut into the solid white rock. Students from the art school occasionally work here. There are examples of the sculpture of an eccentric early 20C miller and primitive artist called Malachier in the gardens of the house nearest the castle.

Facing Lacoste on the hillside across the valley is the distinctive triangular shape of **Bonnieux**, one of the largest of the Luberon villages (1360 inhabitants). In recent years Bonnieux has attracted a great many new residents and second-home owners who, far from destroying the character of the village, seem to have created a livelier atmosphere than that of its neighbours.

History of Bonnieux

Bonnieux is an ancient settlement whose early name was Mitrone (mitre), suggesting a close link with the Church, and it is true that the settlement was a papal protectorate up until the Revolution. This accounts for the relative wealth of the village, seen in the range of substantial houses from the 16C–18C, but it also placed Bonnieux in opposition to the Protestant and Vaudois communities that surrounded it. As a result, there are numerous stories of massacres and reprisals running throughout the history of the village.

🄸 Place Carnot (☎ 04 90 75 91 90).

It is worth looking out for the tourist office, partly because the layout of the village is confusing and you can easily drive up the zig-zag road and out the other side without recognising the main centre. Leave the car in one of the car parks by the main road and make for the Mairie in the 17C Hôtel de Rouville, behind which is a steep lane leading up to the belvedere. At the summit, the 12C **Romanesque church** has some interesting treasures including a carved and gilded retable dating from the 15C and a 17C painting of *St Francis of Assisi* by Nicolas Mignard. Alongside the church is the cemetery enclosed by the old village ramparts and shaded by ancient cedar trees. This was once a primitive citadel but is now a public garden with marvellous views over the Petit Luberon and down the valley to Apt.

In the lower village, at rue de la République, there is an old bakery which now houses an enjoyable **Musée de la Boulangerie** (open Wed–Mon 10.00–12.00 and 15.00–18.30 May–Oct; Sat, Sun only Apr, May and Oct–Dec; closed Jan, Feb) devoted to the history of breadmaking and to the significance of bread in society. On the first floor there is a good library with a terrace from which visitors can see over the village and surrounding countryside. In the summer there are temporary exhibitions of the work of local artists. Finally, at the bottom of the village, the 'new' church (1870) contains an interesting collection of 15C and 16C paintings illustrating scenes from the Passion.

From Bonnieux the D3 leads directly to Apt, the principal town and capital of the region. For a more ambitious excursion, however, take the small road leading uphill to the south of the village to join the *Route du Petit Luberon*, which follows the crest of the mountain along its full length. For most of the way it is shrouded in trees on both sides but it is a fascinating trip into remote areas rich in the distinctive flora and fauna of the Luberon. Care must be taken at certain times of the year, however, especially at weekends, because the local huntsmen stalk wild boar in the woods here and do not always pay attention to other ramblers.

As an alternative ending to the route, the D36 from Bonnieux leads into the D943 and the **Combe de Lourmarin** through the only gap in the Luberon range. This is the main route to the southern side of the mountains. You can return to Cavaillon following the line of the Petit Luberon, passing several very interesting and historic villages such as Lauris and Merindol (see p 162).

13 · Villages of the Grand Luberon

The **Grand Luberon** is a rounded massif rising to well over 1000m at its highest point, Le Mourre Nègre. In some respects it is darker and less picturesque than its neighbour to the west, the Petit Luberon, but in fact the two share a great deal. They are both rich in flora and fauna, both studded with famous archaeological sites and, above all, both marked by a violent history that has shaped the villages and the architecture of the area. It is this combination which prompted the creation of the Parc Régional du Luberon to protect the landscape from modern developments and which make it an excellent area to explore by car (there is very little public transport to talk of). There are numerous places where you can head off from the main roads onto the paths and tracks across the wooded hillsides, or you could plan a more ambitious excursion, perhaps following the *Grandes Randonnées* (National Pathways), two of which, GR92 and GR97, traverse the park at this section. This route, however, has been planned to visit a series of the most picturesque medieval villages, beginning at Apt on the north side and continuing through the Combe de Lourmarin to the villages on the southern slopes of the mountain.

North of the Grand Luberon

Leave Apt by the D48, a minor road which climbs up to the northern slopes of the Grand Luberon arriving, after 4km, at **Saignon**. This is a rugged site which has been occupied since Neolithic times and it is known locally as the *avant garde* or fortress of Apt due to its strategic position overlooking one of the approach roads. As such, it has been fought over by various ruling factions and at one stage in the 12C there were three separate castles perched on these rocks, each one belonging to a different rival family. After 1309, however, much of the district was stabilised under the protection of the Count of Provence who suppressed some of the more unruly groups.

The old village of Saignon is strung out on a saddle of land between the church on one side and the ruined castle opposite, rival symbols of temporal and religious authority. The church, dating from the 12C, has the simple lines that one associates with the early Romanesque but, in this case, it is the details that are worth seeking out. On one outside wall, for example, four antique marble columns have been incorporated into the base, while in the interior to the right of the main doorway there is a puzzling inscription in Greek. The church also possesses an important Gothic reliquary containing a fragment of the True Cross.

One kilometre east of Saignon on the D174 are the remains of the **Abbaye St-Eusébe**, a Benedictine foundation related to St-Gilles-du-Gard. There are several mysteries surrounding this establishment, one being that it was founded in early Christian times by Eusebius himself. More puzzling, however, is the later history of the community. These buildings, now in farmland, were abandoned by the monks in 1471 for reasons that have never been fully explained.

South of Saignon by the D232 and D114 is **Sivergues** (38 inhabitants), a wild and remote village which was once an outpost of the Vaudois. Alongside the remains of the fortifications and the 12C church of St-Trophîme, there are still some ruined houses from the period of the massacres in 1545. There are footpaths from here up to the ridge of the Grand Luberon and the radio mast at **Mourre Négre**, the highest point on the mountains. The climb takes about two hours but provides an outstanding view over the whole region.

Like Sivergues, its neighbour **Buoux** suffered terribly during the religious wars which resulted in the serious depopulation of the village. There are a few surviving monuments including an 18C church with an ancient altar and an impressive castle (private), composed of distinct 13C, Renaissance and 18C wings. The village is also well known for the archaeological discoveries made here which have revealed traces of Neolithic settlements and possibly even Neanderthal man. The principal reason for visiting Buoux, however, is to gain access to two monuments. Further up the D113 and to the left along a footpath is the **Fort de Buoux**, a ruined citadel on a spectacular promontory of rock above the valley of the Aigue Brun. This point overlooks the only pass through the Luberon, thus guaranteeing its strategic importance. In fact, the site has been fortified since Ligurian times and each generation has relied on this stronghold for protection. It was an important bastion of the Protestants during the 16C and was eventually destroyed on the orders of Louis XIV. Even now there is a sense of both the strength and the violence surrounding this position as you clamber over the ruins.

The other monument, some 2km west and also accessible from the D113, is the remains of the 12C Romanesque **Prieuré St-Symphorien**. There are two chapels in the complex but the finest part is the simple square tower, best seen from a distance standing out from the carpet of trees and foliage on the hillside. The D113 rejoins the main road, the D943 south, following the Combe de Lourmarin, the winding pass which, for centuries, was the only route through the 50km barrier formed by the two Luberon ranges. Part of its attraction is the rugged countryside and steep cliffs that still give the area an uneasy atmosphere. The road was certainly prone to bandits who, it is sometimes claimed, still preyed on travellers well into the 20C.

South of the Grand Luberon

On emerging from the pass you arrive at **Lourmarin**, a substantial and rather smart village with an elegant Renaissance château. The **castle** (☎ 04 90 68 15 23; guided tours July–Aug 09.30–11.30 and 15.00–18.00; Sept–June at

110.00 and 14.30–16.30; closed Tues Nov–Mar) was built in two distinct phases, the older wing dating from 1495–1525 and the later 'new château' from 1540 onwards. The two parts are unmistakable; the earlier wing resembles a medieval stronghold with tower, loopholes and a dungeon, while the later wing shows obvious links with the courtly châteaux on the Loire. Nevertheless, they sit very well together. The building was abandoned during the 19C and became a regular staging-post for Gypsies, which attracted a lot of superstitious talk. According to one local legend, the Gypsies cursed the industrialist Robert Laurent-Vibert when he bought the castle in 1921 and began renovating it. He died in a car accident in 1925 but bequeathed the castle to the Academy of Aix to be maintained as a 'Villa Medici' in support of the arts. The interior has some impressive Renaissance fittings, notably the spiral staircase and the fireplaces, some Provençal and Spanish furniture and a modest collection of paintings.

In the village itself, the parish church has some traces of its original Romanesque structure but the bulk of it dates from the late 19C. The writer Albert Camus bought a house in Lourmarin in 1958 and it was from here that he embarked on the car journey to Paris in 1960 on which he and his publisher Gallimard were killed. Camus is buried in the village cemetery.

Notre-Dame-de-la-Purifaction

It is worth taking a short detour of 4.5km to **Lauris**, a substantial village perched on a rock overlooking the Durance valley which is well known locally for its asparagus. Very little remains of the medieval castle which once dominated this area and which was one of the centres of the Catholic suppression of the Vaudois. The surviving château was built in the 18C and now serves as a *maison de retrait* for holy orders. The 18C church of Notre-Dame-de-la-Purification might be overlooked but it has an attractive wrought-iron belfry. Less predictable is the townhouse in front of the church which was built by an Irishman in 1899 and has carved lintels of harps and shamrocks.

To the south of Lourmarin there is Cadenet, the main town in the area, and a bridge over the Durance to the abbey of Silvacane. A more informal itinerary from Lourmarin, however, takes you east through a series of villages on the southern side of the Grand Luberon.

Vaugines, the first village on the D56 out of Lourmarin, is likely to be passed by, but it has a few rather interesting features for such a tiny community. The village is actually on the site of a medieval castle and monastery and, amid the winding narrow streets, there are several historic houses such as the wedge-shaped Capitainerie of 1510. The most picturesque building, however, is the small parish church of St-Sauveur in a wooded area at the eastern edge of the village. Begun in the 11C and much altered thereafter, this small Romanesque structure has the sort of organic disorder that makes it appear to have grown out of its surroundings.

A further 2km on the D56 is **Cucuron**, one of the most important and attractive villages on the southern slopes of the Luberon. It is often proposed as the model for 'Cucugnan' in Daudet's *Letters from my Windmill*, in which the priest, trying to trace some of his flock in heaven, discovers eventually that they have all arrived in hell.

History of Cucuron

The main part of Cucuron is grouped around a small hill which was fortified in the 12C–13C, the tower at the top being all that remains of the medieval castle. The well-preserved walls, although begun in the same period, were mostly built in response to a sudden attack by the troops of Charles V in 1536. Despite this, the 16C was a period of considerable wealth and expansion in Cucuron. The formidable belltower with its decorative lanterna or 'Barabaroto' was built in 1540 and the parish church was substantially enriched at this time to accommodate the relics of St Tulle.

The main part of this **church** consists of a 12C Romanesque nave and a Gothic apse but there are some interesting murals and furnishings including a polychrome wooden *Pietà* from the 15C and an impressive 17C high altar in marble which was originally commissioned for the convent of the Visitation at Aix. Nearby on the square is the 17C Maison des Bouliers which houses the museum and archaeological collection of Marc Deydier (☎ 04 90 77 25 02: **open** 10.00–12.00 and 15.00–18.00; closed Tues am). The surrounding area has thrown up a number of antique remains including a curious inscribed drawing in stone of a Roman ship. Perhaps the most impressive feature in Cucuron, however, is the huge **water basin** outside the walls which was built in the early 15C to drive a flour mill. The mill has long since disappeared leaving a shaded spot in which to relax and feed the ducks.

Continue on the D56 for 4.5km to **Ansouis**, another tightly packed hill-village of winding streets and old stone houses dominated by a delightful **château** which is open to the public (☎ 04 90 09 82 70: guided tours 45min daily 14.30–18.00 Easter–Oct; closed Tues Nov–Easter). The Sabran family have lived here since the 12C and the earliest fortified parts of the castle date from that time. It was altered and extended in the 14C and 17C, however, giving the building an elegant domestic appearance reminiscent of a country house. This effect is greatly enhanced by the beautiful formal gardens of box hedges on terraces around the main buildings. The interior reflects the different periods of the building but the most attractive apartments are those from the 18C, decorated in a light Rococo manner and hung with Flemish tapestries. One room contains mementoes of the two most famous members of the Sabran family, Elzear and Delphine, who in the 14C devoted their marriage to 'God and good works'. For this and their chastity they were canonised in 1365. The guided tour also takes in the old vaulted kitchen and rooms which are still used by the family.

On the place du Château, facing the main gateway of the castle, is the 13C

Romanesque **Eglise St-Martin**, which was built into the castle walls for protection. The plain vaulted interior is much enlivened by decorative mural painting and a range of 17C altarpieces including one devoted to SS Elzear and Delphine. Lower down in the village there is a good 16C belltower and a restored gateway through the old ramparts. At the bottom you will see signs to the **Musée Extraordinaire** (☎ 90 09 82 64: **open** Wed–Mon 14.00–19.00 Apr–Sept; 14.00–18.00 Oct–Mar; closed Tues and Jan, Feb), a curious collection of Provençal furniture, ceramic sculptures and bric-à-brac associated with underwater life. This was assembled by Georges Mazoyer, a diver from Marseille, and reflects his fascination with the sea. The most memorable part is the underwater grotto, a kitsch ensemble of models, stained glass, dangling fabric and coloured lights accompanied by underwater sounds.

La Tour d'Aigues, 9km east of Ansouis, is a substantial if rather dull market town but alongside it stand the remains of the grandest **Renaissance château** in Provence.

History of La Tour d'Aigues

The tower from which the town takes its name was actually an 11C–12C fort subsequently abandoned in the 14C. It was not until 1550, after the lordship passed to the de Bolliers family, that the great château was built on the foundations of the old castle. The architect, an obscure Italian named Ercole Nigra, used the forms and details which were already a feature of the French Renaissance style of Lescot and Delorme at the Louvre in Paris. In this château, however, the strong martial character is preserved with a huge central tower flanked by two wings which advance to enclose a square courtyard at the front. The main gateway to the courtyard is the most striking survival of this original complex.

The legend that this chateau was built out of Nicholas de Bollier's love for Marguerite de Valois, the future Queen of Provence, is entirely apocryphal but the demise of the house is well documented. In 1719 the baronetcy was purchased for 900,0000 livres by Jean-Baptiste Bruni, a wealthy merchant from Marseille. This tight-fisted businessman ran the estate like a commercial enterprise but over-exploited his seigneurial rights to the extent that he was hated by the peasants and workers on the estate. Relations deteriorated even further under his ill-tempered grandson, Jerome Bruni, until a mob attacked and burnt the house in 1780. Things had not settled down by the time of the Revolution and, although Bruni tried to appease his opponents, the house was attacked again in 1792, pillaged and set on fire until it was virtually destroyed.

In recent years it has been declared a historic monument and a programme of restoration is underway but the most impressive parts are still the surviving main gateway, thought to have been inspired by the triumphal arch at Orange, and the huge ramp of buttresses and piers which supported the great house on the east or garden side. There are occasional outdoor performances in the courtyard during the summer months.

From La Tour d'Aigues you can return to Apt by crossing to the north of the Grand Luberon (see p 166). This road, the D956, leads to **Grambois**, a compact oval hill-village enclosed by ramparts dating from the 14C–16C. This village felt the full force of the religious wars and in 1590 it was besieged and sacked by the Duke of Savoy in a campaign to dislodge the Protestants. The old château was destroyed in this siege, but later rebuilt by de Roquesante as a *maison de plaisance* which subsequently received Madame de Sevigné and the Comte de Mirabeau among its visitors. The 13C–14C parish church was also badly damaged but it survived and now contains some interesting pictures including the John the Baptist triptych (1519) and some 14C frescoes. Just outside the village is the 13C pilgrimage chapel of St-Pancrace, which has been decorated with some modern murals. A more poignant sight, however, is the small cemetery alongside with the striking pyramidal tomb of a girl named Honorine Thomelin (1819).

Thereafter, the D956 leads north by La Bastide-des-Jourdans, where you turn onto the D216 to Vitrolles. From there the narrow D33 and D31 climb over the Grand Luberon to Céreste on the north side.

An alternative route from La Tour d'Aigues is to take the D135 eastwards which leads directly to the village of **Mirabeau**. The principal building here is the 16C **château**, a good example of the traditional fortified houses of Provence.

> The village is best known for its association with the Riquetti family who owned it in the 18C. Gabriel-Honoré Riquetti, the orator and tribune known as Mirabeau, hardly ever visited the area and he was roundly disliked by the villagers of his home. It is ironic that while he was lionised in Arles and Aix as the great deputy to the Convention, his own estate workers took the first opportunity to burn the castle on the outbreak of the Revolution. Restored by Mirabeau's son in the 19C, the château was eventually bought by the prolific novelist Maurice Barrès (1862–1923).

St-Pierre, the main church in the village, stands on 13C foundations but the building dates from the 17C and 19C. A more interesting church is the **Eglise Ste-Madeleine**, 2km south of the village by the Pont-Mirabeau on the N96. This building dates from the 12C and has an inscription on the façade recording an eclipse of the sun on 3 June 1239. The Pont-Mirabeau was built in 1947 to replace an earlier suspension bridge of 1835 which had been destroyed in the Second World War. The remains of the earlier **bridge** with its allegorical sculptures can be seen slightly upriver.

The N96 crosses the Durance here leading to Peyrolles on the south bank and the main road to Aix. Remaining on the north bank, however, you can take a direct route to Manosque (21km) by Corbières and Ste-Tulle. This is a particularly fast-flowing section of the Durance where it is joined by the Verdon and there are several hydro-electric schemes and a nuclear power establishment alongside the river. Such scars on the landscape point to the fact that you have now left the Parc Régional du Luberon. Indeed, the whole character of this area is darker and more industrial.

14 · Forcalquier, Digne and Sisteron

This route travels 88km from the protected landscape of the Parc Régional du Luberon to the towns in the 'préalpes' that were once outposts and border defences of an independent Provence. The central part is the valley of the Durance and the broad area of rolling countryside between the Grand Luberon and the Montagne de Lure known as the Pays de Forcalquier. The name might seem odd given the relative insignificance of the provincial market town of Forcalquier. In the 12C–14C, however, Forcalquier was the capital of upper Provence and its impact on the history and building of this area have been considerable. Many quite modest villages, for example, reveal unexpectedly elegant houses amid the simpler rustic buildings, a sign of the wealth that trickled down from the court circles to the outlying districts. Another feature is the number of important Romanesque churches such as those at Ganagobie, Carluc and Salagon established either by courtiers anxious to store up goodwill for the hereafter, or by religious orders who wanted to be near the centre of power. Far from the coast, from the main population centres and the more popular tourist routes, this is one of the least-visited areas in Provence, but it offers a great deal to the traveller whether seeking history, architecture, food or attractive countryside.

From Apt along the Via Domitia

The N100 east of Apt follows the ancient Roman Via Domitia, the main road linking Spain and the Alps in the centuries immediately before and after Christ. This was the route taken by Hannibal in his assault on Italy during the Second Punic War, and also the road along which Pompey and Julius Caesar led their armies in the various campaigns and wars of the Roman empire. There are still some fragments of ancient works in the fields alongside the road and a few Roman remains still in use, such as the bridge at the western edge of Céreste.

Céreste stands on the site of some ancient and prehistoric settlements although the few visible remains, such as the ramparts in the old part of town, are late medieval. The most intriguing monument in the area is the ruined **Prieuré de Carluc**, set in a wooded glade some 2km north of the village on the small lane GR4. Founded in the 11C, this Benedictine establishment had three chapels although only one is still standing. There are fine fluted pilasters at each corner suggesting the quality of the decoration but the interior is closed to the public. Also surviving are the traces of a long gallery and a complex of chambers and tombs cut into the solid rock. This was clearly a place where many people wanted to be interred after death. The isolated cell in the cliff may have been the dwelling of a holy man or anchorite whose fame probably attracted the original monastic community.

The lane leads on to Reillane, once a prosperous village with a selection of good 16C townhouses within the medieval walls. Much more impressive, however, is **St-Michel-l'Observatoire**, further east, standing on a spur of rock which sticks out from the Crau Chetive. This village takes the latter part of its name from the astronomical observatory further up the hill, a national scientific centre that still plays a role in France's space and satellite research although the declining quality of the atmosphere in Provence has limited its capability. The installation can be visited on Wednesdays at 14.00 but it is best to write in advance. In contrast to the modern technology of the observatory with its 13 domes, the village of St-Michel is an ancient centre with a number of interesting remains. At the highest point there is a Romanesque church built by monks from Villeneuve-Lès-Avignon on the site of an early Gallic oppidum. The earliest part of the building dates from the 12C but later additions have not detracted from the chunky arrangement of simple interlocking forms, nor have they obscured such details as the carved capitals, one of which now serves as the font. There is another church in the village, St-Pierre, which was built in the 14C–15C, but it lacks the detailing, the outlook and the sylvan setting of its counterpart. More evocative is the small square chapel of St-Paul in the fields to the south. This 12C rural priory was linked to Carluc.

St-Michel-l'Observatoire stands on the route of the national footpath GR6 running from Tarascon to Sisteron. From here it leads over some reasonable terrain to Mane and Forcalquier. To reach these towns by road, however, you must return to the N100 which leads by the **Château de Sauvan**. This Classical villa was designed by J.-B. Franque in the early 18C for Michel-François de Forbin-Janson, a brigadier of the royal guard. The Forbin-Jansons had close associations with the court and it was to the Marquise that Marie-Antoinette wrote her last letter from the Conciergerie in Paris the night before her execution in 1793. The château has had a similarly troubled history but the building and formal gardens have now been restored to something of their former elegance.

Mane, like several other villages in this area, combines traces of its medieval origins with the bourgeois domestic buildings of an altogether gentler age. At the centre of the old quarter there is a well-defended castle (private) while other parts of the district present the elegant façades of merchants' houses dating from the 15C–16C. The most interesting sight in the whole area, however, is the **Prieuré de Salagon** (open daily 10.00–12.00 and 14.00–17.00 July, Aug; 14.00–18.00 Apr–June; Sat, Sun only 14.00–18.00 Oct, Nov) in the fields to the south of Mane. Established by the Benedictines in the 12C this foundation has a familiar history. After an initial period of success, when the two churches were built, the community went into decline until finally the whole priory was abandoned at the time of the Revolution. In recent years the complex has been restored for use as a centre for ethnological and conservation studies. To this end the church of St-Laurent is now used for accommodation but the church of Notre-Dame, the finer of the two, and some of the early outbuildings are open to the public as a museum in the afternoons. There are numerous fascinating details in Notre-Dame-de-Salagon such as the lively wall reliefs, the fine carved capitals or the 15C rose window, but it is the simplicity and grandeur of the space that is, perhaps, its most notable feature.

Forcalquier and the Montagne de Lure

Forcalquier, once the capital of upper Provence and home to one of the troubadour courts, is nowadays a pleasant market town at the heart of some beautiful rolling countryside.

History of Forcalquier

Its heyday was initiated in 1209 by the marriage of Gersende de Sabran, Countess of Forcalquier, to Alphonse II of Provence, which united these previously independent states. Their descendants, the rulers of Provence for the next two centuries, made Forcalquier their home and divided the court between here and Aix. Sordello, the Italian-born poet and adventurer, was a courtier here as were many other Provençal figures of the period. Raymond Bérenger V built his principal castle here in the 13C and, through a combination of shrewd diplomacy, a strong army and advantageous marriage, consolidated his power base beyond Provence. All four of his daughters were married to kings, one of them, Eleanor, to Henry III of England. This wealth and power made Forcalquier a target in periods of misrule and it was repeatedly attacked by Raymonde de Turenne of Les Baux in the 1380s and then by both Catholic and Protestant forces in the 16C Wars of Religion. The town's final descent was sealed in 1601 when Henry IV of France had the castle pulled down.

❖ Information, accommodation and food

🛈 8 place Bourguet (☎ 04 92 75 10 02).

Hotels. Accommodation in the villages of this area is difficult to find but there are several good hotels in Forcalquier itself. The best of these is the *Hostellerie des Deux Lions*, a 17C coach house at 11 place du Bourguet (☎ 04 92 75 25 30). The *Grand Hotel* at 10 boulevard Latourette (☎ 04 92 75 00 35) is less expensive.

Out of town, you could try the *Auberge Charembeau* (☎ 04 92 75 05 69, open mid Feb–mid Nov) to the east or *Le Colombier* (☎ 04 92 75 03 71), 3km to the south.

Restaurants. The *Deux Lions* (see above) has an excellent restaurant and near it on place Bourguet is another good restaurant, *Le Commerce*, which specialises in local dishes.

For the distinctive liqueurs produced in this area visit the *Distillerie de Haute-Provence* which has a shop in the town centre at avenue St-Promasse.

The remains of the castle can still be seen on the high ground to the south but the single tower gives little sense of its former glory. The centre of town is the place du Bourguet, an open square flanked by the former cathedral of Notre-Dame, a rather austere Gothic church with much later additions, and the 17C town hall. This latter building was formerly a convent but it now houses a local museum and, in the chapel, a small cinema. Superficially similar, but much more rewarding, is the nearby **Couvent des Cordeliers**, a former Franciscan convent (Franciscans took a vow of poverty which extended as far as wearing only a rope or *corde liés* for a belt, hence their name in French). This has restored period rooms and a good museum of medieval art (guided tours Wed–Sun 11.00, 14.30, 16.30, 17.30 July–mid Sept; Sun and holidays only May, June, mid-Sept–Oct). Dating from the 13C, this was one of the earliest Franciscan foundations outside Italy.

The area round the place du Bourguet is at its liveliest on Mondays when the local market takes over the square and many of the surrounding streets. This also spills into the old town, a very attractive quarter of narrow streets running up the montée Ste-Marie to the citadel. Walking tours of this area are offered most days in summer from the tourist office. Grande Rue and the rue du Collège, punctuated by the façades of merchants' houses from the 15C–17C, are among the most attractive streets, and the place St-Michel has a fine Renaissance **fountain** with some rather racy scenes. This is actually a modern copy; the original, dating from 1551, is in the town hall museum. In the gardens at the summit of the hill, near the remains of the citadel and the original cathedral, there is an attractive neo-Byzantine chapel, Notre-Dame-de-Provence, built in 1875. From this spot there are good views out over the Pays de Forcalquier and an orientation table to help pick out the various mountains that encircle the area.

Forcalquier is a good base from which to explore the slopes and villages of the **Montagne de Lure**. This is a quiet area and its attractions are not immediately obvious. If you have a car and time to spare, however, it is worth taking an excursion into the hills to the north and west where you can visit such villages as Limans, Banon or Oppedette, each beautifully situated and containing an array of interesting medieval buildings. **Simiane-la-Rotonde** is a particularly striking village-perché with a formidable 12C castle at its summit. Built by the Simiane family, who controlled much of upper Provence, it is a powerful reminder of the defensive needs of feudal rulers in the Middle Ages.

The most important medieval monument, however, is to the east of Forcalquier along the D12 as it descends to the banks of the Durance and joins the N96. This area is known as the Domaine de Prieuré after the outstanding Romanesque **Prieuré de Ganagobie** (guided tours 30min Tues–Sat 15.00–17.00 in summer; 15.00–16.00 in winter; Sun 11.00; closed Mon) accessible from the N96 by the small D30 off to the left. Ascending the steep wooded slopes of the Bois de Lurs you emerge at the plateau at the top to find a typically modest complex of Romanesque monastic buildings that, on closer inspection, has few equals anywhere.

History of Prieuré de Ganagobie

There has been a priory on this site since Carolingian times (10C) but all the surviving buildings date from a major campaign in the 12C after the foundation was ceded to the Cluniac order. The community further benefited by gifts from the Counts of Forcalquier and its significance in the larger scheme of things was confirmed when it received the sacred relics of St Honoratus from the monks on the Iles de Lérins. This success ended in the 15C when the priory began its long decline until finally abandoned at the time of the Revolution and the abolition of the Cluniac order. After a period of neglect, the 20C has seen a revival of interest in the priory and it is now administered by Benedictines from the abbey of Hautecombe in Savoy.

The most striking feature of the main building is the carved **tympanum** over the main portal depicting Christ in Majesty flanked by the symbols of the four Evangelists. Beneath this, on the lintel, there is a row of figures representing the 12 Apostles. The effect of this ensemble is greatly dramatised by the zig-zag patterns in the archway although these were actually added in the 16C. What gives Ganagobie its distinction over all other Romanesque monuments in this area, however, is the series of **mosaics** in black, white and red tesserae on the floor of the main church. Discovered in the 1960s, they are almost unique and certainly represent the most complete cycle of their type. Most take the form of elaborate curvilinear patterns with fantastic animal and plant forms interwoven throughout but there are a few figurative scenes including two versions of St George and the dragon. In these the saint carries the sort of arms and armour that we have come to know from the near-contemporary Bayeux tapestry. Also in the church is a meretricious mural by the 19C painter Adolphe Monticelli (1824–86). It strikes a wrong note in this context but you can escape to the 12C **cloister** composed of sturdy Romanesque arches and columns, or to the wooded plateau outside which offers excellent views over the Durance valley below.

Just 10km further up the N96 and off to the left by the D101 is another Romanesque priory, the **Chapelle St-Donat** in the foothills of the Montagne de Lure. This is not a match for Ganagobie in terms of its decoration but it is such a majestic and compact church in a beautiful woodland setting that it is worth the detour. The site, which was made sacred by the early Christian hermit Donatus, had four churches in the 11C but only the main abbey church survives. Appropriately, the building is a spare and austere edifice which relies on the simple rhythm of its columns and arches to communicate a sense of order and harmony. Further west on the southern slopes of the Montagne de Lure, Donatus founded another abbey which can be reached from the village of St-Etienne-les-Orgues on the D951. This is much more remote but the site is popular as a pilgrimage destination and for more ambitious walkers who wish to follow the long crest of the mountain from the summit as it curves back towards the river.

The turn off for St-Donat is by the Pont Mardaric, where the main N96 and motorway fork towards two separate destinations. Crossing the bridge to the eastern bank of the Durance at Les Mées, the D4 and N85 lead directly to Digne along the upper reaches of the *Route Napoléon*. **Les Mées** itself is an interesting fortified village with 12C–15C ramparts beneath a series of tall pointed rocks that are thought to resemble the distinctive cowls of penitent monks. According to local legend these are the remains of a procession of monks who were petrified as a punishment for improper desires towards the female slaves brought back by the seigneur from the crusades.

Digne-les-Bains

The N85 follows the Bléone, a tributary of the Durance, to Digne-les-Bains, capital of the *département* Alpes-de-Haute-Provence and a rather smart thermal resort with a long history. The Romans first discovered the curative powers of the waters in this high outpost and it is still popular with those suffering from various ailments from rheumatism to *la maladie moderne*—stress. Unfortunately, the air of a convalescent centre still pervades Digne and it lacks the character or stimulus that you would expect in a town of its size. This is not for the want of trying on the part of the local authority. There is a programme of festivals all year round to attract visitors, the most important being the *Grande Foire de la Lavande* which runs for four days at the end of August. Digne is at the heart of the lavender-growing district of Haute Provence which brings great colour and aroma to the town and the hillsides during the summer harvest.

❖ *Information, accommodation and food*

🛈 Rond-Point du 11ᵉ novembre 1918 (☎ 0492 31 42 73).

Hotels. Accommodation in Digne, like the town, is relaxed and unpretentious. Some of the hotels are linked to the thermal baths and curative centres but the following are all independent and have restaurants of matching quality. *Le Grand Paris*, a restored 17C monastery at 19 boulevard Thiers (☎ 04 92 31 11 15) is regarded as the best, while *Le Petit St-Jean* at 14 cours des Arès (☎ 04 92 31 30 04) and *L'Origan* at 6 rue Pied-de-la-Ville (☎ 04 92 31 62 13) are less expensive.

The main axis of the town is the shaded boulevard Gassendi, named after the local-born 17C philosopher and scientist Pierre Gassendi (1592–1655) who was a friend of Molière and Cyrano de Bergerac, and an opponent of René Descartes. There is a statue to him at the modernised place Général-de-Gaulle where the main local market is held (Wed, Sat). Gassendi's life and work are also celebrated in the **Musée de Digne** (☎ 04 92 31 45 29: **open** Tues–Sun 10.30– 12.00 and 13.30–18.30 July–Aug; afternoons only Sept–June; closed Mon) at the eastern end of the boulevard (No. 64) as well as a rather dull collection of paintings and local history. The main street divides the two old centres of town, each of which is dominated by a major cathedral church. To the northeast, on the site of the old Roman town of Dinia, is the former **Cathédrale de Notre-Dame-du-Bourg**, a striking and unusual building for this part of Provence. The nave and interior are pure 12C Romanesque but the later Gothic façade has the sort of polychrome effects that one associates with Italy. It has been suggested that the frontage was built by masons from Lombardy. The church has been deconsecrated and the various treasures, including traces of 14C–15C murals, are now displayed in a context closer to that of a museum.

The late Gothic **Cathédrale St-Jérôme** in the centre of the old town to the south of the boulevard is less appealing. Begun in the 15C and subsequently enlarged, it has been allowed to deteriorate over many years and is only now being included in a programme of renovation that affects much of the area. It was a bishop of this diocese in the early 19C, Monseigneur de Miollis, whose devotion and modesty inspired Victor Hugo's cleric Bienvenu in the novel *Les Misérables*. The early passages of this great work are set in the area round Digne as the saintly bishop wanders the hills on his donkey in an attempt to save the souls of his atheistic flock. It is also from this cathedral that Jean Valjean steals the silver candlesticks which set the whole narrative in motion.

Appropriately, there is a small **Musée d'Art Religieux** (☎ 04 92 32 35 37: **open** daily 10.00–18.00 July–Sept) on place des Récollets displaying some of the church treasures from the area. There are two other museums in the streets to the rear of the cathedral. The **Musée de la Guerre 1939–45** (☎ 04 92 31 28 95: **open** Wed, Thur 14.00–18.00 July, Aug; Wed 14.00–18.00 Apr–June and Sept, Oct; first Wed of month 14.00–18.00 Nov–Mar or by appointment), in the place Paradis by the Palais de Justice, gives an insight into the confused history of this area under occupation, first by Italian and later by German troops. This is still a sensitive issue and there still appear to be ongoing local disputes about collaboration and the conduct of the Resistance.

The other museum, some distance further out at 27 avenue du Maréchal-Juin, is the curious **Fondation Alexandra David-Néel** set up to promote Buddhist ideals and to house the collection of Tibetan art assembled by the woman whose name is now attached to the centre. Alexandra David-Néel (1868–1969) spent much of her life walking in Tibet, some of it in disguise as a local man, about which she wrote several books and campaigned for a better understanding of this remote culture. On her return to France in 1927 she purchased this house, which she named *Samten Dzong* (Castle of Meditation), and established a small community of emigré Tibetan monks. The foundation, which has been visited twice by the Dalai Lama, is open for guided tours throughout the year (☎ 92 31 32 38: tours daily at 10.30, 14.00, 15.30 and 17.00 July–Sept; 10.30, 14.00 and 16.00 Oct–June).

More in keeping with this region, the **Centre de Géologie** (☎ 92 36 70 70: **open** Mon–Fri 09.00–12.00 and 14.00–17.30 Nov–Mar) on the opposite side of the river Bléone gives an introduction to the rich natural resources and fossil remains of the Alpes-de-Haute-Provence. This wealth has long been recognised and is now protected in the large **Réserve Naturelle Géologique de Haute-Provence** which allows access but controls the use of the ground and rock formations in a 150 square kilometre area to the north of Digne. The centre gives out maps which will guide the traveller to such sights as the 'wall of ammonites' just 4km outside Digne on the D900a towards Barles, or the more remote fossilised skeleton of an ichthyosaurus which is a fair walk beyond the village of La Robine on the same road. The area as a whole is worth exploring and there are numerous sights in the gorges or *clues* of this sparsely populated region to distract the traveller and to allow an escape from the more familiar landscapes and associations of Provence.

From the Pont Mardaric, where the route forked for Digne, you can continue north along the west bank of the Durance on the A51 or N85 by **Château Arnoux**. This village takes its name from the impressive 16C castle which now serves as the Mairie. The Renaissance interior is open to the public in July and August (Tues–Fri; guided tour at 16.00) but the park and botanical garden to the rear are accessible all year round.

Sisteron

At the confluence of the Buech and the Durance, 12km further north, you will reach Sisteron, a fortified town on the border between Provence and Dauphine. It would be difficult to imagine a more expressive boundary between two regions than this point where a chain of mountains presents a huge natural barrier broken only by a gap through which the river runs. On the west bank a rocky outcrop of the Montagne de l'Ubac rises 500m to the Guérite du Diable while opposite this the corrugated Rocher de la Baume has a series of colossal ridges that run up to the distant summit. For these reasons the site has been a fortified bastion since pre-Roman times and as recently as 1944 it proved an obstacle to an invading army.

❖ *Information and accommodation*

🛈 Place de la République (☎ 04 92 61 12 03).

Hotels. The traditional *Grand Hôtel du Cours* on the place de l'Eglise (☎ 04 92 61 04 51) is the best, but *La Citadelle* at 126 rue Saunerie (☎ 04 92 61 13 52) and the *Tivoli* at 21 place du Tivoli (☎ 04 92 61 15 16) are both good value.

The extensive **citadel** (**open** daily 08.00–19.00 July–Aug; 09.00–18.00 Mar–June and Sept–mid Nov) at the top of the hill dates from the 12C but it was repeatedly strengthened, notably by Henry IV's engineer Jean Erard at the end of the 16C. It is still very impressive although the walls and internal buildings, including a 15C chapel, were badly damaged by bombing in the Second World War. A walk along the ramparts in summer not only affords dramatic views over the river but also gives some insight into the practical problems of erecting such heavy defences on thin wedges of rock. There is now an open-air theatre and a museum within the complex which highlights various important events in the history of the castle. One of the most famous relates to Napoleon who passed here on 4 March 1815 on his return from Elba. Despite the royalist sympathies of the population, Sisteron's commander confiscated the ammunition, thus allowing Napoleon to enter the town before proceeding to a triumphant entry to Paris and his nemesis at Waterloo.

Beneath the great assemblage of buttresses that support the citadel, the old town of Sisteron is a charming network of narrow streets, vaulted passageways and tall houses, some of which date back to the 13C. At its heart is the former **Cathédrale de Notre-Dame-des-Pommiers**, an angular 12C Romanesque building with some interesting later furnishings and altarpieces. Much of this area was also damaged by the Allied bombing of 1944 but it has been reconstructed in a sympathetic manner and the large place Général-de-Gaulle is now a lively pedestrian area. The three towers overlooking it are survivors from the medieval town walls. Markets are held at the place de l'Horloge to the north (Wed, Sat) where you can buy local produce such as jam, lavender honey and candied fruits. Sisteron lamb, flavoured with local herbs, is also something of a speciality.

With the building of the A51 motorway most traffic now by-passes Sisteron and its surrounding area. It is, however, still a fairly popular resort giving access to the rivers, mountains and lakes of the Haute-Alpes or marking one end of the national footpath GR6 to Tarascon in the west. One short excursion, by the small D3 on the opposite side of the river towards St-Geniez, leads up to the **Défilé de Pierre-Ecrite**. This gorge takes its name from an enigmatic inscription cut into the rock by the 5C Roman prefect Claudius Postumus Dardanus recording his conversion to Christianity. It goes on to claim that he founded a new settlement called Theopolis, or 'city of God', although no trace of this has been found. Various early religious sites in the vicinity have been proposed as the lost Theopolis, including Dromon near St-Geniez, Vilhosc or Volonne. The last of these, while unlikely to have been Theopolis, is worth a visit for its 12C chapel and 17C château which has very fine interiors.

The central region

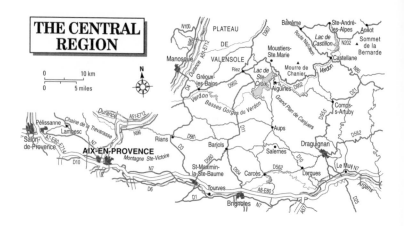

THE CENTRAL
REGION

0   10 km

0   5 miles

N

15 · Salon and the valley of the Durance

Salon-de-Provence sits on the border between two contrasted landscapes. To the west is the open Plaine de la Crau, a mysterious arid flatland formed in the dried-up river bed of the Durance, while to the east is the gentler farming country of the Chaînes des Côtes and the Trévaresse. The area as a whole is one of the main olive-growing districts of France, and Salon has prospered as the market for local produce and, above all, for high-grade olive oil.

To the French, Salon is probably best known as the home of the air force training school. You can see and hear the low-flying aircraft at various times of the week. Internationally, however, Salon enjoys a reputation as the home of the 16C mystic and prophet Michel Nostradamus, whose image is used in various forms throughout the town.

History of Salon-de-Provence

The key to the area's agriculture is the great canal designed in the 16C by a local-born engineer, Adam de Craponne, to bring water from the Durance to irrigate the parched land of the Salonais. This marked a new phase in Provençal agriculture and greatly enhanced the local economy.

Salon lacks the appeal of many similar market towns, possibly due to an earthquake of 1909 which caused considerable damage. There are, nevertheless, many interesting early buildings although a major renovation programme of the 1980s has done much to erase any period atmosphere the old part of the town once had.

At the centre of the old town on the Puech rock is the formidable **Château de l'Empéri** (☎ 04 90 56 22 36: **open** Wed–Mon 10.00–12.00 and 14.30–18.30

❖ *Information, accommodation and food*

🛈 56 cours Gimon (☎ 04 90 56 27 60).

Hotels. Accommodation in Salon is not difficult to find but there is very little variety. In fact the finest hotel is out of town; the *Hostellerie de l'Abbaye de Ste-Croix* (☎ 04 90 56 24 55) is in a restored 12C abbey on the D16 to Val de Cuech in the north. The *Domaine de Roquerousse* (☎ 04 90 59 50 11), not quite as grand, is nevertheless in its own estate 4km out on the route to Avignon

Inside the town, the more modest hotels include *Hôtel d'Angleterre* at 98 cours Carnot (☎ 04 90 56 01 10), the *Grand Hôtel de la Poste* at 1 rue des Kennedys (☎ 04 90 56 01 94) and the *Hôtel Wilson* at 159 rue des Kennedys (☎ 04 90 56 46 20).

Restaurants. The *Robin* on boulevard G. Clemenceau (☎ 04 90 56 06 53) is the smartest and best, and *Le Mas de Soleil* at 38 chemin St-Come (☎ 90 56 06 53) or *La Salle à Manger* at 6 rue Maréchal-Joffre (☎ 04 90 56 28 01; closed Sun, Mon eve) are good for local cuisine.

Apr–Sept; 10.00–12.00 and 14.00–18.00 Oct–Mar; closed Tues), once the residence of the archbishops of Arles who ruled Salon for the Holy Roman Emperors. The fort was begun in the 10C although the principal building campaign was that of the 15C–16C. In modern times it has not fared so well. It was turned into a barracks in the 19C and became one of the principal casualties of the 1909 earthquake. Despite this, it is still an impressive monument, the finest part being the 16C Cour d'Honneur with its Renaissance vaulted galleries. The castle complex houses a military museum comprising the collections of Raoul and Jean Brunon, who concentrated on the history of the French army between the reign of Louis XIV and the First World War. There are copious displays of weapons, uniforms, medals, trophies and paintings and the curators have made a serious attempt to extend the interest of the material beyond the specialist. Needless to say, the *Grand Armée* of Napoleon figures prominently and there are several mementoes related to the Emperor's career, including his short blue bed from St Helena.

On the opposite side of the place de l'Ancienne Halle from the château is the 13C church of St-Michel with its two belltowers. The Romanesque portal carries an interesting tympanum relief of St Michael flanked by two snakes above the Holy Lamb. Behind this church is the Porte Bourg-Neuf, all that remains of the original gate through the 13C ramparts, and an elegant 17C mansion that serves as the Hôtel de Ville. The statue over the fountain is of Adam de Craponne, the engineer whose irrigation canal ensured the prosperity of the whole region.

A few yards to the north of St-Michel and the place de l'Ancienne Halle is the **Maison de Nostradamus** (☎ 04 90 56 64 31: open daily 09.30–12.00 and 14.00–18.30 June–Aug; 09.00–12.00 and 14.00–18.00 Sept–May), the house where the prophet resided for the last 19 years of his life.

Nostradamus

Michel de Nostradamus was actually born in St-Rémy in 1503, the son of a converted Jew. He trained to be a physician at Montpellier and achieved considerable fame for his plague remedies, which were used with some success during epidemics at Aix and Lyon. This alienated him from his professional colleagues, however, and in 1547 he retired to Salon where he took up astrology. It was here in 1555 that he published *Centuries*, the famous book of predictions written in verse quatrains which brought him renewed success at the French court. This was largely due to the supernatural bent of Catherine de Médicis, who depended on horoscopes for everything she undertook and felt that Nostradamus had the key to the future. In fact the prophecies are so elliptical and abstruse that you can read almost anything into them, from the rise of Hitler to the end of the world on any one of several dates. Nostradamus died in Salon in 1566 but speculation over the prophecies has not died down. In the late 20C, with the onset of the millennium, his predictions seem to have been rediscovered by a new generation.

Despite considerable efforts to make the Maison de Nostradamus into a place of pilgrimage, the museum display is rather thin and lacks sufficient original material to bring the subject to life. A more interesting and related site is the **Eglise St-Laurent** some 700m to the north, beyond the colossal mural of Nostradamus and the Porte de l'Horloge. Built by the Dominicans in 1344, this collegiate church is a fine example of the restrained Gothic style which had limited success in Provence. On close inspection you can recognise the persistence of rounded arches in some parts and an overall austerity of design associated with the more popular Romanesque. There are several notable features on the interior but the most famous is undoubtedly the putative tomb of Nostradamus in the fourth chapel on the left. There is an inscription on the wall which begins, 'Here lie the bones of Michel de Nostradamus ...' but according to one local legend he was actually interred in another church which was later desecrated during the Revolution. This is only one of the numerous fables and mysteries that the Salonais like to spin around the life and death of their most famous figure.

If the west of Salon offers only La Crau and the prospect of an unwavering straight road for some 28km to St-Martin, the network of roads to the east through the limestone hills and up to the Durance in the north leads through a series of interesting and attractive villages. Ironically, it is on this eastern side—in a 19C mansion on the avenue de Pivasis—that you find the **Musée de Salon et de La Crau** (☎ 04 90 56 28 37: **open** Mon, Wed–Fri 10.00–12.00 and 14.00–18.00; closed Tues, Sat and Sun am). This is largely a local history museum with some interesting displays related to the life and landscape of the area. Prominent features are the presses and implements used in the olive-oil industry. Connoisseurs tend to recommend the villages outside Salon for the finest olives and oils, particularly La Fare in the south or Aureille, to the northwest on the lower slopes of Les Alpilles. Most of the villages in the area, however, are engaged in some aspect of this industry and all are proud of their own local specialities.

Leaving Salon by the D17, beyond Pélissanne join the D22 which leads directly to the **Château de La Barben**, one of the most romantic of all Provençal castles (guided tours c 40min Wed–Mon 10.30–12.00 and 14.30–17.30; closed Tues). Dramatically situated on a rock overlooking the wooded Touloubre valley, this crenellated fort seems to have been inspired by a medieval romance. It is first mentioned in a document of 1063 but it was later owned by René d'Anjou who, in 1453, gave it to his favourite daughter Yolande, Duchess of Lorraine. In 1474 it was sold to Jean de Forbin, scion of a noble family with, of all things, Scottish origins whose descendants continued to live in the château until 1963. While the exterior retains much of its medieval and Renaissance origins, albeit restored, the interior reveals a more elegant way of life expressed in a series of fine neo-Classical rooms. This is partly due to Pauline Borghese, sister of Napoleon, who lived here in 1807 and employed many of the leading Empire decorators to redesign her apartments. The painter Marius Granet of Aix (1775–1849) was a particular favourite and he was responsible for several works including some hand-painted papers in one of the rooms (see p 188). The castle grounds reveal another great period of French design, the small formal garden having been laid out by Le Nôtre, who was responsible for the gardens at Versailles. Pauline Borghese was reputed to bathe naked in the pool, shielded from prying eyes by sheets held up by her servants. Nowadays, this idyll is marred by the rather sad zoo at the top of a long flight of steps, although nothing can detract from the location and the excellent views from most parts.

Continue east on the D572 to St-Cannat, birthplace of the naval hero Pierre-André Bailli de Suffren (1726–88), whose house is now both the Mairie and a museum, then turn left (north) on the N7/N517 to **Lambesc**. This minor capital, little more than a village, was created by René d'Anjou in the 15C as a location for the General Assembly of the various Provençal district burghs. As a result, there are a number of impressive houses and public buildings that have survived from its age of importance in the 16C and 17C. The elegant Classical church, for example, was designed in 1700 by the prominent Aix architect Laurent Vallon and retains some fine furnishings and fittings. A steeple once completed the overall complex but it collapsed during the earthquake of 1909. There is a small museum of local history on rue du Jas but it is only open a few days each month.

Lambesc stands in the middle of an attractive area, hemmed in by hills on all sides. The tallest and most impressive of these ranges is the **Chaîne des Côtes** to the north but the D15 and D66d (or the D543 north from Rognes) lead through a gap by the Bassin de St-Christophe to the banks of the Durance. Turn left, and just 2km away by the D561 is the medieval **Abbaye de Silvacane**, the youngest of the three Cistercian 'sisters of Provence' (see pp 148 and 195). The Cistercians preferrred solitude and isolation so it is somewhat surprising to come across this major foundation just off the main road. In medieval times, however, this area was a marsh overgrown with the dense reed beds that gave the abbey its name, *sylva cana* (forest of reeds).

History of the Abbaye de Silvacane

The abbey was founded in the 11C by a party of monks from St-Victor in Marseille and over the next three centuries the community prospered due to a series of wealthy and powerful patrons, including Raymond of Les Baux.

Agricultural improvements, land purchase and the creation of a series of minor houses and affiliations all contributed to the success of the abbey to such an extent that in 1289 the monks of Silvacane were drawn into open warfare with the Benedictines of Montmajour near Arles. Reports of this dispute include violent confrontations between the two groups and even the taking of prisoners before the affair was resolved. Thereafter, the wealth of Silvacane made it a target for marauders in the various political struggles of Provence. In 1358 brigands in the service of the Lord of Aubignan pillaged the abbey complex and five years later a severe winter destroyed the olive groves and vineyards. This marked the end of its prosperity and the following centuries tell a story of gradual decline punctuated by outbursts of despoliation. In the 16C it was reduced to serving as the local parish church and by the Revolution the abbey complex had been abandoned. The final indignity came when the buildings and land were sold off to make a farm. It was not until 1949 that it was bought back by the state and even now the process of renovation is continuing slowly.

With its unpromising situation and damaged buildings, Silvacane (☎ 42 50 41 69: **open** daily 09.00–19.00 Apr–Sept; Wed–Mon 09.00–12.00 and 14.00–17.00 Oct–Mar) is perhaps the least celebrated of the great Provençal abbeys. Yet for those very reasons it has retained something of the simplicity, even serenity, that was part of its original aims. The truncated tower and awkward profile of the complex are unmistakeable but the stonework has a warmth which softens the overall effect. The most impressive part is the **church**, the earliest of the abbey buildings, dating from 1175–1230. On entering you immediately recognise the intrinsic nobility of this impressive interior. There is little here to distract attention from the solid lines of the structure; no stained glass or decoration, and only minimal references to Classical motifs in the columns. Even the anomalies, like the absence of a main west doorway, seem to emphasise the harmony and order of the space and the pervasive atmosphere of spirituality.

The **cloister**, dating from the second half of the 13C, is on a lower level than the church and leads on to the other surviving buildings including the chapter house, monks' parlour, dormitory and 15C refectory. Excavation and restoration continues at Silvacane, but it is to be hoped the abbey is not overwhelmed by interpretation and visitor centres. At present, it is the simple beauty of the buildings which preserves the spirit of the Cistercian rule.

One kilometre further along the D561 is **La Roque-d'Anthéron**, a village which shows signs of considerable prosperity in the past. In a park near the centre is the Château de Florans, built in two distinct phases just before and after 1600. It now serves as a medical centre, but in August hosts a well-known piano competition, part of which is held in the abbey of Silvacane. On the place Paul-Cézanne there is a museum devoted to the geology and minerals of Provence. This might normally be for specialists were it not for the fact that the culture and history of this region is so closely bound up with its endlessly varied topography. There is even an example in the immediate vicinity. The rough terrain of the Chaîne des Côtes behind the village offered cover for Resistance activity by the Maquis during the Second World War. As a reprisal, however, there was a notorious massacre of hostages by the Nazis in La Roque-d'Anthéron in 1944.

Continue west on the D561 to the planned village of Charleval, then by the

D22 towards Aurons and Salon. After 6km, beyond the N7 at Cazan, you will see signs for the **Château Bas**, also known as the Château de Vernègues. The 16C castle is now part of farm buildings but there is a small path by the walls which leads to the remains of a 1C BC Roman temple. Built at the same time as the Maison Carrée at Nîmes, this was once an important shrine and sanctuary, as is indicated by the quality of the carving on the Corinthian capital. In the 11C it was turned into a Christian church and a Romanesque chapel was built on to the edge using some of the original Roman masonry. It is, however, the setting of the ruins on a terrace of the wooded hillside which gives them a particularly romantic appeal.

Vernègues itself, a few kilometres to the west, is a new village built after the earthquake of 1909. Nevertheless, it is worth visiting the old village at the top of the hill which shows signs of recent reconstruction. There are remains of a Romanesque church and a medieval castle (11C–14C), but the principal attraction is the view out over the whole valley of the Durance to the north and over to the Alpilles in the west. From here you can return directly to Salon on the D22b and D16 or take the small D68 to Aurons, with its tiny Romanesque church and old priory gardens. The latter route also passes through the gorges of the Cuech valley before arriving at Pélissanne and the main road into Salon.

16 · Aix-en-Provence

Aix is the most relaxed and sedate of the major Provençal centres. It has a strong professional, even bourgeois feel, partly due to its university and legal traditions, but above all because for 600 years it was the old capital of Provence. More recently, however, this slightly superior stance has been shaken by the sense that its role as an administrative and cultural centre has been supplanted by the more dynamic and assertive cities of the region. The Aixois remain aloof from any unseemly civic rivalry but, despite considerable expansion in the light technology industries, there is no doubt that the marginalisation of Aix as a mere sub-*préfecture* does rankle. What this has left however, is the most elegant city in Provence; a network of beautiful 17C–18C streets and squares punctuated by fountains and historical sites that give Aix an unmistakeable atmosphere, in complete contrast to its gritty neighbour Marseille, only 25km to the south.

The university is still one of the dominant features of the town and this partly defines its youth culture, bringing thousands of young people onto the streets and into the cafés all year round. The most famous local event is the music festival held every year in July (Aix was the home of the composer Darius Milhaud), a modest counterpart to the annual theatre festival held in Avignon at the same time, which gives prominence to modern composers. A series of cultural projects is underway in the old industrial area of the cours Sextius, behind the place du Général-de-Gaulle: the conference centre, library and gallery of the Cité du Livre is a restrained and rather belated attempt to remake the image of Aix as a post-Modern cultural centre along the lines of Nîmes or Nice. Even here it seems more likely that the sedate, bourgeois character of Aix will prevail.

History of Aix

Aix was the first Roman settlement in Gaul, founded by Caius Sextius following his victory over the Ligurians at Entremont in 123 BC. The ruins of the citadel at Entremont can be visited to the north of the town but it is little more than a ground plan which the authorities have tried to dramatise with speculation about ritual executions and the Salian cult of decapitated heads. The Romans preferred a more relaxed way of life and fixed on the thermal springs as the site for their town, which they named Aquae Sextiae, later contracted to Aix. From this foothold would grow the complete colonisation of Gaul in the following century, but not without considerable struggle. Just 20 years after Entremont, Marius faced an army of some 200,000 Teutons in the shadow of Montagne Ste-Victoire. His victory, thought to have been near the village of Pourrières to the east of Aix, was widely regarded as the testing-ground that prepared the Roman army for its colonial expansion throughout Europe. In its wake Aix became a major staging-post on the Via Aurelia which traversed southern Gaul. Unfortunately, as the Romans settled in numbers they developed a preference for Arles, relegating Aix to a minor position in the province. Despite being made a bishopric in the 4C its decline continued and it was repeatedly ravaged by Barbarian incursions and later by Saracens during the early Middle Ages. Then, in the 12C, the emerging Counts of Provence declared Aix their capital and this marked the beginning of a period of prosperity and political power that lasted until the Revolution.

The golden age is generally regarded as that under René d'Anjou (1409–80), whose statue stands above the fountain at the eastern end of the cours Mirabeau. According to the cult which has grown up around his name, 'Good King René' was something of a Renaissance man. Cultivated, intelligent, liberal-minded and a considerable artist in his own right, he presided over a famous court at which the new art and learning were encouraged. René was equally interested in politics and science and he is credited with introducing the Muscat grape to Provence, thereby establishing the basis of the flourishing wine trade. A less favourable view sees him largely uninterested in any of these things, and a weak ruler who lost much of his birthright in the narrow-minded pursuit of wealth. In fact he lived most of his life at other castles, spending less than a decade at Aix before his death in 1480.

Even after Provence was annexed to France in 1487, Aix continued to act as a major seat of political power. Much of this was expressed through the judiciary, since Aix was the seat of the Supreme Court of Justice. The city attracted the full panoply of legal support agencies creating a wealthy middle class of magistrates, lawyers and businessmen who dominated the culture of the area. It was this group who built many of the mansions and minor palaces that characterise the townscape of Aix. In the 17C and 18C new districts were created and several older ones were cleared to make way for the elegant streets, squares and fountains of a major centre in the age of Enlightenment. Many scenes in the turbulent life of the Comte de Mirabeau were acted out in Aix.

Ironically, given Mirabeau's celebrity in the town, it was a Revolutionary tribunal of 1790 which declared Marseille as the new capital of Provence, sending Aix into another period of decline. The city has retained its sense of status but little of the substance and political clout that should sustain it.

The 19C saw other cities in Provence expand and develop new industries but Aix remained much as it was. Its most famous son, the painter Paul Cézanne (1839–1906), had a curious relationship with his native city. Aix and its surroundings, particularly the Montagne Ste-Victoire, appear throughout his work but the painter was an independent, rather coarse character, unsympathetic to the bourgeois manners of his fellow Aixois. Indeed Cézanne turned his back on much of the town, preferring the privacy of his own estate, the Jas de Bouffan, which allowed him to pursue his solitary, demanding art. The irony is that Cézanne has now become the dominant feature of publicity and tourism in Aix. The local tourist office advertises 'Cézanne tours' and the pavements are studded with markers which follow the footsteps of the master but they cannot overcome the palpable gulf between the civic character of Aix and the introverted, almost alienated character of the artist's life and work.

❖ Information, accommodation and food

🛈 2 place du Général-de-Gaulle (☎ 04 42 16 11 61).

Hotels. Accommodation of all standards is relatively easy to find in Aix but there are periods of congestion at festival times in high summer. At the top end, the *Villa Gallici* (☎ 04 42 21 29 23) in avenue de la Violette and the *Nègre Coste* (☎ 04 42 27 74 22) at 33 cours Mirabeau are both in 18C mansions near the centre. *Le Pigonnet* (☎ 04 42 59 02 90), with beautiful views and a wonderful atmosphere, is further out at 5 avenue du Pigonnet.

In the middle range, *Le Manoir* (☎ 04 42 26 27 20) at 8 rue Entrecasteaux has a 12C cloister, *La Renaissance* (☎ 04 42 26 04 22) at 4 boulevard de la République occupies the childhood home of Darius Milhaud, while *Le Prieuré* (☎ 04 42 21 05 23), outside town on the route de Sisteron is in a 17C convent.

Among the many cheaper hotels, *Du Casino* (☎ 04 42 26 06 88) at 38 rue Victor-Leydet by rue Espariat, the *Hôtel des Arts-le Sully* (☎ 04 42 38 11 77) at 69 boulevard Carnot, the *Hôtel Paul* (☎ 04 42 23 23 89) at 10 avenue Pasteur, and the *Splendid* (☎ 04 42 38 19 53) at 69 cours Mirabeau can be recommended.

Restaurants. Aix also offers a bewildering range of restaurants and cafés of all types and price range. Perhaps because of the large student population there are numerous bistros in the streets near the Hôtel de Ville. The place des Cardeurs and the rue de la Verrerie have many options, particularly in African and Asian food. For traditional and Provençal cuisine, *Le Clos de la Violette* (☎ 04 42 23 30 71) at 10 avenue de la Violette is considered the best restaurant in Aix while *Le Bistro Latin* (☎ 04 42 38 22 8) at 18 rue de la Couronne is also highly regarded. In general one is advised to avoid the overpriced restaurants on the cours Mirabeau but *Les Deux Garçons* (☎ 04 42 26 00 51) may be worth a visit for its literary and bohemian associations.

Vieil Aix

Any tour of Aix should begin on the **cours Mirabeau**, the most elegant street in Provence. This tree-lined thoroughfare, which actually follows the line of the old walls, bisects the town into the compact medieval centre to the north and the rational grid-plan of the elegant Quartier Mazarin to the south. Fortunately the main car park is by the place du Général-de-Gaulle or Rotonde, at the western end of the *cours*, allowing visitors to explore Aix on foot.

The *cours* was laid out in 1649 as a showplace for wealthy citizens to parade in their carriages. With its broad roadway, its series of fountains and, above all, its four lines of lofty plane trees offering a canopy from the sun, it became immediately the most fashionable address in Aix. Many of the early mansions survive, mostly on the southern side, where they present their finely carved façades and doorways to the street. The finest is the Hôtel Maurel de Pontèves (1751) at No 38, with its Baroque atlantes supporting the balcony. The less impressive Hôtel d'Isoard de Vauvenargues at No. 10 was the scene of a notorious murder in 1784, when the son of the president of parliament attacked his aristocratic wife, Angelique de Castellane, with a razor. In the early days there was an outcry at the mere suggestion of trade in this posh residential avenue but it is now lined with smart shops, banks and cafés. The most famous of these is the **Café des Deux Garçons** at No. 53, something of a literary salon in which the original Empire decorations have been beautifully preserved. Camus and others frequented this place in the 1950s. Further along at No. 55 was the hat shop owned by Cézanne's father and where the young painter was brought up. The shop sign is still visible on the wall. Also on the *cours* are several *patisseries* selling the local speciality known as *calissons*. These biscuits made from almonds and fruit were once distributed in church on feast days, but are now a rather expensive delicacy.

From the cours Mirabeau, you should turn north on the rue Clemenceau, opposite the moss-covered thermal fountain, the Fontaine Moussue, into the old town of Aix. Much of this district is now traffic free and offers a pleasant walk through a succession of interesting streets to the top of the town by the cathedral. At the place St-Honoré turn left into the rue Espariat, where at No. 6 you will find the Hôtel Boyer d'Eguilles, a 17C mansion which now serves as the **Musée d'Histoire naturelle** (☎ 04 42 26 23 67: **open** daily 10.00–12.00 and 14.00–18.00). There are interesting collections of minerals and fossils, including a clutch of dinosaur eggs, but it is the house itself which is most engaging. Begun in 1672 by Magdalene de Forbin, it was completed by her son Jean-Baptiste, a pupil of the sculptor Puget, who supervised the decoration. The house retains much of its original ironwork, *boiseries* and mural paintings. Slightly further along the street on the opposite side is the **place Albertas**, a small cobbled square planned in the 1740s to create an approach to the Hôtel d'Albertas. The result is a delightful, secluded area with Rococo façades on three sides which is sometimes used for open-air concerts.

Continuing north on the rue Aude (note the Italianate Hôtel Peyronetti at No. 13) and rue Maréchal-Foch, the streets emerge into the open area of the **place Richelme** and **place de l'Hôtel de Ville**. This, if anywhere, is the heart of Aix, a lively meeting-place for students and tourists, animated by the fruit and flower markets which often take over most of the lower part of the square. In the middle, dividing the two squares, is the post office, although its grand propor-

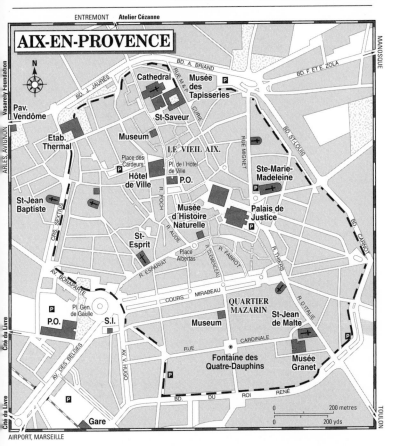

tions and decoration imply a more important origin. In fact it was the old grain market and the 18C sculpture by Jean Chasyel (1726–93) over the façade depicts the rivers Durance and Rhône, symbolising the control of water in the regeneration of the region's agriculture. On the left at the top of the square is the 17C Hôtel de Ville attached to the earlier and more ornate **Tour de l'Horloge**. The bell at the top is enclosed by a fine 16C iron 'cage' typical of Provençal towers, while the astrological clock has a sequence of painted wooden figures representing the seasons. Designed by the Parisian architect Pierre Pavillon in 1655, the **Hôtel de Ville** has some fine sculpture and decorations, notably the wrought-iron gate which leads onto the inner courtyard. Until recently the building also housed two important libraries, both since moved to the Cité du Livre arts complex, but certain treasures are sometimes on display on the upper floors.

Continuing north into the rue Gaston-de-Saporta you come to the **Musée du Vieil Aix** (☎ 04 42 21 43 55: **open** Tues–Sun 10.00–12.00 and 14.30–18.00 Apr–Sept; 10.00–12.00 and 14.30–17.00 Nov–Mar; closed Mon), housed in an impressive 17C mansion designed by Laurent Vallon. This museum has an interesting collection of folklore and local crafts, notably the objects related to the annual Corpus Christi or *Fête Dieu* celebrations. These were established in 1462 by King René and quickly grew into a huge public procession of costumed figures acting out scenes from the Bible and the apocryphal harrowing of hell. The masks employed in this event are very striking and there is a large 18C screen depicting the procession in the early 18C which gives some idea of the scale of the activities. The building itself and the elaborate decoration are equally memorable.

The rue Gaston-de-Saporta was the principal street in old Aix where many of the most powerful and wealthy families built their mansions. Most have since been taken over by the university or the local council, which means that they have lost some of their historic character, but in many cases it is possible to enter and look round the courtyards and interiors. No. 19, the **Hôtel de Châteaurenard**, was built in 1650 and once received Louis XIV although it is now the Social Services Department. Its most remarkable feature is the monumental staircase with *trompe-l'oeil* decoration by Jean Daret (1615–68); the illusionistic architecture and sculpture seems to ascend the whole height of the stairwell culminating in a figure of Minerva distributing flowers. Next is the Hôtel Boyer de Fonscolombe at No. 21, with its courtyard and 17C fountain, followed by the Hôtel Maynier d'Oppède at No. 23, dating originally from 1490.

At the top of the street, in an area still dominated by the old university, is the **Cathédrale St-Sauveur** (open daily 09.30–11.00 and 14.00–16.30). As a piece of architecture it is something of a hybrid, offering a patchwork history of Christian building styles from the 5C, when it was founded, to the Baroque of the 17C–18C which saw the last major campaign. Taken as a whole, therefore, it is not particularly harmonious but it has numerous features which are in themselves excellent. Even the façade tells something of its uneven history. Looking from right to left you can see first the large blocks of the Roman wall, then the 12C Romanesque frontage, followed by the Flamboyant Gothic main façade with its elaborate sculpture (mostly restored using casts), and finally the 14C clocktower with its octagonal crown, the pinnacles of which were completed only in the late 19C. The highlights of this curious *mélange* are the carved wooden doors (1504) by the Toulon sculptor Jean Guiramand representing the prophets and sybils who foretold the coming of Christ. (The doors are protected by shutters which can be opened on request by the sacristan.)

This stylistic diversity, not to say confusion, is carried on throughout the interior but again it seems to follow a sort of chronology. First is the **Baptistery**, to the right on entering by the west door, which dates back to the origins of the cathedral. Few interiors, even in Provence which is well endowed with early Christian remains, can communicate the atmosphere of the early church as strongly as this lofty yet relatively small space. Surrounded by tall columns salvaged from the old Roman forum on this very site, early believers descended the few steps with their priest for a baptism of total immersion in the marble bath. The simplicity and monumentality of this edifice defies the need for any interpretive information panel and one can only hope that the authorities will resist the temptation to provide one.

The main part of the cathedral, and in particular the two naves, follows an unusual plan reflecting the different phases of building. The right or southern nave belongs to the 12C Romanesque cathedral, its simple rhythms evoking the sense of order and clarity that the medieval builders detected in Classical remains. Within a century, however, a grander edifice was needed and a larger nave in the full Gothic style was built alongside, incorporating the old church. The Gothic did not thrive in Provence in the way that it did in northern France but this truncated and at times awkward interior is one of the finest examples in the region.

Among the contents there are several interesting items, such as the 5C sarcophagus of St Mitre in the first bay of the Romanesque nave, or the early 16C tapestries of the life of Christ and the Virgin behind the main altar, which were originally at Canterbury. But the most important treasure in the church is the triptych of the **Buisson Ardent** (Burning Bush), painted in 1476 by Nicolas Froment, court painter to King René. The king is depicted in the left-hand panel accompanied by his patron saints (SS Mary Magdalene, Anthony and Maurice), while his queen, Jeanne de Laval, can be seen on the right panel with hers (SS John the Baptist, Catherine and Nicholas). The central panel shows the Madonna and Child within the Burning Bush with an incredulous Moses below surrounded by his flocks; this juxtaposition of Old and New Testament themes was quite common in the Middle Ages: the 'bush which burned but was not consumed' was taken to symbolise the purity of the Virgin. The painting is hung fairly high up the wall but it is possible to make out the details, the brilliance of colour and the naturalism of the portraits that were a feature of the Flemish schools of this period. If the panels are closed, the sacristan will open them for a small consideration.

At the end of the 17C a third nave of sorts was created by knocking together three chapels on the north side of the main church. Known as **Notre-Dame-de-l'Espérance** this chapel, sometimes regarded as almost a separate church, is perhaps the best example of the Baroque in the whole complex. By contrast, the **cloisters** off the south side of the old nave are the most attractive and uniform section of the early building. Dating originally from the 12C, they are covered by a wooden roof instead of the usual stone vault. The lighter load has allowed for the harmonious arrangement of twinned marble columns around all four sides. Unfortunately, the sculpted capitals have deteriorated badly and, with the exception of the figure of St Peter in the northeast corner, you look in vain for the delicate carving and sensitive characterisation that make St-Trophîme in Arles such a wonderful monument.

Alongside the cloisters on the place des Martyrs-de-la-Résistance is the former Palace of the Archbishops, an impressive 17C building which now houses a theatre and the **Musée des Tapisseries** (☎ 04 42 21 05 78: **open** Wed–Mon 10.00–12.00 and 14.00–17.00; closed Tues). It is a particularly appropriate setting in which to display tapestries. The rooms are suitably spacious and of the right period, and the lighting is relatively low while allowing for close inspection of the weave. The first two rooms display the finest of the sets, that of *Don Quixote*, woven in Beauvais (1735–44) to designs by the French Rococo artist Charles-Joseph Natoire (1700–77). Also interesting are the photographs of the original cartoons, revealing something of the process of transcription involved when reproducing a painted design in threads of different hue. The other two sets, *Russian Games* (1769) after J.-B. Leprince (1734–81) and six *Grotesques* (1689) after designs by Jean Bérain (1640–1711), are hung in the later rooms of the palace.

Returning south on the rue Gaston-de-Saporta towards the cours Mirabeau, turn left at any of the streets after the Hôtel de Ville and you will emerge onto the huge open area of the combined place de la Madeleine, place des Prêcheurs and place de Verdun. This area is dominated by the **Palais de Justice**, an immense neo-Classical building commissioned from the visionary architect Nicolas Ledoux but designed by his follower Michel-Robert Penchaud (1772–1833), for which the old palace of the Counts of Provence was demolished. After the annexation of Provence by France in 1486 the old palace became the principal centre of civil administration and the high court, functions which the new building took over in the early 19C. Much shabbier and rather more grim is the equally large block alongside it to the northwest, also designed by Penchaud. This is the town jail, apparently abandoned but in fact still in use.

> ## Place des Prêcheurs
>
> The place des Prêcheurs was used for public executions and witch-burnings but in the late 18C it was the scene of two even more bizarre events. In 1772, having escaped capture after a night of debauchery in Marseille, the Marquis de Sade was tortured and executed here in effigy. This semi-primitive ritual, purging the town of vice, seems to have given the local citizens a degree of satisfaction because they repeated the exercise 12 years later. In 1784 the son of the president of the parliament murdered his aristocratic wife in their mansion on the cours Mirabeau (see above). He escaped to Lisbon but was tried *in absentia*. The sentence (hands cut off and body broken on the wheel) was carried out on a mannequin dressed in his clothes.

To the north, on the opposite side of the *place* beyond the obelisk and fountain, is the **Eglise Ste-Marie-Madeleine** (open Mon–Fri 09.30–11.30). This building began its life as a Dominican church in 1274 but it has been repeatedly enlarged and altered, particularly in the High Baroque period, so that it has lost virtually all vestiges of its medieval origins. The ponderous Classical façade is entirely 19C. It does, however, have a number of interesting treasures and is occasionally described as a church museum. There is a good marble statue of the Virgin by Jean Chastel in the fourth chapel on the right and a painting of the *Martyrdom of St Peter* attributed to Rubens. But the most important item in the church is the triptych of the *Annunciation*, a masterpiece of the School of Avignon from the mid-15C. Only the central panel, depicting a resplendent Madonna in an elaborate Gothic interior, is original; the wings are copies after paintings now in Brussels and London. The curious symbolism of this work has intrigued many scholars and indeed the whole painting is something of a mystery. If you look closely at the architecture on the left you will notice several diabolical creatures, bats and a dragon, which would normally be out of place at this sacred event. The altarpiece was commissioned by a local draper, Pierre Corpici, but the artist's name is unknown.

The Quartier Mazarin and outskirts

Return to the cours Mirabeau by the small passage Agard at the foot of the place de Verdun. Crossing the *cours* to the south you will enter the **Quartier Mazarin**, a quiet and elegant district laid out in the 17C for the residences of wealthy local families. There are few shops or cafés in this area which means that it is less popular with tourists but it is pleasant to walk in and there are numerous sites of historical and cultural interest. Named after Michel Mazarin, archbishop of Aix and brother of Louis XIV's chief minister, this district has the regular plan and elegant streetfronts that characterise Classical town-planning. Taking the rue du 4e septembre, again opposite the Fontaine Moussue, you will come to the **Musée Paul Arbaud** (☎ 04 42 38 38 95: **open** Mon–Sat 14.00–17.00; closed Sun) on the right at the first junction. Arbaud was a connoisseur and bibliophile who, on his death in 1911, bequeathed his 18C mansion and entire collection to the the city. In honour of this the museum has been kept very much as Arbaud left it, offering a fascinating insight into the life and interests of this man. The collection itself is particularly rich in Provençal ceramics, but there are interesting manuscripts and over 300 portraits of the Comte de Mirabeau. It is easy to understand why Mirabeau should be such an obsession since the *roué* conducted many of his adventures within shouting distance, effecting his first famous seduction at 13 rue Mazarine. On the rue Cabassol, between Mazarine and Goyrand, is the Conservatoire, named after the composer Darius Milhaud (1894–1974) who lived here briefly. Milhaud went to school in the Lycée Mignet at the foot of his street, on the rue Cardinale. Two pupils of an earlier period who struck up a lifelong friendship while there were the painter Paul Cézanne and the novelist and critic Emile Zola.

Mirabeau

Born in 1749, Honoré-Gabriel Riquetti, the Comte de Mirabeau, deserted his noble background to campaign for the new ideals that culminated in the Revolution. In Aix, where the principal street is named after him, he is regarded as something of a colourful, even romantic, figure but he was, in fact, a venal opportunist with a gift for oratory. His amorous adventures drew the greatest approbation and, since he was physically repulsive, this is perhaps all the more remarkable. It was at the Hôtel Marignane in the Mazarin *quartier* that he conducted the very public seduction of the daughter of the house: Mirabeau is reputed to have left his carriage at the door all night to broadcast his affair and compromise the young heiress Emilie de Marignane. This led to his first marriage in Aix in 1772. The relationship did not last long and he was involved in a series of financial and amorous scrapes—including a spell in prison on the Château d'If—before their divorce in 1783. Despite these scandals he was elected to the Estates General in 1789, choosing to represent the Third Estate.

The junction of rue Cardinale and rue 4 septembre is marked by the charming **Fontaine des Quatre-Dauphins**, dating from 1667. In a city renowned for its fountains this group of dolphins spouting water is the most popular and admired. Looking along rue Cardinale to the east you will see the tower and outline of the church of **St-Jean-de-Malte** (☎ 04 42 38 25 70: **open** Mon–Sat 08.00–13.00 and 15.00–19.30, Sun 08.30–12.30 and 18.00–19.30), one of the landmarks outside the old city walls. Dating from the late 13C, this former priory chapel of the Knights of St John was the first true Gothic church in Provence. It is a large building with a famous tall clocktower, but it lacks the interesting details that normally impart charm to the Gothic. For several centuries the Counts of Provence were interred here but their tombs were all but destroyed in the Revolution.

Alongside this, in the old Commandery of the Knights, is the **Musée Granet** (☎ 04 42 38 14 70: **open** Wed–Mon 10.00–12.00 and 14.00–18.00; closed Tues), one of the finest museums and art galleries of Provence. Named after François-Marius Granet (1775–1849), an undeservedly neglected 19C painter, the collection contains Classical and Celto-Ligurian antiquities, including some of the Salian heads from the oppidum at Entremont. The dark and densely hung art galleries on the upper floors display pictures from most of the leading European schools of the 17C and 18C, including interesting works by Rembrandt, Rubens and Guercino (1591–1666). There are also some examples of the School of Avignon and a portrait of *Thomas More* by the Flemish painter Mabuse (c 1475–1533). But the real highlights of the collection are the French neo-Classical and Romantic paintings, many of which were acquired by Granet from his own circle. Ingres' *Portrait of Granet* (1807), one of the artist's masterpieces, grew out of their close friendship while colleagues at the French Academy in Rome. Granet also bought the huge *Jupiter and Thetis*, Ingres' controversial Salon entry of 1811. This curious picture shows the aquiline nymph Thetis imploring a musclebound Jupiter to make her son Achilles immortal. To achieve her aims, she drapes herself across his lap, strokes his chin and allows her naked toe to touch his. Granet's own paintings, particularly his atmospheric, tonal interiors, reveal an aspect of French Romantic art that rarely gets into the main history books. In the mid-19C this gallery also served as the local drawing school, which was attended briefly by Cézanne before he had to give up art in favour of the law. There is one room devoted to a few works by the master of Aix, although they are not his most memorable.

The centre of Aix is circumscribed by its perimeter roadway which closely follows the line of the old city walls. There are, however, many places of interest immediately outside this ring and within walking distance of the town centre. The **Cité du Livre** at No. 8 rue des Allumettes, west of the Rotonde, is a new arts complex containing the two great libraries that were previously housed in the Hôtel de Ville. The earlier of these, the Bibliothèque Mejanes, is an outstanding collection of books and manuscripts assembled by Jean-Baptiste Piquet, Marquis de Mejanes and bequeathed to the town in 1786. The most famous item is the 15C *Book of Hours of King René* which is frequently on display. The other notable collection is that of the author, diplomat and Nobel laureate Saint-John Perse (the *nom de plume* of Alexis Léger, 1887–1975), who bequeathed his own library and papers to the town on his death. Perse was an isolated figure in French literature who worked abroad for much of his life, particularly in the USA, after opposing the collaborationist stance of the Vichy regime.

At the northwest corner of the town by the cours Sextius is the 18C spa on the site of its ancient Roman predecessor, the thermae. A corner tower from the 14C walls survives in the garden. On the other side of the road at 13 rue de la Molle is the **Pavillon de Vendôme** (☎ 04 42 21 05 78: **open** Wed–Mon 10.00–12.00 and 14.00–18.00; closed Tues), an attractive mansion built in 1667 as a country residence for the Cardinal de Vendôme. In the 18C a further floor was added which, far from destroying its proportions, has brought a charm to the building more often associated with the Rococo. The well-kept gardens are open to the public and the house now acts as an art gallery with a programme of temporary exhibitions.

Crossing to the avenue Pasteur in the northernmost part of the old town you come across the bizarre mausoleum of Joseph Sec at No. 6. This monument, built in 1792 at the height of the Revolution, celebrates the rule of law and the ascent of the soul in a series of sculptures and inscriptions. Further up the avenue and off to the right you join the avenue Paul-Cézanne, which leads after 300m to the **Atelier Cézanne** (☎ 04 42 21 06 53: **open** Wed–Mon 10.00–12.00 and 14.30–18.00; closed Tues) behind a wall on the left. The artist bought this plot of land and built the studio in 1901, spending the last four years of his life working here. This was, therefore, the context in which he created his last series of *Bathers*, although there is very little here to suggest the artist's life or working methods. There are no works by Cézanne in the studio and, with the exception of a few props and reproductions, it could be the work-place of any artist. The house which Cézanne painted repeatedly is the Jas de Bouffan, his family home, which is still in private hands. Situated on the right-hand side of the cours Minimes, the main road out of the town to the west, by the avenue du Jas de Bouffan, it is possible to look in through the gates to the line of trees which appear in several of Cézanne's paintings of the 1880s and '90s.

Around Aix

For a better insight into the artist and his works, however, you should visit his most important motif, the **Montagne Ste-Victoire** to the east of the town on the D17 past Le Tholonet. Very little can prepare the visitor for the sheer monu-mentality of this mountain when it is seen for the first time. The huge mass of limestone rock rears out of the ground to take up the whole of your field of vision as you approach. Even from a distance you are aware of the hard, crys-talline material and its huge presence which makes Cezanne's work seem all the more natural. The artist often walked to this area to paint in front of his motif and for a while he had a studio in a farmhouse called the Château Noir, near Le Tholonet, to be close to the mountain.

Travelling eastwards, the D17 follows the line of the mountain's southern face, passing through a series of attractive villages such as St-Antonin and Pourrières, from which you can walk up to the summit. The path from Puyloubier leads up to the 11C pilgrimage chapel of St-Ser, a remarkable site where the eponymous hermit lived in the early Christian period.

On the gentler north slopes of the mountain by the D10 is the 14C–16C **Château de Vauvenargues**, one of the finest fortified houses of a distinctly Provençal type. Square in plan with powerful fortifications and a tower at each corner, the château was the home of the Marquis de Vauvenargues, an 18C moralist and friend of Voltaire. In 1958 the château and estate were purchased by Picasso as a refuge from the increasingly busy Cannes. One anecdote describes Picasso calling his dealer Kahnweiler to announce that he had just bought the Montagne Ste-Victoire. Kahnweiler, who also handled Cézanne's work, asked the painter which version he had acquired to which Picasso replied that he had bought 'the original'. Picasso lived here with his third wife, Jacqueline Roque, for whom he decorated several of the rooms. Although he did not spend a great deal of time at the château, he is buried in the grounds. The castle is still in the hands of his family who are planning to open it as yet another museum to the artist.

There is a circular route back to Aix, looping north by the D11 after Vauvenargues and following an attractive road between the mountains of Concors and Ubac. This leads first to **Jouques**, an important village where the archbishops of Aix had a castle retreat. The castle, dating from 1630, still exists but it is not open to the public. From here the D561 leads to Peyrolles, an industrial town, and the N96 to **Meyrargues**, a similarly ugly centre but overlooked by its 12C castle. This building, transformed in the 17C by the Albertas family who built one of the most beautiful squares in Aix, is now a hotel with attractive painted interiors and a good view over the surrounding countryside and up to the Luberon. In the valley below the castle to the northeast you will find the remains of the Roman aqueduct that once carried water to Aquae Sextiae.

The last section of the road back to Aix, after the ruined village of Venelles, passes several vineyards with traditional *bastides*. One of the finest is La Mignarde, where Napoleon's sister Pauline Borghese stayed; another is the Château de la Gaude near the 14C watchtower known as the Tour de César. Also near this point, to the left or east side of the N96 as it approaches Aix, is the Pavillon de Lenfant, a simple, rectilinear villa dating from 1677 which nevertheless has a rich and elaborate interior. For an alternative to these monuments of Aix's age of elegance, you can leave the N96 by the dual carriageway N296 which leads to the oppidum of **Entremont** (open Wed–Mon 09.00–12.00 and 14.00–18.00; closed Tues), the Celto-Ligurian bastion that was overrun by the Romans in 123 BC. Very little survives of the original fortifications but it is an atmospheric site.

The countryside to the west of Aix has fewer attractions, partly due to the industrial developments and irrigation schemes which have grown up there, but it is a distinctive area overlooked by the impressive **Chaîne de l'Etoile**, the mountains to the south between Aix and Marseille. Excursions to the Vallée de l'Arc, southwest of Aix, should start on the avenue de Belges and avenue de l'Europe leading on to the A51. Before leaving the town at this point, however, it is worth visiting the **Musée Vasarély** (☎ 04 42 20 01 09: open Wed–Mon 09.00–12.30 and 14.00–17.30; closed Tues) on the avenue Marcel-Pagnol at Jas de Bouffan. (Continue up the avenue de l'Europe until it passes under the motorway, then turn first left.) Designed by the eponymous artist himself, this hi-tech, modular building is an alien landmark in the country of Cézanne but it sets the scene for the pictures displayed inside. In some respects Vasarély's work is largely mechanical but there is an ingeniousness to it and, like much abstract art of the post-war period, it is enhanced by scale. If you are accustomed to these Op Art designs as reproductions or even as wrapping paper it is pleasantly arresting to see them blown up to a size that dwarfs the spectator and takes up the entire field of vision. The larger works are complemented by numerous drawings and other material in the smaller galleries on the first floor.

The main route to the Arc valley is via the D9, a turn-off from the A51. There is, however, a small road from the avenue du Jas de Bouffan which joins the D9 at the first point of interest, the Château de Pioline. This is a 16C *bastide* with some surprisingly rich interiors from the 18C when it was remodelled (for information on entrance times, see the Aix tourist office). Further on by the D65, past the industrial centre of Les Milles, is Saint-Pons which has a 17C château, now a hotel. For those interested in the industrial heritage of this region, the **Aqueduc de Roquefavour** is a fine example of 19C civil engineering. Built in 1842–47 to carry the waters of the Durance by canal to Marseille, this series of stone arches bears comparison with its ancient prototype, the Pont du Gard (see p 124).

Finally, there are two picturesque villages which have interesting buildings in themselves but also offer excellent views over the surrounding countryside. **Ventabren**, on the D64, is a tiny *village perché* dominated by the ruins of its medieval castle, once the home of René of Anjou's queen, Jeanne de Laval. In the church there is a painting of the Virgin dating from 1484 by an unknown artist of the School of Avignon. **Eguilles**, another attractive village some 10km to the northeast on the D17, stands on the route of the Roman road to Spain, the Via Aurelia, and there are some Classical remains in the area. Within the village the most important building is the 17C town hall which was once the castle of the Boyer d'Eguilles family.

17 · The Haut Var

The principal route east–west through Provence is the old N7 linking a series of market towns as it makes its way to the coast at Fréjus. This has now been joined by the A8–E80, the *Autoroute La Provençale*, and together they cut a swathe through the centre of the region. Neither provides a particularly scenic journey but they are relatively fast and therefore the most popular routes to the sea and the Côte d'Azur. They also pass near some of the previously remote villages of the Haut Var which have been omitted from many of the obvious tourist itineraries but which represent to many people the older heart of Provence.

The middle section of the N7 passes through St-Maximin, Brignoles, Le Luc and Vidauban, which can all be visited with a simple detour from the *autoroute*. The major villages of the Upper Var (Barjols, Draguignan, Aups) and the important monuments at Entrecasteaux and Le Thoronet involve a more circuitous journey.

Aix to Fréjus ~ the N7 and Autoroute La Provençale

The N7 and A8–E80 leave Aix-en-Provence to the east overlooked by the massive rocky outcrop of the Montagne Ste-Victoire. This area witnessed one of the momentous events in French, not to say European, history. In 102 BC the Roman general Marius defeated a combined Barbarian army of Teutons and Cimbri to consolidate Roman control of Gaul. Livy reported that over 200,000 Barbarians were killed and that the river Arc, which runs by the road, flowed with blood. In an even more macabre tale, Plutarch recorded how for years afterwards the people of the area made their fences from the whitened bones of the dead. The battle itself is thought to have taken place near the village of Pourrières and the *Fête de la Ste-Victoire*, celebrated on 24 April in many of the local villages, has been traced back to the victory celebrations of the Roman legionnaires.

The first town of real interest is **St-Maximin-la-Sainte-Baume**, whose huge Gothic basilica is visible from some distance.

History of St-Maximin-la-Sainte-Beaume

Tradition has it that St Maximinus, who had arrived in Provence with the Stes Maries (see p 84), was martyred in Aix and his relics preserved here. Even more important, Mary Magdalene was believed to have been buried alongside her colleague making this spot, in the words of the 19C theologian Lacordaire, 'the third most important tomb in Christendom'.

The town was certainly a pilgrimage centre from early Christian times and monastery may have been built over the relics. In 716, with the threat of Saracen invasion, these relics were hidden by the monks and it was not until 1279 that Charles of Anjou, reputedly guided by a dream, rediscovered them in the crypt. In the interim period a rival legend had grown up that the relics had been moved to Vézelay in Burgundy, which undoubtedly helped that cathedral to flourish. The confusion created an unseemly dispute which was never fully resolved but there is little doubt that the claims of St-Maximin were stronger. They were also supported by persuasive physical evidence. The Magdalene's body, which was found to be in a remarkable state of preservation, was dismembered to feed the flourishing trade in relics throughout Europe. Only the skull now survives at St-Maximin. Nevertheless, this event restored the fortunes of the town and marked the beginning of a building programme culminating in the huge Gothic basilica and Dominican monastery.

❖ Information and accommodation

🛈 Hôtel de Ville (☎ 04 94 78 00 09).

Hotels. St-Maximin is not the most enticing place to stay but the *Hôtel Plaisance* (☎ 04 94 78 16 74) at 2 place Malherbe is very good.

The **Basilica** (open daily 08.30–12.00 and 14.00–19.00) was begun in 1295 under the direction of Giovanni Baudici, architect of the Count's palace in Aix. Given the importance of the relics and of the rising pilgrimage trade, work progressed quickly on the chancel and nave until 1316. Thereafter work was interrupted for almost 200 years and it was not until 1532 that the church reached its present state. Even now it lacks a façade but the scale of the building is impressive and probably justifies its title as the 'greatest Gothic church in Provence'.

The full effect is only apparent on the interior, its sheer height being one of the most striking features. It does not bear comparison with the great Gothic buildings of the north but there is an order and sobriety to the forms, uncluttered by additional decoration, that reveals the purity of Baudici's design. Mérimée, who had already described the town of St-Maximin as a 'miserable little hole', reserved some praise for the church. He was particularly impressed by the lack of destructive renovation which had blighted so many of the medieval monuments in Provence, so he was keen to protect and develop this building. 'There is not a church in France more worthy to receive works of art', he wrote, and the state responded. As a result, there are several items of interest in the interior, such as the the 13C cope of St Louis of Toulouse or the 16C altarpiece of the *Crucifixion* by François Ronzen with 18 medallions of the Passion, one of which has the earliest known representation of the Palais des Papes in Avignon. The principal feature, however, is the 18C organ. This instrument helped to save the basilica during the anticlerical violence of the Revolution. Napoleon's youngest brother, Lucien, was stationed here and he forestalled a mob intent on demolishing the building by playing the *Marseillaise* on the organ. He later married a local girl in the basilica. The organ continues to serve the town well and good recitals are held here at the annual music festival in August.

The **crypt**, which can be entered by a staircase on the north aisle, was originally the 4C funeral vault and still contains the holy relics. In all five saints are represented here, Mary Magdalene, Marcella, Susan, Cedonius and Maximinus. There are also some good late antique sarcophagi and the 19C helmet-like reliquary containing the cranium of Mary Magdalene. The monastery or **Couvent Royal** adjoining the basilica is a three-storey complex which originates from the 13C although it was substantially rebuilt in the 18C. It now serves as a cultural centre staging exhibitions and performances although there are guided tours to the cloisters and chapter house (☎ 04 94 78 01 93: **open** Mon–Fri 10.00–11.45 and 14.00–17.45, Sat, Sun 14.00–18.45).

Despite Merimée's dismissive comments, the town of St-Maximin has some redeeming features. The area just south of the basilica, for example, has arcaded streets from the 14C and a number of survivals from the old Jewish ghetto. Other items of interest in the area include **Le Saint Pilon**, a 15C stone column to the south of the town which marks the spot where Mary Magdalene received her last communion from St Maximin.

Tourves, the next village which is by-passed on the N7, is dominated by a huge neo-Classical ruin. This is the remains of the **Château de Valbelle**, built in the 1760s by Omer de Valbelle as a modern 'court of love'. Omer's tastes ran to sensual nude statues but his collection was dispersed when the château was burnt down by a revolutionary mob in 1799. One of the figures is reputed to have been placed, inappropriately, on the site of the Magdalene's cave at La Ste-Baume. In the park behind the ruins are a number of monuments including an obelisk and small pyramid in honour of Omer's family.

The name of **Brignoles** is often thought to derive from two Celtic words (*brin* and *on*) meaning 'good prunes'. If this is the source, the town could be described as maintaining its ancient traditions because it is still a trading centre for the fruit and agricultural produce of a substantial area. It has an important fair and market in the first fortnight in April when the local produce is shown and sold. This is also the main celebration of the local wine-growers, which makes the event fairly lively. Brignoles is also the centre of the bauxite mining industry, although this has had little impact on the well-preserved old town.

History of Brignoles

Brignoles was originally a Roman settlement on the Via Aurelia and this position on the main artery across Provence gave it a pivotal role in the region. For many years it was the home of the Counts of Provence whose palace survives at the summit of the old town. For some reason a legend grew up that the air in Brignoles was particularly good for childbirth. This brought many female pilgrims to the town but there is no evidence that the atmosphere had any effect.

St Louis of Toulouse was born and died in Brignoles and this was the seat of the Provençal parliament between the 14C and 18C. As might be expected, therefore, it has witnessed considerable fighting throughout its history. Charles V overran it in 1536 and, to press home the point, renamed it Nicopolis, 'city of victory'. There were similar events during the 16C Wars of Religion when the valuable prune trade seemed to be a constant target for reprisals from one side or another. It was finally extinguished when an uprising against the local landlord destroyed 180,000 plum trees. Nowadays, if you buy Brignolais prunes they come from Digne.

❖ Information and accommodation

🛈 Place St-Louis (☎ 04 94 69 01 78).

Hotels. Accommodation in Brignoles is not difficult to find outside the April fair period and in general it is reasonably priced. *Le Paris* at 29 avenue Dréo (☎ 04 94 69 01 18) or *Le Caramy* on place Caramy (☎ 04 94 69 11 08) are both in the town while *Château Brignoles en Provence* (☎ 04 94 69 06 88) is just outside on the N7.

Despite this turbulent background the old town has remained in a remarkable state of preservation. Spreading out from the 11C church of St-Sauveur at the centre to the remains of the old town walls is a maze of narrow streets punctuated by small squares, fountains and doorways. A helpful map for the confused motorist is available from the *office du tourisme*. At the southern edge of the old town is the palace of the Counts of Provence, dating from the 13C although it was largely rebuilt in the 15C–16C. This building now houses the **Musée du Pays Brignolais** (☎ 04 94 69 45 18: open Wed–Sat 09.00–12.00 and 14.30–18.00; Sun 10.00–12.00 and 15.00–17.00 Apr–Oct; shorter hours Nov–Mar), a curious museum of local history and folklore that should not be missed if only for the bizarre combination of exhibits. As well as the usual collections of traditional furniture, costume, ceramics, dolls, and so on, there is an interesting 3C sarcophagus from La Gayole which is often claimed to be the earliest Christian artefact in Gaul. Nearby is the concrete rowing boat (1840) made by Joseph Lambot—an early failure in marine technology, some dinosaur eggs, an intriguing mechanical crib designed by the Abbé Giraud and displays related to the bauxite industry. The interior of the palace was reorganised when the museum opened in 1947 but it does incorporate some early rooms, notably the 17C chapel of St-Louis with its decorative woodwork and a celebrated figure of the Virgin blackened by smoke. There is also a room devoted to the 17C Parrocel family of painters who were born and worked locally. Among the various 17C–18C mansions in this area the over-restored Hôtel de Clavier on the rue du Palais has some interesting features and now serves as an art centre.

Of the various walks and items of interest in the vicinity, the village of **La Celle** (2km south) has the remains of a Cistercian convent dating from 1060, part of which is now incorporated into a farm. The parish church, originally the 15C convent chapel, has an interesting 11C Italian crucifix with remarkably naturalistic carving for the period. In the opposite direction, 8km northeast of Brignoles, there is a ruined castle with Renaissance details in the village of **Vins-sur-Caramy**. This is under restoration and will be used for concerts.

Brignoles is a good point of departure from the main road for the outstanding 12C Cistercian abbey of Le Thoronet. Other routes to the abbey lead from Flassans-sur-Issoles and, the most direct, from Le Luc. Take the D24 to the east of Brignoles for 15km, turning right into the D13 for 2km, then left into the D79 for 4km.

Set in a secluded glade, as befits the Cistercian rule, the **Abbaye du Thoronet** (☎ 04 94 60 43 90; **open** Mon–Sat 09.00–19.00, Sun 09.00–12.00 and 14.00–19.00 Apr–Sept; daily 09.00–12.00 and 14.00–19.00 Oct–Mar) is the earliest and finest of the 'three sisters' of Provence (see pp 148 and 177).

History of the Abbaye du Thoronet

The Cistercian community first settled in the area in 1136 but chose to abandon their original abbey near Tourtour after only a decade when Raymond Bérenger offered them this site. Such a bold decision must have given the monks a sense of purpose because the main complex of church and outbuildings was completed within 40 years, a remarkably short period for a major building in the Middle Ages. One of the first abbots was the celebrated troubadour poet, Folquet de Marseille, who entered the monastery in 1195 following the death of his muse, the Lady N'Alazais. Folquet went on to become Bishop of Toulouse, from where he led the merciless 'crusade' against the Albigensian heretics in the Languedoc, thus earning himself a place in Dante's *Paradiso*. This militant aspect is unusual in the history of the Cistercians, not least because of their strict vows of humility and seclusion. After an initial period of success, the order went into decline and after the 15C they were often themselves the victims of religious persecution. By 1789 there were only seven monks left, whereupon the buildings were vandalised, sold and threatened with demolition. There seemed little hope for this remote ruin until 1834 when Prosper Mérimée visited the site and recommended that the abbey be purchased by the state. Renovation work has continued ever since.

Le Thoronet is one of the most sublime expressions of the Romanesque style in architecture; a complex of simple, intersecting forms elaborated by the magisterial rhythms of the rounded arch. This effect is further enhanced by the golden pink stone which is used throughout and which seems to reflect the subtle changes in the light at different times of the day. The overall harmony is immediately apparent from the sober façade of the **abbey church** and is emphasised on entering the spacious interior. Typically, there are no furnishings or decoration to distract from the bare masonry. A small door in the north transept leads out to the cloister with, at the top, a hexagonal lavabo or fountain where the monks underwent their ritual washing before meals. Beyond this was the **calefactory**, the only heated space in the abbey, which served as the scriptorium in winter.

The overall plan follows that of St-Gall in Switzerland which provided the model for most monasteries in the period, particularly those of the austere Cistercian order. It is essentially functional with the main facilities for monastic life—church, sacristy, dormitories and refectory—grouped round the cloister. These in turn are linked to the secondary buildings such as the lay brothers' quarters, the cellars, workshops and barn.

These buildings now house a sequence of interesting displays on the history of the abbey and on the repair and restoration work which carries on to this day. This has touched all aspects of the complex, including extensive stone renovation using the original quarries. The work is of the highest standard but, looking at the early photographs of the buildings, you cannot help feeling that some of the atmosphere has been lost. It must have been an impressive ruin, although that would have made for a different experience. The restored buildings are once again in use and it is possible to attend services in the church and occasional concerts and other performances. The best time to visit is probably the late afternoon when the light brings out the contrast of the forms and the stone itself seems to radiate some of the heat absorbed during the hot summer days. At any time, however, Le Thoronet, like its sister houses, offers an unforgettable experience.

Continuing on the N7 east from Brignoles, you pass Flassans-sur-Issoles before approaching **Le Luc**, a modestly prosperous market town and spa dominated by its curious hexagonal tower.

History of Le Luc

As a Protestant centre, Le Luc was continually attacked during the Wars of Religion, culminating in the terrible events of 1589–90 when, after a long siege, most of the population was massacred. Following the Edict of Nantes in 1598 Le Luc became one of only three towns in Provence where Protestants were allowed to practise their religion.

The tradition of radicalism which was evident here in both 1789 and 1848 is celebrated by monuments in the tree-lined place de la Liberté and on a plaque in the picturesque old town recording the imprisonment of 'counter-revolutionaries'. Another monument to this libertarian spirit is the **Château de Vintimille**, a plain if elegant 18C mansion where Jean-Jacques Rousseau was once a protégé. The house was left to the town when the Marquis fled to Germany in 1790, whereupon the populace held their *Fête de la Fédération* in the grounds. This building is now an art centre and a **Musée du Timbre** (☎ 04 94 47 96 16: open Mon–Fri 14.30–1800, Sat, Sun 10.00–12.00 June–Aug; closes 17.30 Oct–May; closed Tues and all Sept), with regular exhibitions devoted to the history of stamps. Another small museum in the old part of town is the **Musée Historique du Centre Var** (☎ 04 94 60 70 12; open Wed–Mon 15.00–18.00 July–Aug; 14.00–17.00 June, Sept; closed Tues), housed in the

17C chapel of Ste-Anne. Exhibits include some ancient archaeological fragments, paintings of the area and material related to J.B. Apollinaire, a local engineer who was responsible for bringing the obelisk of Luxor back to its present site on the place de la Concorde in Paris. The nearby church of Notre-Dame-de-Mont-Carmel has a plain 13C–15C façade although the interior is a fairly elaborate if creepy Gothic revival of the 19C. The **tower** that dominates Le Luc stands over the remains of an 11C priory behind which is yet another religious establishment, the convent of Notre-Dame-de-Nazareth which became first a military hospital in 1794, then a cemetery and is now a wine cellar. The tower may not have been related to either church. Built in 1517–46 it was probably intended as a watchtower to warn the townspeople of approaching danger.

On the opposite side of the *autoroute* is the hilltop village of **Le Vieux-Cannet** which, as well as the splendid view over the plain to the Massif des Maures, has an 11C church with an interesting belltower. The village has been smartened up recently to create a little bourgeois enclave in marked contrast to its earlier history. On the outbreak of the Revolution in 1789 the villagers, carried away with the spirit of the age, attacked and completely destroyed the castle in a single day. So complete was the devastation that even the water tanks were unusable and the villagers were forced to move down onto the plain. The new village, Le Cannet-des-Maures, is a fairly anonymous development along the edge of the main road.

The wine-growing centre of **Vidauban** takes its name from the Latin, *vitis alba* (white vine) but there is very little physical evidence of its ancient history. The most interesting feature of the town is the unusual domed clocktower with its statue of the Virgin which dates from 1898. Just 3km to the north, however, is **Taradeau**, a small village overlooked by a massive square tower and a Romanesque chapel both dating from the 12C. The original village was on the hilltop alongside these impressive landmarks but it was abandoned at the end of the 14C following the ravages of Raymond de Turenne.

Slightly further east and only 2km off the N7 on the D555 towards Draguignan is **Les Arcs**, a prosperous village at the heart of the Côtes-de-Provence vineyards. There are several *caves* open to the public and a Maison des Vins providing information on the routes and vignerons of the area. The most interesting part of the village, however, is the medieval complex on the top of a rock accessible by a series of winding, cobbled paths. The castle at the summit, of which the tower and gateway are the oldest parts, was built in the 13C by Arnaud de Villeneuve, one of the tyrants who ruled this area with a reputation for single-minded cruelty. The 16C clocktower is also very attractive but the whole complex of buildings, including a hotel, *Le Logis des Guetteur* (☎ 04 94 73 30 82), and some excessively quaint houses, has a picturesque quality due to the mottled pink sandstone used throughout. The castle was the birthplace of St Roseline in 1263 and the scene of one of the most popular local legends. In defiance of her cruel father, the same Arnaud, Roseline often smuggled out food from the table for the poor of Les Arcs. On one occasion when challenged by the old ogre she replied that she had only roses in her apron. Forced to reveal her secret consignment, she found the scraps of food had been miraculously transformed into rose petals.

Orphaned at 14, the young Roseline entered a convent at Avignon, later returning to the Benedictine abbey of **La Celle-Roubaud**, just 4km east of Les

Arcs on the D91. This abbey was founded in 1038 by a hermit from Marseille but it has since become associated with the life of St Roseline and the subsequent history of her relics. Following her death in 1329 the body showed no signs of decay and, despite being lost and found during the Wars of Religion, it is still preserved in a glass case inside the rather ugly **Chapelle Sainte-Roseline**. Even more bizarre are the saint's eyes displayed on a wall nearby, one of which has decayed due to the attentions of a surgeon who cut into it on the orders of Louis XIV. Of the other items in the chapel, there are some good 17C choirstalls, a mosaic by Chagall and two bronze sculptures by Giacometti's brother, Diego.

Le Muy, the next town on the N7, is noted for one famous event, a failed attempt on the life of the Emperor Charles V on 23 September 1536 during his campaign to annex Provence. The young would-be assassins hid in the 12C Tour Notre-Dame at the edge of the road but succeeded only in shooting the Spanish poet Garsilaso de la Vega, whom they mistook for the king on account of his sumptuous costume. The terrorists (or freedom fighters) were cornered in the tower, which still survives renamed the Tour Charles Quint, and were eventually overpowered and hanged. Le Muy also has an unusual Gothic church dating from 1500, the fortified appearance suggesting something of the troubled history of the area.

Fréjus is only 17km from here on the N7 but it is worth a detour by the D7 south to see **Roquebrune-sur-Argens** and the impressive deep-red mountain that dominates this area. The village is a warren of old streets, arcades and houses, some dating from the 16C, within the remains of the perimeter ramparts. There is also a late Gothic parish church with two small chapels on the left of the nave, remnants of earlier churches dating back as far as the 8C. Persistent rumours of satanism and heresy have been associated with Roquebrune, partly explained by the repeated Saracen attacks which may have led the demoralised villagers to abandon their religion. Various discoveries in and around the village, such as a Roman marker stone found under the main altar, have been used to support this story but it remains, at best, an intriguing tale quite in keeping with the pagan spirit of the area. Fréjus was, after all, the Roman capital and centre of many cults which continued into the Christian era. For an overview of this unusual district you could make the arduous climb to the top of the Rocher de Roquebrune or visit either of the small chapels, Notre-Dame-de-Pitie or Notre-Dame-de-la-Roquette, signposted from the village, which have good outlooks.

A circuit via Barjols and Draguignan

The short detours from the main N7 road already detailed give something of the flavour of the Haut Var but for a more substantial taste of an area that was historically the heartland of Provence and still has a number of towns and villages of real character, you must leave the main roads behind and head off into the valleys around the Bessillon and Malmont ranges. These are easily accessible by car and the network of small roads offers numerous alternatives to an established itinerary. That suggested here makes a long loop around the main villages and towns starting at St-Maximin-la-Ste-Baume on the N7 and returns to the same road south of Draguignan via Le Muy. There are also exits from the A8 near the same spots. Leave St-Maximin by the D560 to the north which leads directly to Barjols.

Despite its reputation as the Tivoli of Provence owing to the number of springs and fountains in the area, **Barjols** is a quiet town with an air of cultivated gloom. Until recently it was also known as the leather capital of France but the huge tanneries closed down in 1983 leaving gaunt, empty factories looking out from the eastern edge of town.

History of Barjols

There is apparently a long history of unhealthy introversion in Barjols. During the 16C religious wars this was the site of successive reprisals and massacres between Catholics and Protestants, each group using the nearby ravines to dispose of their victims. But in 1799 there was the most spectacular disaster when a depressed saltpeter workman decided to commit suicide by blowing himself up on a barrel of gunpowder. Miscalculating the amount required, or not caring at all, he managed to take a large part of Barjols and many of his neighbours with him. It has been said that his spirit still hangs heavily over the town.

Barjols is perhaps most famous for the festival of St Marcel, held annually on 16–17 January although the full ceremony occurs only once every four years. The day begins with a procession of musicians playing the distinctive flutes and drums (*galoubet* and *tamboulin*) which are made only in Barjols. Following this a cow is decorated with garlands and led through the streets to the cry 'St Marcel, les tripettes!' before being blessed, slaughtered and roasted. This marks the beginning of the 'Tripe Dance' which weaves its way through the streets of the old town. If this sounds like a pagan ritual that is exactly what is often claimed, although its true history stretches back only to 1350 when the relics of St Marcel were first brought to the town and were met by a party of youths preparing tripe.

The church on the main street which houses the relics is an unusual building. Formerly the **Collégiale de Notre-Dame-de-l'Assomption**, it dates from the 11C although it is mainly 16C Gothic and has been altered and enlarged ever since in the most illogical fashion. Access is gained by a flight of steps descending to the dark nave which is flanked by some unusual carvings. There is also a fragment of the original Romanesque tympanum on the altar and some choir stalls carved with a variety of odd characters.

The old town behind the church is a series of narrow streets and small squares, many of which have interesting decorated doorways. The finest of these is that of the 16C Renaissance mansion of the Marquis de Pontèves on the rue Auguste-Guion. (The principal castle of the Pontèves with its four corner towers stands as a ruin in the village 3km east of

Doorway of the mansion of the Marquis de Pontèves

Barjols.) Another feature of the old town are the fountains of which there are 25 in all. The most unusual of these is the **Fontaine du Champignon** (Mushroom Fountain) in the place Capitaine-Vincens, a curious moss-covered monument like a live organism. Some of the abandoned tanneries by the old town walls have been converted into craft workshops producing ceramics and 'leather creations' for the tourist market, although it is difficult to see for whom they are intended.

Cotignac, 15km to the east of Barjols, nestles in the depression below an overhanging cliff face at the top of which are two dramatic ruined towers. During the Middle Ages the crumbly tufa rock provided some protection from marauders leaving a network of grooved and burrowed chambers that are still in use (although felt to be unsafe). In contrast to this backdrop, the village itself is surprisingly elegant. Many of the houses date from the 17C and 18C and the cours Gambetta, with its cafés, fountain and plane trees, is often compared to its counterpart in Aix, although on a much smaller scale. Despite its ugly 18C façade, the church of St-Pierre has an interesting interior dating from the 13C and 17C, the barrel vault illuminated from a cupola in the roof. The rather grand altarpiece by Puget is usually singled out for praise but much more interesting is the large painting of *St Martin and the Beggar*, by Angélique Mongez (1775–1855), one of several women who trained in the studio of David. Religious paintings of this quality in the neo-Classical manner are rare. At the top of the old town, past the charming place de la Mairie, a small open-air theatre has been created in the ramparts. Intimate in scale but enclosed by the immense cliff, it would be difficult to find a more atmospheric setting for the plays and concerts performed here on summer evenings.

On a hilltop 1km south of Cotignac is the **Eglise Notre-Dame-de-Grace**, a pilgrimage church celebrated in the area for a vision of the Madonna in 1519. Its fame was secured by a subsequent vision experienced by Père Fiacre in Paris in 1637, foretelling the birth of Louis XIV. The suggested link between the two manifestations prompted a royal visit to this church by Louis himself in 1660. The sanctuary was badly damaged during the Revolution and despite the beautiful setting amid a grove of tall trees, the rebuilt church is a very dull roughcast building made worse by tasteless modern extensions. A gilt wooden statue above the altar is reputed to have been saved in 1792 by three girls from Cotignac who had been blessed with a miraculous injection of strength, although the size of the figure hardly requires such divine intervention. The diorama telling the story of Père Fiacre and Louis XIV with luridly painted figures is particularly ugly although it does not seem out of place here.

A detour from this route, by the D50 east for 9km, leads to the village of **Entrecasteaux**, grouped round the rock supporting its elegant 17C château (☎ 04 94 04 43 95: **open** Wed–Mon 10.00–18.00 Apr–Oct; closed Tues and at 17.00 in winter).

History of Entrecasteaux

Entrecasteaux was the destination of most of Madame de Sevigné's letters, for her daughter was married to the extravagant Comte de Grignan who built the existing castle on the foundations of an earlier stronghold burned down in 1600. The family remained in residence until 1714 when it passed to Jean-Baptiste de Bruny, a merchant and adventurer who spent the latter part of his life in a Portuguese prison for the murder of his young wife. In

Aix, where the murder had been committed, his effigy was publicly executed. Another member of the family, Joseph de Bruny, died on an expedition in the south seas to find the missing French explorer J.-F. de Galup La Pérouse (1741–c 1788).

Most of the earlier residents and seigneurs, however, are overshadowed by the extraordinary Ian McGarvie-Munn, soldier, diplomat, stockbroker, painter, architect, Scottish nationalist and erstwhile commander of the Guatamalan navy, who bought the ruined château in 1974 and began the difficult process of restoration. It is now a testament to his efforts and, if it occasionally resembles an illustration from the magazine *World of Interiors*, it is nevertheless a believable family home. As if to emphasise this, entrance is gained through the kitchen, leading on to a series of relaxed but gracious rooms, each decorated with a lively combination of paintings, ceramics, Murano glassware, Scottish bagpipes and other curiosities. On the upper floors there is a more formal exhibition of items related to the history of the château and its renovation. Much remains to be done, notably on the outer buildings like the 14C chapel that clings to the edge of the rock, but at least the formal garden immediately below the castle has been restored to its original arrangement. Attributed to Le Nôtre, Louis XIV's garden designer, this is now a pleasant public park. In summer there is a music festival which spills out into the town.

Aups

15km north of Cotignac on the D22, Aups is a village with a history of courageous opposition to authority. Monuments commemorate the victims of several wars and insurrections, the most recent being the Resistance fighters who were executed by the Nazis on the esplanade by the Mairie. An obelisk records the victims of the 1851 insurrection, especially Martin Bidoure who was 'killed twice': the first time was at Tourtour where his wounds were so bad that he was removed to the hospice at Aups; while here, two *gendarmes* took him from his bed to be executed on the square. The Gothic church of St-Pancrace nearby was apparently designed in 1489 by an Englishman, Broulhoui, although the architecture is by far the weakest aspect. Much more interesting is the series of ornate 17C altarpieces dispersed throughout the interior. In the older part of the village there is a good 16C clocktower and a former Ursuline convent which has been converted into a contemporary art gallery, the Musée Simon Segal (☎ 04 94 70 01 95: **open** daily 10.30–12.00 and 16.00–19.00 mid June–mid Sept). The collection itself is fairly weak but, unfortunately, typical of much contemporary French art.

❖ *Information and accommodation*

🛈 Avenue Georges-Clemenceau (☎ 04 94 70 00 80).

Hotels. Accommodation in Aups is generally good if basic, but there is a choice between the *Grand Hôtel* on place Duchatel (☎ 04 97 70 10 82) at the top of the price range and *Le Provençal* on place Martin-Bidoure (☎ 04 97 70 00 24) for economy.

Aups is often felt to be the northern outpost of the Var and it is true that the landscape changes thereafter into rougher and more desolate terrain. This wilder country has an increasing appeal to walkers and those wishing to move beyond the more conventional routes of Provence. As a result, the village has become a centre from which to explore the area and is also within striking distance of the Gorges du Verdon, one of the most spectacular natural sights in the south of France (see p 209).

The main road southeast from Aups, the D557, leads directly to Villecroze, a substantial village with an 11C Templars' chapel on the outskirts, although more people will probably want to take an alternative route via Tourtour. A minor road, the D77, links Aups and Tourtour directly and follows the line of the Montagne des Espiguières. **Tourtour**, known in tourist brochures as 'the village in the sky', has a spectacular setting strung out along the top of a hill between two ruined castles. The village as a whole is now a 'protected site' and this has undoubtedly contributed to its atmosphere as a rather over-restored showpiece. The main square once had two famous elms, planted in 1638 to mark the birth of Louis XIV, but these have been replaced by plane trees. The larger of the castles, at the top of the village, is a traditional four-towered Provençal château which now serves as the Mairie, and beyond it further up the open slope is the 10C parish church of St-Denis. The view from this spot is breathtaking, offering a panorama from Mont Ventoux in the north to the Mediterranean. It is claimed that on a clear day you can even see Corsica and Italy.

Draguignan

The major centre of Draguignan, 20km southeast of Tourtour on the D557, takes its name from the dragon which terrorised the area in the 5C AD. Like its counterpart in Tarascon, the monster was subdued by an evangelist, on this occasion Hermentaire, the first Bishop of Antibes, who converted the population to Christianity.

History of Draguignan

Following its mythical origins, Draguignan played an important role in the history of Provence. Having resisted the Saracens in the 9C, its fortifications became a formidable stronghold against all invaders until Charles V took control of Provence in 1536. By this stage it was one of the major towns in the south of France, becoming the focus of much fighting during the Wars of Religion. On one occasion in 1559 the brutal Antoine de Richieu was cornered by a mob who dragged him from his refuge, stabbed him to death and paraded his ripped-out heart on a pike around the town.

After the Revolution Draguignan was created *préfecture* of the Var and, in accordance with its new status, the town was extended on three sides with rigid boulevards designed by Baron Haussman. This break from the tight organic plan of the old town has been continued into the 20C and, although Draguignan lost its *préfecture* status to Toulon in 1974, it is still an important military and commercial centre. Indeed, the outskirts have an unattractive sprawling character quite unlike the villages of this region, while the town centre is driven more by local business than tourism.

❖ Information and accommodation

🛈 9 boulevard Georges-Clemenceau (☎ 04 94 68 63 30).

Hotels. As the principal town in this area, Draguignan has a reasonable range of accommodation. Among the finest are the *Hôtel Dracenois* at 14 rue du Cros (☎ 04 94 68 14 57) and the *Hôtel du Parc* at 21 boulevard de la Liberté (☎ 04 94 68 53 84). *Les Etoiles de l'Ange* (☎ 04 94 68 23 01), outside town on the road to Lorgues, is probably better and certainly quieter.

The old town is dominated by the formidable turreted **Tour de l'Horloge**, built in 1663 to replace one destroyed by Louis XIV. Below this is the parish church of St-Michel, a dull Gothic-Revival building of 1863–70 which has been showing signs of instability since it was built. The wooden roof, crudely placed on the stone arches, was an early remedy but it has required constant attention ever since. On rue Juiverie, the site of the old Jewish ghetto, there is a façade from a 13C synagogue.

Draguignan has two interesting museums. The **Musée Municipale** (☎ 04 94 47 28 80: **open** Mon–Sat 09.00–12.00 and 14.00–18.00; closed Sun and Mon am), housed in a 17C–18C convent on rue de la République, has a good collection of Sèvres porcelain and some fine 17C–18C paintings and sculpture. Of the more modern works there is a group of watercolours by the sculptor Auguste Rodin (1840–1917), who was also responsible for the bust on the monument to Georges Clemenceau who represented this area in parliament. The **Musée des Arts et Traditions Populaires de Moyenne Provence** (☎ 04 94 47 05 72: **open** Tues–Sat 09.00–12.00 and 14.00–18.00; closed Mon and Sun mornings) on rue Joseph-Roumanille has a major display of traditional furniture, room settings and local industries. The most important of these is agriculture, especially oil-pressing and preparation of cork for the wine industry, which is illustrated in a series of well-displayed galleries.

There is also an artillery museum in the major barracks complex outside the town to the east but it fails to bring military preoccupations to life. A more appealing alternative is a circuit of the Côtes-de-Provence vineyards in the immediate vicinity, for which you can get information at the tourist office. One other feature which may catch your interest is the Neolithic dolmen known as the **Pierre de la Fée** (The Fairy Stone), a huge slab on three stone supports at the northwest edge of town by the D955. It is probably over 3000 years old and still has a certain magic about it.

The Pierre de la Fée

Important as Draguignan was in the administration of Provence, nowadays it is rather isolated at the end of the railway line. To the north, there are a few remote villages such as Châteaudouble, perched over the serpentine gorge of the river Nartuby, but much of the territory beyond that is taken up with the depressing scarred landscape of the **Plan du Canjuers**, now used as a military training ground for tanks and artillery. A journey through this area is certainly unusual but it is hardly picturesque. The village of **Comps-sur-Artuby** in the heart of the *Zone Militaire* is often picked out as an attractive spot but it has the atmosphere of a frontier town, a transit centre for those on their way further north to the Gorges du Verdon.

From Draguignan, the N555 leads directly south to the main N7 and *autoroute* A8 near Le Muy, from where it speeds on to Fréjus. There are, however, many attractions which make this district, known as the **Dracenois**, worth exploring. One of these is the village of **Lorgues**, notable for its medieval gateways, its well-furnished 18C church, and for the celebrated chef Bruno Clement and his very expensive restaurant, *Chez Bruno* on route de Vidauban (☎ 04 94 73 92 19). The Dracenois is noted for its wine, olive oil, truffles and livestock, all of which, figure prominantly in his cuisine.

Another route, to the east of Draguignan by the D562 and turning off to the north on the D225 and D25, leads to a group of attractive small villages with several unexpected features. The first of these is **Callas**, a village of tall 'alpine' houses on a hillside overlooked by the ruins of the Château des Pontèves. In 1579, during one of the periodic massacres which marked this whole country, the people of Callas eventually rose up against their tyrant, J.-B. de Pontèves, and assassinated him and his family. The Romanesque church at the centre of the village has a dull Gothic-Revival façade but there are several treasures inside including the altarpiece of St-Auxile and the figure of Notre Dame de Pennafort, the object of an annual pilgrimage.

The D25 continues through a rolling landscape of wooded hills and valleys before arriving at **Bargemon**, a medieval village with a ruined castle and impressive 10C–12C ramparts. Built into these fortifications is the 15C church of St-Etienne with its Flamboyant Gothic west doorway and a sculpted altarpiece with angels attributed to Puget. The penitents' chapel, Notre-Dame-de-Montaigu, has been the centre of an Easter pilgrimage since the 17C when a miraculous statue of the Virgin was brought to the village from Flanders. Bargemon was noted in Roman times for the purity of its atmosphere and there are still many convalescent homes in the area. The mild climate has also appealed to northern Europeans and there has been a considerable influx of new residents in recent years who have begun to smarten up the village houses and 'improve' its overall appearance.

This tendency is even more marked in the village of **Seillans**, 13km further along the D19. The Surrealist painter Max Ernst (1891–1976) lived here for the last few years of his life, as had the composer Charles Gounod and the author Alphonse Karr before him, but there is little to suggest a bohemian atmosphere. Instead, Seillans is now a pleasant and well-restored hill town with a number of picturesque old buildings and steep cobbled streets leading up to the 12C castle. The process of gentrification began in 1884 when the Viscomtesse de Savigny set up a perfume factory, which is still in existence, and a number of terraced flower gardens. Two kilometres further along the D19 towards Fayence is Notre-

Dame-de-l'Ormeau, an isolated Romanesque chapel with a curious 16C altar-piece in polychrome wood. Depicting the Tree of Jesse with a mass of figures, this unusual piece was carved by an emigré Italian monk who sought refuge in Seillans in 1574.

Fayence is the largest of the towns in the area, a gliding centre and a good base from which to explore the various hill-villages of the Dom de Tourrettes. **Mons**, 14km to the north on the D563, is undoubtedly the most attractive place, combining a tight complex of old arcaded streets with a spectacular view from its hilltop setting. Mons was ravaged by the plague of 1348 with the result that families of Genoese were invited to repopulate the village. For this reason, it has distinctive dry-stone buildings that set it apart from other villages in the area. Even the language is reputed to be a curious dialect that preserves some original Genoese words. The 15C–17C church has some good altarpieces from the 17C. To the east, the villages of Callian and Montauroux, each with a ruined castle and medieval quarter, are worth visiting before the main D562 makes its way down to Grasse.

18 · Manosque and the Gorges du Verdon

This long sweep through the upper reaches of Provence passes through some of the more remote, spectacular and, at times, inhospitable parts of the region. It can be alternately breathtaking and intimidating: when you remember that this was one of the old drove roads and main lines of communication in the medieval world, you are at least impressed by the physical obstacles that early travellers had to overcome. The route takes in the Gorges du Verdon, one of the most famous and awe-inspiring natural sights in the whole of Europe, and a series of important towns and villages each of which is worth visiting for either its historic remains or natural setting.

There is one significant drawback, however. The main road was not built for the volume of traffic that it now carries so you must expect delays in the height of summer when thousands of tourists wish to visit the more popular sites. This is inconvenient but the attractions of the area are so compelling that they easily outweigh such obstacles.

Manosque to Moustiers

The route begins at **Manosque**, the town made famous by the novels of Jean Giono (1895–1970) and an important medieval centre in its own right.

History of Manosque

A legend attached to the town gave rise to the sobriquet, le Pudique (the Modest). On a visit to Manosque in 1516, François I became enamoured of the mayor's daughter, Peronne de Volonde. She did not return this 'compliment' and rather than submit to his advances chose to disfigure her face with sulphur. Giono dismissed the story as stupid nonsense but the name Manosque-le-Pudique is still occasionally used.

❖ *Information, accommodation and food*

🛈 Place du Dr-Joubert (☎ 04 92 72 16 00).

Hotels. Accommodation in Manosque is reasonably plentiful if unadventurous. Modest hotels in the town include the *Mont d'Or* (☎ 04 92 72 13 94) at the place de l'Hôtel-de-Ville or *Le Provence* (☎ 04 92 72 39 38) further out on the route de la Durance, but the best in the area is the *Hostellerie de la Fuste* (☎ 04 92 72 05 95) on the opposite side of the Durance by the D4.

Restaurants. The *Hostellerie de la Fuste* (see above) also has the best restaurant. For something more everyday, there is a good choice in the old town, among which *Chez André* (☎ 04 92 72 03 09) on the place du Terreau is very reasonable.

The old town, oval and compact, is now closed to traffic which makes the exploration of the narrow winding streets even more pleasant and relaxed. Peronne's self-mutilation was reputed to have been enacted in front of the **Porte Saunerie**, a tall crenellated structure and the finest of the two surviving gates from the medieval ramparts. The Porte Soubeyran, less impressive but with an attractive belltower, stands at the opposite, northern edge of the old town. Between these two gates there is a wealth of shopping streets and old buildings, including two rather eclectic churches, St-Sauveur and **Notre-Dame-de-Romigier**, both dating from the 12C but with various later additions. Notre-Dame takes its name from a celebrated Black Virgin claimed to be the oldest in France, although it probably dates from the 12C. A 4C sarcophagus with carved representations of the Apostles now serves as the altar. During the late Middle Ages Manosque was controlled by the Order of Hospitallers who built an important palace on the place du Terreau. Nothing survives of this but there is a silver reliquary bust of Gerard Tenque, founder of the order, in the 18C Hôtel de Ville.

The novelist Jean Giono, author of *The Horseman on the Roof* among others, was born in Manosque and lived here for most of his life, recording the activities of the town and its surrounding area in his early *Pan* trilogy. The redemptive power of nature and the ability of man to overcome the corrupting influence of the modern world is the recurring theme, one which Giono attempted to live out himself in this quiet area. His house at Le Parais just outside Manosque can be visited but there is a more detailed introduction to his life and work in the **Centre Jean Giono** (☎ 04 92 72 76 10: open Tues–Sat 09.00–12.00 and 14.00–18.00) on the boulevard Elemir-Bourges near the Porte Saunerie.

Manosque is at a bridgehead on the Durance which marks the eastern perimeter of the Lubéron national park. The town itself is still within the protected area but as you approach the river you are soon aware of the change in appearance and atmosphere largely due to the major hydro-electric and nuclear power installations which stretch downstream towards Mirabeau. Fortunately, crossing at this point leaves the industrial complex behind and the D6 begins a route through the rolling empty countryside of the **plateau de**

Valensole, punctuated by isolated houses and villages. This sparsely populated area is the setting for many of Giono's later novels and, apart from the spectacle of the lavender fields in summer, it has little in common with the richer districts of southern Provence.

Riez is the major town in the area, a position it has held since Roman times when it was known as Reia Apollinaris. The Roman settlement was originally on the west of the modern town and the principal monuments can be seen by the road as you approach Riez from Valensole. The most famous and enigmatic of these is a row of four Corinthian columns supporting a pediment which formed part of the Roman temple to Apollo. They now stand isolated in a field with little or no trace of any surrounding buildings.

ℹ 4 cours allées Louis-Gardiol (☎ 04 92 77 76 36).

Riez also played an important role in the Christianisation of Gaul, a bishopric being established here as early as the 5C. The finest remnant of this period is the **Baptistery**, an extremely rare Merovingian building of the 6C, on the other side of the river Colostre by the D952. The core is an octagonal structure of eight Roman columns supporting a dome but in 1818 an outer enclosing wall was built. Administered by the local antiquarian society, it now houses a collection of antique fragments and can be visited with a guide from the Mairie, although most of the pieces can be seen through the iron gate. The original 5C cathedral of Notre-Dame-du-Siège was close by, but this was abandoned in 1524 and later demolished in favour of the rather plain new cathedral which was built into the medieval ramparts of the town. Behind it is the Porte Sanson, one of three impressive gateways, and Grande Rue, once the principal street of the old town but now a quiet lane remote from the bustling activity on the market place. Grande Rue has a number of elegant mansions from the Renaissance period one of which, the 16C Hôtel de Mazan, is used as a museum of antiquities. There is already a good small **Musée de Nature en Provence** (open Wed–Mon 10.00– 12.00 and 14.00–17.00; closed Tues) by the Hôtel de Ville and, to the north of the town, **La Maison de l'Abeille** (open daily 10.00–12.30 and 14.30–19.00), a visitors' centre for the local apiary and honey producers.

If Riez has a relaxed and relatively quiet atmosphere, **Moustiers-Sainte-Marie**, only 15km along the road, is possibly the most frustrating and congested spot in the whole region. The reason is simple. It is a small and very picturesque village at one end of the great Gorges du Verdon but there is not enough space for the number of tourists and their cars. Parking areas have been created in the fields on either side of the village but it is still not sufficient to ease the traffic which chokes the narrow roads. This level of popularity has also had a dramatic effect on the life and atmosphere of the village, in which every shop and spare piece of pavement has been turned over to cafés, souvenirs and other services for tourists.

History of Moustiers-Sainte-Marie

Moustiers is probably best known for the ceramics industry which flourished here in the 17C and 18C, largely due to the technical innovations of

Antoine Clérissy, the first major manufacturer of faience in the village. He produced wares with a singular blue glaze but it was not long before others developed the polychrome designs for which the area became known. By the late 18C Moustiers faience was in demand all over France and the distinctive patterns, freely based on ancient grotesque designs, were being imitated by rival potteries. The local trade declined seriously during the 19C in the face of industrial manufacturers and by 1874 the last kiln in Moustiers had closed down. It was in 1927 that the writer Marcel Provence revived the craft and it has flourished ever since, a major element in the interior decoration style known loosely as *le style Provençale*.

❖ *Information, accommodation and food*

🄴 At the Mairie.

Hotels. Accommodation in Moustiers is limited simply because it is a small village but the pressure of tourism has opened up some new hotels and restaurants in the surrounding area. *Le Belvedere* (☎ 04 92 74 66 04) is a reasonable hotel in the village itself.

Restaurants. *Les Santons* (☎ 04 92 74 66 48) in the village is reasonable. The brasserie *Lou Cafetière* is perhaps the liveliest.

Moustiers itself has a dramatic setting near the foot of a great cleft in the rocks, out of which the river Maire cascades down through the centre of the village. The houses cling to the sides of this ravine, supported on a series of bridges and buttresses that would seem improbable under normal circumstances. Above this, suspended between two peaks, is a gilded star that has fuelled much speculation, although its origins are actually quite down to earth. According to legend it was erected around 1250 by a crusader knight from the Blacas family to fulfill a vow he had made to the Virgin while a prisoner of the Saracens. It is an attractive story but the present chain dates from the 1920s (the star replaced in 1957) and several people have claimed that this was actually its first appearance.

The name Moustiers is derived from Monasterium, a small community of monks who settled in the caves here in 432 and who eventually built the series of chapels high up in the rocks overlooking the village. The latest of these is the 12C Romanesque **Chapelle de Notre-Dame-de-Beauvoir**, site of a famous pilgrimage in the first week of September. The main entrance to the chapel, which can be reached by a footpath, has some very good naturalistic carving and a collection of *ex-votos* is displayed on the walls inside.

The centre of the old village is a warren of narrow streets and houses built with the dry pale stone of the nearby quarries. At its heart is the 12C **parish church**, once part of a priory and revealing many of the qualities of Provençal Romanesque. The 14C tiered belltower, one of the earliest of its type, is particularly handsome and is thought to derive from Lombard models. The building was excessively restored in the 1920s but this did strip the interior of later decoration to emphasise the simple lines of the vaulting and the crooked axis of the nave.

Note the altar, a 5C early Christian sarcophagus. There is also a treasury with examples of ecclesiastical porcelain.

Modern Moustiers faience is primarily aimed at the tourist trade and the wares are of poor quality but there is an opportunity to see examples of good early pieces at the **Musée de la Faience** in the crypt of an old monastery at place du Presbytère (☎ 04 92 74 61 64: **open** Wed–Mon 09.00–12.00 and 14.00–18.00 Apr–Oct; closed Tues and winter).

The Gorges du Verdon and the Route Napoléon

Just outside Moustiers to the south you are presented with a choice of routes to view the **Gorges du Verdon**, the largest gorge system in Europe. In all, the Grand CanyoN stretches for some 21km, a great rift or crack in the plateau of Haute Provence through which the rivers Verdon and Artuby flow. It was hardly known outside Provence until recently because there were no roads, and the first journey along its length by river was only completed in 1905 by the explorer and speleologist Edouard Alfred Martel. There is a plaque commemorating this feat at the **Point Sublime**, probably the most spectacular of all the lookout-posts along the whole length of this natural wonder. Since then it has been made accessible by a series of routes including the GR4 which more intrepid walkers may undertake.

The direct road (D952) follows the northern crest of the gorge for much of the way and has the advantage of reaching the Point Sublime. There is a small hotel and café here from which you can contemplate the wild and spectacular landscape. On the other hand, the lower route to the right after Moustiers, known as the **Corniche Sublime** (by the D957, D19 and D71) and following the crest of the gorge on the southern side, remains closer to the line of the cliffs for more of the journey and possibly offers an even greater *frisson* of danger. The belvederes and vantage-points on the southern side are the Falaise de Cavaliers, a colossal limestone cliff of over 300m dropping straight down to the river below, and the Balcons de la Mescla over the confluence of the Verdon and Artuby. Either way, you are guaranteed a thrilling drive and the experience should not be missed.

There are several paths down from the belvederes to the base of the canyon, notably at the Point Sublime, but it is advisable to follow the suggestions about routes and clothing offered by the Bureau des Guides (☎ 04 92 77 30 50) or the tourist office (☎ 04 92 77 32 02) at **La Palud-sur-Verdon** on the north side. A safer and potentially more rewarding expedition would be to take one of the conducted walking tours, of which there are several on offer lasting between two hours and two days. For a different experience entirely, there are canoing and rafting trips along the length of the gorges; again, these should be undertaken with a guide. Information on these can be obtained from Cabanon Verdon (☎ 04 92 77 38 58) or the Verdon Animation Centre (☎ 04 92 77 31 95), both at La Palud. There is a more gentle canoing area at the Pont du Galetas in the lower reaches before the river Verdon flows into the Lac de Sainte-Croix.

Accommodation in this area is well geared up for campers and ramblers and there are several hotels, such as *Les Gorges du Verdon* (☎ 04 92 77 38 26), *Le Provence* (☎ 04 92 77 36 50) or *Le Panoramic* (☎ 04 92 77 35 07), all at La Palud, or the *Grand Hôtel du Verdon* (☎ 04 94 76 91 31), in a very impressive position on the south side.

15km northeast from the head of the gorge (D952) is **Castellane**, a fortified medieval town which has been swamped by the tourism surrounding the Grand Canyon du Verdon. The tourist office is largely devoted to information about the gorges and the various excursions that can be undertaken in this area by land, water or sky (if you have a modicum of experience you are allowed to take a hang-glider over the gorges). This is all very useful but it is unfortunate that such an important and historic town should be subsumed under one heading.

i Rue Nationale (☎ 04 92 83 61 14).

Castellane is dominated by a sheer rock escarpment at the rear of the town which, in the Middle Ages, offered a safe stronghold against Saracen attacks. This settlement was named Petra Castellana and the name was clearly maintained after the inhabitants moved down to the lower ground in the 11C. There was still a need for defences, however, so the new village had a series of impressive ramparts built in the 14C–15C, some of which survive in the towers and gateways that are still a prominent feature. The most important medieval building is the old parish church, the **Eglise St-Victor**, begun in the late 12C by monks from the abbey of St-Victor in Marseille and continually extended until the 18C. It is no longer in use but many of the fittings, including some 17C paintings and Gallo-Roman grave stele, are still intact. (The keys are available from the tourist office.) At the top of the rock is the **Chapelle de Notre-Dame-du-Roc**, built in the 18C but replacing a much earlier medieval building. This was the focus of a famous Easter procession, the 'Way of the Cross', in which the penitent societies would process up the winding path to the chapel at the summit. A collection of *ex-votos* in the chapel depicts some of these processions over the centuries.

Castellane, as any French schoolchild will be able to recount, is on the *Route Napoléon*, that taken by the emperor on his return from Elba in 1815. This is a very scenic journey and at certain points, notably the heights in the south, it offers excellent views over the plateau. In fact, one of the advantages of following the route in reverse is the experience of crossing the **Pas de la Faye** northwest of Grasse where, at the crest of the mountain, a magnificent view opens up before you to the coast and the Mediterranean.

On the south side of the pass, before descending into Grasse itself, it is worth stopping in **St-Vallier-de-Thiey**, an ancient village grouped round its 12C parish church. Napoleon's passage through here on the 2 March 1815 is marked by a column in the main square. The most notable features of this area, however, are the three cave systems that were only discovered as recently as the 1950s. The most spectacular of these is the Grotte de Baume Obscure, off the D5 to the west of the village, an immense sequence of underground galleries oozing moisture and draped with stalactites and stalagmites. The interior of the cave is imaginatively lit to further dramatise the effect of this natural architecture (☎ 04 93 42 69 19: guided tour 1hr daily 10.00–18.00 Easter–Sept). The Grottes de St-Cézaire and the Grotte des Audides, a few kilometres to the south, have similar natural formations and are also open to the public.

The Route Napoléon

The Emperor Napoleon landed at Golfe-Juan from Elba on 1 March 1815 and over the next few days had to negotiate the rather rough terrain of Provence as he made his way north towards Paris. In these early stages it was not a triumphal return because Napoleon did not enjoy widespread support in the south. As a result, his party often had to keep to minor roads and mule tracks, avoiding the centres where he might encounter opposition. This was the case at Grasse, which he passed without attempting to enter. Similarly at Castellane, his party stopped only briefly in the town on 3 March and sped on to Barrême where they spent the night. It was only at Digne and, somewhat nervously, at the military stronghold of Sisteron, that Napoleon made contact with the local populace before heading on to Grenoble.

This was more than a passage from French history: it was a defining element in national pride and self-identity. It was in this spirit that the road was first built in the years after the First World War and opened in 1932, for it is not a trunk road of any significance. Instead, it follows Napoleon's route fairly closely almost as an act of faith and is still popular with French holidaymakers who wish to retrace the emperor's steps, albeit in the family car. The route is marked in bold on every map and there are plaques or monuments along the way carrying the symbol of the eagle.

Along the southern coast

THE SOUTHERN COAST

19 · To Toulon via Cassis and Bandol

The stretch of coast between Marseille and Toulon is less well known than the tourist centres of the Côte d'Azur but it has some of the most distinctive features of Mediterranean Provence. The rugged cliffs and creeks of Les Calanques give way after the Couronne de Charlemagne to a gentler coastline of broad bays and sandy beaches with a series of popular resorts that run right up to the outskirts of Toulon itself. This section has been popular with French holidaymakers since the early 20C but you are constantly aware of the presence of other industries beyond tourism. For that reason there is considerable diversity to the coast here and a number of real curiosities, such as Sanary with its odd literary communities. The hinterland also offers dramatic contrasts, from the rolling vineyards of the Côte de Provence to the lunar landscapes of the Val d'Enfer or the *village perché*, Le Castellet.

Cassis and La Ciotat

Leaving Marseille for La Ciotat, the D559 climbs steeply up the ridge of Mont St-Cyr and the Col de la Gineste, giving an impressive view back over the city and out to the islands in the bay. On this first section the road cuts across country on the inland side of Mont Puget and the Montagne de la Gardiole but there are glimpses of the sea at various points along the way. Just before leaving the outskirts of Marseille you will pass roads off to the south giving access to the first of **Les Calanques**, Sormiou, Morgiou and Sugiton. *Calanque*, a local word meaning a deep cleft or creek which cuts into the rocky coastline, admirably describes these small fjords enclosed by tall limestone cliffs where the Marseillais go at the weekends for picnics and to swim in the clear water. The *calanques* nearer Cassis are the most spectacular, particularly Port-Pin, En-Vau and Port-Miou. Most are signposted and can be reached on foot but there is an excursion by boat from Cassis.

Cassis, the most picturesque of all the resorts on this coast, has a beautiful setting on a deep bay hemmed in on three sides by tall limestone cliffs. The situation has long been admired and the poet Mistral was doing no more than repeating local opinion when he remarked 'What can he say who has seen Paris, my friends, if he has not seen Cassis?' This irresistible appeal, however, has made it extremely busy in summer, when the population increases to five times its normal figure. As a result, no traffic is allowed in the lower part of the town, which is turned over entirely to pedestrians.

History of Cassis

Cassis has an ancient history, this being the site of the Roman Portus Carsicis, which was destroyed in the 5C. It was resettled as an outlet to the sea for the lords of Les Baux in the 13C, when the château on the headland was built. Thereafter, Cassis became a successful port and fishing-village, noted also for its limestone quarries, its seafood and its white wine. Its fame in the last century was largely due to Mistral's epic poem *Calendao* (1867) describing the adventures of a fisherman from Cassis and his love for the princess of Les Baux. Intended as a defiant assertion of traditional Provençal values, it served to make the town even more popular with outsiders. In 1904 the painter André Derain visited Cassis and found here a combination of simple shapes and brilliant colour that suited his art perfectly. Soon he was joined by the other Fauvist painters, Matisse, Dufy and Vlaminck, and as their fame spread Cassis became the haunt of numerous German and British artists. At one time Salvador Dalí (1904–89) worked here, claiming that it reminded him of his home town of Figueras in Spain. There is still a legacy of this art colony but the standard of work on sale in the village is mostly abysmal.

❖ *Information, accommodation and food*

🛈 Place Baragnon (☎ 04 42 01 71 17).

Hotels. Accommodation within Cassis is expensive and best booked in advance. One of the finest hotels is *Les Roches Blanches* on the route des Calanques (☎ 04 42 01 09 30) with an excellent view of the bay, but *Le Grand Jardin* at rue P-Aydin (☎ 04 42 01 70 10) and *Le Clos de Arômes* at 10 rue Paul-Mouton (☎ 04 42 01 71 84) are also very good.

Restaurants. For the distinctive local seafood dishes, particularly sea urchins with the famous white Cassis wine, the best restaurant is *La Presqu'Ile* in Quartier de Port Miou (☎ 04 42 01 03 77). The various restaurants on the *quais* are also of a high standard, *Chez Gilbert* (☎ 04 42 01 71 36), *El Sol* (☎ 04 42 01 76 10), *Nino* (☎ 04 42 01 74 32) and *Le Romano* (☎ 04 42 01 08 16) being among the best and most reliable.

On arriving in Cassis you should make immediately for the lower part of town and the harbour, which offers a pleasant outlook over the bay. Behind this, the old town is graced with a number of surprisingly elegant houses from the 17C and 18C. One of these, an 18C presbytery on rue Xavier-Authier, is occupied by the small **Musée d'Arts et Traditions Populaires** (☎ 04 42 01 88 66: **open** Wed–Sat 15.30–18.30) which has a modest collection of local folk arts, photographs and paintings. Unfortunately it lacks work by the more famous artists who frequented the town in the early 20C. There is also an interesting display on the viticulture of the area emphasising the importance of wine not just to the local economy but to the identity and self-esteem of the town.

Cassis is the point of departure for the *calanques* to the west which are regarded as the most beautiful and remote in the area. **Port-Pin** has the right conditions for swimming while **En-Vau**, with its steep cliffsides right down to the sea, is undoubtedly the most spectacular. From Cassis they can be reached on foot or part of the way by car, but the most enjoyable route is by the boats which ferry people round the point from the harbour. The boat journey is a pleasant trip in itself but it also offers a view of the coastline which was the scene of one of the most remarkable discoveries of recent years. In 1991 a local diver came across a long underwater shaft leading into a deep cavern that was decorated with handprints and pictures of animals and sea creatures. It would seem that these were made before the last Ice Age when the cave would have been accessible from dry land, possibly around 30,000 years ago. Given the location it seems unlikely that this site will ever be accessible to the public but that, in itself, may ensure its survival.

Leaving Cassis for La Ciotat it is best to avoid the main D559 and take the exhilarating if somewhat vertiginous D41a, the Corniche des Crêtes. Climbing up the mountain the road emerges at **Cap Canaille** and follows the line of the clifftop to **La Grand Tête**, at 396m the highest cliff in France. On a clear day the view over the Mediterranean is spectacular but pay close attention to the narrow road. There are few barriers and the line of cliffs drop directly into the sea.

La Ciotat has a different character from the other seaside resorts on the coast. To begin with it was primarily an industrial town with major shipbuilding yards that were only run down to closure in the 1980s. The town has not yet recovered from the shock of this industrial collapse, nor has it really found a new role. It is, nevertheless, a resort with a good beach and a striking natural feature in the huge wedge-shaped rock known as the Bec de l'Aigle (Eagle's Beak) which thrusts out of the water at the west end of the bay. La Ciotat also claims to be the birthplace of cinematography and of that most popular Gallic game, *pétanque*.

History of La Ciotat

The workmanlike character of La Ciotat was not restricted to modern times. The Greeks established a shipyard here in the lee of the Bec de l'Aigle which the Romans expanded into the basin that now forms the centre of the old port. This sheltered position ensured the continuing success of the shipyards and by the 15C La Ciotat enjoyed a measure of prosperity and independence. To protect the natural harbour a small fort was built on the Ile Verte lying just offshore which can be visited by boat from the old port. It was in the 17C, however, that La Ciotat enjoyed its greatest phase, taking over much of the mercantile shipbuilding trade previously centred on Marseille.

❖ Information, accommodation and food

🛈 Boulevard Anatole-France (☎ 04 42 08 61 32).

Hotels. Accommodation in La Ciotat is much cheaper and easier to find than in its more popular neighbour Cassis. In the old town near the harbour, *La Rotonde* at 44 boulevard de la République (☎ 04 42 08 67 50) is very reasonable, while the *Best Western Miramar* (☎ 04 42 83 09 54) and the *Beaurivage* (☎ 04 42 83 09 68) on avenue Beaurivage, both further out, can also be recommended.

Restaurants. The finest restaurant is *L'Orchidée* in the *Best Western Miramar* (see above) but there are good bistros around the old port.

Town mansions on the rue des Poilus and rue Abeille behind the Hôtel de Ville give some indication of the town's prosperity in the 17C, as does the richly appointed Baroque church of Notre-Dame-de l'Assomption. The 17C chapel of the Pénitents-Bleus, facing the sea, is also worth a visit.

By the old port is the **Musée Ciotaden** (☎ 04 42 71 40 99: **open** Wed, Fri–Mon 16.00-19.00 mid Jun–mid Sept; 15.00–18.00 in winter; closed Tues and Thurs) which charts the history of the town and its industry. The decline might be said to have begun in 1720 with a virulent plague which devastated the population and was hastened by the attacks of the British fleet in the Napoleonic wars, after which most of the shipbuiding work returned to Marseille. Several attempts to re-establish the shipyards met with considerable if temporary success and many substantial vessels were laid down here in the later 19C and 20C before the yards finally closed their gates.

The modern docks are clearly visible to the south of the old port. A public park and botanical garden, the Parc du Mugel, behind them leads out to the great **Bec de l'Aigle** rock. A famous ancient naval disaster occurred here when a Roman cargo vessel struck the rock and sank immediately with all hands. This was echoed in 1918 when the French ship *Le Corse* was torpedoed off La Ciotat by a German submarine.

The main beaches at La Ciotat-Plage are at the opposite side of the old town, stretching round towards the eastern end of the bay. Here there is an unexpected footnote to the early history of cinema. In September 1895 the brothers Lumière showed their first films in a theatre here, one of which was of a train arriving at the Gare de La Ciotat. In recognition of this, a monument was erected to the two brothers on the avenue Beaurivage and, since the centenary of the event in 1995, this seems to have become the principal feature advertising the town. A small film festival is held here each year in July.

At the eastern end of the bay is **Les Lecques**, a family resort attached to the older town of **St-Cyr-sur-Mer**. This is thought to be the site of the Greek sea port Tauroentum, where the decisive naval battle was fought between Caesar and Pompey for control of Provence. Between Les Lecques and the small resort of La Madrague to the east there is a **Musée de Tauroentum** (☎ 04 94 26 30 46: **open** Wed–Mon 15.00–19.00 Jun–Sept; closed Tues; Sat, Sun only 14.00–17.00

Oct–May) incorporating the remains of two 1C Roman villas and a range of other Classical artefacts. On the other side of the hill behind La Madrague is the 17C Château des Baumelles, a traditional Provençal *bastide*, with a vineyard producing one of the area's finest red wines. You can visit other vineyards of the notable Bandol *appellation* in the hillsides stretching north from here beyond St-Cyr.

Bandol and its hinterland

Bandol is the principal resort on this stretch of coast, and the reasons for its success are fairly simple; it has three good beaches and an excellent climate giving over 300 days of sunshine each year. This has prompted considerable new building along the coastline and into the hillsides at the rear. It has even extended to the Ile de Bendor, a small island off the town which has been turned into a sort of holiday playground. Despite these developments Bandol is still known primarily as a producer of high-quality red wine and this gives the town and its surrounding area greater range and depth than a simple holiday centre.

History of Bandol

Modern Bandol is a far cry from the small village to which Katherine Mansfield and D.H. Lawrence came after the First World War for the good of their health. Mansfield arrived in 1919 and wrote *The Prelude* in the Villa Pauline by the *quai* while Lawrence came later, somewhat reluctantly, to stave off the effects of consumption. He stayed at the *Beau Rivage* and *Beau Soleil* hotels but did not take to the place. At that time Bandol was famous only for its vineyards, and the principal industry was barrel-making. The natural advantages of this coast, however, and the town's sheltered position beneath the wooded hills of Le Gros Cerveau, made it perfect for the Mediterranean holiday boom. By 1930 there were several hotels, the beginnings of the two elegant promenades, a casino in the Moderne style and several stylish night-clubs such as *Suzy's* which gave Bandol a rather racy reputation. More recently, a huge yacht marina has been added and a rash of new hotel and apartment blocks has spread across the hills to the rear of the town.

❖ Information, accommodation and food

🖫 Allées Vivien (☎ 04 94 29 41 35).

Hotels. Bandol's smartest hotel is the *Ile Rousse* at 17 boulevard Louis-Lumière (☎ 04 94 29 46 86) but much more interesting is the *Master Hôtel* in the rue Raimu (☎ 04 94 29 46 53) which occupies the pink villa that the actor Raimu (Jules Muraire) built for himself in the 1920s. Near this at 3 rue Raimu is the very reasonable *Hôtel Coin d'Azur* (☎ 04 94 29 40 93). *L'Oasis* at 15 rue des Ecoles (☎ 04 94 29 41 69) can also be recommended.

Restaurants. L'Auberge du Port (☎ 04 94 29 42 63) at 9 allée Jean-Moulin is the leading seafood restaurant but there are several more modest bistros with good menus in the port area. The restaurant in the *Master Hôtel* (see above) has the original name of the house, *Le Ker-Mocotte*.

Despite its relentless modernisation, Bandol has retained something of its stylish image and you can find traces of its earlier existence at the Tuesday market or in the more extravagant villas like Le Ker-Mocotte, which have survived from the 1930s. A more recent addition is the **Zoo-Jardin Exotique** (☎ 04 94 29 40 38: open daily 08.00–12.00 and 14.00–19.00; closed Sun morning), a small but attractive zoo with good collections of exotic birds and small mammals, to the northeast of the town.

Just 2km off the coast is the small **Ile de Bendor** which until 1955 was a bare shelf of rock sticking out of the bay. In that year it was bought by the *pastis* tycoon Paul Ricard who set about building a holiday centre that nowadays would probably be described as a theme park. Bendor has an imitation Provençal fishing-village, a craft community and an art gallery as well as three hotels, a marina and a sports centre amid a richly planted and landscaped estate. But the most interesting feature of this curious hybrid is the **Exposition Universelle des Vins et Spiritueux** (☎ 04 94 29 44 34: open Thur–Tues 10.00–12.00 and 14.00–18.00 Easter–Sept; closed Wed), a huge museum devoted to the wines and spirits of the world. Decorated by painters from the local art school, it includes a display of some 7000 bottles from over 50 countries, the stated aim being to represent each and every intoxicant developed by human society.

Bandol is, of course, at the centre of a great wine-growing district with eight communes producing reds that are among the finest in the south of France. For more details of this, the **Maison des Vins** (☎ 04 94 29 45 03) beside the tourist office has a selection of local wines for sale and can arrange visits to the various *caves* and vineyards that stretch back into the hillsides. Among the most notable are the *Domaine des Salettes*, the *Château de Pibarnon* near La Cadière d'Azur and the *Domaine de la Tour du Bon* at Le Brûlat du Castellet. One can very easily form one's own taste, however, from the range of high-quality *maisons* within a few kilometres.

The hinterland of Bandol is a curious and paradoxical area which juxtaposes the rich vineyards of the lower slopes with the rugged and somewhat sinister terrain of **Le Gros Cerveau** (Great Brain).

The caves of Le Gros Cerveau

There are numerous caves in the cliffs to the north of the mountain which are claimed, like many other areas, to have been the haunt of the 18C bandit Gaspard de Besse. Various tales have circulated about this Robin Hood of Provence, most of them improbable, but there is no doubt that the same caves have had some unusual residents over the centuries. In 1614 three old men, probably hermits or refugees, were dragged from here down to Cassis where they were strangled and burned as sorcerers.

This sort of anecdote helps to set the scene for a rather impressive excursion through the countryside to the north of Bandol taking in the fortified village of Le Castellet and returning by the Gorges d'Ollioules. Take the D559b north from Bandol, passing beneath the motorway then turning left after 10km on to the D226 which leads directly to Le Castellet.

Perched on a tall rock rising above the surrounding vineyards, the village of **Le Castellet** presents an impressive sight to anyone approaching. It has been settled continuously since the Bronze Age and the constant building and rebuilding of the outer defences over several epochs has given the settlement the appearance of an elevated castle—hence the name.

History of Castellet

The ramparts skirting the edge of the rock date back to the 11C when the village was under the protection of the bishops of Marseille. They also built the simple Romanesque church and the original castle at the centre of the village; the latter was demolished in the 14C to be replaced by the rather more elegant structure you see today. Appropriately, this beautiful but slightly unreal château was owned by Good King René in the 15C although it is not known if he ever stayed here.

Like many Provençal hill-villages, Le Castellet was ignored and depopulated until the 1950s when an extensive programme of renovation was begun. Since then it has benefited financially from the expanding tourist trade although the blight of craft shops and souvenir stalls has begun to take a serious toll. Already, several of the surrounding fields are given over to car parks during the summer months, suggesting that tourism may be overtaking wine-growing as the principal industry. A further element is the nearby motor-racing track which gives off engine roar, audible for miles, when there are meetings in the summer. It is ironic to hear this in a context that has been felt to typify the quiet rural life of the peasantry. In the 1930s Marcel Pagnol filmed Giono's *La Femme du Boulanger* here and, 50 years later, Claude Berri shot several scenes for *Manon des Sources* in Le Castellet. This combination, however, seems to encapsulate the paradox of Provence as both a rural fantasy and a modern playground for sophisticated tastes.

In front of the castle is the place de la Mairie, a pleasant square that opens out from the narrow winding streets leading up through the village. There are excellent views from here and it is not difficult to appreciate the sense of security that previous residents of this site must have felt.

The network of roads round Le Castellet is confusing at the best of times so you should return to **Le Beausset** by the D226.

History of Le Beausset

This 'new' village, created in the 16C when the inhabitants abandoned Le Beausset-Vieux, has been linked to several illustrious figures including Louis XIV, his chief minister Cardinal Mazarin and, in a later period, Charles X, each of whom stayed at the 17C coaching-inn *L'Auberge de la Gruppi*. The village was also the birthplace of Napoleon's chief administrator, Jean de Portalis, who prepared the *Code Napoléon*, and to complete this roll-call Napoleon himself lodged at 24 rue Pasteur in September 1793 while directing the siege of Toulon.

Le Beausset-Vieux, which you can reach by a narrow road, has little to recommend it on the surface but it has been a place of pilgrimage for centuries due to the miraculous powers of an ancient wooden Madonna in the parish church.

During the Revolution the original figure was taken and burned whereupon a bolt of flame from the Virgin's heart is reputed to have consumed the four iconoclasts. The substitute figure, an 18C Madonna of gilded wood, is now the object of a renewed cult which attracts up to 20,000 pilgrims on the three principal feast days (Easter Monday, Whitsun and 8 September) when there is a midnight mass. Quite separate from this is the strange ritual of the pierced orange on 25 June when the confraternity of St Eligius (Eloi) attends a traditional mass after which an orange is pierced with swords. This is then followed by a pageant of local history involving bands of traditional instruments and a colourful procession. A collection of *ex-votos* recording miraculous cures, most of them painted by the deaf-mute artist Eusèbe, is displayed in the 10C vault of the castle.

Taking the main N8 south towards Ollioules, it is worth making a short detour on the D462 at Ste-Anne-d'Evenos into the **Vallée du Cimai**, one of the most rugged and forbidding areas in the south of France. The road leads to the village of **Evenos** which takes its name from the local word *ebros*, meaning 'mountain spitting fire'. It is an apt description of this weird, volcanic landscape where, according to one legend, 'Satan made his mansion' and St Anne had to be invoked by the peasants for protection. The village itself is similarly forbidding, its medieval houses overlooked by the gaunt remains of a 16C castle high up on the rocks above. This must have been an impressive ruin when the village was virtually abandoned but in recent years the narrow winding streets have shown signs of renovation as the area is colonised for weekend homes. If you have the energy, it is worth climbing up to the castle which has a good view down the gorge to the sea or up to the Massif de la Ste-Baume in the north. There is also a rough path, strewn with boulders and fallen masonry, which leads to the 11C Romanesque church of St-Martin nearby.

Ste-Anne d'Evenos stands at the head of the **Gorges d'Ollioules**, also known evocatively as the 'way of dread'. It is certainly sinister but there is a phantasmagorical aspect to these strange rock formations which Victor Hugo recognised when he came through here in the 1840s. Finding a physical parallel to his own imaginative drawings he likened the terrain to 'the bowels of a mountain hacked open and scorched by the sun'. Even without this Romantic description of the place, you can easily see why it should have been the haunt of bandits and hermits for centuries. As a further test to the nerves you can take the small D220 to the right which leads along the crest of Le Gros Cerveau with astounding views to north and south. All along this route there are caves and landmarks associated with tales of murder or intrigue.

After the drama of the gorge, it comes as something of a surprise to emerge into **Ollioules**, the flower capital of France. Some 35% of the country's flowers are produced in this area and sold in the huge market at the edge of the town. Commanding the entrance to the gorge, Ollioules had considerable strategic importance in the Middle Ages. The Viscomtes de Marseille built the castle whose ruins can be seen above the town and there are some attractive arcaded streets in the old quarter. The most substantial monument, however, is the early Romanesque church of St-Laurent whose solid structure and simple lines are most evident on the interior. The central nave dates from 1096 and the altar is a 3-ton block of stone salvaged from the ramparts by Louis XIV's military architect Vauban.

ℤ 16 rue Nationale (☎ 04 94 63 11 74).

An interesting walk to the north of the town reveals an abandoned 17C chapel which is actually on the site of an Iron Age fort and a Ligurian village known as **La Courtine**. A treasure of over 300 Greek coins was discovered here as was a collection of decapitated statues, interred by the Romans after a fierce battle in 123 BC.

From Ollioules the N8 leads directly into Toulon but you can return to the coast road at Sanary by the D11 to the right.

Sanary and the Cap Sicié peninsula

Less developed than its neighbour Bandol and generally more relaxed, **Sanary-sur-Mer** has many of the advantages found elsewhere on this sheltered coastline. Once a fishing-village, it is now a bathing resort with a picturesque *quai* lined with palm trees and cypresses. There are still a few fishing-boats in the harbour but these are greatly outnumbered by yachts and pleasure craft.

History of Sanary-sur-Mer

The coast around Bandol and Sanary is sheltered from the Mistral wind which partly accounts for its past appeal to foreigners who liked to winter on the Mediterranean. In the 1930s Aldous Huxley had a villa here, still known locally as the *Villa Huley* thanks to a spelling mistake. Another resident at that time was the fashionable painter Moise Kisling (1891–1953) who, like Picasso and Matisse, fled to the south to escape the fervid atmosphere of Paris. If they were typical of the Riviera intellectuals, the community of German emigrés who found refuge here in the 1930s struck a slightly different note. Thomas Mann already knew this area when he decided to settle in Sanary as a refugee from the Nazis. He did not stay long but it must have been enough to encourage other 'displaced persons' and over the next few years Sanary and Bandol accommodated some of the greatest German writers and intellectuals of the 20C. A plaque by the *Hôtel du Tour* records their names, including Heinrich Mann, Bertolt Brecht, Arthur Koestler, Stefan Zweig, Alma Mahler and Franz Werfel. As if to purge the town of this memory, German troops occupying Sanary in preparation for the Allied invasion in 1944 destroyed much of the area round the harbour and drove out the inhabitants.

❖ Information, accommodation and food

ℤ At the Mairie (☎ 04 94 74 01 04).

Hotels. Accommodation in Sanary is both good and reasonably priced for the coast but the resort is becoming more popular. The *Hôtel du Tour* at quai Général-de-Gaulle (☎ 04 94 74 10 10) has an excellent location overlooking the port.

Restaurants. For good seafood try the *Relais de la Poste* (☎ 04 94 74 22 20) on the place Poste.

Since the Second World War the harbourfront has been restored with modern holiday apartments but the steps from the west end of the *quai* lead up to the rue de la Colline and boulevard Courbet which retain something of the 1930s. At the furthest point is the Villa Tranquille, built on the site of Thomas Mann's house, and before this, on the left, is a converted windmill called the Moulin Gris. A plaque records the mill's association with the artist J.G. Daragne (1886–1950) but makes no mention of Franz Werfel and Alma Mahler who lived here in 1938. Almost opposite the mill is a small 16C church with an unusual pedimented entrance. This is Notre-Dame-de-la Pitié, a pilgrimage church for fishermen whose *ex-voto* paintings line the simple nave.

Six-Fours-Les-Plages, the next town on the D559, is really the start of the long conurbation of houses and factories that stretches into Toulon. As such, it has little visual appeal although the early settlement here played an important role in the history of the area. It takes its name from a series of forts built round the Cap Sicié peninsula to protect the southern edge of what had been an important religious area from prehistoric times: there are several interesting archaeological sites, such as the dolmens or cromlechs at Le Brusc. Monks from Marseille settled here as early as the 5C and from these beginnings the collegiate church of St-Pierre-aux-Liens evolved. The church buildings, in a confusion of styles from the 12C to the 18C, are the sole remains of the original town round the fort of Six-Fours which was abandoned in 1580. There are several interesting works of art in the church including an altarpiece in the choir by Jean de Troyes (1520).

Two other early church buildings in this area are also worth a visit. **Notre-Dame-de-Pépiole**, just 3km north of Six-Fours, traces its origins back to the Carolingian period of the 9C. Abandoned during the Revolution, it has been restored in recent years by a Benedictine monk who has established a small retreat here. At the very southern tip of the Cap Sicié peninsula by the radio station is **Notre-Dame-du-Mai**, a pilgrimage chapel dating originally from the 17C. Dedicated to the protection of sailors, this chapel stands at the top of a 300m cliff overlooking the sea and offers a panoramic view of the coast. The development of Six-Fours has put many people off this peninsula but it was once a popular spot for 19C travellers, including George Sand, who loved its exhilarating views, describing Cap Sicié as 'a hand thrown into the sea'.

The **Iles des Embiez**, just off the coast at Le Brusc in the west, were owned by the *pastis* millionaire Paul Ricard who attempted to turn them into a controlled holiday centre causing only minimal damage to the environment. The Fondation Paul Ricard on the main island, for example, is an oceanographic centre set up to research the local sea life and to monitor levels of pollution in the area. There is a certain irony in the fact that Ricard also established a major powerboat-racing circuit nearby.

The eastern side of the Cap Sicié forms the edge of Toulon's outer harbour and has been encroached by the suburbs of the town but there are a few resorts along this stretch of coast. **Tamaris**, taking its name from the tamarisk bushes which grow in such abundance here, was the subject of a novel by George Sand who lived here in 1861. **Les Sablettes** was a fishing-village on the sandy isthmus linking the farther peninsula of St-Mandrier but it was destroyed in 1944. The present village was built in the 1950s in *le style Provençal*, something of a curiosity since it looks out to the deep-water anchorage of France's naval fleet.

20 · Toulon to Fréjus

This route follows a long and at times dramatic stretch of coastline that is punctuated by a variety of small towns and resorts. It spans the Massif des Maures, the huge tract of mountainous land that begins to rise on the edge of Hyères and descends in the east to the banks of the river Argens on the outskirts of Fréjus. Although the route follows the coast, the Massif defines much of its character: at times the rocks drop so close to the sea that the road is almost suspended between the two elements. In theory this is part of the Côte d'Azur. Indeed, Hyères was traditionally regarded as the start of the great Mediterranean playground but it did not benefit or suffer from the huge expansion that the Riviera experienced in the 1950s and '60s. The outstanding exception is the area around St-Tropez which has a separate identity and is covered in the next chapter. The resorts in this section such as Hyères, Le Lavandou, Cavalaire or Ste-Maxime are less cosmopolitan, less developed and less frenetic than their eastern neighbours but they have a distinctive character that deserves to be better known. Before going on to these holiday centres, however, the route starts in the workmanlike port of Toulon.

Toulon

Toulon has an impressive location that has been admired by travellers down the ages. Against a backdrop of tall limestone cliffs, the town spreads round the inner and outer bays, the Petit and Grand Rade, and on to the peninsula of St-Mandrier enclosing a huge natural harbour. This deep-water anchorage is the sole reason for the city's development from an obscure fishing-village to the principal base of the French navy and, since 1974, the capital or *préfecture* of the Var.

History of Toulon
Given the long history of seafaring on this coast it is surprising that Toulon was not developed as a port or harbour until relatively modern times. In the ancient world, this area was known primarily for the production of the purple dye reserved for the clothes of the Roman imperial family. It was only after Provence became part of France that the potential of the bays for shipping was exploited. The first major fortifications were built in 1514, but it was in the reign of Louis XIV that Toulon came into its own as the main naval dockyard in France. In 1679, on the orders of Colbert, the military architect Vauban expanded the Arsenal to cope with the new royal fleet and began the great series of 'star' forts to defend the harbour area.

In this role, Toulon became the base for the royal galleys, fast warships with about 50 oars requiring over 200 men (slaves, convicts and paid volunteers) to propel them into battle. Many of the Protestants who survived the massacres of the religious wars spent the rest of their days chained to the oars. In Victor Hugo's *Les Misérables*, Jean Valjean spends almost 20 years on the galleys for stealing a loaf of bread, a sentence that was not unusual. By the early 18C the galleys had become something of a tourist attraction and visitors would find a vantage-point in the town from which to see the lines of chained and shaven-headed prisoners dressed in their distinctive red-and-green uniform being moved between the shore prisons and the ships moored in the harbour.

In 1793 Toulon achieved notoriety in France by repudiating the Revolutionary government and inviting the British to defend their position. It was in the battle to recapture the town that the young artillery captain Napoleon Bonaparte made his reputation as an audacious commander. Once Toulon was retaken, the Convention imposed terrible reprisals on the people. Thousands were summarily executed, many buildings destroyed and even the name Toulon was erased as traitorous, to be replaced temporarily by Port-de-la-Montagne.

The town had an equally momentous role in the Second World War. In 1942, when Hitler invaded the Vichy zone, the French fleet was caught in Toulon but the sailors succeeded in scuttling most of the ships before they fell into German hands. Two years later, Toulon was again one of the key battlefields of the invasion and much of the old town and harbourfront was destroyed, first by the retreating German garrison and then in the Allied bombardment.

❖ *Information, accommodation and food*

🛈 Place des Riaux (☎ 04 94 18 53 00) and at the railway station on place Albert 1er (☎ 04 94 62 73 87).

Hotels. Accommodation in Toulon is very mixed and, as if to confirm the popular image of a big port, the majority of hotels are fairly seedy. Of the cheaper places, the **Little Palace** at 6 rue Berthelot (☎ 04 94 92 26 62), the **Molière** at 12 rue Molière (☎ 04 94 92 78 35) and **Le Jaurès** at 11 rue Jean-Jaurès (☎ 04 94 92 83 04) can all be recommended. Slightly better are the **Hôtel Continental Metropole** at 1 rue Jean-Racine (☎ 04 94 22 36 26) and the **Dauphine-Arcantis** at 10 rue Berthelot (☎ 04 94 92 20 28), while **La Corniche** at 17 Littoral F. Mistral (☎ 04 94 41 35 12) at Le Mourillon near the beach is one of the best hotels and restaurants.

Restaurants. Apart from the restaurant at **La Corniche** (see above), **Au Sourd** at 10 rue Molière (☎ 04 94 92 28 52) is noted for its seafood menu, while there are many reasonable bistros along the *quais* and on the Littoral F. Mistral at Le Mourillon.

The effects of the Second World War are still evident when you visit the harbour area around the quai Stalingrad. The narrow streets and seedy houses usually associated with most Mediterranean ports have been replaced here by grey concrete blocks that do little to evoke the character or history of this famous port. The sense of loss is emphasised by the two marble atlantes carved by Pierre Puget, one of the finest artists of the French Baroque. These dynamic figures once supported the entrance to the old Hôtel de Ville built in the 17C, but they are now attached to the façade of the new town hall on the *quai*. In the absence of historic remains, you should visit the **Musée Naval** (☎ 04 94 02 02 01: **open** daily 10.00–12.00 and 13.30–19.00 July–Aug; Wed–Mon 10.00–12.00 and 13.30–18.00 Sept–June; closed Tues), also with an elaborate carved doorway, at the western end of the quai Stalingrad beside the Préfecture Maritime. The collection includes a range of ship models from all periods, some interesting carved figureheads, many by followers of Puget who himself learned to sculpt in this trade, and a number of paintings of maritime subjects.

Beyond the museum is the **Arsenal Maritime**, the huge government yards for fitting out and equipping the ships of the French navy. This is still one of the main sources of employment in Toulon but in recent years much naval work has been transferred to the Atlantic port of Brest. It is now a very modern installation although the historic origins of the arsenal are evoked by the impressive Classical gateways in the perimeter wall. Another way to discover Toulon's naval past is to take one of the boat trips round the inner and outer harbours which leave from the *quai*. Not only do these ferry the visitor round the numerous craft still at anchorage (the main naval sections are, understandably, restricted) but there is an excellent view of the town and its fortifications from the sea; a view which many sailors and galley slaves must have experienced when arriving back at their home port.

Behind the modern blocks of the quai Stalingrad you can enter the more atmospheric old town along the pedestrian rue d'Alger, the principal shopping and promenading street. In recent years, this district has been greatly gentrified and over-renovated, but it is still very pleasant to browse or relax in the numerous cafés and bars. At the top, beyond the rue Hoche, is the popular local landmark of the **Fontaine des Trois Dauphins**, erected in 1782 and in Provençal fashion now encrusted with lime and plants.

Parallel with the rue d'Alger to the east is the cours Lafayette where there is a lively flower and vegetable market every morning. The 18C bishop's palace houses the small **Musée du Vieux-Toulon** (☎ 04 94 52 11 07: **open** Mon–Sat 14.30–18.00; closed Sun) which is gradually expanding to display various items from the history of the town as well as some paintings and sculptures by local artists. Between these two main streets, in the heart of the old town, is the rather dilapidated cathedral of Ste-Marie-de-la-Seds, an early Romanesque and Gothic building on which a new Classical façade was placed in the 17C. The interior preserves something of its medieval origins. There are two other churches of note in this area, both dating from the 18C. St-François-de-Paule, on the rue de la République by the harbour, has an impressive polychrome marble altar. More attractive, however, is the neo-Classical church of St-Louis on the rue Louis-Jourdan to the west, which has preserved much of its original decoration intact.

The newer part of Toulon, by which is meant the 19C district, is to the west and north along the broad boulevard de Strasbourg and the avenue Général-

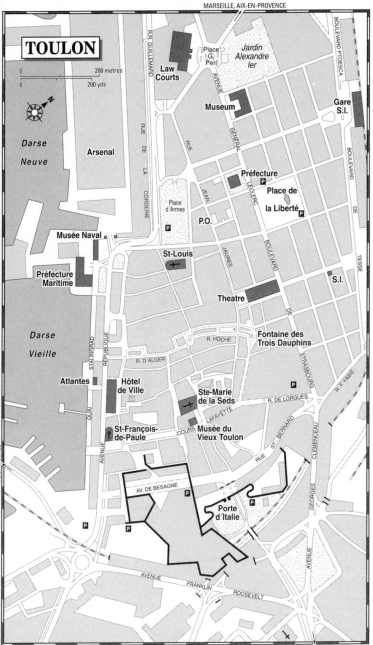

MARSEILLE, AIX-EN-PROVENCE

TOULON

0   200 metres
0   200 yds

Darse Neuve

Arsenal

Law Courts

Place G. Peri

Jardin Alexandre Ier

Museum

Gare S.I.

BOULEVARD PTOESCA

R.R. GUILLEMARD

RUE DE LA CORDERIE

RUE JEAN

AVENUE GÉNÉRAL LECLERC

BOULEVARD DE TESSE

Préfecture

Place de la Liberté

Musée Naval

Place d'Armes

P.O.

Préfecture Maritime

St-Louis

Darse Vieille

JAURÈS

BOULEVARD DE

S.I.

Theatre

R. HOCHE

Fontaine des Trois Dauphins

R. D. ALGER

Atlantes

Hôtel de Ville

Ste-Marie de la Seds

R. DE LORGUES

STRASBOURG

R. F. FABIE

St-François-de-Paule

LAFAYETTE

COURS

Musée du Vieux Toulon

RUE ST. BERNARD

CLEMENCEAU

QUAI STALINGRAD

AVENUE RÉPUBLIQUE

AV. DE BESAGNE

Porte d'Italie

GEORGES

AVENUE

AVENUE FRANKLIN

ROOSEVELT

AIRPORT, FRÉJUS

Leclerc. This is where many of the grander public buldings can be found including the opera house, Conseil Général and the main museum (☎ 04 94 93 15 54), built in 1887 in a sort of Beaux-Arts Renaissance style. In fact, this building houses two separate collections, a museum of natural history (**open** Mon–Sat 09.30–12.00 and 14.00–18.00; Sun 13.00–19.00) and the civic art collection in the **Musée d'art de Toulon** (☎ 04 94 93 15 54; **open** daily 13.00–19.00), filling several galleries with works drawn from all periods between the 16C and the present day. As well as works from the French, Dutch and Italian schools, there is a good selection of sculpture (including work by Puget and Rodin) and wide-ranging displays by artists who worked in Provence such as Ziem and V.-J.-F. Courdouan. There is also a surprisingly rich collection of modern and contemporary art which is displayed in a changing programme of temporary exhibitions.

The forts on the isthmus between the Petit and Grande Rade can also be visited. That to the east is the **Tour Royale** (☎ 04 94 24 90 00: **open** Tues–Sun 14.00–18.00 June–mid Sept; 15.00–18.00 mid Sept–May; closed Mon) built in 1514 and now an extension to the naval museum displaying some cannons and figureheads in the subterranean galleries that once served as a prison. Opposite this, on the western side of the Petit Rade, the **Fort de la Balaguier** was the scene of Napoleon's heroic actions to dislodge the British in 1793. It is also a museum (☎ 04 94 94 84 72: **open** Wed–Sun 10.00–12.00 and 14.00–18.00; closed Mon) with Napoleonic memorabilia and material related to the history of the navy and French colonies. Near this to the south is the district of Tamaris, described by George Sand in her 1861 novel of the same name. Facing the corniche is the Moorish-style Marine Institute, built in 1880 by Michel 'Pacha', a local man who became a prominent figure in the Ottoman Imperial service. The 'Pacha' built several Moorish-style buildings along the coast using the Swiss architect Paul Page, this being one of the finest.

For a spectacular view of the harbour area you should ascend **Mont Faron** behind the town, either by the winding circular road which passes more of the 17C forts, or by the funicular railway from avenue de Vence. At the summit there is a monument and museum to the Allied Liberation of this area in 1944 (☎ 04 94 88 08 09: **open** Tues–Sun 09.30–12.30 and 14.30–17.30; closed Mon and at 16.30 in winter).

Another short excursion is to **Solliès-Ville**, a rather neglected village high on a hill over the busy commuter roads (N97) that run up the valley to Solliès-Pont, Cuers and Le Luc. Solliès-Ville has a distinguished literary past, being the home of the 16C poet Antoine Aréna (c 1500–63) and of the modern Provençal novelist Jean Aicard (1848–1921). Aicard, widely regarded as the true voice of the area of Les Maures, was mayor of the village at his death and there is a small museum in his house. Another museum in Solliès-Ville is devoted to olive oil and the 12C church has fine carved organ shutters dating from 1499. An extension of this route by the D554 will take you up the **Vallée du Gapeau**, a rich fruit-growing district with the pretty village of Méounes-les-Montrieux at the top.

Hyères and the Iles d'Hyères

Hyères is one of the few spots on this entire coastline which retains something of the atmosphere of the great age of the French Riviera. Such was its success in the 19C that virtually every major figure in the travelling literati and aristocracy spent some time here. The Victorian period shaped the new town of Hyères, providing the palm trees, boulevards, grand villas and a casino typical of the Belle Epoque. At the height of its fame, however, it was suddenly eclipsed by the resorts to the east, mainly Cannes, Nice and Monte Carlo, which were racier and more suited to gambling and night life. As a result, Hyères still has an air of faded grandeur that is both relaxing and impressive. The *Grand Hôtel* at Costebelle is now a technical college and many of the villas have been subdivided but the architecture, whether Moorish, Belle Epoque, Modernist or even English parish church, is an unexpected delight.

History of Hyères

There is very little of the Provençal about Hyères, largely because it has been colonised throughout its history. The Greeks from Marseille were the first, establishing a trading-post here c 350 BC which they called Olbia. The site is now being excavated in the area of Costebelle 4km south of the town centre. The Greeks were succeeded by the Romans whose town Pomponiana retained the long-standing link with Marseille. As a result, it suffered along with its ally for supporting Pompey, the loser in the civil war with Julius Caesar. Like most of the towns in this area it was ravaged by repeated Saracen attacks during the Middle Ages but achieved some renown when St Louis landed here in 1254 on his return from the Seventh Crusade. The Knights Templar established their headquarters here and this, accompanied by the demand for salt, gave the town considerable wealth and influence. For a brief period in the mid-16C Hyères became an important centre for the royal court as François I sought to fortify the islands off the coast. The warm climate was such that he encouraged the cultivation of oranges, thus establishing the fruit and flower industry that continues to this day.

As the most southerly town on the French Mediterranean coast, Hyères has been a fashionable resort since the 18C. Indeed, it can probably claim to have been the first true resort on the Côte d'Azur and, during the height of its fame and popularity in the 19C, it was visited by an impressive list of celebrities. Napoleon, his wife the Empress Josephine and his sister Pauline Borghese all spent time in Hyères as did Leo Tolstoy, Victor Hugo, Alphonse de Lamartine and Guy de Maupassant. The historian Jules Michelet died here and Louis Voutier, whose discovery of the Venus de Milo made him a national celebrity, retired to this increasingly smart spot. As was customary, these visitors came for the climate in general and not sea-bathing; the nearest beach is some 5km from the town. This was in accordance with the best contemporary advice for the treatment of consumption and Robert Louis Stevenson had two spells here in the 1880s, describing them later as the happiest days of his life. The climax to this era of high fashion and wealthy convalescence came in 1892 when Queen Victoria took up residence in the *Grand Hôtel* for the summer. There are photographs of her in the grounds being pulled along in her little cart by the Shetland pony she had brought out with her from Britain.

The old town of Hyères, north of the main boulevards, was bounded by two outer walls marked by a series of gates which still span the access roads. It is entered by the 13C Porte Massillon leading into the place Massillon, the market

❖ *Information, accommodation and food*

🛈 Rotonde Jean-Salusse, avenue de Belgique (☎ 04 94 65 18 55).

Hotels. Accommodation in Hyères is split between the old town, the new town and the district near the beaches. In the old town there is the *Soleil* at 2 rue de Rampart (☎ 04 94 65 16 26), while in the new town the *Hôtel de la Poste* at 7 avenue du Maréchal-Lyautey (☎ 04 94 65 02 00) is modest but reasonable. Closer to the seafront, *La Reine Jane* at Ayguade (☎ 04 94 66 32 64) is also fairly simple but, further back at Costebelle, *La Québecoise* on avenue Admiral (☎ 04 94 57 69 24) is recommended.

Restaurants. Hyères has a reasonable range of eating establishments from the bistros on the place Massillon to the more ambitious *Jardins de Bacchus* at 32 avenue Gambetta (☎ 04 94 65 77 63) or *Chez Ma-Mie* at 3 rue de l'Oratoire (☎ 04 94 35 39 20).

square and principal shopping area. Both are named after a celebrated 17C preacher and bishop of Clermont who was born at 7 rue Rabaton nearby. Overlooking the *place* is the curious **Tour St-Blaise**, the last remnant of the Templars' 12C Commandery. The stone staircase by the tower leads into the network of narrow streets, archways and small gardens that characterise the oldest quarter. At its heart is the church of St-Paul, parts of which date from the 10C–12C although the more interesting Gothic nave and columns were only added after 1572. This church still acts as something of a focus for the community and a collection of *ex-votos* and local folk arts is hung round the nave. Alongside the entrance steps of St-Paul is an attractive Renaissance-style house with a turret built over the old gateway. It seems perfectly appropriate to the town's confused history although, in fact, it dates from the 18C–19C.

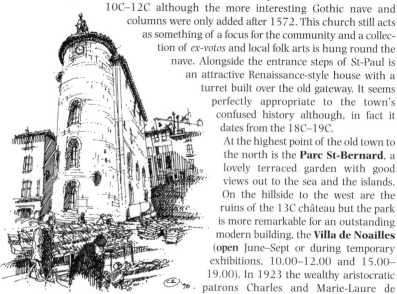

At the highest point of the old town to the north is the **Parc St-Bernard**, a lovely terraced garden with good views out to the sea and the islands. On the hillside to the west are the ruins of the 13C château but the park is more remarkable for an outstanding modern building, the **Villa de Noailles** (open June–Sept or during temporary exhibitions, 10.00–12.00 and 15.00–19.00). In 1923 the wealthy aristocratic patrons Charles and Marie-Laure de Noailles commissioned Robert Mallet-Stevens to design a new villa incorporating all the

Tour St-Blaise

most recent forms and materials of contemporary architecture. The result is an austere rectilinear building with flush geometric planes unrelieved by mouldings, window sills or any type of decoration. The same aesthetic is extended to the garden where a grid of concrete pathways and small flower beds repeats the abstract design. Despite this apparent severity, the whole ensemble is remarkably successful. The clean horizontal drift of the main building has a slightly nautical effect and the large rectangular openings in the outer wall serve almost as picture windows giving excellent views out to sea. Like most of the architects of his generation, Mallet-Stevens kept a firm control over all aspects of the house and he went on to design much of the furniture in keeping with the larger ideals of the building. Neglected and abandoned for many years, the villa has recently been restored to something approaching its original state and is now used for small exhibitions.

Charles and Marie-Laure de Noailles

The Noailles were associated with many leading figures in the *avant garde*, above all the Surrealists, and their circle included artists, writers, musicians and filmmakers who were invited to work at the villa. Cocteau and Alberto Giacometti (1901–66) were just two of the artists who benefited from their patronage. Luis Buñuel and Dalí wrote the screenplay for *L'Age d'Or* here and Man Ray (1890–1976) shot his film *Le Mystère du Château de Dé* in the garden. It is therefore not surprising that Hyères should have a strong and continuing link with French cinema. Jean-Luc Godard shot *Pierrot le Fou* near here (celebrated in a mural on the outside of Hyères public library) and in 1982 François Truffaut made his last film, *Vivement dimanche*, at Hyères. The town's modest film festival helped to launch the careers of many figures in the French *Nouvelle Vague* but it has been dwarfed by the festival at Cannes.

The fiercely modern ensemble of the Villa de Noailles is in marked contrast to the **Castel Ste-Claire**, a short distance to the south, which was the home of the American novelist Edith Wharton (1862–1937). Rebuilding this ruined convent became the great project of her later life and much of the income from her hugely popular novels was poured into the house and garden. Wharton set out to create a relaxing, traditional retreat although it was also intended as a demonstration of her approach to interior decoration. Her taste ran to 18C French, a style that was disseminated to many wealthy American homes through her numerous distinguished guests, such as Henry James and Bernard Berenson. Unfortunately, the house and garden were allowed to deteriorate after Wharton's death and now serve as the offices of the local parks department.

At the edge of the park is the small house called **La Solitude** where Robert Louis Stevenson stayed in the mid-1880s, largely on the advice of his doctor. Stevenson was one of a procession of northern consumptives who sought relief, if not a cure, in the warmer climes of the south. Despite the illness hanging over him, this was a remarkably successful period of his life. While at work on *The Black Arrow* (1888) here he received a number of friends and, more importantly, heard of the colossal success of *Treasure Island*. Five years later, as an exile in

Samoa—again for medical reasons—he wrote 'I have only ever been truly happy once and that was in Hyères.'

If the old part of Hyères presents a picturesque but familiar aspect of Provence, the new town offers a different urban landscape of straight avenues, palm trees, and large Victorian villas. In a bid to recreate some of its Belle Epoque atmosphere, the old station ticket office has been restored and now serves as a tourist information centre. The effect is soon destroyed by the Casino, built in 1907 but remodelled recently for the film festival to include an ugly mirror-glazed superstructure. The **Musée Municipale** (☎ 04 94 35 90 42: **open** Mon and Wed–Fri 10.00–12.00 and 15.00–18.00; closed Tues and weekends) on place Lefèvre to the south is housed in a similarly depressing building but at least its collection of ancient artefacts, natural history and some rather fine 18C–19C paintings and furniture is worth the effort.

For the grander late 19C villas you should wander round the residential district to the east of the old town, where there is a selection of houses in a variety of revivalist styles, many preserving their extensive gardens full of colourful semi-tropical plants. The most interesting houses, however, are the **Neo-Moorish villas** designed by the local architect P. Chapoulart in the western part of the new town. The Villa Tunisienne (1880) on the avenue David-de-Beauregard and the Villa Mauresque, just to the west on the avenue Jean-Natte, combine the arches, crenellations and patterned tiles that were taken to symbolise the exoticism of Arab culture. To make this combination even more unusual, at the corner of the avenue David-de-Beauregard is the **Eglise Anglicane**, designed as an English parish church in the Gothic Revival style.

The beaches of Hyères Plage and the popular racetrack are due south of the town at the neck of the **Giens Peninsula**. This thin strip of land, little more than a sandbank between the rocks of Giens and the shore, encloses the salt pans that were once the main local industry. From a distance the palm-fringed road has a tropical appearance but on closer inspection it is revealed as a rather ugly stretch of abandoned salt flats encroached by holiday camps. **Giens** itself, at the tip of the promontory, is worth a visit although it can be congested and either difficult or expensive to park a car. There is a good fish market here and a lively water-sports centre. A short walk to the west brings you to the ruins of a 16C castle built by the Pontèves family. This spot was much loved by the poet and Nobel Prizewinner St John Perse, and he is buried in the cemetery nearby.

Giens is the departure point for ferries to the **Iles d'Hyères**, some of the most beautiful islands along this whole coast. The three principal islands, Porquerolles, Port-Cros and Levant, are a fascinating combination of rugged rock formations topped by extraordinarily rich vegetation.

History of the Iles d'Hyères

The islands' strategic importance has been appreciated since ancient times and they have been occupied by Ligurians, Greeks, Romans, early Christian monks, Saracens and Corsairs. The most famous inhabitants were a community of criminals given their freedom by Henri II in the mid-16C on condition that they protected the islands against North African pirates. In the way of things, this unruly group took to piracy themselves and terrorised the coast for decades until the army of Louis XIV regained control. Each of the islands is dotted with impressive forts which have been in use up to the 20C. Napoleon relied on them to repulse a British attack and in 1944 the Allied invasion force took these positions before the final push onto mainland Provence. This turbulent history is in marked contrast to the idyllic appearance the islands have from the coast. It was the brilliance of the evening sunlight reflected on their cliffs which gave rise to the popular name of Iles d'Or.

Porquerolles, the nearest and largest of the group, is excellent for walking or cycling. At 7km long and 3km wide it is large enough to explore at leisure, with a range of routes through a richly coloured landscape of eucalyptus trees, umbrella pines and sub-tropical plants. The village of Porquerolles itself has a curiously colonial appearance largely due to the fact that it was founded by Napoleon as a haven for veterans of the *Grande Armée*. Above it is the 16C **Fort de Ste-Agathe** (☎ 04 94 12 82 30; **open** June–Sept 10.00–12.00 and 14.00–17.30) with a small museum on the history of the islands and displays on underwater archaeology. The village and bathing areas to the east were the setting for the climax to Godard's film *Pierrot le Fou*. To the south, a 45min walk to the lighthouse leads through some beautiful wooded countryside before emerging onto the cliffs which line the southern coast of the island. There is also a longer walk along the cliffs to the Calanque du Breganconnet in the west.

The **Ile de Port-Cros**, now a national park in recognition of the variety and richness of its vegetation, is much quieter than its neighbour Porquerolles. In high summer, however, this fragile ecostructure of exotic plants and natural springs must be in grave danger from the increasing number of visitors who wish to explore it. The landscape is rugged but this is no deterrent to the dedicated ramblers who flock through the inappropriately named Valley of Solitude leading from the port to the south coast. This route passes the only hotel on the island, a pale, elegant 18C house known as *La Manoir d'Hélène* after a character in the novel *Jean d'Agrève* by Melchior de Vogue, which is set here. Throughout the summer there are guided tours of the various points of interest along the routes. One walk is the **Sentier Botanique**, a footpath lined with some of the richest Mediterranean and subtropical plants, which leads after 3km to the small bay of La Palud. Another route links the string of forts round the island, the best of which is the **Fort de l'Estissac** above the landing-stage. This was built in the 17C, destroyed by the British in 1793 and rebuilt by Napoleon. It is now a good lookout-point. There is also a clifftop path along the south coast. D.H. Lawrence is reputed to have visited Port-Cros in the 1920s in the company of a high-born English woman. Her tale of an intense love affair with a local labourer has been suggested as the inspiration for another, more famous novel set in an English country house.

The most easterly of the islands, reached from either Giens or Le Lavandou, is the **Ile du Levant**. Much of this is given over to the military but it also contains **Héliopolis**, one of the earliest nudist or naturist colonies, which was set up in 1931 by a Dr Durville.

Bormes, the Corniche des Maures and Sainte-Maxime

From Hyères the main route east (N98) follows the base of the Massif des Maures past more salt pans and industrial developments before branching north into the long valley of the Môle through the mountains to the Golfe de St-Tropez.

At this junction the D559 continues east passing Bormes-les-Mimosas before rejoining the coast at Le Lavandou.

Bormes-les-Mimosas has a beautiful situation on a steep slope above the road looking out over the sea to the Iles d'Hyères. The romantic name, linking the town with the flower which abounds in its streets and gardens, is very much a modern invention, adopted formally in 1968. Indeed, much of the old village has a contrived air in which renovated houses are linked by streets with quirky titles such as 'lovers' alley', 'gossips' way' or 'arse-breaker street'. This can seem rather precious and Bormes has certainly appealed to many celebrities who still have houses here. It has, nevertheless, retained something of its historic character.

History of Bormes-les-Mimosas

The village was repeatedly attacked from the sea throughout the Middle Ages and, as well as the usual incursions from Saracens, Turks and pirates, has the dubious distinction of being sacked first by the Genoese admiral Andrea Doria in 1539 and then by the army of Charles V in the same year. It has also had its share of natural disasters and a monument in the main square commemorates the visit of St Francis of Paola in 1482 when he delivered the village from plague.

❖ *Information, accommodation and food*

🛈 Place Gambetta (☎ 04 94 71 15 17).

Hotels. Accommodation is limited in Bormes but there are four hotels which can all be recommended. The *Grand Hôtel* at 167 route de Baguier (☎ 04 94 71 23 72) is the best, while *Le Provençal* at 37 rue Plaine-des-Anes (☎ 04 94 71 15 25), *La Terrasse* at 19 place Gambetta (☎ 04 94 71 15 22) and *Le Bellevue* at 12 place Gambetta (☎ 04 94 71 15 15), all in the old town, are very reasonable.

There are several other hotels including the excellent *Les Palmiers* (☎ 04 94 64 81 94) at Cabasson nearer the sea.

Restaurants. Bormes has several good restaurants of which *La Jardin de Perlefleurs* (☎ 04 94 64 99 23), *La Tonnelle des Delices* (☎ 04 94 71 34 84) and *La Cassole* (☎ 04 94 71 14 86) are all extremely good.

A chapel dedicated to St Francis of Paola also contains a memorial to Jean-Charles Cazin (1841–1901), a local-born landscape painter who joined the Realist circle in Paris. There are examples of Cazin's work and that of other French 19C and early 20C artists in the **Musée Arts et Histoire** (☎ 04 94 71 56 60: **open** Mon–Sat 10.00–12.00 and 16.00–18.00, Sun 10.00–12.00, also Wed, Fri and Sun 21.00–23.00, July–Sept; Wed 10.00–12.00 and 15.00–17.00, and Sun 10.00–12.00 only, Oct–June), housed in an attractive mansion at 65 rue Carnot. A well-advertised *circuit fleuri* follows a route to the 12C castle where there is a monument to Hyppolite Bouchard, an adventurer from Bormes who drove the Spanish out of Argentina.

Le Lavandou

In contrast to the colour and cultivated prettiness of Bormes, Le Lavandou is a fairly conventional resort which has grown beyond the fishing-village to encompass the beaches stretching out to the Cap Bénat. Like its neighbour, the name has some pretensions, being linked in local publicity to lavender blossom. In fact it refers to the more prosaic activity of laundresses who worked on the seashore here. Le Lavandou was a popular haunt of artists and musicians in the late 19C and the composer Ernest Reyer, who died here in 1909, has given his name to the principal square. There is a small museum devoted to local archaeological discoveries but the dominant activity is undoubtedly water sports, reflected in the large marinas to the south of the town. Behind these is the large promontory culminating in **Cap Bénat**. This has two medieval castles and the summer residence of the late French president François Mitterrand but it is mostly private property with restricted access.

❖ *Information, accommodation and food*

🛈 Quai Gabriel-Péri (☎ 04 94 71 00 61) opposite the bus station.

Hotels. Accommodation in La Lavandou is less interesting and less expensive than Bormes but it is difficult to find in summer. *Les Roches* at 1 avenue des Trois-Dauphins (☎ 04 94 71 05 07) is perhaps the best hotel in the whole area but the *Belle Vue* on the chemin du Four-des-Maures at St-Clair (☎ 04 94 71 01 06) is close in quality and outlook. Among the cheaper hotels *Le Neptune* (☎ 04 94 71 01 01) and *L'Oustaou* (☎ 04 94 71 12 18), both on avenue Général-de-Gaulle, are very reasonable.

Restaurants. Eating out in Le Lavandou offers considerable choice but you should try *Au Vieux Port* at the quai Gabriel-Péri (☎ 04 94 71 00 21) or *Le Pêcheur* at the quai des Pêcheurs (☎ 04 94 71 58 01) for the seafood.

Le Lavandou stands at the start of the **Corniche des Maures**, the long stretch of coast road backed by the dark, tree-covered slopes of the Massif. This road is neither as dramatic nor as glamorous as the corniches further east and it is often congested with holiday traffic but it has good views out to the islands and it passes several small, sheltered resorts such as Cavalière, Pramousquier and Le Rayol. In the early 20C this coastline was popular with Anglo-Saxons who built their villas higher up the hillside to take advantage of the open outlook. There is very little space between the base of the hills and the sea at this point and this has restricted the development of the beaches. As a result most of the resorts have only small bathing areas accessible by staircases, some of which are private.

Cavalaire-sur-Mer at the eastern end of the corniche, however, has some 4km of fine sandy beach. This was probably the site of the ancient Greek town of Heraclia Cacabaria. There are also remains of several Roman villas in the area although this Classical heritage does not seem to have made much impact on the modern resort. Cavalaire is entirely preoccupied with seaside holidays and offers all the facilities for just that.

❖ *Information and accommodation*

🛈 Square de Lattre-de-Tassigny (☎ 04 94 64 08 28).

Hotels. As a family resort, Cavalaire-sur-Mer has some reasonable if unimpressive accommodation. For more interesting hotels, however, *Le Mas* above Pramousquier (☎ 04 94 05 80 43) and *Les Cigales* in rue des Ecoles at Cavalière (☎ 04 94 05 80 32) offer excellent views out over the Mediterranean.

From the Baie de Cavalaire the D559 turns inland by La Croix-Valmer across the neck of the St-Tropez peninsula to one of the most troublesome traffic spots on the whole of the south coast; the junction at La Foux. Several major roads intersect here alongside a funfair which, in summer, gives rise to constant traffic jams. To the right the D98a leads down the coast to St-Tropez but the main N98 turns left round the gulf by the curious new town named Port Grimaud (for more details see p 244), which also contributes to delays on the roads.

Following the perimeter of the gulf, the N98 continues to **Sainte-Maxime**, an unpretentious but lively resort with many of the traditional activities of a seaside holiday in evidence. It faces St-Tropez across the Golfe de St-Tropez and a ferry links the two in summer, but they exist almost as opposites, the lights of one twinkling across the water towards the other at night.

History of Sainte-Maxime

The original settlement of Calidianis was established here by the Phoenicians but by the Middle Ages it was prey to so many attacks by pirates and Saracens that the villagers appealed to the monks of St-Honorat for protection. The monks responded and renamed the village after their patron saint Maxime, a daughter of the Comte de Grasse. There is a *bravade* or *fête* each year on May 15 in which her effigy is carried round the town accompanied by dancers and a party of swordsmen.

The monks of St-Honorat also built a number of defensive towers at Ste-Maxime, the last of which, dating from the 16C, still stands by the marina. This is the solid **Tour des Dames** or **Tour Carrée** (☎ 04 94 96 70 30: open Wed–Mon 10.00–12.00 and 16.00–19.00 July–Sept; closed Tues; closes earlier out of season), one of the town's principal landmarks, which has served variously as a courthouse and prison. It is now a rather quaint museum of local history and folklore complete with draped fishing nets and mannequins dressed in traditional costume. Behind this is the parish church, a fairly conventional 18C–19C building containing one of the many altarpieces dispersed or looted from the Chartreuse de la Verne (see p 246).

In the Forêt des Maures 10km north of Ste-Maxime by the D25 is the Parc St-Donat, a country park round a 12C Romanesque chapel. Near this is the **Musée de la Musique Mécanique** (☎ 04 94 96 50 52: open Wed–Sun 10.00–12.00 and 14.30–18.00 Easter–Oct; closed Mon, Tues and Nov–Easter) one of the most unusual and fascinating museums in Provence. The collection includes some 400 instruments from conventional phonographs to complex hand-cranked musical boxes, mechanical pianos/pianolas, 'orchestrionettes' and an early talking doll, many of which are demonstrated by the keeper. There is also a collection of early typewriters and adding machines. Apart from these various contraptions, however, the collection is housed in two garages which have been decorated by the founder in a personal form of high kitsch. Plaster casts, dolls, old ceramics and plastic plates have been arranged across the façade and painted in a series of vivid colours to create an outrageous Rococo version of Surrealist decoration.

❖ *Information, accommodation and food*

🛈 Promenade Simon-Lorière (☎ 04 94 96 19 24).

Hotels. Since tourism is the main industry in Ste-Maxime, there is plenty of accommodation at reasonable prices but hotels can be busy in high summer. *La Belle Aurore* at 4 boulevard Jean-Moulin (☎ 04 94 96 02 45) is one of the best, but the small *Marie-Louise* in its own garden at the Hameau de Guerre-Vieille in the west (☎ 04 94 96 06 05) is certainly the most attractive.

Restaurants. Besides the very good restaurant at *La Belle Aurore* (see above), *Le Gruppi* on avenue Ch.-de-Gaulle (☎ 04 94 96 03 61) is a classic seafood restaurant while *Le Calypso* nearby is also good and considerably cheaper.

From Ste-Maxime to Fréjus the N98 follows the coastline at the eastern end of the Massif des Maures past a series of small resorts with good bathing and occasional rocky inlets. Les Issambres, for example, has some attractive *calanques* but **St-Aygulf**, the last village before Fréjus, is the most notable. This was a popular spot at the end of the 19C and Sarah Bernhardt lived here for a while, as did the celebrated salon painter Charles-Emile Carolus-Duran (1837–1917), two of whose works are displayed in the church.

Fréjus

Fréjus has perhaps the richest concentration of ancient monuments on the Côte d'Azur, a point which has been taken up in publicity slogans calling it the Pompeii of Provence. As a title this would be more appropriate to either Arles or Vaison-la-Romaine but there is no doubting the rich heritage of Fréjus.

History of Fréjus

The town was founded by Julius Caesar in the build-up to his war with Pompey in 49 BC but it was Caesar's nephew, the Emperor Augustus, who turned it into the major naval base of the province. Augustus settled veterans from his legions here and expanded the dockyards, arsenal and fortifications to such an extent that it had one of the largest harbour areas of the ancient world. The galleys that destroyed Antony and Cleopatra's fleet at Actium in 31 BC were built at Fréjus and it was from here that Roman naval expeditions embarked to suppress the tribes of North Africa and the Iberian peninsula.

Under Constantine, Fréjus became an important early Christian centre and from the 4C it was the seat of a bishopric. Thereafter, however, the fortunes of the town seemed to enter a steady decline. It was devastated first by the Saracens in 940, then by Barbary pirates in the 15C and finally by the troops of the Emperor Charles V in 1536. In the same period the harbour, which had required dredging to make it navigable in the first place, began to silt up leaving an area of marsh that was uncultivable and unhealthy. It was only with the building of canals in the 19C that this was brought under control and the area developed for agriculture and wine-growing.

Fréjus is still a naval base, especially for aeronautics, but it has also become a popular holiday resort with good beaches to the south and a range of activities and festivals held in the Roman arena. In France, however, it is synonymous with one of the worst disasters of modern times. After heavy rain in December 1959 the Malpasset dam at the rear of the town gave way, creating a 50m-high torrent which swept through Fréjus killing over 400 people. The remains of the dam and even the turbines can still be seen littered across the countryside to the north of the *autoroute* by the D37.

❖ *Information, accommodation and food*

🛈 325 rue Jean-Jaurès (☎ 04 94 17 19 19), near the bus station.

Hotels. There is a smaller choice of accommodation in Fréjus than in nearby St-Raphaël but the *Bellevue* at place Paul-Vernet (☎ 04 94 51 42 41) is a reasonable cheap hotel in the centre while *Il était une fois* at 254 rue F.-Mistral is better and nearer the sea. The *Residence du Colombier* on the route de Bagnols (☎ 04 94 51 45 92) is a luxury bungalow complex in pine woods outside the town with good sports facilities.

Restaurants. There are good bistros in the place Agricola and shopping areas of town but *Les Potiers* at 135 rue des Potiers (☎ 04 94 51 33 74) and *La Romana* (☎ 04 94 51 42 41) on boulevard de la Libération at Fréjus-Plage offer something better.

Despite its Classical heritage, the principal monument in Fréjus is the **Cité Episcopale** (☎ 04 94 51 26 30: **open** daily 09.00–19.00 Apr–Sept; 09.00–12.00 and 14.00–17.00 Oct–Mar; closed Tues in winter), a fortified complex of buildings round the cathedral in the heart of the old town. This is one of the great sites of the early Christian church in the west but it has been in constant use and therefore contains elements from every period between the 5C and the 19C.

The guided tour begins at the 16C Renaissance doorway carved with scenes

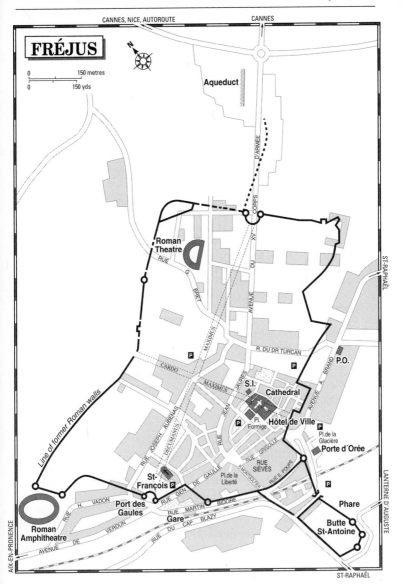

from the life of the Virgin. This leads on to the **baptistery**, the oldest part of the complex and one of the finest early Christian buildings in Western Europe. Eight black granite columns, topped by Corinthian capitals from the Roman forum, encircle the basin where the early bishops baptised new members into the Church. From here the tour follows the route taken by these early catechumens as they ascended the stairs to enter the body of the church to receive communion.

The 13C–14C **cathedral** is a good example of early Gothic in Provence but the forms of the interior are sturdy and handsome rather than beautiful. Defence and strength, after all, were major considerations in every religious building in this region even after the expulsion of the Saracens. The furnishings and fittings, notably the 15C choir stalls and the altarpieces, help to soften this martial effect but it is a far cry from the soaring tracery of northern cathedrals. The **cloisters**, dating from the same period as the main church, offer a more attractive ensemble although they have suffered considerable damage. Originally on two storeys, only one upper range survives. For some reason, during the 15C the stone vaulting was replaced in many sections by wooden beams with delicate painted decoration. Unfortunately, many of these curious pieces were destroyed during the Revolution but some 400 have survived to divert and entertain the visitor.

On the first floor of the cloister there is an **archaeological museum** with some interesting Gallo-Roman antiquities. The finest pieces are the double-headed Hermes and a 1C head of Jupiter but there are also some interesting decorative arts and an attractive Roman mosaic of a leopard.

The Roman town of Forum Julii occupied much of the area now covered by the modern town centre and, as a result, only isolated survivors stand out amid the later building. Sections of the Roman wall, the aqueduct and a theatre can all be seen to the northeast of the town, and in the west, by the rue H.-Vadon, is the **arena** which is still in use for bullfights and public performances. This was the earliest amphitheatre in Roman Gaul, originally seating up to 10,000 spectators, but what remains gives little indication of its original grandeur.

Much of the huge Roman port is still being excavated in the grounds to the south of the old town. All that remains of the citadel is the mound at the Butte St-Antoine and, beyond it, the so-called **Lanterne d'Auguste**, a medieval tower built on the base of a Roman structure that once marked the entrance to the main harbour. Unfortunately, none of these antique monuments bears comparison with their counterparts in Arles, Nîmes or Orange. Lacking both the scale and the detail to make the ancient world tangible, you are thrown back on diagrams and artists' impressions to bring the remains of Fréjus to life.

Given the history of Fréjus it is something of a surprise to come across the clutch of exotic monuments built on the northern outskirts of the town in the early 20C. On the N7 by the remains of the aqueduct (2km out), there is a **Buddhist pagoda** (☎ 04 94 53 25 29; **open** 09.00–12.00 and 15.00–20.30; closes at 17.30 out of season) built by Vietnamese troops as a memorial to the 5000 Annamite soldiers who died in the First World War. Slightly further out of town on the Tour de Mare estate is the **Chapelle de Notre-Dame-de-Jerusalem**, a modern chapel designed and decorated by Cocteau just before his death in 1963 (☎ 04 94 17 05 60; **open** daily 14.00–18.00, closed Tues). Finally, on the other side of the river Reyran, 5km by the D4 towards Bagnols-en-Forêt, there is a **mosque** built in the 1930s in imitation of the great mosque at Djenne in Mali, for the use of soldiers from the former French colony of Sudan. Appropriately, there is both a military museum and a safari park nearby.

21 · Saint-Tropez and Les Maures

In the great sweep of the Côte d'Azur, one section stands out as different or at least as distinctive from the procession of resorts between Hyères and Menton— the St-Tropez peninsula and the area behind it known as Les Maures. One of the reasons for this is the isolation of the area caused by the great Massif de Maures which made land contact difficult until the 19C. But an equal, if not greater reason for the distinctiveness of this region is the fact that for almost 100 years, between 884 and 979, it was controlled by the Moors. This may seem like a very long time ago but traces of that period are still evident in the names of the villages, the architectural remains and, reputedly, in the food and pattern of traditional life.

Nowadays, St-Tropez is one of the most popular holiday resorts in the south of France but since the 1960s it has also been notorious for the practical problems that confront the visitor. It is generally expensive, accommodation can be dificult to find and, above all, the roads are usually congested in summer. There are signs that this may be improving, more through better management than a dropping off in the number of visitors. The area of Les Maures still has a great deal to offer. Bypassed by the main roads and isolated from the communities to the north of the Massif this network of beautiful villages has retained a certain mystique despite the gradual encroachment of the modern tourist boom. The large **Maison du Tourisme du Golfe de St-Tropez et Pays des Maures** (☎ 04 94 43 42 10, fax 04 94 43 42 78) at the junction of the N98 and D559 outside the town is very useful and, despite the traffic jams at this spot, should perhaps be your starting-point before proceeding to St-Tropez itself.

Saint-Tropez

St-Tropez has entered the modern consciousness so completely as a symbol of French high life and permissiveness that it is now difficult to view it with a straight face. People who have never been to France, let alone the Riviera, have an awareness of it that is almost entirely the creation of popular culture. This is not inappropriate since St-Tropez, as we know it today, was largely invented by people from the world of film and fashion. Only now, as many of them die or write their autobiographies, does it emerge how well the town's image was manipulated and projected to a mass audience hungry for the apparent freedom that it represented.

History of Saint-Tropez

St-Tropez takes its name from an obscure Christian martyr called Torpès, one of Nero's centurions who was beheaded at Pisa for refusing to give up his faith. His remains were cast adrift in a boat along with a cock and a dog and eventually washed up at this spot. To celebrate this event each year on 16–17 May there is a *bravade* or *fête* in which a bust of the saint is paraded round the streets accompanied by men dressed in 18C costume who fire off volleys of blank cartridges. Another *bravade* on 15 June celebrates a French victory of 1637 when 22 Spanish galleons were routed in the bay.

These two tales introduce the maritime character of the town. Isolated from the main land routes of Provence, St-Tropez was more easily accessible from the sea. The town was sacked by Saracens in 739 and again in 888, and finally it was one of the landing-points of the Allied invasion force in 1944. This last bombardment reduced the town to rubble; the colourful houses you see on the harbour front were all rebuilt after the Second World War.

Its prosperity dates from 1470 when Genoese merchant families undertook to extend and fortify the town. For 200 years after this influx St-Tropez remained an independent republic. The modern phase of the town's history was probably inaugurated in 1892 when the Pointillist painter Paul Signac arrived here on his yacht. Delighting in the powerful light and atmosphere, he had his friend, the architect Henri van de Velde, design the Villa la Hune for him which still stands on the rue Paul-Signac. From this comfortable haven Signac attracted a succession of younger artists to work in St-Tropez including Bonnard, Matisse, Dufy, Marquet and André Dunoyer de Segonzac. They were followed by Colette, who settled here in the 1920s and set her novels *La Naissance du jour* and *La Treille Muscat* in St-Tropez. She also developed a line in cosmetics and opened a beauty shop by the old port where she was known to make up the more attractive customers herself. By this time the small fishing-village was becoming a summer colony for writers and artists but this development could not compare with the explosion of the 1950s.

While Roger Vadim's 1958 film *Et Dieu Créa la Femme* (*And God Created Woman*) projected an image of St-Tropez as a carefree paradise, it was the off-screen antics of the director and stars that confirmed its reputation for sexual freedom. Brigitte Bardot, who was married to Vadim at the start of filming, moved in with her co-star Jean-Louis Trintignant before it was completed. Vadim married the actress Annette Stroyberg who then left him for the singer and entertainer Sacha Distel. St-Tropez was the hub of this incestuous social group in summer and it soon began to attract a wider circle such as the precocious novelist Françoise Sagan, the millionaire Gunther Sachs and a retinue of Paris intellectuals, actors, writers and hangers-on. Rechristened St-Trop ('too much'), it was the scene of much French fashion and gossip, eagerly promoted by the colour magazine *Paris Match*. Topless bathing was first seen here in 1960 and soon the beaches along the whole Riviera were packed with more exposed flesh than even the bikini would allow.

Tahiti Beach at the Plage de Pampelonne was the most fashionable at that time but it is largely private now. The Vadim/Bardot circle also made a number of bars and clubs famous, notably the *Café des Arts* on the place des Lices (place Carnot), but these are long past their heyday. In fact, this is one of the problems with St-Tropez as a whole. The values and, to some extent, the styles of 1959 are still in evidence, often on people who were in their prime 40 years ago. The concept of beach-wear with heavy make-up and jewellery, accompanied by a miniature dog, is still alive here and, indeed, seems almost fashionable again as kitsch.

Bardot took up residence here, becoming the town's greatest tourist attraction. For the past 30 years she has adopted a fairly reclusive life but this has not deterred thousands of visitors flocking to St-Tropez each year to catch some of the heady atmosphere that she and her early films projected. It was a peculiarly Gallic form of liberation and one which rarely convinces Anglo-Saxons. Nevertheless, if you can overcome an initial aversion to the overdevelopment of the town, St-Tropez still has great appeal.

❖ *Information, accommodation and food*

🛈 Quai Jean-Jaurès (☎ 04 94 97 45 21) and 23 avenue du Général-Leclerc (☎ 04 94 97 41 21).

Hotels. Accommodation in St-Tropez is almost impossible to find in high summer unless you have booked in advance. It is also generally more expensive than anywhere else west of Cannes.

At the top end of the scale there is the fashionable and exotic *Le Byblos* (☎ 04 94 97 00 04) on avenue Paul-Signac, a modern hotel with an Arab flavour. The *Residence de la Pinède* (☎ 04 94 97 04 21) outside town at the Plage de la Bouillabaisse is in an old villa with an excellent restaurant.

One level down from these is *Le Sube* (☎ 04 94 97 30 04) at the quai Suffren, with excellent views, *L'Hermitage* (☎ 04 94 97 52 33) at avenue Paul-Signac or *La Ponche* (☎ 04 94 97 02 53), a fashionable hotel at 3 rue des Ramparts.

The pick of the less expensive hotels are *Le Baron* (☎ 04 94 97 06 57) at the rue de l'Aïoli, *La Romana* (☎ 04 94 97 18 50) at chemin des Conquêtes or *Les Chimères* (☎ 04 94 97 02 90) near the bus station towards Port Grimaud.

Restaurants. Eating out in St-Tropez can be an unreliable and expensive experience. If you want to splash out *Le Chabichou* (☎ 04 94 54 80 00, closed in winter), part of *Le Byblos* (see above) at avenue Foch, is one of the finest, as is *L'Olivier* (☎ 04 94 97 58 16) outside town in La Bastide on the route des Carles. Both are noted for their seafood while *L'Echalote* (☎ 04 94 54 83 26) on rue du Général-Allard is probably best for traditional meat dishes. *Joseph* (☎ 04 94 97 03 90) at 5 rue Cepoun-San-Martin, and *Chez Madeleine* (☎ 04 94 97 15 74) at rue de Tahiti are also good for seafood and *Le Petit Charron* (☎ 04 94 97 73 78) at 6 rue des Charrons serves good Provençal cuisine.

For general café/bistro meals you could try *La Table du Marché* (☎ 04 94 97 85 20) at 38 rue Clemenceau although it is generally busy or, as a novelty, the *Café des Arts* on place Carnot, the haunt of the jet-set in the '50s and still pretending to a 'Left Bank' atmosphere.

As one recent commentator put it, 'St-Tropez is infuriating, tawdry, over-developed, crowded and trashy' but enough of the original character of the old town survives to remind the visitor of its initial attractions. To appreciate it, however, it is best to visit in spring or autumn. In high summer it is generally overcrowded with unbearable traffic jams while in winter it is whipped by the north winds from across the bay.

The best place to catch up on the prevailing atmosphere is on the quayside of

Back street St-Tropez

the old port. Here, if you can afford the price of a drink, is the spot from which to observe the procession of eccentrics, poseurs and 'beautiful people', or to spy on the deliberately public parties on the yachts moored close by. As a contrast, at the corner of the quai de l'Epi there is a 16C monastic chapel which now houses the **Musée de l'Annonciade** (☎ 04 94 97 04 01: open Wed–Mon 10.00–12.00 and 15.00–19.00 June–Sept; 10.00–12.00 and 15.00–19.00 Oct–May; 10.00–12.00 and 14.00–18.00; closed Tues and Nov), one of the finest modern art galleries in France. The core of the collection was bequeathed to the town by Georges Grammont in 1950 and in recent decades this has been augmented by acquisitions which are perfectly in keeping with both the town and the building. It includes some outstanding canvases by Matisse, Signac, Georges Seurat (1859–91), Bonnard, Derain, Braque, Dufy and Vlaminck, most of whom worked in St-Tropez. Indeed, one of the delights of this excellent museum is the sense that many of the paintings depict a scene which can be observed from the gallery windows.

The old town of St-Tropez has retained some of its charm despite the effects of overwhelming tourism. It is true that many of the shops are now boutiques or expensive bars but the alleyways and narrow passages make for pleasant exploring. The place de la Mairie at the north end of the old port is a good spot to start. This is a relatively open area with some grand 17C–18C houses, including the Palais de Suffren, and it leads back into the network of small streets of the Ponche district. To the north, these lanes emerge onto the seafront flanked by the two watchtowers that guarded St-Tropez from invaders. South of the place de la Mairie is the 19C **Eglise St-Tropez**, a substantial neo-Baroque building that seems rather constricted by the narrow surrounding streets. The attractive moustachioed gent in the niche above the main door is the saint although the bust that is carried round the streets during the *bravade* is displayed inside.

Due east of this along any one of several streets is the **citadel**, begun in the 16C as the principal defence of the whole Golfe de St-Tropez. The oldest part is the hexagonal keep in the centre but this was repeatedly extended with a series of moats and ramparts creating a formidable complex. The keep now houses a **Musée Naval** (☎ 04 94 97 06 53: open Wed–Mon 10.00–18.00 June–Sept; 10.00–17.00 Oct–May; closed Tues and mid Nov–mid Dec) devoted to Pierre-André Bailli de Suffren (1729–88), one of France's leading naval heroes, who was born in St-Tropez. (A statue to him stands on the quai de Suffren overlooking the old port, but it is now engulfed by cafés.) The museum has various exhibits illustrating the naval history of the area; if these prove less than enticing it is worth a visit for the view from the walls.

St-Tropez has only one poor beach so the main bathing spots have been developed on the long **plage de Pampelonne**, a great stretch of fine sands some 3km to the southeast of the town off the D93. Tahiti Beach at the top of Pampelonne was the most fashionable in the 1950s but the whole stretch has been parcelled up into private bathing areas which charge for entrance. For free bathing away from the crowds you must go quite far south beyond Cap Camerat where there are a few unmarked and fairly rough tracks leading down to the sea. Navigating round here on foot or by car is a bit unreliable but it can be rewarding.

Around Saint-Tropez

The D93 south from St-Tropez starts a circuit which takes in the hill-villages and vineyards of this whole peninsula. It is a very distinctive area with rich pine-clad hills and remote coastal paths that remind the visitor of a period before the rise of tourism. The reasons for its survival so close to some of the most extreme developments are quite straightforward. Until recently this area was a backwater with few roads to transport the outsider. Allied to this inaccessibility was a strong sense of local identity which to this day can be guarded and suspicious of visitors. Another feature is the turbulent history of the area. It was controlled by the Saracens for much of the 10C and the religious wars of the 16C–17C marked the society in such a way as to leave deep and lasting resentments. It was not so long ago that local tradition forbade marriages between the inhabitants of separate villages due to hostility between communities going back two and three hundred years.

Little of this is obvious now in **Ramatuelle**, a village near the centre and highest point of the peninsula which has been gradually colonised by northern Europeans. The cobbled streets and stone houses follow the plan of the medieval concentric walls and in the main square there is an elm tree which it is claimed was planted in 1598. The church is only slightly older, dating from 1582 and, like many of the houses, was once part of the outer perimeter wall. Its main doorway is an odd feature. Made of a deep green serpentine, it was plundered, like the altarpiece, from the Chartreuse de la Verne after the Revolution. The much-lamented actor and film star Gérard Philipe (1922–59) is buried in the cemetery and this has given the village a curious identity. A small film festival is held in his honour each year.

From Ramatuelle roads lead off in all directions. To the south the D93 passes near the bathing areas of La Bastide-Blanche and Gigaro before reaching **La Croix-Valmer**, where the Emperor Constantine had a decisive vision in 312. A shining cross with the inscription 'By this sign you will conquer' appeared to him, confirming his resolve to fight for control of the empire in Italy and leading to his acceptance of Christianity. A stone cross commemorating this seminal event was erected in 1893. Another route, the D89, loops round to the hilltop in the north by the ruined Moulins de Paillas, where the young lovers of the surrounding villages reputedly met in defiance of local hostilities. The road leads on to **Gassin** a fortified village perched high in the hills and offering panoramic views down to the coastline and bay. This village was controlled by the Saracens and the Knights Templars before gaining a degree of independence in the 16C. The church dates from 1582.

From Gassin the D89 joins the main D559 leading down to Port Grimaud, unfortunately becoming entangled with the notorious intersection at La Foux on the way. Designed by the Catalan architect François Spoerry in 1966, **Port Grimaud** is a closely guarded haven for the *nouveaux riches* in the style of a seaside marina, a form of new town that is becoming quite popular in the south of France. Architects sneer at this entirely bogus Venice of the Côte d'Azur where, in the absence of roads, wealthy residents visit one another's waterside villas by motor boat. There is no charge for entrance but it is difficult to negotiate the various routes into the complex and to park. If you can get access, you may walk round part of this enclosed community looking for such famous residents as Joan Collins. If you want to avoid this area there is a small road from Gassin directly to Cogolin.

Cogolin is unlike most of the villages in this region in that it has retained a number of thriving local industries, many of which have survived since the Middle Ages. Pipe-making, silk-spinning, carpet-weaving and the preparation of corks for wine bottles are all practised here despite the steady influx of tourists. The marvel is that the workshops and factories, which can be visited by arrangement with the tourist office, have not yet degenerated into 'craft shops' for casual spectators.

🛈 Place de la République (☎ 04 94 54 63 17).

The old quarter of the village has several interesting monuments including an 11C Romanesque church with a fairly grand 16C altarpiece that was looted from the Chartreuse de la Verne. The restored castle in rue Nationale dates from the 16C. It is the more modern aspect of Cogolin, however, which projects its true atmosphere. The main square, for example, has a neo-Baroque Mairie dating from 1853 that is well set off by the palm trees and bustling activity around the war memorial. The small **Espace Raimu** (☎ 04 94 54 18 00: **open** daily 10.00–12.00 and 15.00–19.00 June–Aug; 10.00–12.00 and 15.00–18.00 Sept–May), installed in the local cinema, holds an intriguing display of memorabilia associated with this celebrated French actor (real name Jules Muraire). Raimu's daughter set up the museum and she will often show visitors round the still photographs, posters and souvenirs salvaged from film sets of the 1930s.

The carpet workshops of *Manufacture des Tapis de Cogolin* (☎ 04 94 54 66 17: guided tours, **open** Mon–Fri 09.00–12.00 and 14.00–18.00; closed Sat, Sun) on boulevard Louis-Blanc are amongst the most interesting of Cogolin's factories, partly because this serious business is conducted using a combination of traditional French Jacquard looms—of the type which revolutionised carpet and tapestry manufacture in the 18C—and new computer technology to assist in the reproduction of modern paintings by Léger and Matisse. The factory was set up in 1922 to employ Armenian refugees fleeing from the massacres of the Turks. The other industries have a longer pedigree. The cork business was reputedly started in the 10C when Saracens first introduced this simple but effective way of keeping wine fresh. Like cork, the pipe industry relies on the prevalence of briar bushes over the surrounding hills, the briar root being hard enough to withstand heat without flavouring the tobacco. Nowadays, however, suitable woods are imported from all over the Mediterranean. The Cogolin workshops tend to specialise in collectors' pipes, especially those with carved heads (those of former French president Georges Pompidou, Winston Churchill and Voltaire are amongst the most popular) but there is a fair selection of plain bowls for those who like to use their pipes.

Grimaud has an impressive setting at the top of a conical hill standing out against the full sweep of the Massif des Maures. This site overlooking the plain was of great strategic importance, a feature emphasised by the **castle** at the summit whose dramatic silhouette is visible from a considerable distance. This castle could have been a Romantic ruin with a marvellous outlook over the whole valley but the authorities have done such a comprehensive job of restoration that it now seems artificial. The masonry has been repointed, in parts replaced, and some sections have been entirely rebuilt into new arrangements that owe little to the original 11C structure.

History of Grimaud

The village takes its name from the Grimaldis who had control of the area in the 10C–12C but there is some doubt as to whether this was the same branch as the family that became the Princes of Monaco. During the 12C it fell under the control of the Templars and thereafter was repeatedly fought over by the various noble families of Provence.

As a Protestant centre in the Wars of Religion the people of Grimaud and the surrounding villages rose up in 1579 and killed the Catholic commander of the area, in reprisals for which they were in turn virtually wiped out. Finally, in 1655 Cardinal Richelieu ordered the dismantling of the castle.

Following the castle's destruction the Seigneur de Castellane built a lavish new house in the rue des Arcades. This street of Gothic arches, also known as the rue des Templiers because it incorporates the blank square tower of the Templars' Commandery, is a reminder of the age when fortified hill-villages could express both strength and elegance in vernacular architecture. The 11C Romanesque **Eglise St-Michel** is another interesting feature of the village. Entered by steps which descend to a dark interior, this church is notable for its plain vaulting and blind arcades of rough masonry, animated by some modern stained-glass windows by the craftsman Jacques Gautier.

Villages of the Massif des Maures

Grimaud stands at the very threshold of the **Massif des Maures**. The road into the range (D558) ascends through wooded hillsides (past the world's only pigeon museum) to **La Garde-Freinet**, an apparently relaxed and informal village which emerges as one of the more chic addresses in an already fashionable area. The actress Jeanne Moreau has a house here as do several writers, politicians and celebrities, which explains the discreet presence of antique shops, estate agents and art galleries.

The village takes its name from Le Fraxinet, a Celto-Ligurian fortress that was the main bastion of the Moors during their control of this area in the 10C. The remains of the fort, alongside the ruins of a 15C castle, both of which were dismantled for building stone, can be seen on the rough ground above the village. There is a small museum in the Hôtel de Ville and a house once belonging to the novelist Jean Aicard is open to the public. The main church, dating from 1789, is fairly substantial although the interior is a disappointment save for the marble altar pillaged from the Chartreuse de la Verne. Of the other ecclesiastical buildings the medieval chapel of St-Eloi at the southern entrance to the village has been decorated with ugly modern murals and is now a craft centre. There are, however, two Romanesque chapels in the hills outside the village to the south. The closer of these, St-Clement (2km), dates from 1152 while the more remarkable **Chapelle de Notre-Dame-de-Miramar** (5km), a pilgrimage chapel at the top of a steep footpath, is reputed to have been built on the site of the original village following the expulsion of the Moors.

To the north of La Garde-Freinet the Massif descends to a sun-baked plain of gnarled cork oaks reminiscent of some parts of Africa, although the area is being greatly altered by the new motorway which crosses it. The villages on the north side of the Massif, such as Les Mayons, have less to recommend them. Architecturally, they are fairly plain and the business-like outlook of the villagers is not particularly encouraging to outsiders.

An alternative is the spectacular road from La Garde-Freinet along the ridge of the massif to the west. This is the route des Crêtes, leading up to Notre-Dame-des-Anges at the summit of **La Sauvette**, the highest point in the range. The road traverses the mountainsides punctuated by occasional rubbish dumps and emergency water tanks used to control the outbreaks of forest fire that are a constant threat in the summer months. Previous outbreaks of fire are everywhere evident and at some points the hillside is burnt back to the blackened earth. Some trees have their branches reduced to brittle twigs, their trunks scorched and blackened by the smoke, but the new growth of leaves still seems to appear miraculously in spring. Notre-Dame-des-Anges itself is a hideous modern building dominated by a radio mast. A rather grubby courtyard leads to the plain church whose walls are covered with commemorative plaques, embroideries, *ex-votos*, discarded crutches and a stuffed lizard. This apart, the view is breathtaking and it is claimed you can see the Alps on a clear day.

The descent to the south leads to a forested river valley and to the village of **Collobrières**, entered by a graceful avenue of chestnut trees. A 12C bridge near the centre of the village leads to the *Confiserie Azuréenne*, the centre of the confectionary industry of Les Maures and noted in particular for the delicious sugared chestnuts known as *marrons glacés*. The 12C Gothic church has an altarpiece by Puget which was removed from the Chartreuse de la Verne during the Revolution and there is an interesting ruined chapel dedicated to St Pons on a hill overlooking the village.

Collobrières is a calm and relatively quiet village, seemingly in a different country from the coastal developments only 15km away. It is also a good base from which to explore the wild countryside in this part of Les Maures, the finest excursion being to the remote **Chartreuse de la Verne** (☎ 04 94 43 45 41; **open** Wed–Mon 11.00–18.00 in summer; 10.00–17.00 in winter; closed Tues and Nov) some 12km to the east on an unreliable road. You might feel a visit is worth any damage to your car because this charterhouse is one of the most beautiful and haunting sites in Provence. The Carthusians were the most austere and regulated of all the medieval monastic orders, each of their foundations being designed and run according to strictly determined rules. The Chartreuse de la Verne is no exception. Set in the remote forests of this region it is possible even now to sense the atmosphere of seclusion which attracted the original founders. It was established in 1170 by a party of monks from the mother house near Grenoble and soon expanded with gifts of land and stock into a substantial complex. This community, however, was repeatedly attacked over the succeeding centuries by Saracens, local barons and most virulently by Protestants in 1577, before the Revolutionaries of 1792 ransacked the buildings and sold off the contents.

After each of the earlier assaults the monastic buildings were reconstructed and this has left a rather confused history of styles. The oldest building is the chapel of 1174 in the heart of the complex but this is surrounded by various kitchens, refectories, parlours, a bakery, oil press, and even a windmill, as well as the monastic quarters from different periods. There is a useful plan available at the entrance.

A unifying feature is the dark greenish blue serpentine stone used throughout for lintels, mouldings and carved dressings. This deep colour in itself imparts a mood of dolorous melancholy to the buildings, seen at its strongest in the lower cloister and garden where the monks' cells enclose the monastic graveyard. Guy de Maupassant visited the Chartreuse in 1875 on an excursion from his yacht the *Bel-Ami* moored at St-Tropez. Struck by the oppressive sadness of the place, he described the cloisters as 'a walkway of desolation'. At that time the buildings were probably still deserted following the attacks during the Revolution but since 1983 a group of nuns from the Sisters of Bethlehem order have sought to restore it as a religious community.

The buildings are still rather dilapidated but this undoubtedly contributes to the atmosphere. You feel a special sensation while wandering round this complex (which is not eroded by the attempts to reconstruct certain interiors with the furniture and clothing of the original monks), especially when you emerge from the lower 13C gate by the windmill to a view of unrelieved pine forest covering the hills on all sides.

Taking the road south from the Chartreuse, after a confusing series of badly signed roads you will join the main N98 going east to Cogolin. This passes through the tiny hamlet of La Môle beyond which, on the left, is an 11C–18C château with traditional pepperpot towers where Antoine de Saint-Exupéry spent his childhood. After this the road returns to the Golfe de St-Tropez via the La Foux intersection at Port Grimaud.

The Riviera and its hinterland

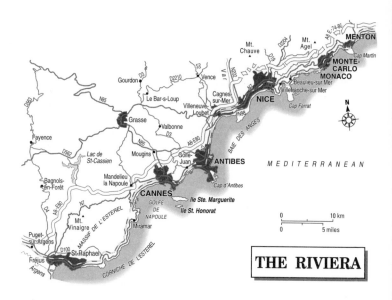

THE RIVIERA

22 · Saint-Raphaël to Cannes

When in 1887 the French journalist Stéphen Liégeard coined the term **Côte d'Azur**, he had in mind the stretch of coastline from Hyères in the west to Menton on the Italian border. At that time there was a greater rivalry between the various resorts, each of which specialised in different types of visitors. While some catered for the sick, others offered gambling or sailing, antiquarian sights or nature study of one form or another; some had high life while others low life. It was not until the 1920s that the culture of the beach and the sun tan took over, at which time the great resorts of Cannes and Nice came to the forefront leaving all their rivals behind. There has even been an attempt to restrict the term Côte d'Azur to just that last group of glamorous resorts. In the mind of most observers, however, the Côte begins at St-Raphaël and this route covers its first 50km as the coast road bends round the Massif de l'Esterel to the broad Golfe de la Napoule leading into Cannes.

Saint-Raphaël and the Massif de l'Esterel

St-Raphaël lacks the glamour of the major resorts further east but it has a long history. Indeed it may have been established as a holiday resort for the Roman imperial officials of neighbouring Fréjus.

History of St-Raphaël

Excavations have uncovered some ancient villas overlooking the coast on the site of the present casino which were probably destroyed during the Saracen raids of the Dark Ages. By the 11C the area had come under the protection of the monks from the Iles de Lérins, who named the settlement St-Raphaël, and they later handed it over to the guardianship of the Knights Templar. To most French people, however, St-Raphaël is best known for the bittersweet role it played in the career of Napoleon. In 1799, the young general landed here on his return from the abortive Egyptian campaign, an event commemorated by a pyramid on the avenue behind the port. It was an inauspicious arrival, made worse when his baggage train was robbed on the outskirts of St-Raphaël. The Emperor passed through the town again 15 years later, bound for Elba and exile.

As a resort, St-Raphaël was largely created by Alphonse Karr, a novelist and retired editor of *Le Figaro* who sang the praises of the town and encouraged many of his friends in the Paris literary world to settle here. Among those who did were Alexandre Dumas, Guy de Maupassant, Hector Berlioz and Charles Gounod, who composed his opera *Romeo and Juliet* at St-Raphaël in 1866. Karr was an enthusiastic gardener who once urged a friend to 'Leave Paris and plant your walking stick in my garden; (next day) when you wake it will already have sprouted roses.' This combination of the climate and the flora made St-Raphaël popular as a winter health resort, especially with the Victorians who flocked here for the sake of their health. They built large villas in and around the town and there is still an Anglican church, all of which tends to confirm St-Raphaël's nickname as the Bournemouth of the Riviera.

❖ *Information, accommodation and food*

🅑 Rue W.-Rousseau (☎ 04 94 95 16 87) near the railway station.

Hotels. Accommodation in St-Raphaël reflects the fact that it is a summer holiday resort: although there are many hotels to choose from, there is not much diversity. The *Pyramides* at 77 avenue P.-Doumer (☎ 04 94 95 05 95) and the *Continental* (☎ 04 94 83 87 87) on the seafront at promenade René-Coty are both reasonable, while the *Hôtel du Soleil* (☎ 04 94 83 10 00) at 49 boulevard du Domaine du Soleil and *La Potinière* (☎ 04 94 95 21 43) in Boulouris to the east are both further out and have gardens.

Restaurants. *L'Orangerie* (☎ 04 94 83 19 50) on promenade René-Coty and *Pastorel* (☎ 04 94 95 02 36) at 54 rue de la Liberté are among the best.

The town still has a reputation for grand villas and exotic gardens but much of this has been swept away in the development of the modern resort. There are some notable buildings, however, when you step back from the seaside promenades. One of the most impressive is the **Eglise de Notre-Dame-de-la-**

Victoire, a huge neo-Byzantine church of pink and white sandstone designed in 1883 by Aublé. The interior is particularly spacious due to the lofty nave and simple rounded arches, an effect made even more striking at the tall crossing and dome. The architect was also responsible for several 19C villas in the area.

By contrast the buildings of the compact old town to the north of the railway line are more discreet. The Romanesque **Eglise St-Pierre** was begun by the monks of Lérins around 1150 but it has some unusual elements. The remains of the Templars' lookout tower is incorporated into the building and there are some 17C frescoes and a curious carved phallus in the choir, possibly dating back to a Dionysiac cult. The painted wooden bust of St Peter is the centrepiece of the annual *fête* held at the beginning of August when it is carried round the town in procession to the accompaniment of trumpets and gunfire. Alongside the church is the **Musée d'Archéologie et de Préhistoire** (☎ 04 94 19 25 75: open 10.00–12.00 and 15.00–18.00, closed Tues, mid June–mid Sept: 10.00–12.00 and 14.00–17.00, closed Sun, rest of year), displaying a surprisingly interesting collection of Roman antiquities and local history material. The area is noted for underwater archaeology and this has provided a number of the exhibits.

In the pine-clad hillsides to the north of St-Raphaël is the upmarket residential quarter of **Valescure**. Popular with wealthy English residents in the late 19C, it still features a number of grand villas from the Belle Epoque amid the recent pastel developments and golf courses. Finest among these is the Villa Magali (private), the home of Gounod's favourite singer Caroline Miolan-Carvalho, who designed the exotic garden to incorporate fragments from great French houses, including the Palais des Tuileries, which were sold off at auction in 1882.

The area between St-Raphaël and La Napoule is the **Massif de l'Esterel**, a great mass of volcanic rock which has cracked and fissured to create a network of ravines and caves. It is a rugged and inhospitable landscape that was largely ignored until the present century. The original Roman road, the Via Aurelia, swung around the northern side of the massif on the route followed by the modern N7, so the coastal villages were only accessible by boat. As a result, the craggy interior became the haunt of mystics, escaped convicts and bandits. The most famous of these was Gaspard de Besse, a colourful character often described as a Provençal Robin Hood, who preyed on the coaches passing by the foot of Mont Vinaigre. Gaspard was eventually caught in 1780, broken on the wheel and decapitated, and his head was nailed to a tree near the scene of his exploits.

Nowadays narrow roads make the interior of the Esterel more accessible but it is worth the extra effort to explore the peaks such as Mont Vinaigre, Pic du Cap Roux or Pic de l'Ours on foot. These hillsides were largely covered with cork oaks and pines until a series of forest fires in the 1980s laid waste to the vegetation leaving the outcrops further devastated by scorching. The porphyry rocks produce a range of colours in the sunlight and the deep gorges and craggy skyline make this a spectacular area of unusual harsh beauty with exceptional views out over the sea.

The event which opened up the Esterel was the creation of the coast road, the *Corniche d'Or*, by the Touring Club in 1903. It was a considerable feat in itself since the steep descent of the massif to the sea leaves little room for building. The road is therefore often squeezed to the very perimeter between rockface and sea as it follows a meandering line around the promontories and inlets.

Despite these constraints, several small resorts have been able to prosper along the Esterel, usually round one of the inlets or near a scrap of beach. **Agay** has at least the advantages of a small bay and deep anchorage which has been used since ancient Greek times. This was where a large American force landed in 1944. Other resorts, such as Anthéor, Le Trayas and Miramar, have less space for development although this has not hindered a rash of hotel building on both sides of the road. The most extreme of the modern resorts along this stretch, however, is **Port-La-Galére**, an entirely new complex of apartments built to a modular system looking like a honeycomb. Designed by the architect Jacques Couëlle, it is the object of much local pride although to many it seems to represent the worst excesses of the 1970s in an area noted for bad taste. Further east, **Théoule** has the unusual combination of a thriving harbour and an 18C soap factory equipped with battlements to look like a castle.

La Napoule-Plage, the seaside suburb of the rather dull town of Mandelieu, is itself a fairly conventional resort with good sandy beaches. It is distinguished, however, by one curious monument, the fanciful château on the sea by the harbour. This was a ruined Saracen tower when in 1918 the wealthy American sculptor Henry Clews acquired it as a home and studio for himself and his architect wife. In essence, he was seeking an appropriate context for a fantasy life that included adopting the title of Grand Knight of La Mancha Supreme Master Humormystic. Having rebuilt much of the castle in a sham medieval and Ottoman style he extended his Hollywood antiquarianism into designing exotic costumes for his wife and servants in preparation for lavish entertainments. The inscription over one of the doors, 'Once upon a time', sums up both his own outlook and a phase in Riviera life when Anglo-American millionaires dominated the social life of the whole coast. Clews died in 1937, having already designed his tomb, and his wife later opened the castle as a museum and foundation for artists, the **Musée Henry Clews** (☎ 04 93 49 22 93: guided tours of 45min Wed–Mon 15.00 and 16.00 Mar–Oct; also 17.00 July, Aug; closed Tues and Nov–Feb). Throughout the house and gardens there are examples of Clews' sculptures, which combine elements from ancient, medieval and Asian art in a style that is at least memorable if nothing else.

From La Napoule the long sweep of the bay stretches some 7km, punctuated by ugly modern hotels, fairgrounds, hoardings and temporary structures. It is a sort of seaside wasteland and an unfortunate approach to Le Suquet and the main resort of Cannes.

Cannes and the Iles des Lérins

Throughout the 20C century Cannes has confirmed its position as the most successful and cosmopolitan of the Riviera resorts. It has some of the most spectacular hotels and is conspicuous in its wealth and extravagance but it has equally been a refuge for artists, musicians and writers. Renoir, Bonnard and Picasso each lived and worked here for long periods, and F. Scott Fitzgerald set part of his classic Riviera novel *Tender is the Night* on the palm-lined promenade known as La Croisette. Stretching out along the bay to the east, La Croisette is still the focus of the town's social life and for two weeks in May it becomes the stage upon which the more public aspects of the film festival are acted out.

History of Cannes

Cannes was, according to Tobias Smollett, 'a little fishing town' until 1834 when Lord Brougham, the Lord Chancellor of England, was halted here due to an outbreak of cholera in Nice. He was enchanted by the place and his decision to build a villa here marked the beginning of Cannes' expansion into a fashionable international resort. Over the next few decades the British began to colonise the town and to build substantial villas in the land round the edge. It was not long before others saw the appeal of this spot. In 1879 the Tsarina Maria Alexandrovina came to Cannes for her health and started a fashion among the Russian aristocracy that spread throughout much of the Riviera and is still recognisable in the Orthodox churches. After 1917 there was a widespread rumour that many of the taxi drivers and hotel porters were Russian aristocrats bankrupted and stranded by the Revolution.

The increasingly international character of Cannes in the late 19C was not without friction. There were many complaints from the local residents, and from other French visitors such as Prosper Mérimée, that Cannes had been taken over by foreigners. But, despite the sense of chauvinistic outrage, there was no doubt that the new residents were good for business. Mérimée had in fact visited the town around the same time as Lord Brougham in his capacity as an inspector of ancient monuments and he later returned to live there, affecting an English style of dress and manners. There are statues to these two men, each in their way founders of the modern town, on the promenade near the harbour.

❖ *Information, accommodation and food*

🆔 Palais des Festivals et des Congrès (☎ 04 93 39 24 53) and at the railway station on rue Jean-Jaurès (☎ 04 93 99 19 77).

Hotels. The seafront hotels, above all the palatial *Carlton* (☎ 04 93 68 91 68) at 58 La Croisette but also the fashionable *Majestic* (☎ 04 92 98 77 00) at 14 La Croisette, are colossally expensive for what they offer.

More reasonable are the *Bleu Rivage* (☎ 04 93 94 24 25) at 61 La Croisette, the *Alnea* (☎ 04 93 39 39 90) at 20 rue Jean-de-Riouffe or the *Hôtel Ruc* (☎ 04 93 38 30 61) at 15 blvd de Strasbourg. Of the cheaper hotels, most are fairly anonymous but *Le Chanteclaire* (☎ 04 93 39 68 88) at 12 rue Forville and the *Cybelle* (☎ 04 93 38 31 33) at 14 rue du 24-Août are both good, while the *Hôtel National* (☎ 04 93 39 91 92) near the station at 8 rue Marechal is a popular budget choice.

Restaurants. La Palme d'Or in the *Hôtel Martinez* (☎ 04 93 94 430 30) at 73 La Croisette and the *Royal Gray* (☎ 04 93 99 79 60) at 6 rue des Etats Unis are the establishments for the highest haute cuisine in Cannes but there are plenty of restaurants to choose from lower down the price scale. *La Croisette* (☎ 04 93 39 86 060) at 15 rue du Commandant-André and *Lou Souléou* (☎ 04 93 39 85 55) at 16 blvd Jean-Hibert both concentrate on seafood while *La Mère-Besson* (☎ 04 93 39 59 24) has Provençal specialties. *Au Bec Fin* in the *Hôtel Cybelle* (see above) and *La Brouette de chez Grand-Mère* (☎ 04 93 39 12 10) at 9 rue d'Oran are noted for their wholesome meals so you must book in advance, while *La Pizza* (☎ 04 93 39 22 56) is a lively trattoria by the old port at 3 Quai St-Pierre.

The old town of Cannes, known as **Le Suquet**, is at the western end of the harbour, stretching up the hill towards the 12C castle and square lookout tower. This was the citadel of the abbots of Lérins and now houses the **Musée de la Castre** (☎ 04 93 38 55 26; open Wed–Mon 10.00–12.00 and 15.00–19.00 July–Sept; 10.00–12.00 and 14.00–18.00 Apr–June; 10.00–12.00 and 14.00–17.00 Oct–Mar; closed Tues and Jan) with its collection of archaeological remains and local history. There is also an unexpected collection of Egyptian and Oriental art left to the town by the Dutch explorer and adventurer Baron Lycklama, who died in Cannes in 1900. Also in this complex is the small Romanesque chapel of Ste-Anne and nearby a more substantial Gothic church, Notre-Dame-d'Espérance, dating from the 16C and 17C. Linking Le Suquet and the modern town is the pedestrianised rue Meynardier, an attractive shopping thoroughfare with more to offer the casual stroller than the more flashy and crass rue d'Antibes.

The modern part of Cannes is not notable for its monuments or for its architecture. Most of the villas and clubs which once lined the seafront of **La Croisette** have been replaced by anonymous apartment blocks or hotels, memorable only for their prices. This is unfortunate because it gives modern Cannes the appearance of any Mediterranean holiday centre and strips it of the associations of the Belle Epoque when it was truly extraordinary. The Cercle Nautique, most exclusive of all Riviera clubs, overlooked the sea from here until it was demolished to make way for the original film festival building (now the *Noga-Hilton Hotel*). The Cercle was where Edward, Prince of Wales always stayed when holidaying in Cannes, much to the annoyance of his mother, and where he was joined by many similar heirs to the crowns of Europe. One dazzling survivor from this period is the **Carlton Hotel**, a white, neo-Baroque palace designed by Marcellin Mayère in 1907. The distinctive tiled domes at each corner are reputed to have been modelled on the breasts of La Belle Otero, one of the leading courtesans of the period. This link with sex and the high life is kept alive in the hotel's excellent restaurant which is named after her.

Redevelopment and expansion has taken its toll on many of the finest 19C villas, notably

The Carlton Hotel

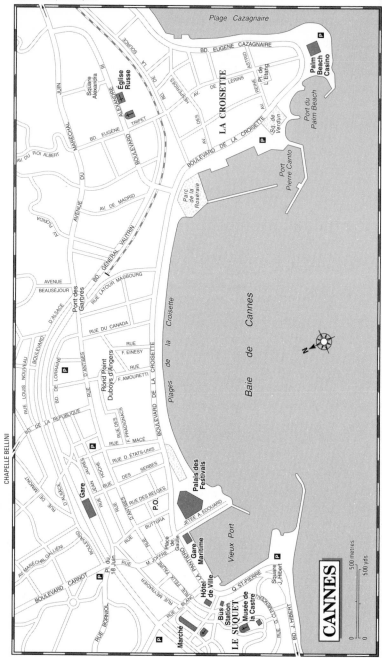

JUAN-LES-PINS, ANTIBES, NICE

CHAPELLE BELLINI

Plage Cazagnaire

BD. EUGÈNE CAZAGNAIRE

LA CROISETTE

Palm Beach Casino

Port du Palm Beach

Port Pierre Canto

Square Alexandra III

Église Russe

Sq. de Verdun

Parc de la Roseraie

Baie de Cannes

AV. DU ROI ALBERT

AV. DE MADRID

Pont des Gabres

AVENUE BEAUSÉJOUR

RUE LATOUR MAUBOURG

RUE DU CANADA

Plages de la Croisette

Rond Point Dubovs d'Angers

RUE F. EINESY

RUE F. AMOURETTI

RUE DES F. PRADIGNACS

RUE F. MACÉ

RUE D. ÉTATS-UNIS

DES SERBES

Palais des Festivals

RUE DES BELGES

P.O.

JETÉE A. EDOUARD

BUTTURA

Place de Gaulle

Gare Maritime

Vieux Port

Gare

Square J. Hibert

Hôtel de Ville

Musée de la Castre

Bus Station

Marché

LE SUQUET

Q. ST-PIERRE

AV. MARÉCHAL GALLIENI

Pl. du 18 Juin

BOULEVARD CARNOT

RUE BORNIOL

CANNES

500 metres

500 yds

The Cannes Film Festival

The annual Festival International du Film was launched in 1939 but because of the Second World War it did not become established properly until 1947. Since then it has grown into a curious combination of trade fair and publicity stunt in which the actual screenings and prize-giving seem to be sideshows to the real business. Its classic period was the 1950s and '60s when the perceived hedonism of the Riviera attracted attention to the festival as a permissive and slightly *risqué* event. American stars such as Marlon Brando flew in to give it an international flavour and starlets were photographed along the seafront wearing less than a bikini, all of which prompted the famous quip that Cannes was the place 'where you can lie on the beach and look at the stars, or vice versa'. In recent years the festival has attracted greater American interest which has, in turn, stimulated financial activity and prompted the rebuilding of the Palais des Festivals et des Congrès, a huge and tasteless building on the promontory beside the harbour. As the focal point for much of the high level festival and civic activities this is something of a centrepiece for Cannes, marking the division between the old and new towns while overlooking the marina with its flotilla of expensive yachts.

Lord Brougham's huge Villa Eleanore behind Le Suquet which was demolished in the late 19C. It is, however, still possible to find survivors from the Belle Epoque in the residential areas beyond the town centre. Lord Woolfield's neo-Gothic pile, the **Villa Victoria**, for example, renamed the Château Vallombrosa when he sold it to a Spanish nobleman, has survived as flats at 15 avenue du Dr-Picaud. This was one of the most glamorous of all the residences, setting the tone for the luxurious lifestyle of the British in Cannes. Woolfield started the fashion for croquet and had the turf for his lawn shipped out from southern England. The public library nearby was originally the Villa Rothschild, built in 1880.

The area of **Super Cannes** to the west of the town also retains some of the impressive villas built by the super-rich of the late 19C and early 20C although they are now usually subdivided and their once-spectacular gardens parcelled off into minor developments. Amongst these are Lochabair (rue Cdt-Bret, now a school), the Villa Fiorentina (4 avenue de Poralto) with its Italianate painted chapel in the park, and the huge Villa or Château de Fayère (14 boulevard de Saissy).

South of Super Cannes is the equally opulent district of **La Californie** and the Pointe de la Croisette, the main focus of the Russian community at the turn of the century. The clearest reminder of this is the blue onion dome of the Orthodox church on the boulevard Alexandre III[e]. In contrast, the avenue du Roi-Albert to the north had mostly English residents who have been survived by a Gothic-Revival Anglican church and a series of half-timbered villas. Nowadays it is the **Palm Beach Casino**, a white building on the tip of the Pointe, which attracts most attention. It has dancing, a swimming pool and a cabaret but is nothing like its heyday in the 1930s when stars like Marlene Dietrich were regular guests and occasional performers.

The most famous resident of this area was Pablo Picasso, who bought the 19C villa named **La Californie** in 1955. Over the next six years he produced some of the finest works of his later career, often depicting his studio and garden here in the grand mythological themes that he felt were still alive in the Riviera. It takes quite a leap of the imagination to detect that spirit nowadays but forays outside Cannes do reveal places in which the history of the area is still a powerful influence.

One of the most interesting excursions from Cannes, and certainly a serene alternative to the brash street culture of the city, can be made to the **Iles de Lérins**, two wooded islands just 2km or 15min by boat from the old harbour by the Palais des Festivals. The nearer and larger of the two is the Ile Ste-Marguerite, overlooked by the impressive **Fort Royal** built in the 17C by Cardinal Richelieu and his military architect Vauban.

On the ground floor the **Musée de la Mer** (☎ 04 93 38 55 26: open Wed–Mon 10.30–12.00 and 14.00–18.30 in summer; earlier closing in winter; closed Tues) has antiquities and everyday items from the various ships which have been wrecked here since pre-Roman times. In recent years the island has seen some tourist and housing development, a pattern begun in the 19C when Napoleon III installed his English mistress here. Fortunately, this has not eroded the pine woods and plants and shrubs which cover most of the island. There are guided tours for those who wish a more detailed introduction to the flora.

The Man in the Iron Mask

Although it served an important military purpose, the Fort Royal is better known as a prison. Huguenots and prisoners of war were incarcerated here but its most famous inmate was the 'Man in the Iron Mask', described in numerous tales and films. Voltaire was one of the first to claim that this intriguing figure, who was moved from prison to prison in secrecy, always kept in isolation, hooded and accompanied by his own attendant, was actually the elder brother of Louis XIV. Another element in the story was the report of his gaoler who claimed that his orders were to keep the prisoner safe and well but, in the last resort, to kill him immediately if the secret was threatened. The unfortunate man, thought to have gone by the name of Dauget, eventually died in the Bastille in Paris in 1703, whereupon his remains were removed in a sealed coffin and all trace of his existence obliterated. His prison cell is open to the public as are other parts of the castle complex.

The other main island in the group is the **Ile St-Honorat**, only a mile across at its widest point but the site of one of the most important monastic foundations in the Mediterranean.

History of the monastery

The original monastery, founded by St Honoratus in the 4C, had a considerable reputation as a pilgrimage centre and mother house to a network of priories throughout France and Italy. In 732, however, the community was overwhelmed and massacred by Saracens, the first of a series of incursions which threatened the monastic tradition on the island. To counter this, the fortified monastery was built on the south shore in the 11C.

The later history of the monastery was similarly turbulent and by 1786 there were only four monks where once there had been almost 4000. Abandoned and deconsecrated, the island was bought in the 19C by an actress from the Comédie Française who had a high old time in the monastic remains. Then in 1859 a community of Cistercians from Sénanque took over the island and they have flourished here ever since.

The **Monastère Fortifié** (☎ 04 93 48 68 68: **open** daily, except Sun am, 10.00–12.00 and 14.15–16.30) is now the most impressive of the surviving buildings, a tall crenellated structure like a castle keep enclosing a series of galleries and Gothic cloisters. At one time the only access was by a gate 3.5m above the ground with a retractable ladder for security. It is still a formidable bastion and from the battlements the outlook that originally protected the community now offers beautiful views out to sea or back over the Golfe-Juan to the snow-capped peaks of the Alps.

The Cistercian monks now occupy some of the old monastic buildings in the centre of the island, parts of which, although clothed in modern additions, are open to the public. There are also seven minor chapels dotted about the island, the most interesting of which is the **Chapelle de la Trinité** at the eastern end, a much-restored building dating from the 5C. There is a legend that the violinist Niccolò Paganini was buried in secret on the tiny islet of St-Ferréol just off the east coast here, but this is disputed.

The direct route from Cannes to Antibes (N7) follows the coast after the Pointe de la Croisette but it is not a particularly interesting stretch of road. Instead it may be worth following the D803 beyond Super Cannes and La Californie to Vallauris (see p 266).

23 · The Cannes hinterland

Like most cities of the south, or indeed anywhere, the outskirts of Cannes have little to offer but the unsightly evidence of urban sprawl. Several excursions can be made beyond the suburbs, however, to the outlying towns and villages of the hinterland, many of which are beautiful and historic yet within 20 or 30km of the coast.

These routes can all be undertaken by car or public transport, although the latter does restrict flexibility in your itinerary. One note of caution: this area is highly developed and the woods and hillsides of even apparently rural districts conceal private houses. One of the effects of this is to increase the amount of local traffic on the roads. The area is prone to traffic jams, especially at rush hours, which can mar any day out, especially if the weather is hot. It should not be a deterrent, however, because some of the destinations in this route are unmissable if you want to experience the true character of the Riviera, both as history and as a society that lives to create and dispose of wealth.

The quickest way out to the hills above Cannes is by the boulevard Carnot, a broad highway that drives a straight line due north from the place du 18^e juin. Near the top is **Le Cannet**, once a separate and fairly exclusive village but now an overcrowded suburb. In 1926 the painter Pierre Bonnard bought the Villa du Bosquet near here but it wasn't until the onset of war in 1939 that he took up residence. From then until his death in 1947 he worked constantly in the house and garden, producing a series of sun-drenched landscapes and shimmering female nudes, usually of his wife Marthe as a young woman.

Mougins

The real money has now moved further out to the village of Mougins, a genuine *village perché* but one that is expensively maintained and well-supported by a country club, golf courses and a string of outstanding restaurants.

❖ *Information, accommodation and food*

🚩 Avenue Charles-Mallet (☎ 04 93 75 87 67).

Hotels. Accommodation in Mougins, like the village itself, tends towards the exclusive and expensive. *Le Moulin de Mougins* (☎ 04 93 75 78 24) at 424 chemin de Moulinn at Notre-Dame-de-Vie, and *Les Muscadins* (☎ 04 93 90 00 43) at 128 blvd Courteline are both excellent but very pricey. For something more modest, still beyond many travellers, there is *Les Liserons de Mougins* (☎ 04 93 75 50 31) at 608 ave St-Martin.

Restaurants. Of the restaurants here, the most famous is the *Moulin de Mougins* (☎ 04 93 75 78 24), established by chef Roger Vergé in 1969 and now one of the greatest restaurants in the world. Getting to eat here is not easy. It will cost a small fortune and you must book several months in advance but you will be guaranteed something truly outstanding. In the 1970s Vergé opened another restaurant, *L'Amandier de Mougins* (☎ 04 93 90 00 91), with slightly lower prices although they are still high by normal standards.

Elsewhere in this gastronomic paradise, *Les Muscadins* (☎ 04 93 90 00 43) is highly regarded as are the *Bistrot de Mougins* (☎ 04 93 75 78 34) and the *Relais à Mougins* (☎ 04 93 90 03 47), each probably better than restaurants in much larger towns.

At one time Mougins was more important than Cannes and the surviving ramparts and 15C Porte Sarrasin testify to its power in the Middle Ages. Inside the walls there is a Romanesque church, much extended in the 19C, and a series of expensive shops and restaurants in the ancient houses along the winding streets. There are also two museums, the **Musée Municipal** (☎ 04 92 50 42: **open** Mon–Fri 09.00–12.00 and 14.00–18.00) devoted to local history and the more recent **Musée de la Photographie** (☎ 04 93 75 85 67: **open** Wed–Sun 14.00–23.00 July–Aug; 13.00–19.00 Sept–June; closed Mon, Tues) which has an impressive collection of classic 20C images.

Mougins has been very popular with artists throughout the present century, many of whom stayed at the *Hôtel Vaste Horizon*. The list includes such figures as Isadora Duncan, Léger, Cocteau and the Surrealists Man Ray, Francis Picabia (1879–1953) and Paul Eluard. The most famous in this company is Picasso who, in 1961, bought a farmhouse by the ancient hermitage and chapel of Notre-Dame-de-Vie just 2km east of the village. This was the artist's favourite residence during his last years and where, with the help of the Crommelynck brothers, master printers in Mougins, he produced a huge amount of new work. Picasso died at Notre-Dame-de-Vie in 1973 and is buried at Vauvenargues near Aix (see p 189).

Just south of Mougins, in a huge hangar-like building off the D3 by the motorway, is the **Musée de l'Automobiliste** (☎ 04 93 69 27 80: **open** daily 10.00–18.00), an automobile museum founded by ESCOTA, the company which runs the French motorway system. The collection includes many historic cars such as Bugattis and Hispano-Suizas as well as a range of modern racing machines but, having little interpretation, it speaks only to the enthusiast.

Grasse

Travelling north from Mougins, the N85 passes through Mouans-Sartoux, with its restored 16C castle, before climbing through terraces of exotic plants and flowers towards Grasse, the 'perfume capital of the world'.

History of Grasse

According to one legend, Grasse was founded in the 1C AD by a community of Jews expelled from Rome and Sardinia by the Emperor Tiberius. Having fought the indigenous people to establish their community they adopted Christianity and received the 'grace' which gave the name to their town. In the Middle Ages Grasse was an independent city state with powerful allies in Genoa who helped to control much of the sea trade along the Esterel and Italian coasts. Then in 1227 an alliance with Raymond Bérenger brought the town back into the political orbit of Provence.

Thereafter, Grasse prospered as a tannery for leather hides and the centre of the glove-making trade, and this was the curious origin of the perfume industry. In the 16C Catherine de Médicis introduced a fashion for scented gloves which the local craftsmen took up, using a distilling process derived from Florence. By the 19C most of the surrounding countryside was turned over to the cultivation of exotic plants and the great perfumeries were the principal employer in the area.

Napoleon passed by Grasse in 1815 on his return from Elba but it was not an auspicious visit. Fearful of a hostile reception he camped at the edge of the town and quickly sped on to Digne (see pp 170 and 210). A few years earlier, however, his sister Pauline Bonaparte had spent the winter here and helped to create its reputation as a winter resort. The terraced garden where she liked to sit is named after her. Later in the 19C Queen Victoria spent three winters here, usually staying in the *Grand Hôtel*, and Grasse soon caught on among the English. H.G. Wells was a regular, as was the Belgian poet Maurice Maeterlinck and the American painter Mary Cassatt (1844–1926).

❖ *Information, accommodation and food*

🛈 Cours Honoré-Cresp (☎ 04 93 36 66 66).

Hotels. The *Hôtel des Parfums* (☎ 04 93 36 10 10) on boulevard Eugène-Charabot and the *Panorama* (☎ 04 93 36 80 80) on the place du Cours are probably the best hotels although lacking in character.
　More interesting and less expensive is the *Hôtel du Patti* (☎ 04 93 36 01 00) on place du Patti, while *Le Printania* (☎ 04 93 36 95 00) on rue des Roses and the *Pension Michele* (☎ 04 93 36 06 37) at 6 rue du-Palais-de-Justice are the best at the budget end.

Restaurants. In contrast to Mougins, Grasse is lacking in top restaurants but *Maître Boscq* at 13 rue de la Fontette (☎ 04 93 36 45 76) is extremely good and specialises in local dishes such as 'Lou Fassam', a sort of stuffed cabbage, while the baker *Maison Venturini* at rue Marcel-Journet is noted for *fougasses* flavoured with orange blossom.

Grasse has a lot to offer the passing visitor or those who wish to stay for longer. There are wonderful views down to the bay of Cannes, a colourful daily market on the arcaded place aux Airès and, despite some rather slick modern development, a surprisingly well-preserved old quarter of narrow lanes and tall medieval houses. The 12C **Cathédrale de Notre-Dame-de-Puy** is an impressive if plain building but it has some remarkable treasures. There are three important pictures by Rubens, painted in 1601 when the artist was in Rome, a triptych by Louis Bréa and a rare religious work by Jean-Honoré Fragonard, *Christ Washing the Feet of His Disciples*.

Fragonard was born at 23 rue Tracastel in 1732 but he spent most of his career in Paris where he became the greatest Rococo artist of the later 18C. With the onset of the Terror he returned to Grasse in 1790 where he sought the protection of Evariste Maubert, a wealthy glove-maker and perfumier. Maubert's elegant villa and garden, just a few minutes' walk to the south, is now the **Musée Fragonard** (☎ 04 93 40 32 64: open daily 10.0019.00 June–Sept; 10.00–12.00 and 14.00–17.00 Oct–May; closed Mon, Tues in winter and all Nov) containing a modest selection of pictures by the artist and his painter son. Unfortunately the greatest of his paintings, the five canvases depicting *The Pursuit of Love* which were installed here after Madame du Barry had refused them, are now in the Frick Collection, New York. Copies are on display in the villa to give something of their luscious, exuberant flavour.

There are three other museums close by, each housed in an 18C mansion. The **Musée de la Marine** (☎ 04 93 09 10 71: open same times as the Musée Fragonard) in the Hôtel de Pontèves consists mostly of ship models and memorabilia relating to the career of Admiral de Grasse, a hero of the American War of Independence. Almost next door is the **Musée International de la Parfumerie** (☎ 04 93 36 80 20; same times as the Musée Fragonard), an introduction to the history and techniques of perfume-manufacturing from the ancient world to the present day. There is also a large display of perfume bottles and flasks. Finally, the **Musée d'Art et d'Histoire de Provence** (☎ 04 93 36 01 61; same times as Musée Fragonard) in the Hôtel de Cabris or Petit Trianon on rue Mirabeau has good collections of furniture and ceramics, as well as paintings by artists such as Granet, Maurice Denis (1870–1943) and Berthe Morisot (1841–95) who worked in the area. To the rear of the museum a series of gardens leads down to the cours Honoré-Cresp and have excellent views out to the sea.

The manufacture of perfume still relies on flowers, particularly wild mimosa, jasmine and roses, but to these are added an exotic cocktail of ingredients including musk, civet secretions, ancient oils and, where necessary, a touch of whale vomit. The techniques are explained on the informative tours of any of the principal **perfume factories** (*Fragonard, Molinard* and *Galimard*), which are usually free. Nowadays the factories rarely produce the finished article but send the essence to the fashion houses of Paris for blending and packaging. The tourist office has information on many of the parfumerie tours.

Grasse sits at the centre of a network of small villages in the slopes leading up to the Plateau de Calern, the 'balcony of Grasse'. Among the most notable is **Cabris** in the west, with its ruined castle offering spectacular views out to the sea. The *Hôtel l'Horizon* became very fashionable with writers and intellectuals in the 1950s attracting Gide, Camus and Jean-Paul Sartre to its gardens. To the south of Grasse are Pegomas and Auribeau, and to the east Opio, all with interesting medieval remains amid lush countryside that is gradually being encroached upon by housing. **Valbonne**, also to the east of Grasse, has some attractive old streets but the most interesting feature is the remains of a major monastery founded in 1199. The Chalaisian order, a branch of the Cistercians, preferred an austere, contemplative life which is perfectly expressed in these plain Romanesque buildings. The area of Valbonne was chosen some 25 years ago to be a centre of new industries and technology. What has emerged in this silicon valley of the Côte d'Azur is a new town and science park named **Sophia Antipolis**.

Wilder and more spectacular landscape lies on the D2085 to the northeast of Grasse leading up to the **Gorges du Loup**. The gorge itself is one of the most striking natural features in Provence, a torrent plunging down narrow clefts in the limestone rock which can be viewed from various points on the road on either side. Towering some 450m above it on a rock pinnacle is the picturesque village of **Gourdon**. The site was fortified by the Romans and then again by Raymond Bérenger in the 13C to form a virtually impregnable bastion. So strong was it, in fact, that a tiny force was able to resist the army of Charles V. Much of the château was dismantled by later occupying forces but it has been reconstructed in the present century by an American woman, Miss Norris, and now houses a local history museum, with some minor paintings and furniture, and a museum of highly questionable naïve art (☎ 04 93 09 68 02: guided tours Wed–Mon 11.00–13.00 and 14.00–19.00 June–Sept; 14.00–18.00 winter; closed Tues).

The most interesting picture in this area is a curious 15C *Danse Macabre* in the Gothic church of St-Jacques in **Le Bar-sur-Loup** at the foot of the gorge. The artist has depicted five courtly couples dancing the traditional Provençal *tambourin* while the skeletal figure of Death picks them off with a bow and arrow. An inscription in Provençal reminds the spectator of the shortage of time for those who enter the dance and of the terrible vengeance of God.

Further east along the D2210 is **Tourrettes-sur-Loup**, whose old stone houses can be seen crammed onto a steep rocky escarpment over the river valley. The medieval quarter, a network of sinuous passages winding down the slope behind the main square, has been colonised by craft shops but it is not yet overdeveloped. Amid this maze of old lanes is the rather blank castle complex which originates from the 13C although it was largely rebuilt in the 18C. The main route into the old quarter is through the belfry gate, an interesting building in its own right. During the 1950s the composer François Poulenc lived in the small house beneath it where he composed his most profound religious work, *Les Dialogues des Carmelites*. The countryside round Tourrettes is noted for the cultivation of violets and there is a colourful *fête* and procession in March to celebrate the harvest. It is sometimes claimed that this ritual stretches back to ancient times and, it is true, there is a pagan shrine in the Romanesque church of St-Grégoire on the main square. The *fête*, however, like so many in Provence, is actually a quite recent innovation.

Vence, Saint-Paul-de-Vence and Cagnes-sur-Mer

Vence, beyond Tourettes on the same road, is an ancient town with Ligurian and Roman origins but it has expanded rather haphazardly in modern times to fill a large area at the head of a valley noted for fruit- and flower-cultivation. Fortunately its beautiful old centre, enclosed by an impressive medieval wall, remains virtually intact if rather over-restored. It is also a good base from which to explore the hill-villages in the vicinity as well as the coast only 9km to the south.

History of Vence

Throughout the 20C Vence has been a popular winter resort, particularly with artists and writers. D.H. Lawrence died here in 1930 and the Russian painter Marc Chagall spent the last 15 years of his life in Vence until his death in 1985. Both are buried nearby: Lawrence in Vence and Chagall in St-Paul-de-Vence. One of the dangers of accommodating major artists in the 20C is that their work becomes associated with a place and soon the army of artists and craftspeople moves in to perpetuate the idea of a colony. It has happened in many of the villages along this part of Provence and nowhere more so than in Vence. Galleries have sprung up and there are numerous stalls and exhibitions in the street presenting all types of art. The work is generally meretricious and in many respects this process has contributed to the stagnation in French art over the last few decades. Despite this obsession with art tourism and the trivia that surrounds it, however, Vence has many attractions.

❖ *Information, accommodation and food*

🛈 Place du Grand-Jardin (☎ 04 93 58 06 38).

Hotels. The tourist office can book rooms in the private houses of the area. *La Roseraie* at 14 avenue H.-Giraud (☎ 04 93 58 02 20) is one of the best and most reasonably priced hotels while *La Closerie des Genêts* (☎ 04 93 58 33 25) at 4 impasse Maurel and the *Auberge des Seigneurs* (☎ 04 93 58 04 24) at place du Frêne, both by the old town and with good restaurants, are also highly recommended.

Restaurants. The *Château du Domaine St-Martin* (☎ 04 93 58 02 02) at route de Coursegoules is the finest restaurant and this is reflected in its prices. *La Farigoule* at 15 avenue Henri-Isnard (☎ 04 93 58 01 27) is best for local dishes and a good atmosphere.

The best place to start a tour of the town is the place du Frêne, a busy thoroughfare which takes its name from the huge ash tree in the centre. This spot is overlooked by the outer walls of the 15C–17C castle but the nearby gate leads into the beautiful place du Peyra. This was the site of the old Roman forum and there are several antique fragments in the masonry of the surrounding buildings. Overlooking this is the tall square tower and castle of the Villeneuve family, lords of Vence since the 13C. There is a museum in the castle, the **Fondation Emile Hughes** (☎ 04 93 58 15 78: **open** Tues–Sun 10.00–19.00 July–Sept; 10.00–12.00 and 14.00–18.00 Oct–June; closed Mon), with examples of the work of artists associated with the area such as Dufy and Chagall.

At the heart of the old town is the former **cathedral**, built in the 11C but extensively altered in the Baroque period. This was partly due to Bishop Godeau (1605–72), a famous wit and friend of Cardinal Richelieu, who took up the bishopric as an escape from the court. Inside, there are some choir stalls (1455) with lively carving by Jacques Bellot and, in the baptistery, a mosaic of *Moses in the Bullrushes* by Chagall.

By far the greatest monument to modern art in Vence, however, is the **Chapelle du**

Place du Peyra

Rosaire (☎ 04 93 58 03 26: **open** Tues, Thurs 10.00–11.30 and 14.30–17.30; closed Nov–mid Dec) to the northwest of the town centre. Designed and decorated by Henri Matisse between 1949 and 1951 as a gift to the Dominican nuns who had nursed him through a serious illness, this is one of the most profound religious monuments of the 20C. Perhaps the chapel's most remarkable feature is its economy of means. Employing simple linear decoration animated by the strong clear colours of stained-glass windows, Matisse succeeded in creating an atmosphere of tranquillity and peace that survives even the packed tourist groups who pass through it. A small exhibition of drawings in the ante-room is particularly revealing of the artist's working methods for this project.

Three kilometres south of Vence is **St-Paul-de-Vence**, one of the most remarkable villages in the south of France. Perched on a spur of rock, this medieval village occupied an important strategic position overlooking the border between France and Savoy. So important was it that in 1537 François I had many of the houses pulled down to supply masonry for the impressive outer ramparts. These fortifications still survive, largely intact, as does much of the old village. It has, however, been excessively cleaned and prettified which gives the place a rather artificial air.

It is ironic, therefore, that in an age that thrives on the fake, much of St-Paul is genuinely old. The Gothic **Eglise de la Conversion de St-Paul** dates from the 13C–14C and contains a number of ecclesiastical treasures including a magnificent Baroque chapel and an altarpiece attributed to Tintoretto. There are also numerous attractive buildings and doorways in the rue Grande which testify to the wealth and importance of the community in the 16C and 17C. Traffic is restricted in the old part so you can walk freely round the arcaded streets, most colonised by a rash of craft shops, or visit the **Musée d'Histoire de St-Paul** (☎ 04 93 32 53 09: **open** daily 10.00–18.00 mid June–mid Sept; 10.30-17.00 mid Sept–mid June; closed mid Nov–mid Dec), in which the folklore and history of the region are recounted in a series of tableaux.

After the First World War, St-Paul became the centre of an artists' colony frequented by many of the leading figures of the School of Paris. Picasso, Braque, Léger, Rouault, Derain, Chagall and many more converged on the village, partly due to the presence of a sympathetic hotelier. This was the formidable Paul Roux whose hotel and restaurant, the **Colombe d'Or**, would offer board and lodgings in exchange for works of art. Roux built up one of the finest private art collections of the 20C, examples of which are still displayed around the simple interior of his restaurant. By 1954, when Roux himself died, the *Colombe d'Or*'s reputation as a centre of bohemianism was still intact although by this time only celebrities could afford the prices. Nowadays, if you wish to see the collection you must book a table and expect to pay a hefty bill.

Alternatively, you can visit the **Fondation Maeght** (☎ 04 93 32 81 61: **open** daily 10.00–19.00 July–Sept; 10.00–12.30 and 14.30–18.00 Oct–June), an excellent modern art museum in the pinewoods to the northwest of the village. Built in the 1960s by the art dealers and publishers Marguerite and Aimé Maeght, this is a monument to the great figures of the French art world of the 20C. Within the galleries there is an outstanding collection of paintings, sculpture and decorative arts by such figures as Picasso, Matisse, Léger, Derain, Bonnard and Chagall. A particular feature is the terraced sculpture gardens where works by Giacometti and Alexander Calder (1898–1976) are arranged against both the woodland landscape and the series of emphatic buildings designed by the Catalan architect J.L. Sert. More recent artists such as de Staël and the modern School of Nice are also represented but perhaps the most engaging pieces on display are works such as the fountain by Miró which was specifically executed for this setting. The galleries are regularly reorganised to rotate the collection and there is a programme of major retrospective exhibitions devoted to the work of individual artists.

South of St-Paul is the sprawling town of **Cagnes-sur-Mer** which has been subdivided into three distinct sections: Haut-de-Cagnes, the old settlement on a steep hilltop, Cagnes-Ville, a dull commercial area, and Cros-de-Cagnes, a brash seaside development. Needless to say, **Haut-de-Cagnes** is the most attractive. This medieval hill-village has a lovely situation approached by steep paths climbing up to the castle at the summit. Built by the Grimaldis of Monaco when they became lords of this area in 1309, the **Château Grimaldi** (☎ 04 93 20 85 57: **open** Wed–Mon July–Sept 10.00–12.00 and 14.30–18.00; shorter hours Oct–June; closed Tues and mid Oct–mid Nov) formed an impressive bastion that withstood numerous onslaughts and sieges. In the early 17C Henri Grimaldi undertook extensive renovations to convert the fortress into a more elegant residence. As well as altering the buildings to create the triangular inner courtyard, he invited two Genoese artists, J.B. Carlone and Giulio Benso, to decorate the interior. They undertook the elaborate illusionistic fresco of the *Fall of Phaeton* which dominates the main hall. The other rooms of the castle are given over to an unusual combination of museum displays. One is devoted to olive culture, one to a mediocre collection of modern Mediterranean art and a third, housed in the boudoir of the Marquise, to the curious art collection of the singer and artist's model, Suzy Solidor. There are over 40 paintings in this collection by such artists as Kisling, Cocteau, Dufy, and van Dongen, all of them portraits of Solidor.

Like Vence and St-Paul, Cagnes was something of an artists' colony in the 1930s. The English writer Cyril Connolly was here then and, as Trou-sur-Mer, Cagnes appeared as the setting for his only novel *The Rock Pool*. It is difficult now to understand why this account of bohemian life should have caused such offence, but in 1936 it was refused publication in Britain on the grounds of obscenity.

The reputation of Cagnes among painters was due to two major figures of the Impressionist group who worked here during the latter part of their careers. Pierre-Auguste Renoir came to Cagnes in 1903, partly to find relief from his progressively crippling arthritis, and then in 1907 he bought the old olive grove known as Les Collettes to the east of the old village. Here he built a house and studio where he lived until his death in 1919. Of all artist's houses in the south of France, the **Musée Renoir** (☎ 04 3 20 61 07: **open** Wed–Mon 10.00–12.00 and 14.00–18.00 May–mid Oct; 10.00–12.00 and 14.00–17.00 mid Nov–Apr; closed Tues and mid Oct–mid Nov) has retained most of the atmosphere of its owner, partly because the paintings are fairly ordinary and seem to be more appropriate for his house rather than a gallery. The effect of domesticity is further emphasised by a number of everyday items such as the painter's coat, cane and wheelchair which are left on display much as they were when Renoir was alive. It is not difficult to imagine the aged painter working in these rooms as he struggled to overcome the restrictions of his arthritic hands. There is also a strong sense of the whole Renoir family who are pictured in photographs as well as paintings. Both the artist's sons had considerable reputations in their own right, Jean as a film director and Pierre as an actor. But perhaps the best part of this museum is the garden, still containing many of the original olive trees and studded with a few of Renoir's sculptures. It is a quiet spot in an otherwise busy town.

In the 1880s another Impressionist painter, Claude Monet (1840–1926), worked briefly by the old fishing-village of Cagnes-sur-Mer. He would not recognise it now. This stretch of coastline has seen the full impact of modern seaside development where hotels, apartment blocks, supermarkets, hoardings and an urban motorway have sprawled without any apparent control. The pattern continues on the eastern side of the river Var, past the airport and along the full length of the once-beautiful Baie des Anges to the outskirts of Nice itself.

24 · To Nice via Vallauris and Antibes

The short stretch of coast between Cannes and Nice has not escaped the intensive seaside developments which have overtaken the whole Riviera. Quite the reverse, in fact. Most of the towns on this route are highly developed as resorts for the tourist trade and the roads between them can be very busy in summer. Nevertheless, the area is not short of history and indeed was one of the great centres of French art in the 20C: the small towns of Biot, Cagnes-sur-Mer (see p 265) and Antibes each have excellent museums recording their close associations with major artists. This route begins on the outskirts of Cannes at Vallauris, a centre that personifies this curious blend of the ancient and the modern.

East of Cannes and the Cap d'Antibes

The bustling town of **Vallauris** has a colourful history but it was in serious decline when Pablo Picasso came here in 1948 to discover the traditional craft of hand-ceramics.

History of Vallauris

Ceramics have been at the heart of the town's history since ancient times and there is evidence to suggest that the Romans had potteries here to exploit the clay reserves. During the Middle Ages Vallauris was under the control of the abbots of Lérins who built it up into a substantial market centre but in 1364 the marauding troops of Raymond de Turenne razed it to the ground and drove off the population. It remained a virtual desert until the early 16C when, in a campaign to stabilise the area and re-establish the pottery industry, a number of Genoese families were encouraged to settle there. This original group of some 400 Italians was responsible for the traditional grid plan of the town and for the Renaissance-style castle completed in 1568.

Picasso first visited Vallauris in 1936 but it was not until after the Second World War, when he had settled in Cannes, that he returned to take up an entirely new interest in painted ceramics. In 1949 he met the potters Georges and Suzanne Ramié of the Atelier Madoura and it was their work which proved to be an inspiration, prompting a collaboration between painter and craftsworkers. They produced vessels to Picasso's specification and he began to decorate them with an astonishing range of subjects and designs. Typically, this released an immense burst of creative activity in the 68-year-old-painter. Such was his enthusiasm that he took a studio on the rue de Fournas where in one year alone he produced over 2000 pieces.

This phase in Picasso's work was so successful that he has been credited with single-handedly reviving the hand-ceramic industry in Vallauris. That is probably an overstatement but there is no doubt over his influence. Now the town centre is packed with shops and studios selling what are generally fairly inferior, not to say vulgar, products in the wake of Picasso.

For a good indication of the inspiration behind it all, there is an excellent display of Picasso's ceramics in the **Musée Municipal** (☎ 04 93 64 16 05: **open** Wed–Mon 10.00–12.00 and 14.00–18.30; closed Tues) now housed in the 16C castle. In the simple Romanesque chapel at the heart of the fort there is a large painting of *Peace and War*, executed by Picasso on plywood screwed to the wall, and an enlarged photograph of the artist where the altarpiece should be. Other parts of the museum display a range of international ceramics, including prizewinning pieces from the biennial competitions held in Vallauris, and a collection of paintings, prints and collages by the Italian abstract artist Alberto Magnelli (1888–1971). A further mark of Picasso's presence in Vallauris is the bronze statue of a *Man with a Sheep* in the main square, beside the 19C church of St-Martin. As a gesture of gratitude, in 1950 Picasso presented this work to the town which had inspired his ceramics and ushered in a new phase to his work. For more information on the various potteries active here you might visit the commercial **Musée de la Poterie** (☎ 04 93 64 66 51: **open** daily 09.00–18.00 in summer; shorter hours in winter) on rue Sicard. There are, however, several workshops open to the public in the hope that you will buy some of their wares.

From Vallauris the D135 leads back down to the coast at **Golfe-Juan** where in 1815 Napoleon disembarked from the frigate *L'Inconstant* after his escape from Elba. This was the beginning of the '100 days' which ended on the battle-field of Waterloo. There is a commemorative column and a plaque marking the start of the *Route Napoléo*n which retraces the returning emperor's journey from the coast to his glorious re-entry to Paris (see p 210).

Antibes

With a population of over 63,000, Antibes is one of the largest towns on the Côte d'Azur, yet it still has a reputation as a rather stylish resort with a harbour well stocked in luxury yachts.

History of Antibes

The original settlement, known as Antipolis (City Opposite) due to its position facing Nice across the Baie des Anges, was established by the Greeks in the 4C BC as an outpost for trade with the Ligurians. In the Middle Ages it was controlled by the Grimaldi family who built the castle by the harbour in the 12C, and was successively besieged and bartered by warring factions until eventually sold to the French king Henry IV in 1608. From then on Antibes prospered and for protection it was provided by Vauban with the impressive Fort Carré, just to the north of the harbour, and with the sea wall which still skirts the front.

Over the years it attracted a number of celebrated residents including Napoleon, Guy de Maupassant, Picasso and the English novelist Graham Greene, who lived here until his death in 1992. In the late 19C it seems to have been popular with artists. Monet worked here, producing a number of vivid paintings of the bay from the west side of the town. On arrival in January 1888 he had his doubts, writing home to Giverny, 'I definitely see that this area is not for me.' Although he found much to attract his brush, he never felt entirely comfortable on the Riviera. In another letter he writes 'It is so beautiful here, so clear and luminous! You are bathed in blue air; it's frightening.' The people who made Antibes famous and glamorous, however, were the wealthy American expatriates of the 1920s, who included Gerald and Sara Murphy and Scott and Zelda Fitzgerald.

❖ *Information, accommodation and food*

🖪 11 place Général-de-Gaulle (☎ 04 92 90 53 00), at the edge of the old town south of the railway station.

Hotels. Accommodation in Antibes is fairly expensive but the *Mas Djoliba* at 29 avenue de Provence (☎ 04 93 34 02 48) is a good hotel in its own grounds not far from the beach.
    Among the less expensive hotels are the small *L'Auberge Provençal* at 61 place Nationale (☎ 04 93 34 13 24) and the *Belle Epoque* in the centre at 10 avenue du 24ᵉ août (☎ 04 93 34 53 00).

Restaurants. Eating out in the town can be reasonable, especially along the rue James-Close, but *Le Clafoutis* at 18 rue Thuret (☎ 04 93 34 66 70), *La Tour chez Laurent* at 6 cours Masséna (☎ 04 93 34 07 70) and *L'Oursin* at 16 rue de la République (☎ 04 93 74 13 46) are all worth seeking out for seafood. *L'Eléphant Bleu* at 28 boulevard Aiguillon (☎ 04 93 34 28 80) is more exotic. *L'Auberge Provençal* (see above) also has an excellent restaurant.

Antibes' medieval quarter survives and although it has lost many of its older buildings, it has a lively atmosphere that seems rather more substantial than many of the famous resorts on this coast. The most important building is the 12C–16C **Château Grimaldi** whose rugged stonework and square tower form a striking silhouette on the seafront. In 1946 it was being used as a warehouse when the mayor of Antibes offered Picasso the keys to set up his studio. Jaded from the war years which he had passed in his dull Paris apartment, the 65-year-old artist entered an intense burst of creative activity inspired by the warmth of the south and by his new lover, Françoise Gilot. Themes of Classical mythology, love and the life of the Mediterranean coast crowded into his pictures, culminating in the large painting *Joie de Vivre*. Three years later he presented most of these works to the town as well as several tapestries and ceramics which are now beautifully displayed here in the simple whitewashed rooms of the **Musée Picasso** (☎ 04 92 90 54 20: open Tues–Sun 10.00–18.00 mid June–mid Sept; 10.00–12.00 and 14.00–18.00 in winter; closed Mon and Nov). Another interesting feature of this collection is the large group of drawings which reveal Picasso's working methods. In essence they are little more than doodles but they reveal the constant variation and development of a theme which is typical of Picasso at his moments of greatest innovation. There are also a number of works by Picasso's contemporaries, notably Léger and Ernst as well as a group of sculptures by Miró, Arman and Germaine Richier (1904–59) laid out on the terrace and ramparts. Appropriately, there is a good collection of works by Nicolas de Staël, who took over Picasso's studio on the second floor. He was the great hope of French painting in the 1950s but committed suicide in Antibes in 1955 aged 41.

Immediately beside the musum is the former **Cathédrale de-l'Immaculée-Conception**, whose 19C Baroque façade conceals a fairly plain Romanesque and Gothic interior. Among the early altarpieces there is one from the 15C which was discovered in the walls in 1938, having been concealed during the Revolution. Antibes has several other museums which may also be of interest. The **Musée de la Tour** (☎ 04 93 34 50 91: **open** Wed, Thurs and Sat only 16.00–19.00 Apr–Sept; 15.00–17.00 Oct–Mar), part of the old town gates in the cours Masséna, is a local history museum; in the place Nationale the **Musée Peynet** (☎ 04 92 90 54 30; **open** Tues–Sun 10.00–18.00 mid June–mid Sept; 10.00–12.00 and 14.00–12.00 and 15.00–19.00 mid Sept–mid June; closed Mon) is a celebration of Gallic sentimentality in the form of rather fey drawings of young lovers by Maurice Peynet (1908–). In marked contrast, the Bastion St-André, part of the 17C ramparts and sea wall to the south of the château, houses the **Musée d'Histoire et d'Archéologie** (☎ 04 92 90 54 35: **open** Tues–Sun 10.00–12.00 and 14.00–18.00; closed Sat, Sun, and Nov) with an interesting display of ancient and medieval discoveries in two dark, vaulted chambers.

To the south of the town is the peninsula of **Cap d'Antibes**, which has become associated with the glamorous and wealthy lifestyle of the Riviera.

History of Cap d'Antibes

The Cap's origins as a playground of the rich and famous are well documented. In the mid-19C a Russian, Count Fersen, and an Englishman, James Close, began the development by building villas on this green stretch of land. They were followed by a Scotsman, James Wyllie, who laid out the gardens of the Eileen Roc (see below). It was not until after the First World War, however, that it really took off.

In 1923 the painter Gerald Murphy (1888–1964) and his wife Sara, who were in the habit of wintering on the Riviera, paid to have the *Hôtel du Cap* opened up for the summer. Until then, the cult of sunshine and water sports was hardly known to the upper classes but the Americans set a precedent which soon caught on. Scott Fitzgerald, a close friend of the Murphys', was drawn to this and gave a fairly close account of how it started in the opening passages of *Tender is The Night*. The Murphys were soon joined by a procession of stylish and fashionable New Yorkers including Cole Porter, Dorothy Parker and Ernest Hemingway. Before long other upper-rank hotels were opening in the summer months for a new clientele of rich and beautiful young people who liked the distinctive markings of a sun tan, Chanel clothes and the cycle of parties and drinking that characterised the whole scene.

In the 1920s the main swimming area was the Baie de la Garoupe on the eastern side of the peninsula, which has some small beaches, but the real centre for the celebrities was the **Hôtel du Cap** with its restaurant the *Eden Roc*, at the southwestern point of the Cap. It is still one of the smartest hotels on the whole coast and its guest list has included many leading writers, musicians and film stars, as well as politicians, millionaires and aristocrats. Fitzgerald recalled sitting here working on his short stories while Zelda swam in the sheltered bay.

In the old coastal fortifications nearby there is a **Musée Naval et Napoléonien** (☎ 04 93 61 45 32: open 09.30–12.00 and 14.15–18.00, closed Sat pm and Sun) with mementoes of Napoleon's landing at Golfe-Juan. Further east is the Eileen Roc, a 19C villa designed by Charles Garnier (1825–98), the architect of the Paris Opéra. Its name is a reverse of Cornelie, the wife of its first owner. Beside this is the Château de la Croe, a large private house owned successively by the Duke and Duchess of Windsor and Stavros Niarchos. As a contrast to the expensive and mostly concealed villas, the semi-tropical gardens of the **Parc Thuret** (☎ 04 93 67 88 66: open Mon–Fri 08.00–18.00 in summer; 08.30–17.00 in winter; closed Sat, Sun) by the boulevard du Cap offer a pleasant retreat at the very centre of the Cap. Just to the east of this, the sanctuary of La Garoupe has two chapels, dating from the 13C and 16C, displaying a large collection of *ex-votos* and primitive paintings.

At the top of the Cap is **Juan-les-Pins**, a fashionable resort and yachting base that has been allowed to degenerate into a loud and congested holiday centre. It was reputedly a wasteland in 1881 when 'discovered' by the Duke of Albany, who wanted to call it Albany-les-Bains. It was, however, the American millionaire Frank Jay Gould who established this resort when he built the hotel and casino in the 1920s, largely to entertain his Californian wife. Juan-les-Pins has a reputation for racy night life but most of it is hollow. The liveliest time of year is July when the international jazz festival is held.

To the north of Antibes, past the large marina of Port Vauban and the formidable 16C Fort Carré, the road follows the gentle curve of the coast to La Brague, best known for its zoo and for Marineland, where whales and dolphins perform.

At this point it is worth turning inland on the D4 to the small pottery-making centre of **Biot**.

🛈 Place de la Chapelle (☎ 93 65 05 85).

This medieval walled village has preserved something of its original character, particularly in the steep cobbled pathway which leads up from the 16C Port de Tines. In the old centre, beside the 16C church of Ste-Madeleine, is the place aux Arcades with 13C–14C arcades enclosing a series of traditional small shops. Near this is the tourist office which gives access to the small local history **museum** (☎ 04 93 65 54 54: Wed–Sun 14.30–18.30 June–Oct; 14.00–18.00 Dec–May; closed Mon, Tues and Nov). Housed in an old chapel of the Pénitents-Blancs, this collection introduces the history of the pottery industry in the area. There are also several shops specialising in glass and pottery nearby but for the best of the local product it is preferable to visit the workshops or *verreries* below the old town.

The principal feature of Biot however, is the **Musée National Fernand**

Léger (☎ 04 93 65 63 61; **open** Wed–Mon 10.00–12.00 and 14.00–18.00; closed Tues; closes 17.00 in winter) set up by the artist's widow to display a representative collection of his work. Fernand Léger (1881–1955) died just two weeks after buying this plot of land with the intention of producing some ceramic sculptures. Perhaps the most noticeable feature of the large concrete building is the huge glazed ceramic mural in the vivid primary colours championed by Léger, which spans the façade. The collection covers most of his career but there are few of the early Cubist works which established his reputation. Instead, there is greater emphasis on the later period when the artist turned to images of workers to express his socialist and anarchist ideals. There is also an interesting display of drawings and decorative arts which are rarely exhibited in the mainstream modern art museums where Leger's paintings have pride of place.

From La Brague, the **Baie des Anges**, one of the most evocative names on the Riviera, follows a gentle curve round towards Nice. Unfortunately this stretch of coast is also one of the most scarred by unplanned development. It is not helped by the fact that three major roads and a railway track run alongside one another for part of it, punctuated by intersections and turn-offs for Cagnes and Nice airport. Hotels and adverts scream for the attention of the passing motorist. This is not an auspicious entrance to Nice itself but the city nevertheless has its own character in contrast to the more crass developments on its periphery.

25 · Nice

Nice is the oldest and still the most diverse of all the great resorts on the Côte d'Azur. To think of it solely as a resort, however, is to underestimate its size and significance. As the fifth largest city in France, second only to Marseille in the south, it occupies a position in the administration and economy of the region that belies its more famous role as a holiday centre. It is also the most cosmopolitan of southern French towns, largely due to its position and turbulent history, pitched somewhere between Provence and the city states of northern Italy. Indeed, Nice often seems more Italian than French, its architecture, layout, pattern of life, dialect and particularly its cuisine offering strong parallels with such maritime cities as Genoa or Pisa.

History of Nice
The city was founded by the Greeks in the 4C following their victory over local tribesmen. Appropriately named Nikaia (after Nike, the goddess of victory) it was at that time a small trading-post on the sea. The Romans had greater plans for it and established a settlement at Cimiez (Cemenelum) which grew to some 20,000 inhabitants. As with all the ancient towns on this coast, however, it was repeatedly overrun by Barbarian incursions and virtually obliterated by the Saracens in the 10C.

The town that grew up in the wake of this was the present city of Nice, re-established on the sea by the counts of Provence. It was hardly a peaceful location, uneasily placed between warring factions in both Italy and Provence, and in 1388 the people of Nice elected to join the Duchy of Savoy from which they enjoyed considerable independence as the capital of their own county. The French continued to press claims on Nice, however, and it was repeatedly besieged and bombarded until annexed in 1792 by the new French Republic. Returned to Savoy after the collapse of the Empire in 1814 it was eventually ceded to France in 1860 following a plebiscite prompted by the political unification of Italy. One irony of this last act was that in 1807 Guiseppe Garibaldi, the hero of the Risorgimento, had been born in Nice, in a house by the old port. He campaigned vigorously to keep his native city in the new Italian state but his fellow citizens were not convinced.

Of other famous Niçois, local legend picks out Catherine Segurane whose bravery helped repulse an army of Turks, French and Austrians under Frederick Barbarossa in 1543. Having forced back several soldiers from the battlements she turned her back in a gesture of defiance, lifted her skirts and displayed her backside to the enemy.

As early as the 1760s the mild climate of Nice was beginning to attract winter visitors. One of the earliest was the dour Scottish doctor and writer Tobias Smollett, nicknamed Smelfungus by Laurence Sterne, whose *Travels in France and Italy* (1766) helped to publicise this part of the coast. It was not until 1864, however, with the arrival of the railway, that Nice was launched as the great winter resort for the aristocracy of Europe. Between then and the First World War most of the crowned heads passed at least one season in Nice to be followed by all sections of wealthy and fashionable society. Queen Victoria and her family were at the forefront but Nice was equally popular with the Russians, who developed a strong community here after the Revolution.

This glittering procession of monarchs and their extensive retinues required a major building programme to provide the necessary comforts. Hotels, casinos, theatres, racetracks and an opera house were built to ensure that the full range of entertainments was available. Before this, in 1820, an English pastor had had the idea of relieving unemployment among orange-growers by setting up a project to build a new breakwater and walkway along the seafront to the west of the old town. This was to become the promenade des Anglais, providing a stage on which the international high life could be enacted in the greatest of all the Mediterranean playgrounds.

Nice had attractions other than a good climate and casinos. To begin with there was considerable local colour best expressed in the festival held every year in the weeks before Lent. In 1873 this was expanded into the Carnival, two weeks of riotous street activities, a spectacular procession of floats and wildly costumed figures, culminating in a 'battle of flowers' and fireworks display when King Carnival is burned in effigy. Like the Mardi Gras and carnivals of the Caribbean it relies on the rivalry of different districts whose supporters work all year round to prepare their floats and costumes.

Nice continued to attract tourists throughout the 20C but rarely for the usual reasons. The beach at Nice is entirely shingle and not particularly good for bathing. Instead, the city cultivated a reputation for rather flashy public display embracing cultural events, high-profile popular entertainments and a fairly expensive nightlife. It would be wrong to see this as some innate character weakness in the Niçois. In fact it has been part of the civic policy of a city that was virtually ruled for over 60 years by two generations of the Médecin family. Their longstanding control of local government gave great prominence to Nice, particularly with major civic projects like the huge Acropolis and modern art gallery, but equally a reputation for sleaze and corruption. In 1982 Graham Greene wrote a famous book, *J'Accuse*, exposing the links between the mayor Jacques Médecin and organised crime syndicates, but this did little to damage Médecin's reputation. He was often seen out in public with shady company and seemed to invite the attention of photographers when escorting the most fashionable and scantily dressed young women. It was not until 1990, when tax investigators got close to his illegal income—said to be over 300 million francs obtained from the building of the opera house, that Médecin fled to Uruguay. He is now back in France serving a long prison sentence but many Niçois still regard him as a victim of central government prejudice. This vacuum in a city that has always been politically to the right has left a fertile breeding-ground for Jean-Marie Le Pen and the Front National.

This development is perhaps to be expected. After all, Nice seems to be run largely for the rich and its pleasures are offered to people who can afford them. It does, however, have a stronger and more distinctive identity than any other resort on the Côte d'Azur. It has never been dominated by tourists and the old town still presents an image of the traditional Mediterranean community, tightly packed and defiant within the warren of narrow streets. Even the hotels and squares of the Belle Epoque or the new public buildings like the ugly conference centre seem to contribute to the life of the town that is shared by residents and visitors alike, creating a real sense of vibrancy and spirit that is infectious.

❖ Information, accommodation and food

🛈 Avenue Thiers (☎ 04 93 87 07 07) by the railway station, 1km or 15min walk to the northwest from the old town and at 2 rue Massenet (☎ 04 93 87 60 60), at Nice-Ferber (☎ 04 93 83 32 64) towards the airport and in Terminal 1 of the airport itself (☎ 04 93 21 44 11).

Hotels. There is perhaps a better choice of reasonable accommodation here than at any other spot on the Riviera. At the top end, the most famous hotel is the *Negresco* on the promenade des Anglais (☎ 04 93 88 39 51) but the *Beau Rivage* at 24 rue St-François-de-Paule (☎ 04 93 80 80 70) has an equally illustrious history while the *Elysée Palace* (☎ 04 93 86 06 06), also on the promenade des Anglais, is a modern hotel with a great address and a rooftop pool.

Less expensive but very good and characterful are the *Windsor* at 11 rue Dalpozzo-Royale (☎ 04 93 88 59 35), the *Nouvel Hôtel* at 19 boulevard Victor-Hugo (☎ 04 93 87 15 00), *La Perouse* at 11 quai Rauba-Capeu in the old town (☎ 04 93 62 34 63), and the *Vendôme* at 26 rue Pastorelli (☎ 04 93 62 00 77). The *Relais de Rimiez* at 128 avenue de Rimiez

(☎ 04 93 81 18 65) is a small hotel with its own garden in the heights beyond Cimiez. For good hotels in the economy bracket you might try the *Cronstadt* at 3 rue Cronstadt (☎ 04 93 82 00 30), the *Drouot* at 24 rue d'Angleterre (☎ 04 93 88 66 15), *Au Picardy* at 10 boulevard Jean-Jaurès (☎ 04 93 85 75 51) or the charming *Porte Bonheur* at 146 avenue St-Lambert (☎ 04 93 84 66 10).

Restaurants. Nice is regarded, justifiably, as the most distinctive culinary centre on the Riviera, and not merely for *salade Niçoise*. Its cuisine covers a huge range and is the more special because of the combination of so many different types of cooking and ingredients. The palace of *cuisine Niçoise* is the *Chantecler* restaurant in the *Negresco* (see above) which has nurtured a sequence of great chefs. It now has a less expensive sister in *La Rotonde*.

You will also find many interesting places in the old town. *L'Ane Rouge* (☎ 04 93 89 49 63) by the port at 7 quai des Deux-Emmanuel is pricey but, *Don Camillo* (☎ 04 93 85 67 95) at 5 rue des Ponchettes and *Chez Flo* (☎ 04 93 80 70 10) at 4 rue Sacha-Guitry are more reasonable; all have local specialities, particularly seafood and variations on the delicious ravioli.

Finally there are two very distinctive restaurants that offer an experience more than a meal. *La Mérenda* at 4 rue de la Terrasse and *Barale* (☎ 04 93 89 17 94) at 36 rue Beaumont are hangovers from the tradition of large popular refectories where the people of Nice would eat. These two are now quite famous restaurants and, while not cheap, have an earthiness and character missing from most of the others.

When planning an itinerary or even an overall approach to the city it is best to think of it in three distinct sections; the old town by the port and château, the 19C town behind the promenade des Anglais in the west, and the later developments or suburbs inland to the north, which include Cimiez.

The Vieux Ville

The Vieux Ville (Old Town) occupies a triangle of land bounded by the sea in the south, the old port or port Lympia in the east and the broad boulevard Jean-Jaurès running up the Paillon rivercourse to the place Garibaldi in the north. There is a statue to the Italian patriot in this 18C square but Garibaldi was actually born in 1807 at 2 quai Papacino in a house overlooking the main basin of the old port. Ferries to Corsica operate from here and there is still a fishing-fleet as well as the predictable yachts and pleasure craft. Indeed, there is still something of a port atmosphere in the cafés and shops along the quays and narrow streets, although Nice has long since ceased to carry much shipping or industry.

Overlooking the main harbour to the west is the castle hill, a tall outcrop of rock which was the site of the original Greek acropolis. As an easily fortified position this has seen several castles, but the last one was dismantled in 1707 on the orders of Louis XIV and his military architect Vauban. Oddly enough, the person responsible for the demolition was the Maréchal de Berwick, bastard son of James II of Great Britain. The hill itself is still known collectively as the **Château** although there are few traces of the old fortifications. Instead, the summit and site of the ramparts is now a pleasant terraced garden offering good views over the bay and the coloured rooftops of the old town. The Tour Bellanda, a 16C bastion in the southwest corner, is the only substantial survivor and this is given over to a **Musée Naval** (☎ 04 93 80 47 61: open Wed–Mon 10.00–12.00 and 14.00–19.00 June–Sept; 10.00–12.00 and 14.00–17.00 Oct–May; closed Tues and mid Nov–mid Dec) with collections of ship models, paintings and memorabilia from the city's history. Beside this a lift operates between the Château and the eastern end of the quai des Etats-Unis, some 80m below. Another attraction of the Château is the old town cemetery at the north side which has a fascinating collection of 19C tombs and gravestones. Garibaldi and 19C prime minister Léon Gambetta are both buried here alongside wealthy local families and a fair sprinkling of northern visitors whose cure on the Riviera proved unsuccessful. There is also a Jewish cemetery commemorating the long-standing Jewish community in Nice.

The old town, below this to the west, was once squeezed within a defensive wall which explains the tight network of narrow streets and dark passageways at its centre. Even now it retains a strong Italianate character with a range of small shops and cafés amid tall buildings bedecked with washing lines and window boxes. What is remarkable is the number of important and rather grand buildings in this warren including the 17C cathedral of Ste-Réparate on the place Rossetti, the church of St-Jacques, based on the Gesù in Rome, and the chapel of the Annunciation, confusingly known also as either St-Giaume or Ste-Rita. All three have impressive Baroque interiors with the full panoply of stucco work, polychrome marble, *boiseries* and illusionistic painting. The finest building in the old town, however, is the **Palais Lascaris** (☎ 04 93 62 05 54: open Tues–Sun 09.30–12.00 and 14.30–18.00; closed Mon) at 15 rue Droite, an Italianate palace built in the 17C for the Vintimille family. The façade and interior have a profusion of high Baroque decoration including a fresco cycle of mythological scenes on the second floor by Genoese artists. The building now houses a museum of local arts and crafts with an attractive 18C pharmacy from Besançon reconstructed on the ground floor. Further up the rue Droite, the place St-François has a lively fish market supplied by the local fleet.

The main market, however, is in the lower part of the old town on the cours Saleya. This open space, overlooked by the huge palace of the Sardinian kings (now the Préfecture), hosts a fruit and flower market every morning, complemented on certain days by second-hand clothes and bric-à-brac stalls. Also by the *cours* is the 18C Baroque chapel of the Pénitents and the **Galerie de Malacologie** (open Tues–Sat 10.30–13.00 and 14.00–18.00; closed Sun, Mon and all Nov) with its collection of molluscs but the greatest attraction is the street itself, offering a pleasant walk of some 600m animated by cafés and the general bustle of Mediterranean city life.

At its western end is the **Opéra** dating from 1885. It is not an architecturally distinguished building but several famous composers including Guiseppe Verdi, Giacomo Puccini, Camille Saint-Saens and Dmitri Shostakovitch all conducted their work here. Nice has been an important music centre for over 200 years. Niccolò Paganini died here in 1840; Hector Berlioz was a great enthusiast, claiming 'I have found my city and it is Nice'; while Richard Wagner, who conducted the French premier of *Lohengrin* here, apparently planned an opera to be called *Les Français devant Nice*.

The Russian playwright Anton Chekhov stayed near the opera house at the *Hôtel Beau Rivage* in the rue St-François-de-Paule where he wrote *The Seagull*, and Matisse was also a guest here on his first visit to Nice in 1916. When in 1921 he decided to settle here he took the small yellow house close by in the place Charles-Felix which had a view over the *ponchettes* to the sea. This became his home and studio for the next 18 years, frequently appearing as the sensual interior in his paintings, until he moved to the comparative splendour of the *Hôtel Regina* in Cimiez. In 1950 Matisse held a small exhibition of his work in an old commercial building at 77 quai des Etats-Unis. This is now the **Galerie-Musée Raoul Dufy** (☎ 04 93 62 31 24: **open** Tues–Sat 10.00–12.00 and 14.00–18.00; closed Sun mornings and Mon) showing a collection of paintings, drawings and prints which were presented to the city by Dufy's widow after his death in 1953. These light, decorative works capture something of the spirit of the Riviera without any of the pretensions of many weaker artists who have

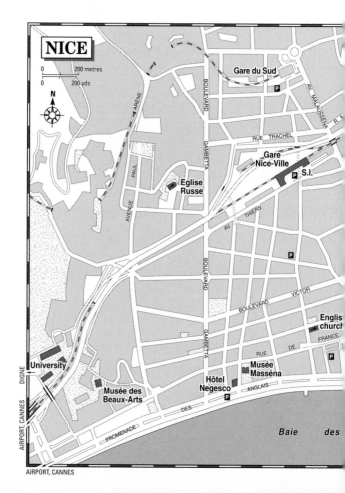

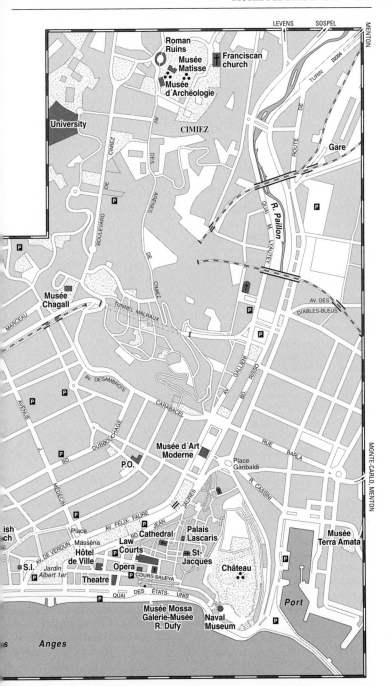

chosen to paint here. A few doors along at No. 59 is the **Musée Mossa** (☎ 04 93 62 37 11: **open** same times as Galerie-Musée Raoul Dufy) a collection of sexy Symbolist paintings and designs for carnival floats by the father and son artists Alexis and Adolf Mossa.

The Jardin Albert Ier facing the sea marks the western end of the old town. It is also the start of a long strip of gardens and boulevards running northeast and known as the Paillon. This is actually the dry bed of the river Paillon which has been covered to create a series of 'hanging gardens', underground car parks and *Grand Projets*, the large public buildings and prestige developments designed to celebrate the reign of the Médecins. Largest of these, about 1km back from the seafront, is the **Acropolis**, a huge music and conference centre that has served to enrich many local officials. Just before it, near the place Garibaldi, is a new complex containing the theatre and the **Musée d'Art Moderne et d'Art Contemporain** (MAMAC), sometimes described as the Promenade des Arts.

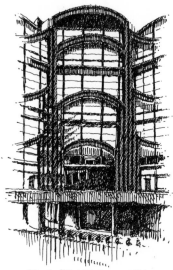

Musée d'Art Moderne et d'Art Contemporain

The museum (☎ 04 93 62 61 62: **open** Mon, Wed, Thur, Sat, Sun 11.00–18.00, Fri 11.00–22.00; closed Tues) is the most striking of all these buildings, composed of four white pavilions linked by steel walkways enclosed in a curtain wall of plate glass. Unfortunately, within five years of its opening it has revealed cracks that threaten its very existence. The collections are uneven but quite lively, offering an interesting alternative to the colourful sensuality of Matisse and Picasso. Alongside the more witty efforts of the modern School of Nice (Arman, Raysse and César), there is a good collection of European and American art (Fluxus, Pop, Minimalist), and a section devoted to Yves Klein, the most radical French artist of the post-War period who was born in Nice in 1928.

19th-century Nice

The lower end of the Paillon offers a more relaxed and elegant cityscape. Just above the Jardin Albert Ier is the huge place Masséna, an arcaded 19C square which is the entrance to the avenues, shops and hotels of the **Ville Moderne**. The main shopping street is the avenue Jean-Médecin but the key to the development of this whole area was the promenade des Anglais. Initially a built-up road which offered a good surface for carriages along the seafront to the west, in the late 19C it became one of the great streets of Europe. Successively widened to cope with the ever-increasing traffic of wealthy visitors wishing to parade along this playground of aristocrats it is now an eight-lane dual-carriageway still crowded with flashy traffic. Along this, a series of grand hotels and casinos were built with names like *Le Westminster*, *Le Victoria* and *Le West-End*, clearly aiming for the English market. Greatest of all, however, is the **Hôtel Negresco**, opened in 1913 and still famous for its Belle Epoque architecture, its restaurant and its residents. Scott Fitzgerald stayed here as did many visiting royal families. In the Salon Royal there is a huge chandelier designed for Tsar Nicholas II by Baccarat. In the 1920s Isadora Duncan was forced to extend her stay indefinitely because she could not afford to pay her huge bill and, closer to our own times, Paul McCartney is reputed to have composed *The Fool on the Hill* on the ballroom piano. The later history and glamour of the promenade des Anglais is perhaps best represented in the **Palais de la Méditerranée** (1929), a couple of blocks to the east. This Art Deco casino was the most stylish and fashionable spot in Nice when it opened in 1929. More recently, however, it was at the centre of a notorious scandal when a take-over in the 1970s led to the murder of Agnes le Roux, daughter of one of the owners. Several local politicians and organised crime syndicates were implicated, prompting Graham Greene to write *J'Accuse*, but the case remains unsolved. In the aftermath, the building lay derelict and its once lavish interior was stripped, although it is now partially restored and has reopened.

Alongside the *Negresco* in its own formal gardens is the Palais Masséna, an impressive mansion built in 1901 by Prince Victor Masséna, grandson of Napoleon's general. Donated to the city after the First World War it is now the **Musée Masséna** (☎ 04 93 88 11 34: **open** Tues–Sun 10.00–12.00 and 14.00–18.00 May–Sept; closed Mon and all Nov) a local history museum with a wide range of exhibits including paintings, particularly those of the school of Louis Bréa, furniture and decorative arts, some exotic items and memorabilia of such people as Garibaldi and Masséna.

The area around the promenade des Anglais has several fine museums. Most important is the **Musée des Beaux-Arts—Jules Chéret** (☎ 04 92 15 28 28: **open** Tues–Sun 10.00–12.00 and 15.00–18.00 May–Sept; 10.00–12.00 and 14.00–17.00 Oct–Apr; closed Mon and Nov), Nice's main art gallery, occupying a large mansion at 33 avenue des Baumettes, off the rue de France. The house, looking rather like a Renaissance palace, was built in 1875 for the Russian Prince Kotschoubey. Later owned by an American millionaire, James Thompson, it was bought by the city in 1925 to display the collections given to Nice in 1860 by Napoleon III. Since then the interior has been altered and renovated although it retains much of its late 19C grandeur. The collection is also fascinating since it combines an interesting selection of works drawn from various schools and periods, much of which reveals some link with the city. There are, for example, some good 17C and 18C pictures in the ground-floor galleries including works by Robert, Fragonard and J.-B. Van Loo. The bulk of the paintings, however, are 19C and 20C with examples of work by Eugène Boudin (1824–98), Edgar Degas (1834–1917), Alfred Sisley (1839–99), Rodin, Monet, Renoir, Signac and Bonnard. Jules Chéret (1836–1932) was primarily a designer of posters, which is apparent in his more sentimental pictures, but there are other, more substantial artists who lived and worked in Nice. Félix Ziem was a prominent landscape painter of the mid-19C whose richly coloured views are often compared to those of J.M.W. Turner. Dufy is better known largely because his pictures, although inspired by the Fauves, seem to celebrate the bourgeois leisure pursuits and sunny atmosphere of the Riviera. Van Dongen's *Tango of the Archangel* (1927), depicting a woman dressed only in stockings and garter dancing with an angel in a dinner jacket, suggests a more decadent taste, as does the work of Adolf Mossa

(1883–1971), a late Symbolist drawn to mysticism, sex and death (see above).

Further west, in a villa built for the perfumier François Coty, is the **Musée International d'Art Naif** (☎ 04 93 71 78 33: same hours as Musée des Beaux-Arts but closed Tues), on avenue Val-Marie off the avenue de Fabrona, with a collection of over 600 naïve paintings donated by the Russian collector Anatole Jakovsky.

The suburbs

The districts of La Buffa and St-Etienne to the north of the promenade des Anglais are largely residential suburbs and although many of the houses are fairly splendid, most are either sealed off from view or swamped by modern developments. There are, however, several buildings worth seeking out, the most interesting of which is the **Cathédrale Orthodoxe Russe** (☎ 04 93 96 88 02: **open** daily 09.00–12.00 and 14.30–18.00 May–Sept; 09.30–12.00 and 14.30–17.00 Oct–Apr) off the appropriately named boulevard du Tzarevitch. This remnant of the Russian community in Nice was designed in 1903 by Preobrajenski, a Russian architectural historian, who produced a miniature version of St Basil's in Moscow, complete with onion domes and polychrome majolica tiles. Finished in 1914, only three years before the Revolution, it served many of the exiled White Russians who saw out the last of their days on the Riviera and continues to draw a congregation.

The other smart residential districts of Nice offer some unexpected architectural treasures. Mont Boron, to the east of the old port, has a number of extravagant 19C residences including the pink **Château de l'Anglais**, an Oriental fantasy built in 1858 for Col. Robert Smith of the Indian Army. To the north of this, the **observatory** at Mont-Gros was designed in 1881 by Charles Garnier, the architect of the Paris and Monte Carlo opera houses. The client, a keen amateur astronomer, also wanted two domes with astral maps, for which he engaged Gustave Eiffel.

The most important of these suburbs, however, is **Cimiez** on the site of the old Roman town of Cemenelum. This area was already attracting a number of wealthy residents when Queen Victoria decided to spend a couple of winters here in the 1880s. From then on its prestige was assured, the queen giving her name to a boulevard and to the huge *Hôtel Exelsior Regina Palace* (now apartments). She is also represented in a large statue overlooking the approach road. For traces of the old Roman town you can visit the ruined amphitheatre and the large baths complex in the park and there is a new **Musée d'Archéologie** (☎ 04 93 81 59 57: **open** Tues–Sat 10.00–12.00 and 14.30–18.30 May–Sept; 10.00–12.00 and 14.00–17.00 Oct–Apr; closed Sun morning, Mon and Nov) recording the history of this important settlement.

Alongside this, in a charming 17C Genoese villa, is the **Musée Matisse** (☎ 93 81 08 08: **open** Wed–Mon 11.00–19.00 Apr–Sept; 10.00–17.00 Oct–Mar; closed Tues), one of the most enjoyable 20C art museums in the south of France. Consisting of the artist's own collection of paintings, drawings, prints and bronzes, which he bequeathed to the city, this museum offers a comprehensive survey of Matisse's long career from his early still-lifes of the 1890s to the paper cut-outs of his last years. Highlights include several important Fauvist pictures such as the *Portrait of Madame Matisse* (1905) and the sensual interiors produced in Nice in the 1920s and '30s like *Nude on an Armchair* (1936) as well as a series of drawings and models for the Chapelle du Rosaire at Vence (1952; see p 263s). Matisse once claimed that his work should be as relaxing as an armchair and, as if to emphasise this, there is a painting of a Rococo armchair as well as some of his own furniture and personal effects. Indeed, the whole collection is a reminder of how Matisse celebrated the light and colour of the Côte d'Azur, and how, by extension, he encouraged the idea of a lifestyle based on sensuality and hedonism.

Matisse spent most of his working life in Nice, the latter part, until his death in 1954, in an apartment in the nearby *Hôtel Regina*. He is buried in the Franciscan cemetery at the eastern edge of the park, as is his fellow Fauve, Raoul Dufy. Alongside this is the complex of **monastic buildings** consisting of a 15C church, two cloisters and an attractive garden. The Franciscans have been in Nice since the 13C and a museum (**open** Mon–Sat 10.00–12.00 and 15.00–18.00; closed Sun) celebrates their history in a collection of early church treasures, including several altarpieces commissioned in the late 15C from Louis Bréa.

At the lower end of Cimiez on the avenue du Dr-Menard is the **Musée National Message Biblique Marc Chagall** (☎ 04 93 53 87 20: **open** Wed–Mon 10.00–18.00 July–Sept; 10.00–12.30 and 14.00–17.00 Oct–June; closed Tues). The core of this museum is 17 large canvases depicting Old Testament subjects which were given to the state by the artist's children in 1966. Since then the collection has been expanded with other works by Chagall on a religious theme, including tapestries, mosaics, stained glass and a grand piano which he decorated and which is now used for recitals. Even the temporary exhibitions are devoted to religious art from around the world which gives the gallery the dubious effect of being a quasi-religious foundation. Chagall's childlike pictures do lend themselves to this sort of pious atmosphere although a visit can seem more like the devotions of a cult than modern art. The building certainly helps, offering a cool and relaxed ambience when it is not overcrowded.

26 · The Corniches, Monaco and Menton

The final stretch of coast from Nice to Cap Martin and on to the Italian border is one of the most spectacular sights in the Mediterranean. Sheer limestone cliffs rise sharply from the sea to heights over 300m providing an immense screen of rocks behind the beaches and inlets. Quite apart from the sheer scale and breathtaking beauty of some of these sights, attempts to settle and develop this area have created some impressive, man-made additions to the landscape. Villages like Eze, perched high over the sea, are salutary reminders of the inge-nuity and persistence of local communities to settle, defend and exploit this apparently impossible rocky terrain. What is even more remarkable is that, in the past, Eze was primarily a fishing-village. No doubt it was easy to defend from its vantage-point on the pinnacle of a rock, but one wonders at the difficulty of getting to the sea from the village and back again.

Along the Corniches

The challenges posed by this landscape to a medieval community were exchanged for slightly different problems when the area first became part of modern France and later became attractive to the tourist market. Far from needing the safety of the rugged outcrops, tourists wanted to see and experience the impassable stretches of cliff which offered spectacular views over the sea and coast. In the 19C, therefore, the local authorities were faced with the problem of creating a route through this area and providing access to the wildest and highest parts for tourists who, nevertheless, could still get back to their hotels in the evening. The solution was the three **Corniches**, roads cut into the rockface and following the line of the cliffs to link Nice and Roquebrune. To these three famous roads has been added the easternmost section of the *Autoroute La Provençale*. Although its views out to sea are intermittent, this is also a spectacular route to drive due to the sequence of soaring bridges and tunnels which have enabled the roadway to traverse the rough terrain.

If you are driving along the Corniches it is important to remember that certain towns are only accessible by one or another road although at certain points all three roads may be visible in parallel. The difference in heights between them means that you often have to travel a considerable distance to find a link allowing you to transfer. The roads make for an exhilarating drive but can be both confusing and tiresome due to congestion in high summer.

The earliest of the roads, and the highest, is the *Grande Corniche* (D2564) which follows the Roman Via Julia Augusta by La Turbie to Roquebrune. This is still the most spectacular of the three routes and numerous signs along the way offer panoramic viewpoints or belvederes such as that at Col d'Eze. It is worth turning off to appreciate the view and to avoid the frequent accidents caused by stationary cars.

La Turbie (18km from Nice), overlooking Monte Carlo, is dominated by a single and very impressive Roman monument. The so-called **Trophée des Alpes** (*tropaea*) from which the village takes its name was built by Augustus between 13 BC and 5 BC to celebrate his subjugation of the Cis-Alpine tribes. Originally 50m high, it consisted of a square base and a circular colonnade supporting a stepped roof at the top of which was a colossal statue of the emperor. There is a model of the completed monument in the nearby museum (☎ 04 93 41 20 81: **open** daily 09.00–19.00 Apr–Sept, 09.00–12.00 and 14.00–16.30 Oct–Mar). Only one other such monument has survived (at Adam-Klissi in Romania) which suggests something of its importance. Throughout the Middle Ages the trophy acted as a fort and lookout-post for the small community but it was repeatedly attacked and vandalised. The monks from Lérins disposed of the statuary as pagan idols and finally Louis XIV ordered the dismantling of this 'château' which marked the border between France and Savoy. Not even this could destroy it entirely. The upper sections have disappeared, mostly into buildings in the medieval village below, but a substantial section of the colonnade survives up to a height of 35m. It is now surrounded by a public park which offers wonderful views down to the Mediterranean.

The village of **La Turbie** below also has a few interesting features. In plan it follows the ancient processional route leading up to the trophy and you can see fragments of Roman masonry built into the 18C Baroque church of St-Michel-Archange.

❖ *Information and accommodation*

🛈 At the Mairie (☎ 04 93 41 10 10).

Hotels. Accommodation and a reasonable meal can be found at the *Hôtel Napoléon* (☎ 04 93 41 28 93).

The **Moyenne Corniche** (N7), built at the height of the tourist boom in the early 20C, is perhaps the most glamorous of the three roads and its cliffside route with occasional tunnels has often appeared in films set on the Riviera. It is a considerable feat of engineering and, when not overcrowded, offers an exhilarating drive above the sea.

This is the direct route to **Eze**, some 10km from Nice, the most improbable village in the whole region. Situated at the tip of a tall narrow rock some 450m over the sea, Eze is said to be 'balanced on the point of a spike'. Needless to say the views are unparalleled and the effect of looking down to the sea below sometimes vertiginous.

History of Eze

The modern history of Eze is better told in events rather than physical remains. Nietzsche is reputed to have formulated the latter part of his famous but little-read text *Also Sprach Zarathustra* while on holiday here in the 1880s. The path leading down through ravaged woods to Eze-sur-Mer on the Corniche Inférieure is named after him. Eze and its surrounding area was also a popular site for the villas of wealthy aristocrats who wished to escape from the public glare of the boulevards and casinos. The Russian Grand Duchess Anastasia was one such, but her villa by Eze was kept mainly for the stream of young men she picked up on daily trips to the seafront. During the Second World War the Fort de la Révere 2km north of Eze was used by the Germans as a prisoner-of-war camp. On two occasions in 1942 there were large escapes, the latter involving 66 Allied airmen, which is still a subject of some pride among the local residents.

❖ *Information and accommodation*

🛈 Place Général-de-Gaulle (☎ 04 93 41 26 00) near the car park.

Hotels. Eze can be a spectacularly expensive place to stay. The *Château Eza* (☎ 04 93 41 12 24) and the *Château de la Chèvre d'Or* (☎ 04 93 41 12 12) are in that category but their restaurants are worth it. More reasonable accommodation can be found at the *Golf* (☎ 04 93 41 18 50) or at the *Auberge des Deux Corniches* (☎ 04 93 41 19 54) just outside.

With this degree of natural spectacle, it is perhaps not surprising that Eze is very commercialised, the old houses festooned with card and craft displays and the shops taking up virtually every spare metre on the narrow streets. Eze was once a Ligurian stronghold but what you see nowadays is largely the restored medieval village. At the summit are the ruins of the 14C citadel which have been given over to a Jardin Exotique specialising in cacti (☎ 04 93 41 10 30: **open** 08.00–20.00 in summer; 09.00–12.00 and 14.00–18.00 in winter). The most interesting building is the 14C chapel of the Pénitents-Blancs on place du Planet. This was renovated in the 1950s when the decorative enamels were added but it retains several early treasures, among them a rather cheery-looking Christ on a Catalan crucifix (1258). Near the chapel there is a 13C–16C mansion which once belonged to the Riquier family.

Villefranche-sur-Mer

The *Corniche Inférieure* (N98) is actually the coast road giving access to all the beaches between Nice and Roquebrune. As such it is often congested but there is a lot to see in each of the resorts, many of which have been developed from modest fishing-villages. The first of these, just on the other side of Mont Boron, is Villefranche-sur-Mer. Despite its proximity to Nice, this picturesque village with a wonderful outlook to the cliffs on the opposite side of the bay has retained something of an independent character and a surprisingly unspoiled appearance. The 18C Italianate houses which line the quai Courbet give an attractive backdrop to an area that still works as a fishing-port although the deep-water bay attracts everything from yachts to warships.

❖ *Information and accommodation*

🛈 Jardins François-Binon (☎ 04 93 01 73 68).

Hotels. Villefranche has a modest range of accommodation but, given its location, could be a good base for this coast. *Hôtel Welcome* on quai Amiral-Courbet (☎ 04 93 76 76 93), where Cocteau stayed when painting the nearby chapel, has a wonderful outlook and is near the seafood restaurants on the harbourfront. *La Résidence Carlton* at 9bis avenue Albert 1er (☎ 04 93 01 06 02) and *Le Provençal* at 4 avenue du Maréchal-Joffre (☎ 04 93 01 71 42) are more reasonable.

Also by the *quai* is the small 14C **Chapelle St-Pierre** (☎ 04 93 76 90 70: **open** Tues–Sun 09.30–12.00 and 14.00–18.00; closed Mon), the interior of which was entirely painted by Jean Cocteau in 1957. This is one of his finest decorative schemes, employing the distinctive linear manner that he used in all media to achieve a balance of subtlety and humour. Historically, the chapel was maintained by the local fishermen so the small charge for entrance goes to one of their charities. Cocteau spent part of his childhood in Villefranche and retained fond memories of the village and its surroundings. In 1959 he returned to film part of *Orphée* here.

Behind the *quai* the network of streets offers various routes into the old town, the heart of which is the rue du Poilu and the 17C Baroque church of St-Michel. The most interesting of the streets, however, is the narrow rue Obscure, an arcaded passageway dating from the 13C under which the inhabitants sheltered from the bombardment in 1944. A couple of hundred metres south of the old town and also overlooking the coast is the formidable **Citadelle St-Elmo** (☎ 04 93 76 33 44: **open** Mon, Wed–Sat 10.00–12.00 and 15.00–19.00 July, Aug; Sun 15.00– 19.00; earlier closing other times; closed Tues), built by the Dukes of Savoy in 1560 to protect the harbour of this, their principal port in the west. The fort was apparently much admired by Vauban who decided to retain it as the main defence for the area after destroying most of the fortifications in Nice. From the base of the moat, now a car park, it is easy to appreciate the inherent strength of the structure as the great walls of dark masonry rise up on all sides. The effect is, at least, intimi-

Chapelle St-Pierre

dating. On the inside there are several civic offices, the Hôtel de Ville, the old chapel of St-Elmo, a museum of underwater archaeology and two minor art collections (closed Tues and Sun morning). The first of these consists of a number of rather pretentious sculptures, mostly large female figures, by a local artist called Volti which are displayed in the main courtyard. The second is devoted to the collection of the painter-printmaker Henri Goetz and his wife Christine Boumeester which is supplemented by works presented to the couple by Picasso, Miró and Hans Hartung (1904–89). Unfortunately, all of the displays are rather disappointing in this powerful context.

Cap Ferrat and Beaulieu-sur-Mer

The eastern side of the bay of Villefranche is formed by **Cap Ferrat**, one of the most glamorous and romantic spots on the Mediterranean coast and an essential element in the myth of the Riviera. It is a peninsula measuring some 3km from the corniche (N98) to Cap Ferrat itself, the southernmost tip. Much of this can be covered by following the circuit of the boulevard Général-de-Gaulle or the path round the coast, but it is a disappointing journey since it is virtually impossible to detect anything of the past or present grandeur. The great houses are either sealed off from view with severe warning notices or else broken up into smaller units. Only the Villa Ephrussi Rothschild retains the scale and opulence of the Belle Epoque and that is now a museum.

History of Cap Ferrat

The central figure in the modern history of Cap Ferrat is Leopold II, King of the Belgians (1835–1909) who bought a house here when pursuing one of his innumerable mistresses. This was the Villa les Cèdres and he proceeded to buy up most of the land on the whole peninsula. Leopold's lifestyle was certainly carefree thanks to the enormous wealth he obtained from Belgium's African colonies and his complete lack of concern about public opinion, least of all that of his own subjects. He became a virtual resident on Cap Ferrat where he would swim in the sea every day, his long beard stuffed into a rubber envelope. He also established a superb garden of exotic plants which survives, although the lake has been drained and replaced with a rather sad zoo.

After Leopold and the international super-rich, the next generation to settle on the cape were more popular and worldly. Charlie Chaplin had a house here, as did David Niven, and Winston Churchill was a regular visitor who loved the area for his hobbies, painting and bricklaying. One of the most celebrated residents was the English novelist W. Somerset Maugham who lived for much of his life in a house called the Villa Mauresque near the base of the cape. Maugham found life on the Riviera less restrictive than in England, particularly in view of his homosexuality, and he enjoyed something of an idyll here surrounded by his art collection and garden. He was also able to entertain lavishly and stories of his parties are recounted in many memoirs, not least his own. Finally, the peninsula attempted to reinvent itself in the 1950s when the small fishing-village of St-Jean-Cap-Ferrat, on the eastern side, was developed into a modest but expensive resort.

❖ Information and accommodation

🛈 59 avenue Denis-Séméria (☎ 04 93 76 08 90).

Hotels. There are several affordable hotels such as the *Brise Marine* at avenue Jean-Mermoz (☎ 04 93 76 04 36), the *Clair Logis* on allée des Brises (☎ 04 93 76 04 57) or *La Costière* at avenue Albert 1er (☎ 04 93 76 03 89).

On a raised site overlooking the sea to the north of Leopold's Villa les Cèdres is the magnificent Villa Ile-de-France, now the **Musée Ephrussi de Rothschild** (☎ 04 93 01 33 09: **open** daily 10.00–19.00 July–Aug; 10.00–18.00 Mar–June and Sept, Oct; Mon–Fri 14.00–18.00 Nov–Feb). Built for the daughter of the Rothschild family and her husband in 1905–12 to the designs of an architect named 'Messiah', this villa imitates the style and patronage of the Italian Renaissance princes. The baroness was fairly eclectic in her tastes, acquiring medieval, oriental and Impressionist works, but she had a particular interest in the fine and decorative art of the Rococo period. On her death in 1934 the house and collection were bequeathed to the Académie des Beaux-Arts. It was not until 1960 that they did anything with it, but it is now open to the public as a museum.

The most memorable aspect of the villa is the gardens which cover some 7ha with a rich planting of exotic flowers and shrubs. At the centre, by a cascade, there is a small 'temple of love' in imitation of a similar garden building at Versailles. But it is the views out to sea, particularly to the west in summer evenings, that are most beautiful and provide the greatest reminder of what this paradise offered to the wealthy in the early 20C.

There are some good beaches on or near the peninsula and the St-Jean tourist office has details of walks and other sights.

Beaulieu-sur-Mer, the first town after Cap Ferrat on the *Corniche Inférieure*, is a fairly quiet and mature resort that avoids much of the pace and excess of this coast. In many respects it still looks back to its heyday in the late 19C and early 20C when its sheltered location made it attractive to elderly British visitors in winter. There are, for example, still numerous exotic gardens and palm-lined walks which evoke an earlier era and the grand hotels with such English names as Bristol still seem to thrive. There are also many splendid villas from the Belle Epoque.

History of Beaulieu-sur-Mer

In 1890 the British prime minister Lord Salisbury built his Villa Léonine (La Bastide) in the hills behind Beaulieu where, on one occasion, he received Queen Victoria. Just north of the town, in the area known as La Petite Afrique, is the Villa Namouna built by James Gordon Bennett, the proprietor of the *New York Herald* who sent Henry Stanley to find David Livingstone in Africa. Stories of Bennett's wealth and extravagance are often repeated; he reputedly bought a restaurant in Monte Carlo in order to be served without delay and then presented it to the waiter as a tip. In Beaulieu he lived well and paid for extensions to the harbour in order for his yacht to anchor.

❖ *Information and accommodation*

🛈 Place Clemenceau (☎ 04 93 01 02 21).

Hotels. There is some reasonable accommodation in Beaulieu amid the expensive hotels but it is hard to find. *Le Havre Bleu* at 29 avenue Maréchal-Joffre (☎ 04 93 01 01 40) is good as is the cheaper *Riviera* on rue Paul-Doumer (☎ 04 93 01 04 92). At the top of the range, *The Métropole* (☎ 04 93 01 00 08) and *La Réserve* (☎ 04 93 01 00 01), both on boulevard Maréchal-Leclerc, have excellent facilities and restaurants.

The most interesting house in Beaulieu is the **Villa Kérylos** (☎ 04 93 01 01 44: **open** daily 10.00–19.00 July–Sept; 10.30–12.00 and 14.00–18.00 Mar–June and Oct; varied hours in winter), built in 1902–08 by the German archaeologist Théodore Reinach. Basing his design on a Greek villa of the 4C BC, Reinach took great pains over its accuracy and materials. There is a richly decorated interior and an attractive garden, the whole ensemble being set off by its location on the headland above the Baie des Fourmis with views along the coast to Monaco. In 1928 Reinach left it to the state and it is now open as a museum with a small collection of ancient art.

Monaco

Few countries in the world, or cities for that matter, can have generated such contempt and hostile criticism as the tiny sovereign state of Monaco. Katherine Mansfield described it as 'Real hell' inhabited by pimps, governesses, old hags, ancient men, rich fat capitalists and 'little girls tricked out to look like babies'. Queen Victoria could not bring herself to stop when forced to drive through Monaco. S. Baring-Gould, still the most entertaining commentator on the Côte d'Azur, felt his religious calling rise when he saw the casino and described the miniature state as 'the moral cesspool of Europe'. For a while during the late 19C there was even a society for the closure of Monaco with branches in London and Paris. But it is hardly surprising that this moral crusade had little effect since the younger sons and daughters of those same objectors were drawn to the excitement of gambling and the hedonistic *demi-monde* that surrounded it.

Even modern commentators have adopted a censorious tone towards the intensively developed late 20C Monaco, and the English novelist and translator Anthony Burgess, a resident for much of his later years, felt obliged to mount a defence of the country and its relentlessly high-profile royal family. It didn't have much effect on the Anglo-Saxons who continue to regard Monaco with disdain, while those with excessive amounts of money still seem very happy to spend it there.

History of Monaco

The Grimaldis are the oldest monarchy in Europe and have been resident in Monaco since the 12C. At that time they had extensive lands along the Mediterranean coasts of modern France and Italy but over the years this was whittled away by bad management and the emergence of more powerful neighbours. As late as the 1840s the entire estate of Monaco was available for purchase but the British ambassador thought the price of four million francs rather a lot for an area that produces 'nothing other than lemons'.

This state of affairs was soon to be remedied when Prince Charles III (reigned 1856–89) decided to launch Monaco as a gambling centre. He began building on the barren rock to the east of the city, renamed Monte Carlo, and after the arrival of the railway in 1868 it became a huge success. Soon Monte Carlo had a casino, an opera house and a series of hotels to accommodate the aristocracy, the plain wealthy and the procession of secretaries, chefs, servants, adventurers and courtesans that followed in their train. The following year the prince announced the abolition of taxes. Monaco had been launched as one of the great centres of aristocratic pleasure and indulgence.

The spin-off from this fabulous expenditure formed the basis of the economy and to this day there is a curious system that keeps taxes down while restricting the actual number of citizens. By 1949 when Prince Rainier was crowned, however, the economy was in decline. It is a measure of his foresight, or luck, that he has transformed the state into an international business centre with huge banking interests in which gambling represents less than 5% of the income.

During the last 40 years the appearance of Monaco has been altered drastically. Whole sections of the old town have been demolished to make way for huge high-rise office blocks and conference centres which are in turn surrounded by a series of flyovers and underpasses. A large section of the coastline around Fontvielle in the west was extended by reclaiming some 24ha from the sea and this has been built upon to create a skyline that rivals that of Hong Kong.

Rainier also raised the profile of the royal family into a spectacular global soap opera in which their everyday lives are reported in magazines throughout the world. The process began in 1956 when he married the Hollywood film star Grace Kelly, herself the daughter of a wealthy Philadelphian industrialist, who brought considerable style and glamour to the throne. Their children have kept up the relentless media attention, particularly daughters Caroline and Stephanie, who lead often controversial lives. In 1982 Grace was killed in a car accident and it is still widely believed that she was being driven illegally by Stephanie, who was then under age.

The death of Princess Grace was a great blow to the people of Monaco who had developed a deep affection for her. There was national mourning but it has not been allowed to dampen the rather frivolous floating world of conspicuous expenditure, festivals and Grands Prix. Visiting Monaco you cannot fail to notice the number of luxury cars and attendants or to sense the discreet presence of police and security systems. Juxtaposed with the colourful uniforms of the official guards, with the Prince's palace in all its Ruritanian absurdity, or with the decorative buildings of the Belle Epoque, the new world of business creates an unreal effect that must be experienced.

❖ Information, accommodation and food

🛈 2a blvd des Moulins (☎ 377 92 16 61 66). When telephoning from France, all Monaco numbers have the prefix 377.

Hotels. The *Hôtel de Paris* (☎ 377 92 16 30 00) on the place du Casino and the *Hermitage* on the sq. Beaumarchais (☎ 377 92 16 40 00) are the most opulent hotels in the principality but the slightly faded *Balmoral* (☎ 377 93 50 62 37) at 12 av de la Costa is more evocative of the great age.

For a more reasonable price range, the *Hôtel de France* (☎ 377 93 30 24 64) at 6 rue de la Turbie, the *Cosmopolite* (☎ 377 93 30 16 95) at 4 rue de la Turbie, both near the station, and the *Hôtel Helvetia* (☎ 377 93 30 21 71) at 1 rue Grimaldi can all be recommended.

Restaurants. The *Louis XV* in the *Hôtel de Paris* (see above) is the most celebrated of the old restaurants in Monaco because it was here that a crêpe intended for the Prince of Wales was accidentally set alight. The future George V apparently like this novel concoction and christened it after his dinner guest: hence 'crêpe Suzette'. The *Belle Epoque* in the *Hermitage* (see above) is similarly impressive and expensive, while *Le St-Bénoit* (☎ 377 93 25 02 34) at 10 ave de la Costa is excellent for seafood.

For something more modest, the *Polpetta* (☎ 377 93 50 67 84) at 2 rue Paradis is noted for its excellent pasta dishes and *Le Perigordin* (☎ 377 93 30 06 02), at 4 rue de la Turbie, for its French rural dishes. The *Castelroc* (☎ 377 93 30 36 68), at place du Palais, has a local Monegasque menu at lunchtime.

To stay in Monaco comfortably is generally expensive, especially if you are spending your own money. For the day visitor, however, there is plenty to see in a relatively small area. The most interesting district is the old town, **Monaco-Ville**, containing the palace, cathedral and administrative centre grouped along the huge promontory of rock between the two harbours.

The rock itself has been occupied since Neolithic times and there is a series of chambers cut deep into the stone, one of which has been extended to create the underground Parking des Pêcheurs. From here an excellent lift transports passengers up to the elevated level of the streets, emerging close by the **Musée Oceanographique** (☎ 04 93 15 36 00: **open** daily 09.00–20.00 July–Aug; 09.00–19.00 Apr–June and Sept; 10.00–18.00 Oct–Mar). Founded in 1910 by Prince Albert I, a passionate collector of marine life and minerals, it is housed in a huge white Beaux-Arts building that seems to rise out of the cliffs. Although it is one of the main tourist attractions of Monaco, the museum is still regarded as one of the world's foremost oceanography centres and until recently was directed by the popular underwater explorer Jacques Cousteau. The aquarium in the basement is the most popular section but there are lively displays on the upper floors devoted to all aspects of marine life and to underwater exploration, as well as an excellent view from the terrace at the top.

To the west of the museum, past the Jardins St-Martin, is the **cathedral**, a neo-Romanesque building designed by local architect Charles Lenormand in 1875. A 13C Romanesque church was demolished to make way for this clumsy edifice because the pope conferred a bishopric on the principality, which it was felt deserved something grander. There are several fine paintings inside, notably the St Nicholas altarpiece and a *Pietà* by the 15C School of Nice painter Louis Bréa, but the principal attraction is the tomb of Princess Grace which is generally littered with flowers and tributes.

Behind the cathedral are the narrow streets of the old town, which are worth exploring. On the rue Princesse-Marie-de-Lorraine the colourful chapel of the Miséricorde contains a sculpture of the recumbent Christ which is carried round the streets on Good Friday. Nearby, on the rue Basse, a different note is struck with the Historial des Princes de Monaco, a waxwork museum of the Grimaldi family (☎ 04 93 30 39 05; **open** daily 09.30–19.00). At the top of these streets is the Place du Palais, an open esplanade where you can see the changing of the guards before midday.

The **Palais Princier** (☎ 04 93 25 18 31; **open** daily 09.30–18.30 June–Sept), which looks more like the work of a pastry chef than an architect, actually has its origins in the 13C. The bulk of it, however, was built in the late 19C and the pastel colours on the exterior were chosen by Princess Grace in 1956. The interior, in which period rooms bear the unmistakeable sign of extensive remodelling in the 19C and 20C, has a similarly unreal effect. The Cour d'Honneur and the Galerie d'Hercule are perhaps the finest rooms and contain frescoes by the 17C Italian painters Luca Cambiaso and Orazio Ferrari. Otherwise, the tiresome but compulsory guided tour is mostly concerned with the associations of the current royal family. One room takes its name from the Duke of York, brother of George III, who, while in pursuit of a mistress in Genoa, was taken ill on his yacht and brought ashore here to die. This room has several fine portraits but there are very few works of art worthy of attention in the palace as a whole. In one wing there is a museum devoted to Napoleon, who was

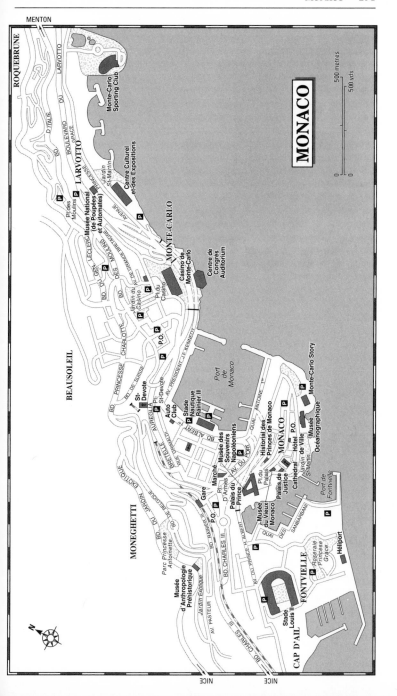

The Hermitage hotel overlooking the main harbour

related to the Grimaldis by marriage. This contains personal items belonging to the emperor such as his hat and tobacco pouch as well as some attractive portraits of him and his wife Josephine. Above this are the palace archives with a small museum of the history of Monaco.

Of the other sights and attractions in Monaco, the **Jardin Exotique** (☎ 04 93 30 33 65: **open** daily 09.00–19.00 May–Sept; 09.00–18.00 Oct–Apr) on the heights to the west is very impressive. The deep grottoes are used to good effect and there is a museum of anthropology in the grounds. There is also Princess Grace's Rose Garden in the heart of the intensively developed Fontvieille district. **La Condamine** is the main shopping and commercial area and has the added attraction of the port where most of the luxury yachts are berthed. As ever, the life of a yacht in harbour is a fairly public one and you can often see groups of people watching other groups of people having a meal or cocktail party on board. Near the northwest corner of the port is the 19C **Eglise Ste-Dévote**, not a particularly interesting building but the most popular church in Monaco. On 26–27 January each year there is a festival in which a boat is burned to celebrate the return of the saint's relics from robbers.

The principal attraction in Monaco nowadays, just as it was a century ago, is **Monte Carlo** on the opposite (north) side of the port from the old town.

History of Monte Carlo

This was a barren crag with little to recommend it when in 1856 Prince Charles III decided to launch a casino as a source of much-needed revenue. At that time gambling was restricted or illegal in many European countries but there was good evidence of the potential profits from the example of the German casinos at Baden-Baden. In fact, the first few years of the enterprise were a complete failure and three successive entrepreneurs went bankrupt over the scheme. It was not until 1863, when a shrewd French businessman named François Blanc bought the concession, that the casino took off. Operating under the superficially healthy title of the Société des Bains de Mer et du Cercle des Etrangers, the new proprietor took full advantage of the approaching railway line and within a few years Monte Carlo became the principal gaming and society resort on the Côte d'Azur. When the casino was extended in 1878–79 to designs by Charles Garnier, the architect of the Paris opera house, the gaming-rooms became the most opulent and glamorous in Europe.

Some of the rooms in the **Casino** have degenerated into simple money-pits, notably the Salle de Jeux Américains which is crammed full of slot machines, but the *salons privés* retain some of their Belle-Epoque grandeur. This was the setting for many dramatic events although most of the stories of suicides after spectacular losses were exaggerated. (One theory was that the rival authorities of Nice used to dump corpses in the sea around Monte Carlo to discredit the casino.) There were, however, several men who did break the bank. One of those was a Yorkshireman, Charles Jaggers, who fixed on a very practical solution to the question of probability. Instead of looking for mystical or mathematical patterns in the results he decided that the simple mechanics of each wheel would produce certain outcomes. After a few weeks he was able to identify different probabilities at each of the roulette tables. Having narrowed the odds he took to gambling with high stakes until the authorities intervened and reformed their system of maintenance.

The casino looks a very imposing building but anyone can go in to look round or to visit the café or restaurant. It seems to thrive although there is little obvious sign of outrageous wealth. Indeed, it is often claimed that the casino must be mixed up in some way with the corruption that is endemic on the Côte d'Azur. This is always fiercely denied on the principle that, since it is now state owned, it is closely monitored and can make a healthy profit quite legally. Despite these assurances, it is slightly unsettling to see that one of the recent owners was Aristotle Onassis and that one of the gaming rooms is still named after the erstwhile mayor of Nice, Jacques Médecin (see p 273).

To the rear of the casino, Garnier's principal addition was the **Salle Garnier**, a sumptuous theatre and opera house which in its early years saw many famous performances by the actress Sarah Bernhardt and the singers Adelina Patti, Nellie Melba, Enrico Caruso and F.I. Chaliapin, and was particularly closely associated with the composer J.E.F. Massenet.

The Ballets Russes at Monte Carlo

The Salle Garnier's most celebrated period, however, began in 1911 when Sergei Diaghilev's Ballets Russes performed here for the first time. By 1926 the company that included Nijinsky, Karsavina and some of the greatest choreographers and designers of the modern stage was so closely associated with this theatre that it was renamed the Ballets Russes de Monte Carlo. Diaghilev's originality was in bringing together great artists from unrelated fields to collaborate on his productions. In this he succeeded spectacularly, engaging such figures as the composers Igor Stravinsky, Maurice Ravel, Francis Poulenc and Erik Satie and the artists Picasso, Braque, Ernst, Miró, Juan Gris (1887–1927), Naum Gabo (1890–1977) and Giorgio De Chirico (1888–1974).

The casino and opera house are surrounded by a beautiful terraced garden within which numerous contemporary sculptures are displayed. This continues to the rear of the building (actually the main façade) where there are excellent views over the sea above the new conference centre. On the other side the high life of Monte Carlo revolves around the place du Casino. Many of the expensive cafés and hotels are around here, notably the *Hôtel de Paris* which set the style for high-class catering as early as 1865. At 17 avenue Princesse-Grace, to the north of the casino, there is another building designed by Garnier. This villa now houses a fascinating **Musée National des Poupées et Automates** (☎ 04 93 30 91 26: **open** daily 10.00–18.30 Easter–Sept; 10.00–12.15 and 14.30–18.30 Oct–Easter) with a collection of some 2000 dolls and automata, many of which can be set in motion by the attendants. There are also a number of interesting sculptures in the garden.

Roquebrune, Cap Martin and Menton

The avenue Princesse Grace runs along the coastal strip at the eastern end of Monaco and overlooks a series of recent sport and beach developments, but the main road is the boulevard d'Italie which becomes the *Corniche Inférieure* again as it sweeps round the bay towards Roquebrune and Cap Martin. There has been much hotel and tourist development on the coast but the old town of **Roquebrune**, set back from the road on a hilltop, is a maze of narrow streets and stairways with a very early castle at its summit.

History of Roquebrune

Dating originally from the 10C, when it was erected by the Dukes of Ventimiglia to repulse the Saracens, this stronghold was extended by the Grimaldis who took control of the area in 1308. In this early period the fortress enclosed the village but in the 15C the population was ousted to establish a proper castle. Thereafter a series of towers and battlements was erected, some of which survive to this day as heavy masses of stone rising out of the rock.

Not all of it is particularly historic, however. By the late 19C the castle and much of the village was an abandoned ruin having been sold off in 1861 by the Grimaldis to raise cash. It was in this state that it was bought by a wealthy Englishman, Sir William Ingram, in 1911. Over the next decade he rebuilt some of the towers and walls without paying too much attention to the original design or layout. On his death in 1926 Ingram bequeathed the castle to the town.

❖ Information and accommodation

🛈 20 avenue P.-Doumer (☎ 04 93 35 62 87).

Hotels. Accommodation here can be as expensive as anywhere on the coast, especially if you wish to stay at the spectacular *Vista Palace* (☎ 04 93 35 01 50) on a high cliff by the *Grande Corniche*. A more reasonable option is the *Westminster* at 14 avenue Louis-Laurens (☎ 04 93 35 00 68) near the beach and the Monaco border.

The castle or **Donjon** (☎ 04 93 35 07 22: **open** daily 10.00–12.00 and 14.00–19.00 in summer; closes 17.00 and Tues in winter) remains one of the most striking monuments on the Riviera. The so-called baronial apartments on the upper floors are unimpressive but there is a spectacular view from the artillery platform at the top out over the rooftops of the old village to the sea.

Roquebrune holds two famous annual festivals on Good Friday and 5 August. The latter, fulfilling a vow made in 1468 after the town was delivered from plague, is quite an elaborate affair in which the townspeople re-enact the Passion of Christ in the streets of Roquebrune. The same cast and costumes are used on Good Friday to portray the entombment of Christ, again through the streets of the town. Details of these can be obtained from the tourist office.

Like Roquebrune, **Cap-Martin** was a virtually abandoned piece of ground until 1889 when an English entrepreneur, M. Calvin White, bought it with a view to developing an exclusive resort and convalescent centre. Its success was ensured when two empresses, Eugénie of France and Elisabeth (Sissi) of Austria, began to frequent the cape and built houses there. From this it grew in popularity and attracted many of the leading figures from British society and the arts. W.B. Yeats died here and Winston Churchill was a frequent visitor. The cape is studded with luxurious villas, many of which were designed by the Danish architect G.-H. Tersling (1857–1920). A notable exception is the severely Modernist villa **E-1027** designed in 1926 by Eileen Gray. Her close friend Le Corbusier was a regular guest and it was while swimming from the rocks here in August 1965 that the architect drowned. He is buried in the local cemetery and the coastal path, which offers a lovely view over the sea, is named after him.

Menton

Menton is the last resort on the French Riviera, a title that suggests more than just its proximity to the Italian frontier. Sheltered in a beautiful, wide bay it has the warmest climate all year round, which made it particularly attractive to northern Europeans. This was where the affluent sick from London, Berlin and Stockholm flocked to spend their winters in the late 19C and early 20C. The often quoted epigram 'Cannes is for living, Monte Carlo for gambling and Menton for dying' pretty well sums it up.

History of Menton
It was not always so but, as a minor fishing-village and lemon-growing district in the Grimaldi territories, Menton had little of note in its early history. The real celebrity of the town began in the 19C, and arguably only in 1861 when an English doctor, James Henry Bennet, published a book recommending this part of the coast for the treatment of consumption. *Winter and Spring on the Shores of the Mediterranean* was soon translated into several languages and by 1875 there were over 30 hotels in Menton, two Anglican churches and a foreign convalescent community of over 1600. Thereafter, Menton became a desperate refuge for some of the wealthiest and most famous consumptives in Europe. Robert Louis Stevenson came here twice, as did D.H. Lawrence, and Queen Victoria wintered here in the 1880s with her haemophiliac son Leopold and her cantankerous Scottish retainer John Brown. A lasting symbol of this royal presence is the statue of the queen which was only unveiled in 1939. The Russian nobility also favoured Menton, particularly Prince Youssoupoff, who achieved some fame as the assassin of Rasputin.

With so many visitors suffering from an incurable wasting disease it is not surprising that Menton had a high mortality rate and the local cemetery is punctuated with foreign names. Aubrey Beardsley (1872–98) arrived in November 1897 and died just four months later after a passionate religious conversion which saw him destroy many of his drawings. Katherine Mansfield spent her last years here, raging against her fate at the small Villa Isola Bella, and the Spanish novelist Blasco Ibàñez retired to Menton where he died in 1928.

❖ *Information, accommodation and food*

🛈 Palais de l'Europe, 8 avenue Boyer (☎ 04 93 57 57 00) with branches at 5 rue Ciapetta (☎ 04 93 10 33 66) near the harbour and at the coach station on Esplanade du Carei (☎ 04 93 28 43 27) to the northwest above the Jardin de Bioves.

Hotels. Accommodation in Menton is reasonably priced for the coast but often difficult to find in summer. The *Napoléon* at 29 porte de France (☎ 04 93 35 89 50) is one of the best while the *Chambord* at 6 avenue Boyer (☎ 04 93 35 94 19) and *Le Magali* at 10 rue Villarey (☎ 04 93 35 73 78) are more reasonable. *The Bristol* at 24 avenue Carnot (☎ 04 93 57 54 32) and *Claridges* at 39 avenue de Verdun (☎ 04 93 35 72 53) are also good and the names, at least, are a reminder of past times. The *Pension Beauregard* at 10 rue Albert 1er (☎ 04 93 35 74 08) is the best in the cheaper range.

Restaurants. Dining out in Menton is surprisingly unimpressive: *L'Auberge des Santons* on the Colline de l'Annonciade (☎ 04 93 35 94 10) is probably the best restaurant while *Le Chaudron* at 28 rue St-Michel (☎ 04 93 35 90 25) and *de la Poste* on impasse Bellecour (☎ 04 93 57 13 79) can be recommended.

Menton has long since lost the atmosphere of the sanatorium but attempts to make it a younger, livelier resort have had only limited success. Nowadays it is a curious blend of the genteel and the modern that is pleasantly diverting in contrast to its brasher neighbours in the west. Even the beaches are rarely as packed and noisy as you might expect for this part of the world and the entire seafront is backed by a promenade fringed with palm trees and other exotic plants.

Behind this, the old town is a real gem worth exploring on foot. Begin by ascending the flight of steps from the quai Bonaparte near the harbour which leads up to the place de l'Eglise, a beautiful square decorated with mosaics. Open-air concerts are held here during the music festival in July and August. Dominating the square or *parvis* is the painted façade and campanile of the **Eglise St-Michel**, the 17C parish church that stands out in the skyline of the old town. In contrast to the pale painted exterior, the interior presents a sump-tuous display of rich colours and textures piled up in a truly Baroque ensemble. As well as the traditional combination of marble, frescoes, altarpieces and stucco decoration, on important occasions the nave and chapels are draped with old silk damask giving an overwhelming effect of faded opulence and High Church ritual.

A few steps to the west of the *parvis* is another 17C church, the beautiful chapel of La Conception, built by the Penitents Blancs in 1685 although substantially restored after repeated damage. At the very top of the hill, amid the remains of the 12C–13C castle, is the **town cemetery** from which there are excellent views over the whole area. Described by Guy de Maupassant as 'the aristocratic cemetery of Europe', the tombs carry the names of many prominent Russian and British families. One of the best kept is that of William Webb-Ellis who, as a schoolboy in the 1820s, first ran carrying the football and thus invented the game of rugby.

Of the various picturesque streets in this district the most notable is the rue Longue, once the main street where the town mansions of all the leading citizens were located. No. 123, in fact, was the Prince's palace dating from the 16C–17C and it still has vestiges of its earlier existence. It was in use as the town hall until the 19C.

The modern and shopping centre of Menton is below the old town to the west along the rue St-Michel and rue de la République. This has been taken over by fashionable boutiques but there is some evidence of the traditional activities of the town in the nearby markets around the place du Marché. Menton's fish-market in the rue des Marins is still supplied by the local boats which fish for sardines and anchovies off the coast in spring and early summer. Beside the main harbour at the bottom of the quai de Monleon is a small orange bastion built in 1636 to ward off the French. This is now the **Musée Jean-Cocteau** (☎ 04 93 35 49 71: **open** Wed–Mon 10.00–12.00 and 14.00–18.00; closed Tues), devoted to the painter, poet and film-maker and containing a selection of his drawings, ceramics, tapestries and stage designs as well as a large mosaic of a salamander which he installed in 1962.

Cocteau was declared an honorary Mentonnais largely due to a rather odd commission from the mayor. In 1957, despite his reputation as a drug addict, homosexual and Nazi collaborator, he was invited to decorate the **Salle des Mariages** in the Hôtel de Ville on the rue de la République. The completed work is as absurd and amusing as you might expect. Within this formal 19C building, largely occupied by civic offices, Cocteau has depicted a saucy local fisherman with his Niçois bride and Orpheus and Eurydice in bright pastel colours reminiscent of an ice-cream parlour. The entrance fee gives access to the Musée Jean-Cocteau (see above).

To the rear of the Hôtel de Ville, on the rue Loredan-Larchey, is the **Musée du Préhistoire régionale** (☎ 04 93 35 84 64: **open** Wed–Mon 10.00–12.00 and 14.00–18.00; closed Tues), a local history museum with archaeological collections including the 30,000 year old skull of 'Menton Man' discovered in 1884. There are a few pictures here but the main art gallery is housed in the **Palais Carnolès** (☎ 04 93 35 49 71: **open** Wed–Mon 10.00–12.00 and 14.00–18.00; closed Tues), a delightful 18C mansion at the extreme west end of the town on the avenue de la Madone. Built in 1717 as a summer palace for Prince Antoine of Monaco, it was altered and remodelled as a casino and private residence before being turned into an art gallery in 1969. The collection of paintings is interesting if unspectacular and there are some notable early French and Italian pictures. There is also a group of modern works, mostly from the School of Paris, which were bequeathed to the town in 1959 by Wakefield Mori, a wealthy English resident.

One of the most attractive features of the Palais Carnolès is the beautiful garden which is typical of Menton as a whole. Not only are the streets decorated with exotic plants and palm trees but there are numerous public gardens which take advantage of the climate to cultivate rich displays of exotic plants and flowers. The most spectacular of these is the **Jardins Bioves** stretching back from the promenade du Soleil behind the casino in an overwhelming and, at times, oppressive onslaught of colour and scent. Menton is widely known as the lemon capital of the Mediterranean and every year in February there is a *Fête du Citron* in which elaborate floats decorated with thousands of oranges and lemons parade round these gardens and out into the streets of the town.

Of the other notable gardens perhaps the finest are two personal creations in the affluent residential area of Garavan to the east of the old town. The **Jardin Botanique** or Val Rameh (☎ 04 93 35 86 72; **open** 10.00–12.30 and 15.00–18.00 May–Sept; 10.00–12.30 and 14.00–17.00 Oct–Apr) on avenue St-Jacques, created by a Scottish woman, Miss Campbell, in the early years of the 20C, is a demonstration of the range of exotic plants which can be cultivated in this exceptional climate. But the garden that is most admired by the Mentonnais is the **Domaine des Colombières**, designed and laid out as an act of devotion by the artist Ferdinand Bac (1859–1952). This is a true Mediterranean garden, slightly decaying, with terraces and cypress banks traversed by pathways and occasional statues in a style intended to evoke memories of Classical poetry. The villa has frescoes of mythological scenes by Bac but it is private property and not always open to the public. This domaine may be neglected but it has remained intact. The same cannot be said for the house of the Spanish writer Blasco Ibàñez (1867–1928) who lived in Garavan in the 1920s where he created a writers' garden at the Villa Fontana-Rosa, which has now been divided into private apartments (guided tours by appointments ☎ 04 93 10 33 66). Katherine Mansfield also spent her last years in Garavan in the Villa Isola Bella on the street now named after her. The house has a small museum and a plaque recording her statement in a letter of 1920, 'when I die you will find the words Isola Bella inscribed in poker-work on my heart.'

The last French territory before the border with Italy is the promenade Reine-Astrid, named after the Queen of the Belgians who was killed in a traffic accident in 1935. Nowadays the border—once fiercely guarded and fought over—does not mean very much because Menton has chosen to unite its commercial and civic affairs with Ventimiglia as a gesture of international collaboration. To this day you can still find remnants of the Maginot Line which stretched down to the sea here but this reminder of the old Europe is unmarked.

Into the mountains

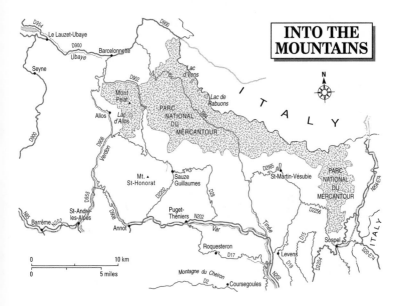

27 · To Haute-Provence along the Var

The hinterland behind Nice is dominated by the rugged chain of rocks known as the pre-Alps, stretching north for some 50km before crossing the Parc National du Mercantour and joining the Alps proper. This territory of hard, crystalline rock is pierced by huge cracks and gorges through which the river courses of the Var, the Vésubie and the Paillon make their way down to the sea. It is a dramatic landscape, snow-covered for much of the year and partially forested, but even this is ravaged occasionally by fires which break out in the hot summer months. Amid this hard terrain there are many impressive sights and the area is dotted with ancient hill-villages perched on the most improbable ledges.

The best routes to visit the area are those along the course of the rivers. The main road, following the line of the Var, is the easiest and leads quickly into the heart of the mountainous region. This is an ambitious journey if taken in its entirety and leads eventually to the very northern villages of Auron and Barcelonnette. It is not essential to see this route to the end, however, and there are many attractive spots such as Entrevaux or Utelle along the way to make the journey worthwhile. Other routes offer circuits round the mountain villages of the Paillon and Mont Chauve which are within reasonable distance of the coast. An alternative to driving on this area is to take the train, the Chemin de Fer de Provence, which runs between Nice and Digne. This is undoubtedly a more relaxing way to experience the landscape of the pre-Alps.

Nice to Barcelonnette and the pre-Alpes

Leaving Nice by the N202 or route de Grenoble in the west of the city (by the airport), you travel north past the new market complexes which have spread out to the suburbs. For a taste of the wilder countryside you could try a detour by the D2565 to the right above Plan-du-Var before the defile de Chaudan. This road leads along the impressive **Gorges de la Vésubie** to St-Jean-La-Rivière. From here the D32 winds up to the substantial village of **Utelle** with its handsome 16C church in the main square. This has some interesting carvings including a frieze of the life of St Véran over the doorway. Some 6km further along this road, with a spectacular outlook over the whole of the Alpes Maritimes, is Madone d'Utelle, an early medieval chapel which was largely reconstructed in 1806 as a pilgrimage centre. The valley of the Vésubie has some impressive views particularly in its upper reaches but if you are prepared to travel this far you would find more of interest along the main N202 as it sweeps westwards to Entrevaux.

Beyond the hydro-electric schemes at Plan-du-Var, the N202 enters some of the hardest terrain in Provence, where solid rock faces apparently split apart to create steep gorges with only the narrowest of passes. Following almost any route from here will lead you through some spectacular sights in which the road seems either balanced on the edge of a steep chasm or squeezed alongside the riverbank by sheer cliffs. Even the main road continues through the narrow defile de Chaudan and beyond this, by the D2205 to the north, there are a series of similar gorges leading up into the mountains. This is perhaps the most remote and, at times, the eeriest part of the Alpes Maritimes but the road leads through the Parc National du Mercantour to Auron and St-Etienne-de-Tinée, truly distinctive and unusual mountain villages, and yet further to Barcelonnette.

Remaining on the main N202 to the west you will follow the line of the river Var, passing near a series of interesting villages such as Malaussène and Villars-sur-Var. The main point of interest along this stretch, however, is **Entrevaux**, once a border town between Provence and Savoy, which explains the impressive fortifications that confront you from the opposite side of the river. Having been taken twice by enemy forces in the 16C, Entrevaux was chosen as the pivotal position in Louis XIV's defences and in 1693 his architect Vauban was directed to construct the ramparts and twin-towered **Porte Royale** that commands the bridge. The tourist office just beside the gates has details of various activities and excursions in the area.

The citadel at Entrevaux

Within the walls many of the early buildings have survived unrestored and, as you walk through the narrow streets, there is a wonderful sensation of entering a medieval town enclosed and protected by the ever-present battlements. The former cathedral church of **Notre-Dame** has some Romanesque and Gothic remains but the main part of the building and the sculpted façade date from the town's expansion in the 17C. The furnishings and altarpieces, including a fine *Assomption* by François Mimault, are also from this period, offering an appropriate context for the festival of Baroque music held in August. By contrast and, given the streetscape, somewhat surprisingly there is a motorcycle museum in the rue des Douaniers. The most dramatic feature of the town, however, is the citadel, or at least the approach ramps which zig-zag up the hill at the rear to the fort. From the top there are excellent views out over the hills and up to the Alps.

ℹ Port Royale (☎ 04 93 05 46 73).

Entrevaux and Puget-Théniers are at the foot of a series of rugged mountain groups (Mont St-Honorat, the Dôme de Barrot and Les Clots) which are separated by spectacular gorges. The most impressive of these is the **Gorges du Cians** which can be followed on the D28 leading north from the N202 to the east of Puget-Théniers. Not only is the landscape breathtaking, a journey in this area allows you to visit many village churches which house some fascinating treasures. **Lieuche**, just off the road to the east, has one of the finest examples of the School of Nice in Louis Bréa's polyptych of the *Annonciation* (1499) while Beuil, a *village perché* at the head of the gorge, has some interesting 17C altarpieces.

The **Gorges de Daluis**, on the D902 to the west of Entrevaux, is similarly spectacular and presents an exciting prospect in the village of **Daluis**, itself on a tall spur of rock. This was regarded as the northern limit of olive-growing culture, for many the defining feature of the Mediterranean lands and, therefore, the boundary of Provence. It is worth proceeding further north into this territory, however, where you find a curious combination of Alpine and Mediterranean elements in the architecture, the way of life and even the landscape.

Colmars-les-Alpes, on the D2202 and D78 from Guillaumes, north of Daluis, is a small fortified town set within the wooded slopes of the pre-Alps.

History of Colmars-les-Alpes

There was a Roman outpost here and, in fact, the name Colmars derives from a temple to Mars built on the nearby hill. In the late Middle Ages, however, it became a stronghold on the border between Provence and Savoy and thereafter its defences were repeatedly strengthened and extended. François I was responsible for the 16C ramparts that encircle the town but the two castles, the Fort de Savoie (**open** in afternoons in summer) and the largely ruined Fort de France, were designed by Vauban in 1693.

Despite its martial history, the interior of the old town is very calm and relaxed with a series of squares and fountains to divert the aimless pedestrian. This whole area is something of a refuge from the more aggressive pace of the south and the tourist office has details of various walks in the hills and woods around

❖ *Information and accommodation*

🇮 By the Porte de Savoie (☎ 04 92 83 41 92).

Hotels. Accommodation in Colmars is limited but there are two hotels, *Le Vauban* (☎ 04 92 83 40 49) and *Le Chamois* (☎ 04 92 83 43 29). Allos has been developed as a winter resort and has more hotels and *gîtes* which can be booked through the tourist office there (☎ 04 92 83 02 81).

Colmars. The **Lac d'Allos**, one of the highest lakes in France, and the vallée du Verdon are both recommended for simple or strenuous treks, as are the routes into the western edge of the Parc du Mercantour for their pervasive solitude.

Further north on the D908, amid the mountains and ski stations of the Grand Berard range, you reach **Barcelonnette**, perhaps the most curious and unexpected place in the whole of northern Provence.

History of Barcelonnette

The town takes its name from Barcelona in Catalonia, ancestral home of Raymond Bérenger V, who established this settlement in 1231 as a bastion on the northern border of his territory. He and his successors were overreaching themselves at this point and in 1388 the town fell to the Counts of Savoy, under whom it remained until 1713. Throughout this long period it was repeatedly attacked, sometimes with devastating effects. In 1628 the Marquis d'Uxelles led a French force which set a raging fire that destroyed most of the town centre. After its return to France there was a major rebuilding programme which explains the unusual mixture of medieval and 18C–20C buildings.

The genuinely curious aspect of Barcelonnette, however, derives from the emigration of many of its citizens in the 19C. The lead was taken by the three Arnaud brothers who in 1821 left for Mexico, where they established a textile works and trading empire. Soon they were joined by others from this region until, by one estimate, there were some 5000 'Barcelonnettes' in Mexico. The effect of this on their native town came largely from the returning emigrants who, having made their fortunes in the new world, chose to build substantial villas and farmhouses in the Mexican style along the valley towards Jaussières.

❖ *Information and accommodation*

🇮 Place F. Mistral (☎ 04 92 81 04 71).

Hotels. Of the local hotels, the *Grande Epervière* at 18 rue des Trois-Frères-Arnaud (☎ 04 92 81 00 70) is one of the best, while *L'Azteca* at 3 rue François-Arnaud (☎ 04 92 81 46 36) is, as its name suggests, in one of the Mexican-style houses.

There are further examples of this Mexican heritage in the **Musée de la Vallée** (☎ 04 92 81 27 15; **open** daily 10.00–12.00 and 15.00–19.00 July–Aug; afternoons only Sept–June), which has displays of Mexican folk art, in the restaurants specialising in Tex-Mex food, and even in the names and signs which lend this remote town a sort of hybrid exoticism. One of the streets, for example, is named avenue Porfirio-Diaz.

Nowadays Barcelonnette is a centre for the various ski resorts in the area, although it continues to attract many visitors all year round for walking trips in the mountains and the Parc National du Mercantour. Details of these are available from the tourist office, which can also book accommodation.

A circuit of the Paillon

This shorter excursion explores the Paillon basin, a depression between the foothills to the northeast of Nice, into which the three branches of the river Paillon drain off the melted snow from the upper mountains.

There are many tortuous routes through this area but you can make a circuit by leaving Nice on the route de Turin, joining the D2204 past La Trinité and then the D15 past Contes. The fortified village of **Contes** has expanded into a substantial centre for this district but it retains some of its historic appeal as a medieval market for olives and ceramics. The large 16C church of the Magdalene has a good retable by François Bréa, although missing its central panel, and outside there is an elegant Renaissance fountain. Contes was once plagued by caterpillars which were exorcised by the Bishop of Nice in 1508, an event celebrated in the *Fête-Dieu* at the end of May when small lamps made from snail shells are lit in every window.

On the opposite side of the river (by the D815) and overlooking the valley from its high position is **Châteauneuf de Contes**, a historic medieval village that traces its origins back to an outpost of the Roman Empire. The 11C Romanesque church, which is on the site of a pagan shrine, has some interesting sculpted and painted decoration. Beyond the main village (2km) are the remains of the oxymoronic 'Old Châteauneuf', a fortified stronghold that was finally abandoned after the incursions of Revolutionary armies in 1803. The ruins of the church, citadel and houses can be explored, usually in complete isolation.

The D15 continues to **Coaraze**, one of the most remote and therefore unspoilt villages in the area. It is also one of the most attractive with a series of narrow vaulted streets winding up to the 14C church at the top of the rock. The traditional crafts of this village include ceramics, which has attracted some outsiders including Jean Cocteau, but it has retained a distinctive character and way of life. One legend attached to the village is particularly macabre. When Queen Jeanne came to Coaraze for Christmas mass her enemies murdered her two young sons and made soup from the corpses. Returning from mass the queen supped the soup before being told of the contents. Driven mad she fled into the night and cursed the village.

After Coaraze the D15 winds round from the Paillon de Contes towards another branch of the river, the Paillon de l'Escarène on the eastern side of the basin. This stretch of road is not for the faint-hearted. Crossing the Col de St-Roch it rises to 1000m, descending sharply by the D2566 in a series of convoluted hairpins with a steep drop alongside. At the end of this stretch is the village of **Lucéram**, a true medieval complex of streets arranged in tiers along a narrow ridge overlooking the valley. Despite its isolation Lucéram seems to have been a crossroads on the old mule tracks through the mountains and many religious orders had foundations here. The church of Ste-Marguerite at the apex of the village dates from the 16C but the interior was decorated some 200 years later in an elaborate Italian Rococo manner. There are also some interesting treasures including several 15C altarpieces by the School of Nice, one in particular by Louis Bréa.

From Lucéram the D2566 follows the river to **L'Escarène**, another village of unexpected variety which benefited from Italian influence in the 17C and 18C. The parish church of St-Pierre and its attendant chapels have some rich Baroque painting and stuccowork on the interior. The D21 takes up the line of the Paillon from here, running south through some impressive gorges before reaching two of the most famous villages in this area. Peille and Peillon are closer to Nice than the villages of the high valley and, as a result, they show more signs of colonisation by the business class of Nice. Nevertheless, they are both very picturesque.

Of the two, **Peille** is perhaps the more independent, largely due to the rougher terrain of the 'badlands' which stretch out towards Blausasc in the west. The village still has a number of buildings dating from the 14C–16C, the finest of which are in the place de la Colle where the medieval court of justice sat. The name la Colle may refer to the hangman's noose. The Romanesque parish church has some interesting treasures including a retable of 1579 by the Niçois painter Honoré Bertone and a picture with a view of Peille in medieval times. Contact the hospice next door for access.

Peillon, 14km south of Peille and also off the main road (this time on the D121), is an archetypal *village perché*, huddled on a rock spur overlooking a valley of olives and pines. The main street is a winding ascent to the church and square at the top, from where you can look out over the whole area. Near the entrance to the village is the **Chapelle des Pénitents-Blancs** which has a fascinating group of frescoes of the *Passion* from 1485 by the painter Giovanni Canavesio. One scene, for which there is a counterpart at La Brigue, depicts Judas hanging from a tree with devils being pulled from his abdomen. From Peillon there are several walks into the countryside. The more ambitious can reach La Turbie, some 18km to the south, although it does mean crossing the motorway. Another arduous walk to Peille in the north reputedly follows an old Roman road.

A circuit of Mont Chauve

For those with less time or perseverence this 51km excursion into the hills behind Nice runs round Mont Chauve (Bald Mountain), the dome-like mountain immediately to the north of the city. The circuit can be completed in two to three hours but it provides a taste of the whole region, taking in gorges, modest mountain passes and several historic villages.

Leaving Nice by the avenue de Gairaut and D14 towards Aspremont, it is worth making a slight detour just beyond the motorway to the Cascade de Gairault off the road to the left. This waterfall is, in fact, the Vésubie canal pouring into a large basin to provide the freshwater for Nice. There is also a good view over the city from this point. **Aspremont**, the first of the hill-villages, forms a series of concentric circles around its rock pinnacle. There was once an important castle at the summit but this was demolished in 1792 leaving a good open viewing area from which to survey the valley and coast. There are two churches; the 13C–16C Gothic church of St-Jacques and a smaller 17C chapel dedicated to St-Claude at the foot of the village. Claude was invoked against the plague, a recurrent danger in these parts which devastated many isolated communities. An earlier village nearby called Villevieille was abandoned after an outbreak in 1327. The ruins include a Romanesque chapel which can be visited although there is not much to see.

After Aspremont take the D719 over the pass between Mont Chauve and Mont Cima to **Tourrette-Levens**. This *village perché* has been swollen with incomers from Nice with the result that a new town has developed at the foot of the rock leaving the old town partly abandoned. The 18C church has an altarpiece of the *Pietà* (1624) by Jan Rocca and the old village with its restored castle (private) offers good views over the surrounding hills. **Falicon**, 7km south of here through the Gorges du Gabre, is a smaller village with narrow winding streets that was the setting for Jules Romain's novel *La Douceur de la vie*. Queen Victoria liked Falicon and her visits to take tea in the village are recalled by the restaurant named *Au thé de la Reine*. About 2km southwest of the village at **Ratapignata** on the D114 there is a curious pyramid that was discovered in 1803. This covers the entrance to a cave that is thought to have been an ancient shrine. Its precise date and function are unknown but it remains an intriguing site in this landscape.

Falicon is almost on the outskirts of Nice but before returning to the suburbs it is worth taking the D214 north of the village up to the top of **Mont Chauve**. There is an abandoned fort on this bald summit but the real attraction is the panoramic view to the Alps in the north and over the coastal resorts and Mediterranean in the south.

28 · The Roya and the Vallée des Merveilles

The valley of the Roya to the north of Nice and Menton is a curious area not at all like the rest of Provence. Running parallel to the Italian border and leading up to the great rugged wilderness of the Parc National du Mercantour, it seems closer to Alpine regions and this is borne out in the pattern of the villages, the architecture and even the dialect which are all quite different from those of the gentler districts near the sea. The valley has also had an unusual history during the last two centuries which has no doubt contributed to its exceptional character. As a result this is one of the more unusual and, at times, challenging routes but it offers a refreshing alternative to the familiar pursuits of the coast.

History of the Roya Valley
When the county of Nice was ceded to France in 1860, the Italian prime minister Cavour held back the Roya valley as a royal hunting-ground for the king, Victor Emmanuel II. It therefore remained a part of Italy, despite its obvious links with the surrounding territory, and became the scene of much political activity during Mussolini's reign. It was not until after the Second World War that the issue was addressed and, following a plebiscite

in 1947, the new border was fixed at the watershed of the mountains to the east. This restored the three villages of Tende, St-Dalmas and La Brigue to France and unified a region that seems to combine many features from all the surrounding countries.

There are two different ways of seeing the full length of the valley; by car, which offers greater freedom and a lively if exhausting drive, or **by rail** on the breathtaking line that runs between Nice and Cuneo or Turin, one of the great railway engineering feats of the 20C. Between Nice and the Italian border at Col de Tende there are over thirty tunnels including three which complete a full 360° circle within the rock to emerge hundreds of feet higher up on the mountain. The line was built in the 1920s but it was badly bombed during the war and only reopened in 1978; many locals believe its reconstruction was deliberately hindered by politicians in Nice who saw it as a distraction from the development of tourism on the coast. It now offers a more relaxed way to travel through some spectacular mountain scenery and has a few genuine oddities along the way, such as the oversized station at St-Dalmas (see p 308).

Menton to Saorge

By car, the most direct route is from Menton through the winding Carei river valley on the D2566 to Sospel. On this first stage, however, you can take the parallel D24 on the eastern side of the river to **Castellar**, a picturesque village on a plateau dating back to the 15C. There was an earlier village on the rock nearby but it was abandoned for this more favourable setting, which allowed the residents to lay out the streets on a rational plan. Some of the original arcades and corner towers survive from this early piece of urban planning. The small road out of Castellar to the north rejoins the D2566 from where you can proceed past the new village of Castillon (the old village was destroyed in 1944) and through the first of the major tunnels towards **Sospel**.

History of Sospel

Standing at the confluence of two rivers and two valleys, Sospel has been an important crossroads since the Middle Ages. By the 16C it had a population of 8000 as well as several palaces, churches and centres of learning. At the end of the 19C Sospel became a fashionable resort due to the clarity of the air which was felt to be invigorating. The Austrian Emperor Franz-Joseph, for example, stayed in the *Golf-Hôtel* designed by the popular Danish architect Tersling.

❖ *Information and accommodation*

🛈 Vieux Pont (☎ 04 93 04 15 80).

Hotels. There are few hotels in the area: the *Hôtel de la Gare* (☎ 04 93 04 00 14) is reasonable but the *Hôtel des Etrangers* (☎ 04 93 00 04 09) is better and has a good restaurant.

Changed priorities and easier transport through this rugged territory mean that Sospel is now mainly a summer resort but there are echoes of its former self at every turn. The most famous landmark is the 11C **Vieux Pont** across the Bévéra with its distinctive tower or toll-gate over the middle pier. This was partially demolished by the retreating German forces in 1944 but has been faithfully restored. The bridge is in many ways the main axis since Sospel is divided by the river into two separate districts; St-Nicholas, the medieval village on the north bank, and the 'new' town on the south. In fact, both districts have a good selection of old houses and arcaded streets to wander among. The most delightful and unexpected landmark in the town is the **Eglise St-Michel**, its elaborate Baroque façade (17C) contrasting with the much earlier Romanesque tower. Inside there are several fine altarpieces including an *Assumption of the Virgin* (1520) by the Niçois painter François Bréa.

The *Golf-Hôtel* is now an apartment block but the village is still something of an outdoor centre and a base from which to embark on walks and excursions to the surrounding areas. Mont Agaisen, overlooking the town, is the closest ascent but the valley of the Bévéra and the Gorges de Piaon are not far to the northwest and lead up to the extensive Forêt de Turini.

Just south of the town on the D2204 is the **Fort St-Roch** (☎ 04 93 04 00 70; guided tours Tues–Sun 14.00–18.00 in summer; closed Mon; Sat, Sun only in winter), an underground bastion built in the 1930s as part of the chain of defences known as the Maginot Line. This complex of passageways and subterranean chambers, which housed over 200 soldiers, now serves as a military museum devoted to the destructive campaigns in this area during the Second World War.

The D2204 continues northeast across the Col de Brouis after which it descends to join the main road from Ventimiglia as it follows the railway line along the banks of the Roya. If not speeding to the upper valley, it is worth turning south on the N204 for a couple of kilometres to visit the village of **Breil-sur-Roya**. This is a modest manufacturing centre but it has, among other things, an impressive and very ornate 18C Baroque church dedicated to Sancta-Maria-in-Albis. Breil was previously on the border between Italy and France and offered an opportunity to display the achievements of the Fascist state. It therefore has a rather oversized railway station which now serves as a local museum with an emphasis on ecology and transport (☎ 04 93 04 99 76: **open** daily 10.00–12.00 and 15.30–18.30 July, Aug; Sat, Sun only Sept, Oct, May, June; closed Nov–Apr).

Proceeding north, the N204 weaves through the series of narrow gorges that were once the haunt of bandits and sorcerers before emerging to a wonderful view of **Saorge**, stretched out improbably along the steep hillside above. From the road it looks inaccessible and, in fact, you must either take an earlier turn-off or drive on to the next village of Fontan before turning back to Saorge. Even then, the car has to be parked at the edge of the village leaving visitors to explore the steep streets and piled-up houses on foot.

Although there are traces of earlier settlement, Saorge was created by the Dukes of Savoy in the Middle Ages as a stronghold to control the pass south from the Col de Tende. As such, it was virtually impregnable and it was not until 1794 that it was first taken by Napoleon's army. There are some remains of the old fortifications but it is the narrow streets and pastel-coloured houses, most of which date from the 16C–18C, that are most interesting. So steep is the setting that you can enter a building at street level only to find that you are on the fourth or fifth floor on the side overlooking the valley. There are also several churches of note. The parish church of St-Sauveur in the centre of the village dates from the 15C but it was extensively remodelled and decorated during the 18C in a vigorous Italianate manner. To the eastern side is the 17C convent church of the Franciscans, offering a good view from its terrace, while below the village is the isolated Romanesque sanctuary of the Madone del Poggio, a curious building with a tall belltower and some 15C altarpieces and decoration. There are no hotels in Saorge but *L'Auberge de la Roya* (☎ 04 93 04 50 19) in Fontan to the north has rooms and a good restaurant.

The Parc National du Mercantour

Returning to the main road at Fontan, the N204 proceeds north through the Gorges de Bergue and emerges into a broader valley before **St-Dalmas-de-Tende**, another border village which became the focus of much activity in the 1930s. This was the spot chosen by Mussolini as his triumphal entry to France and he proceeded to build an oversized neo-Classical railway station with powerful rusticated stonework. It seems rather ridiculous now that the border has been pushed back leaving the pompous monument as a sort of folly in this small community. St-Dalmas is not deserted, however, because this is the main point of departure for visits to the **Vallée des Merveilles** in the Parc National du Mercantour.

History of the Parc

It was at the end of the 19C that the English botanist Clarence Bicknell began documenting a series of engraved marks that had been discovered several centuries earlier in the valley between Mont Bégo and Grand Capelet to the west of St-Dalmas. After a lifetime's work he had identified some 14,000 designs scratched into the rock, all seemingly done as part of a cult by some prehistoric tribe. Following Bicknell's death in 1918 (from eating a poisonous mushroom) an Italian scholar, Carlo Conti, took up the work and identified a further 20,000 markings. The total now stands at over 100,000 designs, all executed within this remote valley miles from the coast and the other population centres of pre-history.

The designs are mostly abstract but specialists and amateurs have identified a series of stylised animals and figures, including one group thought to represent a sort of 'first coupling' along the lines of Adam and Eve. Another theory relates the designs to the Mediterranean bull cult, since the name Bégo seems close to an Indo-European word meaning mountain of the bull god. The dating of the designs is similarly unclear. While most theories put the period of their creation as Bronze Age, the possible dates vary from c 1700 BC to c 1000 BC, and they may have been produced over several hundred years spanning the full range of these proposals.

It is not easy to visit the Vallée des Merveilles but it is an unforgettable experience, made all the more memorable by the arduous journey and various difficulties to be overcome. As it is in a national park subject to certain restrictions there are only two ways to get there on your own. You can walk from Lac des

Mesches, the closest point on a public road, to the refuge at the foot of the valley, a journey of about 2–3hrs. From here you can explore the main part of the valley to the north in the company of a guide. Some care should be taken since this is fairly high (over 2500m) and likely to test even experienced walkers. It may be advisable to allow two days for the trip, spending the night at one of the hostels which can be booked in advance. Otherwise you can start from Val Casterine further north from Lac des Mesches on the D91, which is an equally if not more arduous route. There are a few hotels at Casterino such as *Les Melèzes* (☎ 04 93 04 64 95) or *La Marie-Madeleine* (☎ 04 93 04 65 93).

The alternative is to take one of the jeep excursions from St-Dalmas or Tende, led by a guide and lasting for a full day. This method is definitely easier and ensures that you will see some of the more important sights but it can be expensive and lacks the sense of personal discovery that walkers generally experience. Full information on travel to and within the park is available from the tourist information offices at Tende or Nice.

Just 3km east of St-Dalmas-de-Tende on the D43 is **La Brigue**, an unspoiled village of cobbled streets and stone houses built using the local green schist rock. There are three interesting church buildings here, all grouped together in the main square. The two chapels dedicated to the Annunciation and the Assumption were both founded by the Pénitents-Blancs in the 18C and each has some good stucco decoration. Standing between them is the 15C–16C parish church of St-Martin built in a late Romanesque style derived from Lombardy. This church is well furnished and has a good collection of painted altarpieces by artists of the School of Nice, including several works by François Bréa.

There is, however, a more remarkable group of paintings in the nearby **Chapelle de Notre-Dame-des-Fontaines**, 4km to the west at the end of the wooded D143. Ask at the Mairie for the key before going down the road. On entering you will see one of the liveliest and most important fresco cycles in Provence. Two artists were at work here. In the choir and on the archway before it are scenes from the *Life of the Virgin* painted in the 1470s by the obscure Italian painter Jean Baleison. Slightly later and much more vigorous are the scenes from the *Passion* round the walls, by another Italian, Giovanni Canevesio. At his finest, for example in the *Crucifixion* and *Last Judgement*, there is an expressiveness and angularity to the figures that is rare in Franco-Italian painting but more often associated with contemporary German art. Note the scene of *Judas Hanged*, his stomach ripped open and a spiky demon dragging out the small figure personifying the victim's soul (compare the similar scene at Peillon, p 304).

The road north from St-Dalmas-de-Tende previously culminated in **Tende** itself, the largest village of the Roya valley and something of an outpost. Perched on the steep face of the Ripe de Bernou, Tende served as a border stronghold, a base for the local herdsmen and a refuge for travellers attempting the near insurmountable path over the Ber Rouge. Since the early part of this century, however, a tunnel has opened up a direct route through the mountain to Station de Limone Piemonte on the other side and made this a popular staging-post on the way to Italy. Despite this, the village still has a brooding, isolated atmosphere, partly due to the dark schist rock which has been used in many of the early buildings piled up on one another across the mountainside.

❖ *Information, accommodation and food*

🛈 Avenue du 16^e septembre (☎ 04 93 04 73 71), by the railway station.

Hotels. Tende is quite well provided with accommodation partly because it caters for through-traffic to Italy and for those who wish to explore this area. The *Cheval Blanc* (☎ 04 93 04 62 22) at 18 rue Maurice-Sassi is one of the best but still reasonable in price. The *Hôtel du Centre* (☎ 04 93 04 62 19) at 12 place de la Republique and the *Miramonti* (☎ 04 93 04 61 82) at 5 ave Vassalo are less expensive.

For eatting out, the Italian restaurant and pizzeria *La Margueria* on ave du 16^e Septembre is the most distinctive.

A jagged spike of masonry sticking out above the village is all that remains of the 14C castle of the Lascaris, destroyed in 1692 and now the site of the local cemetery. There is an excellent view from here over the slated rooftops and tight street pattern to the valley stretching out to the south. Lower down is the **Eglise de Notre-Dame-de-l'Assomption**, a large parish church built in the early 16C and including a fine Renaissance doorway with carved decoration. The richly painted interior houses the Lascaris family tombs and some 17C wooden statues which were part of an altarpiece presented to the church by Charles-Emmanuel II of Savoy.

Tende is the capital of the valley and one of the main centres from which to embark into the Parc National du Mercantour. There is also a new museum, the **Musée des Merveilles** (☎ 04 93 04 73 71; **open** 10.30–18.30 May–Oct; 10.30–17.00 mid Oct–Apr; closed Tues and for 2 weeks in mid Nov and mid Mar), which has displays on the turbulent history of the area and, specifically, on the geology and carvings of the Vallée des Merveilles.

Index